# Critical Criminology in Canada

**LAW AND SOCIETY**

## Law and Society Series
W. WESLEY PUE, GENERAL EDITOR

The Law and Society Series explores law as a socially embedded phenomenon. It is premised on the understanding that the conventional division of law from society creates false dichotomies in thinking, scholarship, educational practice, and social life. Books in the series treat law and society as mutually constitutive and seek to bridge scholarship emerging from interdisciplinary engagement of law with disciplines such as politics, social theory, history, political economy, and gender studies.

A list of the titles in this series appears at the end of this book.

# Critical Criminology in Canada

New Voices, New Directions

...... Edited by Aaron Doyle and Dawn Moore

**UBC**Press · Vancouver · Toronto

21 20 19 18 17 16 15 14 13 12 11    5 4 3 2

Printed in Canada on FSC-certified ancient-forest-free paper (100% post-consumer recycled) that is processed chlorine- and acid-free.

**Library and Archives Canada Cataloguing in Publication**

    Critical criminology in Canada : new voices, new directions / edited by Aaron Doyle and Dawn Moore.

(Law & society, ISSN 1496-4953)
Includes bibliographical references and index.
ISBN 978-0-7748-1834-6 (bound)
ISBN 978-0-7748-1835-3 (pbk.)

    1. Critical criminology. 2. Criminology – Study and teaching (Higher) – Canada. 3. Criminology – Canada. I. Doyle, Aaron II. Moore, Dawn, 1974- III. Series: Law and society series (Vancouver, B.C.)

| | | |
|---|---|---|
| HV6019.C75 2011 | 364.01 | C2010-903473-2 |

e-book ISBNs: 978-0-7748-1836-0 (pdf); 978-0-7748-5958-5 (epub)

Canadä

UBC Press gratefully acknowledges the financial support for our publishing program of the Government of Canada through the Book Publishing Industry Development Program (BPIDP), and of the Canada Council for the Arts, and the British Columbia Arts Council.

This book has been published with the help of a grant from the Canadian Federation for the Humanities and Social Sciences, through the Aid to Scholarly Publications Programme, using funds provided by the Social Sciences and Humanities Research Council of Canada.

UBC Press
The University of British Columbia
2029 West Mall
Vancouver, BC V6T 1Z2
604-822-5959 / Fax: 604-822-6083
www.ubcpress.ca

# Contents

# Acknowledgments

There are a number of people and organizations who have lent support to the creation of this collection. Special thanks to the Departments of Law and of Sociology/Anthropology at Carleton and the Department of Sociology at the University of Alberta, as well as the Faculties of Arts and Social Sciences and of Public Affairs at Carleton and Arts and Social Sciences at the University of Alberta for funding to assist with the workshop that sparked this book.

We offer a very special thank you to the sorely missed Law Commission of Canada (LCC), which also provided generous funding for that workshop. The LCC was a shining light in the world of critical research on the law in Canada. We are particularly indebted to Yves le Bouthillier for his direct participation in the workshop, as well as to Gordana Krcevinac from the Social Sciences and Humanities Research Council of Canada (SSHRC) for her valuable assistance. Thanks to SSHRC and to the Canadian Federation for the Humanities and Social Sciences for their support of this book.

Akwasi Owusu-Bempeh provided indispensable assistance in organizing the workshop and putting together the manuscript. Thank you, Akwasi.

Our editor at UBC Press was Randy Schmidt. We appreciate how solidly he supported us throughout this project; without that support, it is likely this collection would never have seen completion. We owe a large debt of gratitude to Randy. Likewise, many staff at UBC from copy editors to promotions people deserve our thanks for all their hard work, in particular Ann Macklem. We also want to thank the Editorial Board of the Law and Society Series and especially Wes Pue.

Aside from the contributors, many others were directly involved in the discussions about the future of critical criminology that led to this book. At the risk of forgetting some of the participants, we would like to thank Dale Ballucci, Larry Buhagiar, Carolyn Côté-Lussier, Paul Datta, Erin Dej, Sylvie Frigon, Neil Gerlach, Michael Gulayets, Michael Handelman, Alan Hunt,

Jennifer Kilty, Maeve McMahon, Mike Mopas, Pat O'Malley, Justin Piché, and Jennifer Whitson. Again at the risk of omitting some, special thanks to Bryan Hogeveen, Joane Martel, Bob Ratner, and Andrew Woolford for their various efforts at building collaboration among Canadian critical criminologists over the years, and to Laura Huey and Paul Paré for organizing the follow-up "Bridging Divides" workshop in 2009 at the University of Western Ontario.

Kevin Haggerty was a key part of this project, co-organizing the workshop and helping with the early stages of the book manuscript until he was overtaken by his many other scholarly commitments. As always, it was a great pleasure collaborating with Kevin and this book would not have happened without him.

A special thank you to our families for offering the support and making the sacrifices that families so often do. Liz, Gen, Charlie, Carrie, and Kier, thanks for seeing us through one more time!

Over the course of putting together this collection, our community lost four members who will be greatly missed both as people and as scholars. We want to close by remembering Jean-Paul Brodeur, Richard Ericson, Robynne Neugebauer, and David Sealy.

# Critical Criminology in Canada

# Introduction:
# Questions for a New Generation
# of Criminologists

*Aaron Doyle and Dawn Moore*

Criminology in Canada is bigger than ever before, but at the same time faces its most severe challenges. The contributors to this book are members of a newer generation of criminologists emerging this century who are increasingly sharing leadership (or perhaps having leadership thrust on them). Far more university students are studying criminology than ever before, yet ironically, Canada's Conservative government is dismissive of criminological expertise that does not support its law and order agenda. This reflects the broader marginalization of criminology from public policy questions globally (Garland and Sparks 2000, Haggerty 2004, Currie 2007). The Harper government's aggressive law-and-order package of bills features, for example, new mandatory minimum prison sentences for a range of crimes, extending even to possession of a small number of marijuana plants. Other measures include a major reduction in conditional sentences. These measures will cram Canadian jails and prisons even more, with a price tag in the billions of dollars (Tibbetts 2010), while Canadian crime rates have been falling since the early 1990s. The vast majority of Canadian criminologists are ignored as we point out that research shows overwhelmingly that such measures are both inhumane and counterproductive (see, for example, Tonry 2009). Meanwhile, the Ottawa-Carleton Detention Centre has already been so overcrowded that inmates have been living in the showers, and triple bunking is a feature of many Canadian penal facilities. We watch the spread of security certificates and surveillance cameras, hear of a teenaged Canadian citizen imprisoned in Guantánamo with no due process protections, and read repeatedly of people dying after being tasered by Canadian police.

We criminologists proliferate, even as we struggle to define just what criminology should be. How can we overcome our own internal divisions and polarizing tendencies, for example, among English Canadian and French Canadian scholars, or among "critical" and "positivist" thinkers? We face urgent and vital questions about what we should now research and how we should theorize it, what our duty is to our thousands of new students, and, perhaps most pressingly, what our roles should be in shaping the politics of crime, in the news, in policy talk, or in mobilizing dissent.

Our aim in this book is to give voice to some of the newer people who are now shaping Canadian critical criminology and will help shape it in the years to come. We seek to gather some of the newer voices in Canadian criminology and related disciplines, but we do not presume to be representative of, or speak on behalf of, that generation. This is simply a collection of writing by one set of interesting newer criminologists we know.

These writers will continue to help shape important theoretical and practical debates about policing, criminalization, and punishment in the years to come. The book joins other efforts to get this newer generation to think about the future of criminology, such as the 2006 special issue of the *Canadian Journal of Criminology and Criminal Justice* on critical criminology and socio-legal studies (Woolford, Hogeveen, and Martel 2006), the 2010 special issue of the same journal entitled "Bridging Divides in Canadian Criminology" (Huey and Paré 2010), plus various ongoing efforts to organize spaces at national meetings for critical scholars working in these areas.

The editors and contributing authors have spent hours in passionate discussion in various settings about broader themes that colour this book. This introduction draws out these themes. We editors pose a set of questions that face the new generation of Canadian criminologists. Note that we define "criminologist" broadly and in an interdisciplinary way, consistent with our roots at the Centre of Criminology at the University of Toronto, rather than restricting the term to a narrower, institutionally based definition. We do not seek to protect the term so it applies only to those based in criminology departments or with criminology PhDs. Instead, we also include those in other disciplines, here notably sociology and law, who are working substantively on criminal justice issues. The perspectives captured here are wide ranging on the matter of criminology and offer assorted glimpses into some of what the future might hold for a movement whose only constant over the last thirty years has been change. The beginnings of this project were at a workshop at Carleton University entitled "The Criminological Promise." As Bryan Hogeveen notes in Chapter 2 in his meditation on the "criminological promise," we are still haunted by the promise of earlier generations of criminologists to control crime scientifically, a promise most of us would now disavow. But what can and should we promise instead, then? Perhaps the most urgent recurring points in our talks, the key points in this introduction, are the need to avoid polarization and to build intellectual alliances that accommodate difference, and the need to turn our critical scholarship more often into meaningful practice beyond the campus.

In the first section of this introduction, we consider the future of "critical criminology" and what that term means and could mean. In the second section, we look at how geographical and institutional locations shape Canadian criminologies. In the third section, we briefly identify some of the other key theoretical and substantive issues crosscutting contemporary critical research. In the fourth section, we highlight some of the advances and continued struggles of feminist criminology, and emphasize its continued importance for the discipline. In the fifth section, we talk about the challenges facing criminologists as teachers at a time that has seen massive expansion of undergraduate criminology programs. In the sixth and final section, we address the role of criminologists in questions of politics and criminal justice policy.

## What Is the Future of Critical Criminology?
## What Does Critical Criminology Mean? What Should It Mean?

One key question we considered in the discussions around this book is what the future holds for "critical criminology" and, indeed, what exactly "critical criminology" should mean. What has resulted, as is often the case when a lot of useful dialogue occurs, is a series of partial answers and further questions.

To begin with, we define criminology broadly as academic study of "crime" and social and governmental reactions to it. Depending on how it is defined, some see critical criminology globally as something whose moment quickly passed in the 1960s and 1970s, a product of radical times that came and went. Others see it differently, for example, Jock Young, one of the founders of the critical criminology movement with the landmark neo-Marxist book *The New Criminology* (Taylor, Walton, and Young 1973) and someone who remains one of the most avid, acute, and prolific contributors decades later. Young (2002, 259-60) sees the movement blossoming far beyond its neo-Marxist origins and writes: "Critical criminology is flourishing ... Critical criminology has been at the cutting edge of the discipline and is international in its scope ... think of the burgeoning literature on governmentality ... on masculinities ... or the extraordinary flourishing of cultural criminology ... and feminist criminology." Some reject the term "critical criminology" as too much associated with the original neo-Marxist tradition. Others use the term, like Young, in a more inclusive way that incorporates a broad rainbow of academics who research, question, and challenge current criminal justice institutions and practices, including not only neo-Marxists but also feminists, Foucauldians, legal geographers, anarchists, and numerous others who generally resist classification.

Younger twenty-first-century criminologists live in the aftermath of grand intellectual revolutions. For many who came later, the original neo-Marxist form of the critical criminological project lost its shine, and they sought to move criminological inquiry beyond what they saw as structural determinism into a realm that focused more on varicoloured power relations and on the gendered and racist aspects of crime control, as well as on complex matrices of governance. The optimism of the heyday of neo-Marxism, the vigour and moral certainties of second wave feminism, and the sheer intellectual vibrancy of postmodernism are all, to some extent, part of history now.

Critical criminology remains fundamentally concerned with researching and theorizing power relations in crime and criminalization, power relations that lead to social injustice. Critical criminology also arguably implies a commitment to put theory into practice. Yet, the dimensions of these power relations, how they are theorized, and what putting theory into practice actually means are all ongoing topics of furiously animated exchange among critical criminologists. Even so, all that talk should occur with the sense that there is a common project that holds a very valuable heterogeneity. It can be argued that the term "critical criminologies" more accurately captures this radical heterogeneity (Sumner 2004). Like Woolford, Hogeveen, and Martel (2006), we thus want to celebrate "plurality and irreducible diversity" in our work. Another way to characterize a critical criminological orientation is that it tries to be actively self-conscious of its own margins and exclusions, continually trying to interrogate silences, omissions, and exclusions both from its research and theoretical approaches and from its politics and policy agendas. Although critical criminologists might be drawn toward such a common identity out of a sense of solidarity, we also see that categories constrain and foreclose possibilities. We are also conscious of the problems of organizing such a collective identity. Our senior colleagues recount that earlier efforts to recognize and develop critical criminology in Canada were sometimes painfully divisive and we are aware of this past.

One way we who contributed to this book have jokingly described our commonality is by saying that we are all people who might wander around the poster session at the American Society of Criminology (ASC) meetings and be horrified by much of what we see. (We are not denying there are also many excellent papers at the ASC meetings, especially in the critical crimin-ology section. We will continue to go there!)

Critical criminology has defined itself to a large degree by what it is not, situating itself against what it sees as the mainstream criminological enterprise. Indeed, all of us in this book have been influenced by Michel Foucault and a range of other key thinkers who problematized the discipline of criminol-ogy itself, who portrayed criminology (other than the criminology they did, of course) as fundamental to the apparatus of repression and punishment (Foucault 1977), and pushed to dismantle what they saw as "managerialist" criminology. Where do we now sit, then, in relation to criminology alto-gether? Is the mainstream criminological project fatally problematic? What of value might be salvaged from it?

There is clearly a conscious rejection among critical criminologists of managerialist criminology, leaving the more difficult question of what exactly constitutes managerialist criminology in the Canadian context. How should critical criminologists engage with a rather large group of broadly liberal Canadian criminologists who certainly do not fit neatly into the reduc-tive dichotomy of critical and managerialist camps? How, then, do we relate to the many criminologists out there who may not talk about Foucault, and may do quantitative research, but who share many of the same fundamental criticisms that we have of the criminal justice system as very often harmful and counterproductive and unjust, and whose research, teaching, and work beyond the university tries to make things better? A lot of those so-called mainstream or positivist people are just as concerned as we are about issues such as overcrowded jails and prisons and about the futility of long sentences. They are arguably sometimes more engaged and effective advocates than many people who identify as "critical." Yet, critical criminologists sometimes end up set apart from these other critics, at a time when it might be much more productive to ally ourselves with them strategically on pressing crim-inological issues over social justice concerns we share.

This observed split between critical and liberal mainstream criminologies fits with a broader view that academia is inherently polarizing and tends strongly to drive wedges between positions that are not that far apart, so that people who really have a lot in common end up instead fighting about rela-tively small differences. Rather than Kuhnian paradigm shifts, as academic knowledge evolves, there is instead a continuous fracturing of positions that are not very far removed from one another, leading to a process of more and more fragmentation. This is an argument that Andrew Abbott (2001) makes in his book *Chaos of Disciplines*. Heterogeneity is very healthy, as long as we listen to each other instead of shouting each other down.

Does the term "critical," then, perpetuate an outsider status in the discipline? Does it promote polarized relations with others with whom critical criminologists have a fair bit in common and need more than ever as strategic allies? Here in Canada, are critical criminologists really outsiders anymore? Is the problem the supposed marginalization of critical criminology in academia from mainstream criminology, or is the problem the marginalization of criminology in general from a role shaping criminal justice practice (Garland and Sparks 2000; Garland 2001; Haggerty 2004)? One advantage of recent calls for a "public criminology" (Chancer and McLaughlin 2007; Currie 2007) is that they may push criminologists beyond debating such internal differences and toward finding common progressive goals in the world of criminal justice politics beyond the university.

## Locating Criminology in Canada
Defining critical criminology in Canada is bound up with questions of geographical and institutional location. National identities remain key in criminology. We live in an increasingly globalized world, but the nation-state remains central in some of our research questions, for example, around national penal cultures (O'Malley 1999; Pratt et al. 2005). The nation-state is also central in understanding and defining trajectories in criminology itself. Global criminology continues to be dominated by academics from the North and West, especially the United States and Britain, in a way that is problematic. Also, critical criminology has taken somewhat different pathways, in the United States, say, versus in Britain. Previously, we used the example of being appalled by much of mainstream American criminology. Martel, Hogeveen, and Woolford (2006) give extensive evidence of the marginalization of critical criminology but focus narrowly on the American context. It might be argued that the critical criminology section of the ASC, as strongly institutionalized as it is, has a tendency to reproduce the separation of critical from mainstream criminology in the United States. There is an open question about the pros and cons of setting up a similar formal institutional structure for critical criminologists in Canada; some argue that it is healthier not to institutionalize critical criminology as separate here.

Canadian critical criminologists tend to look with disdain on much of the American criminological enterprise as blinkered, methodologically fetishistic, and compromised by its close alignment with the criminal justice system.

Looking at a good deal of the criminology work of our southern neighbours, it is often as if the postmodern turn, with its critical interrogation of grand narratives and presumptions about scientific certainty, never occurred. This is a frustrating situation to those of us who cut our intellectual teeth on Foucault, Donna Haraway, and Dorothy Smith. We tend to wince at unreflexive appeals to truth and scientific methodology and are immediately suspicious of the power politics inherent in appeals to established categories.

However, although this is still the case for too much American criminology, we must also acknowledge that it too is a very diverse enterprise that contains important currents of critical thought. Even so, critical criminology seems to be much more obviously marginalized in the United States than here in Canada or in Britain. It might be argued that outside the United States there has been movement to close the schism between critical and mainstream criminology, with a few key scholarly examples being the advent of journals such as *Theoretical Criminology* or the 2000 special issue of the *British Journal of Criminology*, edited by David Garland and Richard Sparks, on criminology and social theory (Garland and Sparks 2000) or the prominent place in the *Oxford Handbook of Criminology* of criminology rooted in broader critical social theory (Maguire, Morgan, and Reiner 2007).

Like a large portion of Canadian sociology, much of Canadian critical criminology is more oriented toward European theory, and particularly the work of Michel Foucault, than that of our American counterparts. It may be argued that the dire state of American criminology has led many to look to Britain in particular for inspiration. Yet, this British influence too has presented its own difficulties. The immersion of Canadian criminologists in the robust history of British radical criminology and left realism means that many of us are strangely familiar with developments that are iconic in British criminology, such as the miners' strike, the Thatcherite revolution, left realist statistical surveys, the increasing influence of the Home Office on British crime policy, and the unflinching embrace in the United Kingdom of closed-circuit TV cameras. The problem is that these developments occurred thousands of miles away in a very different political climate and were motivated – at least in part – by uniquely British historical factors. Many of these stories were not paralleled in Canada or took on very different forms across the Atlantic. The end result has been a form of intellectual colonization where junior Canadian critical criminologists can be more familiar with developments overseas than with what has happened in their own country. This situation is exacerbated by the precarious state of Canadian academic publishing, which can make it difficult to communicate uniquely Canadian observations to a Canadian audience.

Canadian criminologists also face the particular research issue of exploring the distinctiveness of Canadian penal culture (Hatt, Caputo, and Perry 1992; Doob and Webster 2006). Although we live in an increasingly globalized world, the question of national differences in practices of punishment and the reasons for them remain very important. "Neo-liberalism" is often used as a blunt conceptual tool to talk about continuity across nations in recent penal practices – how and why, then, do penal politics vary by nation-state (O'Malley 1999)? Some claim Canada has "missed the punitive turn" compared with other jurisdictions (Meyer and O'Malley 2005). This is highly debatable (Moore and Hannah-Moffat 2005), but at least Canada has thus far offered somewhat of a favourable contrast to the nightmarish penal politics and prison population explosion of our neighbour to the south. Given our proximity geographically and socially to America, it is important to understand sociologically why, at least so far, we are sometimes not so punitive as the United States is, but also why sometimes, as in the case of our overcrowded provincial jails, Canada may be just as bad. Furthermore, we need to understand fully as researchers the socio-politics behind the Conservative government's current drive toward more American-style penal policies that will swell our prison population at great cost. These policies come despite Statistics Canada telling us that Canadian crime statistics have been declining since the beginning of the 1990s, and even as the State of California's finances are in ruins partly because of its own parallel laws leading to massive prison overcrowding (S. Moore 2009; The Economist 2009).

In Canada, critical criminologists sometimes make a straw figure of much mainstream positivist or managerial criminology and romanticize the marginalization of more critical scholars. Some critical criminologists (including ourselves) are highly frustrated with the tendencies toward reduction, conflation, and parody that too often characterize the repetitive and simplistic debate between "positivists" (our thoughtless pejorative term for them) and "postmodernists" (their thoughtless pejorative term for us). Critical criminologists too often unfairly characterize everyone doing any kind of quantitative research as automatically atheoretical, unreflexive, and conservative, when it is easy to think of quantitative criminologists who are none of these things. Meanwhile, others characterize anyone doing qualitative research informed by critical theory as "postmodernists" incapable of any empirical rigour, in so doing collapsing the whole history of interpretive social science, and of social theory, into the now-exhausted 1990s debates around postmodernism.

Of course, there persists managerialist criminology that helps reproduce and reinvent oppressive and brutal features of criminal justice. Prevalent in the US, such criminology is less vital and hegemonic here in Canada, with the exception of a small number of academic departments. Historically, the civil service and its research branches have also often served as moderating influences on Canadian crime policy (Hatt, Caputo, and Perry 1992). The problem instead is the current federal government ignoring not only the vast majority of criminologists but also its own internal research. The government thus disregards the recommendations of officials in its own Public Safety ministry that "credible research shows that longer sentences do not contribute to public safety" and that "there is little or no empirical evidence to support the premise that hiring more police, as proposed in the platform, will have the result of reducing victimization" (Tibbetts 2006).

In considering whether critical criminology is marginalized in Canadian universities, it is important to look across the whole country. Historically, Canadian criminology has been oriented around four main departments, at the Université de Montréal, University of Ottawa, University of Toronto, and Simon Fraser University. The bleak and poignant account by Dorothy Chunn and Robert Menzies (2006; Menzies and Chunn 1999) of the marginalization of critical criminology at Simon Fraser, once a radical fountainhead, and of their departure from the School of Criminology along with two critically leaning colleagues, fortunately seems to reflect mostly their grim local experience. Criminology at Simon Fraser represents the extreme, not the situation of Canada as a whole. At other universities – for example, the Centre of Criminology at the University of Toronto, where both of us completed graduate degrees – there is much more of a healthy coexistence and collegiality between criminologists of varying theoretical and methodological persuasions. Critical and theoretical criminologists also now play a strong role at the University of Ottawa. Historical accounts arguing that critical perspectives have been marginalized in Canadian criminology also seem to ignore major, extremely influential figures such as the late Richard Ericson or Mariana Valverde, perhaps because of a difficulty in situating them neatly.

There have also long been blurred boundaries between criminology and socio-legal studies, and thus crossover with various law schools as well (D. Moore 2002). Socio-legal studies seems very institutionally healthy in

Canada, thanks in large part to the vibrant Canadian Law and Society Association (CLSA), and is a space where feminist scholarship is prominent. The CLSA is a key home for critical criminologists, with a number of criminologists on the board, and many of the presentations at national conferences being criminological.

The institutional bases of criminology in Canadian universities are also shifting. In part because of the expansion of criminology undergraduate programs, there are also new institutional foci at other universities (for example, at Carleton University, which both of us call home) and often in other disciplines, especially sociology and legal studies. In many of these emerging places, critical criminology seems to be thriving among professors and graduate students alike. Some argue that criminology should fundamentally be the province of those with doctoral degrees in the discipline itself; others, including ourselves, see critical criminology as more interdisciplinary. Sociology has always been perhaps the most prominent discipline informing criminology, especially in North America, and it goes without saying that Canadian critical criminology is also a sociological criminology and one connected to broader social theory. It is always a critical move to connect private troubles to public issues (Mills 1959). Sociological criminology battles the profound social tendencies to individualize wholly the problem of crime, tendencies that are prominent in the criminal justice system, in the media and wider culture, and in other disciplines such as psychology. In Canada, there is also strong interplay between criminology and thriving work on political economy, on risk, on governmentality, on security, on legal geography, and in surveillance studies, much of which is substantively concerned with criminal justice. Much of this work is done by people with graduate degrees in disciplines other than criminology.

All of this is encouraging, but there are also some very significant negatives. The destruction by the Harper government of the Law Commission of Canada, one of the sponsors of the conference that was the starting point of this book, kicked out one key support for research that asked tough questions about criminal justice policies.

Martel, Hogeveen, and Woolford (2006) cite studies demonstrating the marginalization of scholarship by women and African Americans in criminology. In Canada, a parallel problem is the marginalization of French Canadian criminology. The strong tradition of French Canadian criminology, centred at the Université de Montréal and the University of Ottawa, continues to operate very far away from Anglo-Canadian criminology, as Benoît Dupont discusses in Chapter 1, and this is one very important gap for us to work to bridge.

## Theoretical and Substantive Debates

As is clear from impassioned discussions at the conference, our critical criminology also features numerous other theoretical and substantive debates. For instance, what should be our object of study: something called crime, or processes of criminalization, or something tied to a broader notion of harm or social justice? Several chapters here extend the focus to people and topics that have not historically been studied by criminologists, such as genocide (Andrew Woolford's Chapter 5). Stacey Hannem (Chapter 7) likewise proposes extending the critical ambit empirically to incorporate research on the families of prisoners, even as she extends it theoretically to bring in an earlier sociological tradition of research on stigma. Others offer new ways of thinking about existing fields. James Williams (Chapter 4) offers novel and important approaches to corporate and white-collar crime. Diana Young (Chapter 6) takes a fresh look at the implication of social services in the criminal justice system.

More questions: Does critical criminology mean abandoning the question of the etiology of crime or simply refocusing etiological analyses on the criminogenic properties of late capitalism or of contemporary masculinities? Where should critical criminologists stand on the restorative justice movement? How much can the heterogeneity of critical criminologies incorporate both realist and strong constructionist ontologies? One position is that people on both sides of these realist-constructionist debates should nevertheless acknowledge that their critical projects have a great deal in common. George Rigakos and Jon Frauley argue otherwise in their provocative chapter (Chapter 9) on critical realism.

Certainly, there is sometimes validity to the intellectual criticisms people have of critical criminology, to the things people say about us. These include, as we have said, not only reductionism and adopting "straw figure" opponents without fully engaging with those positions but also other failures: inverse functionalism; fetishization of social theory and key theorists, especially Foucault, in a way that is inaccessible; retreat into obscurantism (see Boyd 2007), lack of methodological rigour; empirical studies with outcomes preordained by theory; and perhaps most crucially, lack of meaningful practice.

Criminological work in governmentality studies is critical of political economy for narrowly focusing on the state as opposed to a broader focus on governance beyond the state (Williams and Lippert 2006). Governmental-ity studies is criticized in turn for its lack of realist ontology and praxis (Balfour, this volume; and Rigakos and Frauley, this volume). One approach is to argue that a more pressing question is a lack of ability by either to turn critical theory into practice.

What kind of truth claims can we criminological experts make in the world beyond academia? With initiatives such as the Conservatives' introduc-tion of new mandatory minimum sentences, should we be saying, for example, that a decisively large body of research shows convincingly that long prison sentences do not reduce crime – or are we somehow trying to destabilize the machinery of truth that makes such statements possible? We are on stable enough ontological and epistemological footing to say that prisons and cap-ital punishment do not accomplish their alleged goals, and it is very import-ant to say this. This leads to the next question. If we say that "tough" sentencing regimes mostly do more harm than good, how and where do we say this?

## Feminist Criminology: Advances and Challenges

Feminists made key contributions to the early critical movement in the United Kingdom and the United States, yet often their work was marginalized and ignored within "malestream" critical criminology that routinely treated women, especially women in conflict with the law and issues of women's victimization, as ancillary to the larger project (Naffine 1996; Ratner 2006). Naffine (1996) describes the critical criminological project as one that takes maleness as the accepted norm of criminological inquiry, applying an "add women and stir" strategy that routinely fails to appreciate how women's experiences differ in criminal justice as both victims and offenders. Feminist criminology has often been marginalized in Canada also (see Gillian Balfour's Chapter 8), but it has progressed considerably nevertheless, and we celebrate the growing and important body of feminist criminological research here.

Feminist scholarship is taking its place more and more in undergraduate and graduate criminology programs across the country. This is overdue but still so far insufficient. Meanwhile, women students often predominate num-erically in these programs. For example, of the 200 or so students a year entering criminology as a major at Carleton, about two-thirds are women. The rates for female enrolment in criminology run ahead of the rates of women entering the social sciences more generally. Encouragingly, courses on women and the law, if not core curriculum, are now standard fare for most criminology/law and society programs, and young women scholars are being hired consistently as professors in criminology programs across the country. Of course, we cannot assume that every woman scholar is interested in feminist scholarship (just as it is wrong to assume that men in the academy are not feminists). However, there is sometimes a sense that departments have an informal quota of feminist-oriented criminologists (typically one or two). Given this, emerging scholars (male or female) may be disinclined, at least initially, to frame their work as feminist lest they render themselves less marketable. Meanwhile, introducing feminism in the classroom remains sometimes a precarious endeavour. Some students appear willing to accept one week of feminism taught in a survey course but become resistant and in some cases belligerent when faced with more extensive feminist interventions (D. Moore 2008). This seems especially true when the professor is a woman whom the students read (rightly or wrongly) as a feminist. Thus, feminist thought does not always appear to enjoy the same degree of legitimacy among the student population as it does in select academic circles. One encouraging example has been the third-year sociology of gender and justice course at Carleton, which has been taken mostly by criminology students using it to fulfill a core course requirement and which has been very popular. (One factor was that the class was taught for many years by the late Robynne Neugebauer, an outstanding teacher who won multiple awards and was much loved by the students. Her sudden and untimely death in 2007 was a huge blow to many.)

We also faced challenges in including feminist criminology in this collection. When we organized the workshop on the future of critical criminology that was the starting place for this book, we foresaw a key role that feminist criminology would play in our event, but in the end this did not happen to the extent we wanted. Two women presenters withdrew fairly close to the workshop, one citing as the primary reason her need to provide child care, unfortunately still too often a constraint for women academics in particular. Although feminist concerns were repeatedly raised and some of the authors featured here take up feminist frameworks elsewhere, there was little explicitly feminist work among the papers presented at the event. This absence bothered us a lot. This book is not intended to be a comprehensive survey but is merely meant to provide an outlet for one set of new voices, and, as with many such works, the selection is biased toward people we know. There are other key exclusions in the book, both geographical (no one from eastern Canada) and substantive, for example, not enough on questions of racialization and First Nations people. Nevertheless, we decided that it would be wrong to put together a collection intending to speak to the future of the critical criminological movement without acknowledging the centrality of feminist work. At our request, Gillian Balfour kindly agreed to contribute a revised version of her previously published piece.

Feminist criminology is still engaged in ongoing and, in some cases, losing struggles (D. Moore 2008). Perhaps this is most obvious in the uneasy relationship between feminist criminologists and criminal justice reforms. Feminist criminologists are arguably among the most successful critical criminologists in putting theory into practice, and the Canadian criminal justice has offered many opportunities in the last thirty years – for example, the Prison for Women, Jane Doe, rape shield laws, police inattention to violence against women, the acute marginalization of Aboriginal women, including the many missing and murdered "Stolen Sisters," such as Pamela George. There is not only much more work to be done but also huge cause for concern that earlier feminist work has been co-opted or is now under threat in an increasingly conservative political climate.

For example, Minaker and Snider (2006) offer an apt consideration of the rise of "husband abuse" as a perceived cause for concern by the criminal justice system. They take issue with claims that wives' abuse of their husbands is anywhere near as pervasive and egregious a problem as wife assault. Minaker and Snider raise timely concerns for feminists, suggesting that equality claims can have deleterious effects on women, often working to bring them closer to the male norm, resulting in a system that ignores gender differences and thereby constitutes women as equally violent (and equally worthy of punishment) as men.

The Harper government has also attempted to claw back gains made specifically for women. The Correctional Service of Canada has moved to close the only minimum security facility for federally sentenced women in the country, Isabel McNeill House in Kingston. The Harper crime package cut against previous bids for decarceration, instead calling for a more Americanized system of criminal justice that relies on heavy funding for law enforcement and a range of mandatory minimum sentences. Such legislation will have terrible effects on the system as a whole and impact not only women in conflict with the law but also the mostly female partners of the largely male population that will be incarcerated as a result (see Hannem, this volume).

The Task Force on Federally Sentenced Women and its aftermath is a fundamental example of the co-optation of feminist ideals in the Canadian criminal justice system. Feminist activists and scholars were called to the table to address the egregious circumstances of federally sentenced women. However, more than a decade after the task force report was released (and close to a decade after the infamous Prison for Women in Kingston was finally closed), the same activists and scholars are deeply concerned about new manifestations of gendered discrimination and institutional violence endemic in the system (Hannah-Moffat and Shaw 2000). The human rights complaint launched by the Canadian Association of Elizabeth Fry Societies is a case in point. This complaint cited myriad human rights abuses, including holding women in much more extreme security conditions than warranted and failing to meet women's basic health, cultural, and educational needs (Marriner and Moore 2006). Similarly, the superintendent of the Ottawa-Carleton Detention Centre testified in April 2006 in a case alleging human rights abuses at that institution. The superintendent indicated that women prisoners often faced what was essentially an extra punishment, being housed in the segregation unit, simply because there were no other facilities for them (Doyle and Walby, unpublished).

Feminist criminology also has its internal debates, the most contentious of which over the last ten years or so concerns the massive influence of Foucault – the "Foucault effect" that has swept much of the social sciences – and how this can interfere with feminist politics and praxis. As Gillian Balfour points out in this collection, the core issue is a tension between standpoint feminism and what Carol Smart (1995) describes as "postmodern feminism." The trouble, according to Balfour, is that the Foucault effect is anaesthetizing, dampening the feminist activist spirit and lacking any clear political agenda. Balfour's concerns (echoed by Snider 2003 and others) are worthy of consideration. At the same time, perhaps, as Clare Hemmings (2005) suggests in her consideration of the "waves" of feminism, feminist scholars and activists are better served by drawing on their commonalities rather than focusing on their differences. Hallway conversations at conferences reaffirm that we share similar political and intellectual concerns and that scholars are very capable of strategically adopting different positions when the situation warrants. Thus, regardless of their intellectual divisions, feminist criminologists have been close to unanimous on major issues such as the condition of women in prison.

## Teaching Critical Criminology
We also need to reflect critically on the huge growth in undergraduate criminology programs across Canada, as Laura Huey discusses in Chapter 3. Our

duty to these students in the coming years is extended discussion and analysis: Why has this happened? What should we do about it?

Criminology undergraduate programs seem to prove very attractive to university administrators in the current marketplace, apparently because of their extreme popularity with students. Yet, the reasons for the rapid rise and popularity of these programs are not well understood. Is it a "CSI effect," as some claim, in which the massive popularity of the various ubiquitous TV series since 2000 has glamorized criminology? Are such criminology programs popular just because of their alleged vocational or perceived vocational orientation? Although criminology undergraduates are often stereotyped as wannabe cops, the students and their motivations are clearly diverse and, like the rest of our student populations, increasingly so. What accounts for the high proportion of women in undergraduate criminology courses?

Even if we are teaching a good proportion of the next generation of police, correctional, and probation officers (though, equally, we are teaching a good proportion of current and future activists, policy makers, defence lawyers, academics, and social workers), many universities, as opposed to colleges, reject the notion of skills-based training in favour of an analytical stance that problematizes crime and its control.

Our experience, having taught hundreds of criminology students, is that the current appeal by post-secondary institutions to students who are only interested in "getting a job" in criminal justice is actually targeting only one segment of criminology students. It was never the case that students (even in ostensibly applied criminology programs) went exclusively into criminal justice careers. As early as the 1980s, in one of the first empirical studies of an undergraduate criminology program in Canada, it was found that fully 40 percent of the students in an applied criminology program envisioned themselves going on to further education, including graduate school, law, and teacher's college (Buckley 1986). The BA criminology programs at the University of Alberta and at Carleton fit with this pattern – a large portion of these students during the course of their degrees come to be attracted to further education. The field placement coordinator at Carleton estimates that of eighty students each year in the placement program, forty will go on to further education once completing their criminology bachelor's degrees. And, of course, many of the contributors to this book were criminology undergraduates at one time.

Another implication of the explosion of criminology programs is that there is a furious scramble to find qualified people who will teach these courses and, more difficultly, to fill full-time faculty positions. Is it possible that one consequence is that more people are being hired into criminology positions from a wider range of fields and subfields than has historically been the case? This is an open empirical question, but, if it is indeed the case, it might mean that students are exposed to an even wider range of perspectives and viewpoints from ostensible criminologists? Would those new faculty members be inclined toward (or even capable of) teaching "applied" criminology?

At Carleton, the undergraduate criminology program is shared between the departments of sociology and anthropology, of law, and of psychology, allowing the students to triangulate between different disciplinary perspectives. Our experience is that the resulting disjunctures in vision often raise troubling questions for the students in the program, disjunctures that we see as creating very valuable and important "teachable moments."

In such programs, perhaps the goal is to foster more amicable relations between the varying camps and disciplines and to dream of doing away with such divisions altogether. This does not mean that the promise has to be one of cohesiveness. Rather, as we all participate in developing curricula, this offers the possibility of opening up dialogues with those with whose work we may find ourselves in conflict. This move is as much for ourselves as for our students. Such a situation helps keep us honest. A key is not to force the students to take sides or to be entrenched. One way those on one side of the realist-constructionist debate see this situation is that none of us produces truth in the classroom; that, at best, we give our students different ways of seeing the world. The goal, then, is not to usurp the teachings of other disciplines but to offer a heterogeneous array of viewpoints. In other words, we need to teach our students to think critically, but that is not necessarily the same thing as teaching them some kind of critical criminology party line, if there is or could be such a thing. Critical thinking means thinking for oneself, not just "thinking critically like we do." At the same time, it goes without saying that it is crucial to get students to re-examine and question much of what they understand as "common sense" about criminal justice coming into our courses – system definitions of crime, and popular and media understandings of who criminals are and how law enforcement and deterrence works. It is our experience that this is best done through classroom methods that promote critical discussion and active learning, rather than by simply memorizing a new orthodoxy to replace the old one. Although there are numerous critical criminological textbooks, critical criminologists seem to have focused mostly on producing appropriate content for their courses, rather than on reflecting very much on pedagogy. Indeed, there is something of a silence in critical criminological literature about pedagogy. Concerns with social justice have not connected up with the literature on critical pedagogy, the work of people such as Paulo Freire (1970) and Henry Giroux (2006). We need to theorize more about the ways in which students themselves are often a marginalized group. In hallway talk, faculty sometimes seem to take on board the notion that undergraduates are privileged consumers who hold sway over us disempowered professors, and there is too much of a culture of disdain at many universities about undergraduates in general and criminology undergraduates in particular, often stemming from faculty members who themselves have little actual contact with criminology students. We need to take more account of the ways in which undergraduates are disempowered and exploited and how this is tied with the point that teaching is very undervalued in our universities.

Another social justice issue needs to be addressed in the area of pedagogy: the long history of exploitation of the cheap post-Fordist "flexible" labour force of non-tenure-stream sessional faculty in the two-tier teaching system of Canadian universities (Rajagopal 2002). Huge criminology programs are a prime context in which this has been occurring. The sessional phenomenon is a good example of what we call "the gap": the inability to apply critical social theory to the things right under our noses.

## How Do We Put Critical Criminology into Practice?

Teaching is one of the most important ways we put criminology into practice. But it is not enough. What role can and should criminologists now take in criminal justice politics and policy making? Academically, at least, as we have argued, critical criminology is thriving in many ways in Canada. Even though some veteran critical criminologists (see, for example, Cohen 1988) tend to focus only on what was not achieved as part of a tremendously ambitious agenda outlined in the 1960s and 1970s, many notions previously considered radical are now widely accepted, at least intellectually within the discipline itself. Yet, in the bleak account of David Garland (2001, 65-68), although the intellectual influence of critical criminology has been long lasting, perhaps its most significant medium-term consequence in practice was to help undermine penal welfarism, opening the way for more punitive approaches to criminal justice in Western states. In this narrative, critical criminology, rather than being marginalized within the discipline, simply shares the fate of the discipline as a whole: institutionally strong but increasingly irrelevant beyond the campus.

The weak voice of criminology in criminal justice policy making has been attributed to the rise of neo-liberal governance, the ascendance of a punitive popular politics (though historically perhaps somewhat less prominently in Canada than elsewhere), and the growth of a technological infrastructure tied to other disciplines (Haggerty 2004). Criminologists themselves, as Garland (2001) argues, along with the structure of the university reward system, must also take some of the responsibility. In an academic world with increasing pressure on our time and pressure for publishing productivity, there is a tendency to limit our focus to publications that build one's CV but speak only to a narrow audience of the scholarly converted, rather than to work that reaches an audience beyond the university but is of more ambiguous currency in the tenure stream (Currie 2007).

Another source of ambivalence: critical criminology has also always been characterized by a tension between abolitionism versus reformism. Are these goals indeed mutually exclusive though? The body of sociological research on social movements suggests that radical change is more likely to occur when conditions are improving rather than worsening, as in the final years of the Soviet Union, when the reforms of Gorbachev were followed by the dismantling of the entire oppressive Soviet system (Tarrow 1998). One can argue that working for criminal justice reform is "propping up the system"; the danger is that this can simply become a handy rationalization to avoid doing demanding work that pushes us out of our comfort zones. Early reforms might be steps toward more thorough-going changes that address the fundamental difficulties at the heart of the system.

We recognize the potential danger of having one's work co-opted in policy makers' hands in contexts like the Task Force on Federally Sentenced Women, for example, contributing to the kind of nightmare that George Pavlich (1999) would call left-wing managerialism. Some argue we lose an important political sensibility because we end up working within rather than outside the system. Pavlich reminds us of the importance of people standing on the outside.

Others argue that such co-option is an unlikely scenario. Instead, many of us who are critical have developed a sensibility that is immediately suspicious or dismissive of any policy option that has any realistic chance of being implemented as compromised and likely to be co-opted. It is possible that "left-wing managerialism" has become an overblown chimera. In the current political situation, is it really a valid concern that critical scholars will be so successful in shaping crime policy that we have to worry about oppressing people through misguided liberal coercion? Instead, the real dilemma may be exactly the opposite one – that for assorted reasons we find ourselves in a situation where critical criminologists make very few concrete proposals for policy development that have a realistic chance of being implemented. Moreover, critical criminologists may be inherently suspicious of those who try to make such proposals. Indeed, the types of cautions that Pavlich advances further reinforce habits of thought that effectively predispose critical criminologists from ever getting involved in the messy, compromised real-world pragmatics of policy development. The end result is a situation where the role of critical researchers in policy debates is typically a form of "trashing" (to use the critical legal studies lexicon) or deconstruction of existing options. Yet, there are simple reforms we can push for – reforms that might not revolutionize the system or get to the root of problems but that would incontrovertibly make the justice system somewhat more humane. Battling to keep conditional sentences rather than scrap them, introducing bail reform to keep more people accused of relatively marginal offences out of our jails as they await trial, or bringing in reforms to stop incarceration of impoverished offenders for non-payment of small fines, or improving conditions in institutions like detention centres, infamous for overcrowding, vermin, chaos, and violence, are a few examples of changes that could make a giant difference in the lives of marginalized people.

Another arena of political engagement that pushes critical criminologists out of our comfort zones is speaking to the news media. The work we do does not always translate easily into the short "talking point" needed to reach the ears of the public or policy makers, and this is one way in which reaching beyond the campus is risky. It is also fair to say that critical criminologists are not always the best communicators. Gregg Barak's (1994, 2007) call for critical criminologists to engage in "newsmaking criminology" has never really been explicitly taken up to any great degree in Canada (or elsewhere). There has long been ambivalence in university culture toward those who are seen as seeking the media spotlight, and, in particular, there is at times ambivalence toward those few criminologists who get a good deal of media attention in Canada, even though these same criminologists are often effective public advocates for humane and progressive approaches to crime. Increasingly, university administrators are pressuring faculty to get involved with the media. Indeed, the University of Alberta has established a media liaison office responsible for linking the national and local media with experts on campus. Although this provides new opportunities and institutional support for a form of "public criminology," such encounters remain intermittently frustrating because of the ongoing structured limitations inherent in trying to convey a critical message in the mainstream media (Ericson, Baranek, and Chan 1989; Doyle 2003). Such constraints are exacerbated by profound media misperceptions about what criminologists do. Nevertheless, as Hackett (1991) argues, following Gramsci, if the news media are not a level playing field, sometimes it is still possible to win playing uphill. The rise of "do-it-yourself" media such as blogs also opens spaces for different forms of newsmaking criminology.[1]

A final point on this theme: discussions of practice in critical criminology tend to focus on taking an insider role working on criminal justice policy rather than on activism working outside the system. The book closes with two interesting chapters by Lisa Freeman (Chapter 10) and Kevin Walby (Chapter 11) on their more anarchic political projects. The notion of radical flanking suggests complementary and mutually supporting roles for more mainstream versus more radical activists in promoting social change, and such projects may be seen as a complement rather than an alternative to the work of others in more mainstream settings. Critical criminologies are defined by an urgent sense of social justice. How this successfully translates into impact beyond academia is perhaps, we argue, the most difficult question facing us.

NOTES

1 See, for example, Justin Piché's blog, "Tracking the Politics of Crime and Punishment in Canada," at http://tpcp-canada.blogspot.com, which is increasingly read by media, politicians, and other audiences.

REFERENCES

Abbott, A. 2001. Chaos of Disciplines. Chicago: University of Chicago Press.

Barak, G., ed. 1994. Media Process and the Social Construction of Crime: Studies in Newsmaking Criminology. New York: Garland.

–. 2007. Doing Newsmaking Criminology from within the Academy. Theoretical Criminology 11(2): 191-207.

Boyd, N. 2007. Letter to the Editor. Canadian Journal of Criminology and Criminal Justice. 49(1): 125-26.

Buckley, D.L. 1986. What Does the Future Hold for Criminology Undergraduates in Canada: A Look at Past Trends and Future Prospects. *Journal of Criminal Justice* 14(1): 47-60.

Chancer, L., and E. McLaughlin. 2007. Public Criminologies: Diverse Perspectives on Academia and Policy. *Theoretical Criminology* 11(2): 155-73.

Chunn, D.E., and R. Menzies. 2006. So What Does All of This Have to Do with Criminology? Surviving the Restructuring of the Discipline in the Twenty-First Century. *Canadian Journal of Criminology and Criminal Justice* 48(5): 663-80.

Cohen, S. 1988. *Against Criminology*. New Brunswick, NJ: Transaction.

Currie, E. 2007. Against Marginality: Arguments for a Public Criminology. *Theoretical Criminology* 11(2): 175-90.

Doob, A.N., and C.M. Webster. 2006. Countering Punitiveness: Understanding Stability in Canada's Rate of Imprisonment. *Law and Society Review* 40(2): 325-68.

Doyle, A. 2003. *Arresting Images: Crime and Policing in Front of the Television Camera*. Toronto: University of Toronto Press.

Doyle, A., and K. Walby. Unpublished paper. The Forgotten Worst Third: The Neglect of Jails in Theorizing Punishment.

*The Economist*. 2009. Canada's Criminal Justice Policy: Prisoners of Politics; Less Crime, More Punishment. December 17.

Ericson, R.V., P. Baranek, and J. Chan. 1989. *Negotiating Control: A Study of News Sources*. Toronto: University of Toronto Press, 1989.

Foucault, M. 1977. *Discipline and Punish*. New York: Vintage.

Freire, P. 1970. *Pedagogy of the Oppressed*. New York: Herder and Herder.

Garland, D. 2001. *The Culture of Control: Crime and Social Order in Contemporary Society*. Chicago: University of Chicago Press.

Garland, D., and R. Sparks. 2000. Criminology, Social Theory and the Challenge of Our Times. In *Criminology and Social Theory*, ed. D. Garland and R. Sparks, 1-22. Oxford: Oxford University Press.

Giroux, H. 2006. *The Giroux Reader*. Ed. C. Robbins. Boulder, CO: Paradigm.

Hackett, R. 1991. *News and Dissent: The Press and the Politics of Peace in Canada*. Norwood, NJ: Ablex.

Haggerty, K. 2004. Displaced Expertise: Three Constraints on the Policy-Relevance of Criminological Thought. *Theoretical Criminology* 8(2): 211-31.

Hannah-Moffat, K., and M. Shaw, eds. 2000. *An Ideal Prison? Critical Essays on Women's Imprisonment in Canada*. Halifax: Fernwood.

Hatt, K., T. Caputo, and B. Perry. 1992. Criminal Justice Policy under Mulroney, 1984-90: Neo-Conservatism, Eh? *Canadian Public Policy* 18(3): 245-60.

Hemmings, C. 2005. Telling Feminist Stories. *Feminist Theory* 6(2): 18-41.

Huey, L., and P.-P. Paré. 2010. Bridging Divides in Canadian Criminology: Some Thoughts on a Possible Future. *Canadian Journal of Criminology and Criminal Justice* 52(3): 237-41.

Maguire, M., R. Morgan, and R. Reiner. 2007. *The Oxford Handbook of Criminology*. 4th ed. Oxford: Oxford University Press.

Marriner, S., and D. Moore. 2006. Women's Imprisonment: How Getting Better Is Getting Worse. In *Humane Prisons*, ed. D. Jones, 112-39. Oxford: Radcliffe.

Martel, J., B. Hogeveen, and A. Woolford. 2006. The State of Critical Scholarship in Critical Criminology and Socio-Legal Studies in Canada: An Introductory Essay. *Canadian Journal of Criminology and Criminal Justice* 48(5): 633-46.

Menzies, R., and D. Chunn. 1999. Discipline in Dissent: Canadian Academic Criminology at the Millennium. *Canadian Journal of Criminology and Criminal Justice* 41(2): 285-98.

Meyer, J., and P. O'Malley. 2005. Missing the Punitive Turn? Canadian Criminal Justice, "Balance" and Penal Modernism. In *The New Punitiveness: Trends, Theories, Perspectives*, ed. J. Pratt, 201-17. Cullompton, UK: Willan.

Mills, C.W. 1959. *The Sociological Imagination*. Oxford: Oxford University Press.

Minaker, J., and L. Snider. 2006. Husband Abuse: Equality with a Vengeance. *Canadian Journal of Criminology and Criminal Justice* 48(5): 243-78.

Moore, D. 2002. What Exactly Is It You Do? The Problem of Spanning Jurisdictional Divides in Law and Society Scholarship. *Studies in Law, Politics and Society* 24(2): 33-48.

–. 2008. Feminist Criminology: Gain, Loss and Backlash. *Sociology Compass* 2(1): 48-61.

Moore, D., and K. Hannah-Moffat. 2005. The Liberal Veil: Revisiting Canadian Penality. In *The New Punitiveness: Trends, Theories, Perspectives*, ed. J. Pratt, D. Brown, M. Brown, S. Hallsworth, and W. Morrison, 214-35. London: Willan.

Moore, S. 2009. The Prison Overcrowding Fix. *New York Times*, February 11.

Naffine, N. 1996. *Feminism and Criminology*. Philadelphia: Temple University Press.

O'Malley, P. 1999. Volatile and Contradictory Punishment. *Theoretical Criminology* 3(1): 175-96.

Pavlich, G. 1999. Criticism and Criminology: In Search of Legitimacy. *Theoretical Criminology* 3(1): 29-51.

Pratt, J., D. Brown, M. Brown, S. Hallsworth, and W. Morrison. 2005. *The New Punitiveness: Trends, Theories, Perspectives*. London: Willan.

Rajagopal, I. 2002. *Hidden Academics: Contract Faculty in Canadian Universities*. Toronto: University of Toronto Press.

Ratner, R.S. 2006. Pioneering Critical Criminology in Canada. *Canadian Journal of Criminology and Criminal Justice* 48(5): 647-62.

Smart, C. 1995. *Law, Crime and Sexuality: Essays in Feminism*. London: Sage.

Snider, L. 2003. Constituting the Punishable Woman: Atavistic Man Incarcerates Post-Modern Woman. *British Journal of Criminology* 43(2): 224-43.

Sumner, C. 2004. The Social Nature of Crime and Deviance. In *The Blackwell Companion to Criminology*, ed. C. Sumner, 3-31. Oxford: Blackwell.

Tarrow, S. 1998. *Power in Movement*. 2nd ed. Cambridge: Cambridge University Press.

Taylor, I., P. Walton, and J. Young. 1973. *The New Criminology: For a Social Theory of Deviance*. New York: Harper and Row.

Tibbetts, J. 2006. PS Experts Opposed Tory Crime Agenda: Party Ignored Advice That Get-Tough Policies Don't Protect Public. *Ottawa Citizen*, August 9.

–. 2010. Tories' Planned Prison Legislation to Cost Billions. *Montreal Gazette*, April 28.

Tonry, M. 2009. The Mostly Unintended Effects of Mandatory Penalties: Two Centuries of Consistent Findings. *Crime and Justice* 38(1): 65-114.

Williams, J., and R. Lippert. 2006. Governing at the Margins: Exploring the Contributions of Governmentality Studies to Critical Criminology in Canada. *Canadian Journal of Criminology and Criminal Justice* 48(5): 703-20.

Woolford, A., B. Hogeveen, and J. Martel. 2006. Introduction: An Opening. *Canadian Journal of Criminology and Criminal Justice* 48(5): 631-32.

Young, J. 2002. Critical Criminology in the Twenty-First Century: Critique, Irony and the Always Unfinished. In *Critical Criminology: Issues, Debates, Challenges*, ed. K. Carrington and R. Hogg, 251-74. Cullompton, UK: Willan.

# Canadian Criminology in the Twenty-First Century

Textbooks often present the discipline of criminology as having developed through a procession of conceptual and theoretical advancements. Such an orientation can overlook how institutional processes help to fashion an academic field. In Part 1, Benoît Dupont, Bryan Hogeveen, and Laura Huey accentuate some of those processes in the context of Canadian criminology. In so doing, they draw attention to issues of language, pedagogy, and institutional history, all of which structure the discipline and will undoubtedly inform the possible futures of Canadian criminology.

Benoît Dupont focuses on criminology in Quebec, outlining several reasons why the vibrant works of francophone criminologists remain marginalized within the anglophone scholarly community. Language differences play a role here, but how language operates among French criminologists is more complicated and surprising than might have been anticipated. For example, Quebec has secured a notable position in a wider global intellectual geography because it is physically located at the crossroads of a unilingual North America and a multilingual Europe. Paradoxically, Quebec has become an intellectual hub for visiting international francophone scholars who seek to access English language publications. Indeed, scholars arriving in Montreal from France and Belgium have been known to fill their computer hard drives with downloaded English-language publications that are unavailable in their home countries.

Since the 1970s, the often passionate linguistic politics in Quebec have helped establish French as the language used in most provincial workplaces. Things, however, are more complicated in the academy where English dominates the world of scientific publication. Quebec social scientists publish in French comparatively more than is the practice in other disciplines. For example, approximately 75 percent of the publications associated with Montreal's International Centre for Comparative Criminology are published in French. That said, the publishing market for Quebec criminologists is highly differentiated and characterized by three distinct linguistic markets. The most prestigious caters to an international audience of English speakers, and French-speaking junior scholars are often pressured to publish in that market. There is also a fragmented international French-language market, also prestigious, but which tends to be politicized and policed by gatekeeping mandarins. Finally, a local French-language market in Quebec serves as a secondary option for senior scholars and as a testing ground for students and younger researchers.

This variegated linguistic marketplace produces pressures that help keep Quebec scholars out of Canadian English publications, which do not offer the same level of returns on their investment as international publications. Likewise, there are few incentives for English scholars to enter into Quebec's French-language publishing market. Such linguistic divides are unfortunate for many reasons, including that they often thwart the possibility of comparative research on the many distinctive attributes of criminal justice in Quebec.

The contemporary field continues to be structured by tensions that have characterized the historical emergence of criminology in Quebec. Dupont notes that institutions are built by individuals and that the idiosyncratic biographies and personal motivations of these individuals inform the evolution of all disciplines. The most notable figure in the rise of criminology in Quebec is Denis Szabo. A Hungarian immigrant, Szabo was instrumental in introducing an MA and subsequent PhD program at the Université de Montréal. An energetic institution builder, Szabo sought to establish criminology as an unassailable attribute of Quebec higher education. He did so by capitalizing on wider developments related to education, occupational structures, and criminal justice. Notable here were a series of governmental inquiries and royal commissions on crime and criminal justice and the attendant growth in the rehabilitative ideal. The dramatic expansion of post-secondary education in Quebec and the professionalization of the criminal justice system also produced career opportunities for graduates of criminology programs – a development that, as Laura Huey accentuates in her chapter, has been a mixed blessing.

To secure the disciplinary standing of criminology, Szabo hired graduate students from potential rival departments. He also championed a dual model of criminology that embraced both the treatment focus of the medical model and the analytical concentration on the social origins of crime. This dual model not only allowed the institute to emerge largely unscathed from historical vacillations in intellectual currents, but it also fostered an ongoing identity crisis, a feature that emphasizes the precursors to contemporary debates among criminologists about interdisciplinary subjects.

In the past decade, Quebec criminology has undergone a series of transformations related to its professional standing. As the state has progressively withdrawn from welfare provision, new interdisciplinary criminal justice projects in higher education have emerged. Many of these programs exhibit a pragmatic treatment focus. Notwithstanding that the Université de Montréal's criminology program became a professional school in 1972, the rise of these new programs appears to have contributed to a markedly different professional orientation for criminology. This came to a head in the hearings of a government of Quebec committee on the professions in the health and human relations sector in 2000. Concerned about the potential social harms that criminological practitioners might produce, the committee proposed further professionalization as a way to mitigate these risks. Remarkably, the committee's definition of "criminologist" was almost completely aligned with the medical model's focus on treatment, assessment, and risk profiling. In this model, many Quebec academics who self-identify as criminologists and who have taught in criminology programs for years would not qualify as professional criminologists.

Bryan Hogeveen also interrogates some of the legacies of initiatives by an earlier generation of Canadian criminologists. More specifically, he investigates the promises made by certain seminal Canadian criminologists when criminology was burgeoning as a discipline in this country in the 1960s, and how these may structure and constrain contemporary criminology.

Some key members of that generation of Canadian criminologists promised institutional and political audiences that the emergent discipline could help to control crime, something it would accomplish through effective research, teaching, and policy advice. This promise entailed appeals to scientific understandings of truth, knowledge, objectivity, and mathematical certainties, with relevance to government and policy as a driving force.

Hogeveen quotes pioneering criminologist Tadeusz Grygier (1963, 42): "The main problem ... is the scientific control of criminal behaviour." Although such gestures helped legitimate the nascent discipline, they also imposed continuing expectations that criminologists justify their investigations in light of the standards of the natural sciences. Early Canadian criminologists made promises about relevant research, where the standard of relevance was set by the administrators of the criminal justice system. Frank Potts (1963, 8), director of psychology for the Department of Reform Institutions of the province of Ontario, suggested that "the problem for research usually is one that has been identified by, or in consultation, with, the policy maker, the administrator or the practitioner in the field." Promises of pertinent teaching were also espoused, where education was characterized as a form of professional training, stimulated by and relevant to the field. Finally, there were promises of ongoing consultations with legislators and administrators, who would be provided with practical advice about managing the criminal justice system. These promises continue to haunt contemporary criminology

– for example, when we are contacted by the media or compete for research grants – despite that many criminologists have conspicuously disavowed the feasibility or desirability of such undertakings.

Particularly distasteful to Hogeveen is that, as he argues, early criminological promises were bound up with a project that implied and required otherness. Rejecting the Other from "society" through criminological praxis has taken many forms. Ironically, though, the successful realization of the criminological promise would require the death of both the discipline and the Other. In lieu of these inaugural promises, Hogeveen advocates for a criminology that negates the appropriation of the Other. Such a project would continually open up to alterity. For this project to advance, we must develop new standards to evaluate the relevance of criminological research that embraces a promise of emancipation and of being continually open to difference, as well as a restructured praxis. Hogeveen's second key argument concerns disciplinary identity. Hogeveen argues that we should rework disciplinary boundaries such that nothing is beyond question, critique, or deconstruction. Hogeveen looks back at the diverse disciplinary backgrounds of those advocating for an institute of criminology in the 1960s: law, forensic psychiatry, social work, psychology, psychoanalysis, and theology, among others. Criminological problems were so complex they required a multidisciplinary solution. This interdisciplinary aspect of criminology is still seen as essential in today's criminology textbooks. Hogeveen laments, however, how instead some contemporary Canadian criminologists and departments now seem increasingly myopic and concerned with policing disciplinary boundaries. A tendency during the burgeoning of criminology to want to pull "crime" away from other disciplines and give its study scientific legitimacy has increasingly resulted in a narrowing and limiting of criminological thought; critical scholars are migrating to other disciplines. Hogeveen advocates instead a "post-disciplinary" criminology, an expanded scholarly space not circumscribed by the traditional criminological promise. He not only urges a restructured promise that is opened up to otherness but also cautions against too much fixity being imposed on it. Hogeveen urges instead a constant reworking of established limits, a "criminology of possibility."

Laura Huey highlights ways that the contemporary university system works against the emergence of such a radically utopian criminological project. As she notes, the growth of criminology in Canada has been spectacular, but this expansion has foregrounded a deep tension inherent in the very idea of the university. Although universities have long been associated with professional training, this mission has been augmented over the past several decades by the liberal notion that universities should train individuals in critical thinking and help transmit cultural capital. Contemporary criminology programs exemplify the reascendancy of the professional training model, one that is often pushed to its extreme as university degrees risk becoming little more than consumable products.

A funding crisis in higher education has exacerbated these tensions, forcing university administrators to embrace a more entrepreneurial orientation to secure resources and meet enrolment quotas. University programs are now advertised through transparent appeals to student careerist aspirations. Some of the more distasteful of these overtures include championing criminology programs by referring to the remarkable "growth capacity" of the criminal justice system. The coterminous rise of a public discourse on the "knowledge economy" has intensified students' consumerist orientation, as they are encouraged to see university education predominately as an investment in career advancement.

These tensions come to a head in the classroom. Instructors schooled in critical orientations encounter students quick to vocalize their distaste for both theory and abstraction, which they see as being at odds with pragmatic career training. Facing the prospect of poor teaching evaluations and, for junior faculty, the always stressful tenure process, instructors are pressured to quietly shelve their critical orientation in favour of narrow forms of applied criminology.

For students, the promise of such applied criminology programs is a career in criminal justice, including work in policing, courts, and corrections. Questions remain about whether this promise can be fulfilled – if there are enough desirable jobs to employ the reserve army of criminology graduates being churned through the diploma mill. The employment that awaits many of these students is less of a career and more of a low-level job in the expanding world of private security. It is a formula almost consciously designed to foster student resentment.

REFERENCES

Potts, F. 1963. Institute of Criminology. *Canadian Journal of Criminology and Corrections* 5(1): 7-10.

Grygier, T. 1963. Dimensions of Criminology. *Canadian Journal of Criminology and Corrections* (5)1: 40-46.

# 1

# The Dilemmas of "Doing" Criminology in Quebec: Curse or Opportunity?

*Benoît Dupont*

This chapter is not about two criminological solitudes. Analogies between the history of the discipline and the broader political and cultural contexts of two distinct societies unable to understand each other would simply be too reductive. The history of criminology in Canada is a short one, but more importantly, its first pages were written by academics in exile whose cosmopolitanism was a living contradiction to the re-emerging Canadian and Quebec nationalisms. However, one cannot help but notice that since these early days, Anglo-Canadian and French Canadian criminologies have developed in different directions and at different paces. This explains why, despite frequent intellectual exchanges between scholars of the two communities, a clear disconnection remains at the institutional level: academic and student mobility between both fields is very limited, conferences that integrate both groups tend to be the exception rather than the rule, and research projects that cross over are fairly rare. Academic presses are also predominantly monolingual, with the notable exception of the *Canadian Journal of Criminology* and the *Canadian Journal of Law and Society*. The local institutional contingencies experienced by the discipline in very different environments account to a large extent for this situation. Taking Quebec criminology as an example, this chapter shows how particular constraints, such as the competition with more established fields of research, the need to ensure employability for graduates, and the language issue, can create still unresolved dilemmas that shape the interactions with Anglo-Canadian criminology.[1]

It is those dilemmas – and how they resonate in Quebec – that I want to explore in the following pages. The language of science being English, how can French-speaking criminologists reconcile the need to engage their international peers in a constructive dialogue with their duty to contribute to policy debates in their own communities? The stratification of the academic markets on which they trade forces them to make choices in terms of resource allocations that could result in the scientific ideal or their fellow citizens being shortchanged. The process through which criminology conquered its autonomy is also central to our understanding of the intellectual models that inform its evolution. The early compromises that had to be made and the entrepreneurial inclination of the Université de Montréal's School of Criminology's founder have produced lasting effects, whose relevance in the current context of the discipline's transformation is in question. Finally, the early professional orientation given to Quebec criminology is culminating with its formal integration into the provincial system of professions (Abbott 1988). If this outcome would seem to establish the status of criminology and its graduates, the bureaucratization and compromises involved will test the resilience of a discipline that has so far thrived on its openness. Thus, to paraphrase Latour (1987), I want to explore criminology as it is being done, instead of exploring "done" criminology.

To do this, I must first specify the position I occupy in the field described in this rather introspective chapter. The notion of field, central to Pierre Bourdieu's (1993) sociology, expands on Émile Durkheim's work on the social division of labour and Max Weber's differentiated spheres of activity (Lahire 1999). Bourdieu's definition of a field relies on a number of core properties: fields are professional microcosms within broader social macrocosms. Each field is a system of positions that obeys a set of stakes, interests, and rules distinct from those found in other fields. For example, to assess success in their chosen field of practice, criminologists employ different criteria than bond traders, politicians, or artists. The actors of a field struggle to occupy the most authoritative positions, mobilizing specific forms of capital (social, cultural, political, and symbolic) and developing a *habitus*, which represents a set of beliefs and dispositions. Strategies in each field lean either toward conservation, for those occupying the most desirable positions, or subversion, for those least endowed in capitals and *habitus* (Bourdieu 1993). Even if fields are relatively autonomous, because of their unique internal architecture, they nonetheless face numerous external constraints. As we will see, the field of criminology emerged from the defection of actors from more crowded fields, including psychology, psychiatry, and sociology. Competition with those neighbouring fields proved a defining parameter to the development of criminology. In Quebec (and the rest of Canada), the criminological field is occupied by university professors and administrators; funding agencies (Social Sciences and Humanities Research Council, National Crime Prevention Strategy, and Canadian Institutes of Health Research); and practitioners in police organizations, correctional services, and other criminal justice institutions; as well as journalists covering the crime beat and public affairs. One of the weaknesses of the notion of field is that it ignores to a large extent the contribution of those who do not exercise professional activity within a field, such as criminology students or prison inmates (Lahire 1999, 35). The notion of field being coarsely defined, the reader should be warned that my credibility to reflect on the history and structure of the Quebec criminology field is legitimately questionable, being neither a criminologist by training nor having lived in Quebec for a very long time. So here is the caveat: It might well be that the views expressed here are heterodox interpretations of Quebec's criminological microcosm and social macrocosm, resulting from cultural and institutional short-sightedness. However, none of my experienced colleagues who has read earlier drafts of this chapter has objected so vigorously to my arguments that I felt compelled to reconsider them.

## The Language Dilemma: When the Lingua Franca Is No Longer French

Scientists who work in non-English-speaking environments must juggle two diverging sets of interests. The scientific ideal requires that they make their discoveries known to the broadest possible audience and to their peers, who can then falsify their work (Popper 1959). However, they must also ensure that their society of origin benefits from the research investment that was consented and therefore disseminate their work in their native language (Martel 2001).

### Languages' Political and Scientific Dimensions

Language in Quebec is a particularly sensitive issue. In the nineteenth century and for most of the twentieth, English was the language of many workplaces, including government offices, despite the fact that a majority of the population used French at home. The Quiet Revolution placed a high priority on changing this perceived imbalance, and the enactment of a language law became a high priority for the Parti Québécois when it was voted into power in 1976. A year later, Bill 101, also known as Charte de la langue française, made French the sole official language of the province, to the dismay of anglophones. In later years, rulings from the Supreme Court of Canada invalidated some of the most controversial sections of the act. Meanwhile, a government agency – the Office québécois de la langue française – was created to ensure compliance with the law and to monitor the state of the French language in Quebec society. Frequent studies have been conducted to determine the evolution of the language at work, in schools, and at home, and performance indicators such as linguistic persistence, attractiveness, vitality, and substitution have been designed. The quality of French used in the media or taught by educators is also the subject of frequent public debates, signalling the underlying concern for the future of the language (Stefanéscu and Georgeault 2005). In this context, Bill 101 and the policies associated with it are perceived not only as legitimate means to stop the erosion of French but also as necessary tools to protect Quebec's cultural heritage.

The latest census data indicates that in 2001, native French speakers in Quebec accounted for 81 percent of the total population, while native English speakers (8.3 percent) had been overtaken over the previous five years as the main minority group by immigrants whose native language was neither French nor English (10.3 percent) (Office québécois de la langue française 2005). In sharp contrast with the situation that prevailed until the 1950s, French has regained most of its lost status as the language used in the workplace: in 2001, it was used most often by 86.8 percent of the Quebec workforce (whatever the language spoken at home), and an additional 7.3 percent declared they used it regularly (Statistics Canada 2003). If the vitality of French as the language of everyday life seems assured in the near future in Quebec, the situation is much more contrasted in the scientific realm, where English has become the universal language.

The need to communicate the results of scientific discoveries so that they can be debated and thus integrated to the cumulative process of knowledge creation has always led a particular language to dominate the field of ideas. Long after the Roman Empire fell, Latin remained the language of choice among European scientists and philosophers, only to be replaced in the eighteenth century by French and to a lesser extent by national languages, which were revived by the Romantic political philosophy. The decline of French as the *lingua franca* at the beginning of the twentieth century coincided with the rise of English, reflecting the economic and industrial power of the British Empire. In 1880, the proportion of articles published in English in the hard sciences (medicine, mathematics, physics, chemistry, biology, and earth sciences) accounted for slightly more than 35 percent of the total output, while French ranked second with 28 percent and German third with 25 percent. English crossed the 50-percent threshold during the 1920s and, by 1980, its hegemony was undeniable, accounting for more than 70 percent of all publications in the natural sciences (Tsunoda 1983). Eugene Garfield, the founder of the Institute for Scientific Information (ISI), provides an even blunter assessment: according to his analysis of 900,000 items indexed from 6,100 scientific journals in 1984, the share of English had reached 84.7 percent of publications and an even more impressive 97.4 percent of citations over the following four years (Garfield and Welljams-Dorof 1990, 13).

The domination of English as the scientific language would seem to confirm William Mackey's (1983) hypothesis, which establishes a negative correlation between the intensity of intellectual exchanges and the number of languages used to support those exchanges. He also suggests that the increased specialization of exchanges narrows the number of diffusion languages. As a result, researchers in non-English-speaking countries have little choice but to publish their work in the dominant language if they want to be read and cited, an effect compounded by impact factor bias toward journals published in the United States, which represents an additional incentive (Van Leeuwen et al. 2001). In Quebec, for example, 98 percent of natural sciences contributions published in 1993 were written in English (Godin 1996, 58). As a backdrop to this total domination, the social sciences seem to offer more resistance, with 16.4 percent of Quebec's scientific output in this field written in French during the same year, which amounts to a ratio of ten to one. However, important variations occurred from one discipline to another: economics and public administration publications, for instance, were entirely printed in English, while the fields of planning and development and political science had the highest rate of French publications – respectively 41.7 and 39.1 percent (ibid.). No specific data can be found in the bibliometric literature on criminology, but a very limited survey of the publications listed in the International Centre for Comparative Criminology's annual reports can yield valuable insights.

The French Criminologist's Choices

The International Centre for Comparative Criminology (ICCC) was founded in 1969 to complement the teaching activities of what was then the criminology department (founded in 1960), with an administrative structure exclusively dedicated to research. Since its inception, the centre has published an annual report listing the scientific output of its members. A summary analysis of the publications listed for 1970, 1980, 1990, 2000, and 2005 places criminology among the disciplines where French remains the first language in terms of quantity: after having fluctuated widely in 1970 (50 percent) and 1980 (84 percent), since 1990, the peer-reviewed articles and book chapters published in that language by the centre's membership (thirty-one principal researchers) 'has stabilized at around 75 percent of the overall production, unaffected by a productivity increase of more than 148 percent during the same period (from 47 to 117 items recorded). The stability extends to edited and sole-authored books (around 92 percent written in French since 2000) and to scientific communications done at conferences (around 82 percent done in French since 2000), despite an increase in productivity of 100 percent for the earlier and 400 percent for the latter. This incomplete data suggest two things beyond the confirmation of a more output-oriented academic market in the criminology field: first, Quebec criminology seems to resist the trend toward a more integrated knowledge market where the exchange currency is English, and, second, an equilibrium seems to have been reached, despite the continuing growth in the volume of publications and scientific exchanges.

This apparent contradiction between a more active group of researchers and a stable and limited presence in the English world can be explained by the specific location of Quebec at the crossroads of a unilingual North America and a multilingual Europe, besides underlying factors observed in the social sciences. Such general factors include a more important focus on local social, political, and economic problems, which are more readily written about and dissected in national outlets, as well as the lesser emphasis placed on international peer-reviewed journals by comparison with the natural sciences. As a result, books are still viewed as a valuable academic output in the social sciences. These factors help social scientists reach a broader audience of non-experts beyond the small circle of their peers (Whitley 1984; Godin 2002). But more importantly, the comparative strength of French in the Quebec criminology field can be explained by the role of intellectual "broker" between North American and European scholars that the School of Criminology and the ICCC assume. Ever since the creation of the school and the ICCC in 1960 and 1969 respectively by Denis Szabo, a Hungarian-born sociologist trained in Belgium who started his career in France, a constant flow of francophone scholars from France, Belgium, Switzerland, and the rest of continental Europe has used Montreal as a privileged platform from where to chart the latest theoretical and empirical "discoveries" made by English-speaking criminologists, and either adopt them or respond with a more skeptical stance (Laplante 1994). This situation can partly be attributed to a favourable budgetary environment on this side of the Atlantic, which resulted in more comprehensive library collections or the availability of fully funded visiting fellowships that appealed to criminology scholars starved of resources in their own countries (Mucchielli 2004; Poupart 2004). Even today, many visiting scholars from Continental Europe who have a more limited access to academic journals view their stay as an electronic harvest, taking advantage of their temporary access to expensive scientific databases to load up their laptop hard drives with full-text contents. Beyond this utilitarian attraction, the blend of up-to-date English sources and French-speaking local colleagues able to point them out and discuss them forms an attractive combination that brings Montreal much closer to European capitals than to some of its Canadian neighbours.

In this context, Quebec criminologists trade their cultural capital on several academic markets: a local French market supported by the peer-reviewed journal *Criminologie* and several academic presses with very limited distribution outside Quebec, an international English market dominated by US and European publishing interests backing powerful professional associations such as the American Society of Criminology, and finally, a more fragmented international market based in Paris and serving the Francophonie, a heterogeneous group of First World countries and former French colonies.[2] This three-tier system leads to positioning strategies built on its inherent hierarchy and the simultaneous need to maintain a presence in the three markets. At the top of this hierarchy, English-language journals and presses with prestigious editorial boards, impressive impact factors, and professional editing (and marketing) services, are a magnet for innovative and ambitious papers (and more rarely books) that have the potential to establish or reinforce an international reputation. For those who do not routinely write in English, the investment in a translator is deemed a worthwhile cost to enter such a market. The second tier of this informal hierarchy is composed of journal and publishing houses based in France, whose existence is more precarious, and which are generally controlled or managed by mandarins or research centres rather than through the rotating and plural system of editorial teams found in the English world. This secondary market is by nature idiosyncratic: less open to empirical material and more politicized, its gate-keepers use it as a strategic tool to maintain their grip on the field. The rationale for their decisions to grant or refuse publication depends as much on personal likes and dislikes or institutional affiliations as on the scientific quality of the proposed contribution. In that market, Quebec criminologists are usually well received by virtue of their proximity to the innovative North American market and of their marginal involvement in the local power struggles of the discipline. Despite its dysfunctions, the international French market bestows vast quantities of symbolic capital and, as such, remains attractive. Finally, the Quebec market is the third rung of this hierarchy. A survey of 1,714 Quebec academics (42 percent of whom originated in the social sciences) administered in 1994 enquired about the opinions the respondents held on the fifty-two academic journals published in the province: on a scale of 1 to 5, social science journals scored slightly better than their natural sciences counterparts but failed to achieve exceptional marks, obtaining less than 3 for reproducibility of results (2.82) and methodology (2.93), and performing best in "social, economic, and political relevance" with 3.54.[3] However, in terms of diffusion and international relevance, they barely reached the average, with respective scores of 2.43 and 2.76 (Godin 2002). This mediocre reputation means the Quebec market is essentially perceived as a secondary option by experienced academics and as a testing ground for gifted students and aspiring young researchers.

## BUILDING BRIDGES INSTEAD OF WALLS

The market stratification described here is in no way absolute, and as one's career progresses, loyalty for colleagues in less attractive markets will often prevail over objective assessments of one's best interests. The decision to publish in French rather than in English is also sometimes based on emotional considerations: for a few (becoming fewer), it constitutes a political statement in defence of French and Quebec culture; for others, it reflects their embeddedness in complex webs of professional and personal affinities that steer their publications predominantly toward French. Even then, the stratification delineated above always plays a role – sometimes reduced to a cameo appearance – in a Quebec criminologist's decision to publish in French or in English, in Quebec or abroad. This three-tier system places powerful constraints on academics: for a majority of French speakers, the acknowledgment of the importance of English publications appearing on their CV does not make it any easier to write in that language. Translators are often expensive, and their expertise in specialized fields such as criminology is limited. As it is almost impossible to trade simultaneously on the three markets, efforts must be focused on one or two of them, producing a tacit hierarchy among academics themselves that is reflected in the distortion of their career opportunities (which are unfortunately much less influenced by community service or teaching excellence). Furthermore, this particular market structure explains to a large extent the relative absence of Quebec criminologists from Canadian forums, which require proficiency in English without offering the same levels of international returns.

For the same reasons that the stratification of the publication markets deprives Quebec society of its most innovative cultural capital in the field of criminology (Bourdieu 1986), the very limited presence of Quebec scholars in Canadian criminology perpetuates a segmentation of the national field, which could very well use a more unified approach to interpret the regional variations in crime and social control patterns. For example, the criminal justice indicators report that Statistics Canada released in December 2005 clearly highlights Quebec's distinctiveness on several dimensions, including criminal victimization rates (both in the violent and acquisitive categories), the frequency and length of probation sentences for adult offenders, the average and mean length of incarceration for adult offenders, the length of detention sentences imposed on young offenders, fear of crime, public opinion toward the police, and financial compensation of crime victims (Gannon et al. 2005). Although it has been instrumentalized by generations of politicians for electoral gains, this distinctiveness is a core feature of Quebec society that can bear scientific benefits, facilitating the design of quasi-experimental research protocols, the evaluation of competing crime-control policies, and the falsification of criminological theories. One of the reasons this particular social feature has not yet been fully taken advantage of resides, in my view, on the asymmetrical nature of the language dilemma.

Whereas French-speaking scholars have an obligation to outgrow their local market, English-speaking scholars have very few incentives to trade on the Quebec market and, as a result, underestimate (or sometimes ignore) its effective and potential contributions to a broader understanding of crime and deviance in Canada. They must also wait (sometimes for years) for translations in order to access significant research produced outside the Anglo-Saxon realm. In that context, Quebec criminologists could harness the language dilemma to provide the same knowledge transfer platform to their Canadian counterparts that they already offer to their francophone colleagues. The institutional similarities that Canadian and Quebec criminologists analyze should certainly match – if not prevail over – the false sense of familiarity created by both groups' linguistic attachments.

## Criminology: The Cannibal Discipline and Its Hungry Cousins

The above considerations on the impacts of English as the language of science for Quebec criminology would have been unnecessary if the efforts to establish it as an autonomous discipline had failed forty years ago. However, its successful institutional development at the Université de Montréal, which was far from assured, did not occur in an academic vacuum. The more established social sciences, such as psychology and sociology, were also developing an interest in crime and deviance, and these antecedents have produced repercussions that are still being felt today, in terms of both the discipline's methodological diversity and its search for unique perspectives that would consecrate its autonomy and assert its growing scientific credibility. A historical overview of the creation of the School of Criminology and the ICCC at the Université de Montréal will help illustrate this point, complemented by an assessment of the discipline's current condition at the university and in other Quebec tertiary institutions. These two particular moments fall short of telling properly the whole story of criminology in Quebec, but the emphasis on the foundation and contemporary transformation are useful keys to understanding the place occupied by the discipline.[4]

## THE FOUNDING FATHERS OF QUEBEC CRIMINOLOGY

Quebec's interest in criminological theory came relatively late, compared to the European and North American early contributions to this field. The first criminological study was published in 1949 by Father Beausoleil: it attempted to understand the "criminal person" and the ways to correct his or her character through a psychological framework (Laplante 1994). It should not come as a surprise that the first Quebec "criminologist" was a member of the clergy: until the Quiet Revolution of the 1960s that led to its secularization, every aspect of French Quebec society was controlled by the powerful Catholic Church, which had reached a tacit pact with the political conservative elites to maintain the working classes in a state of temporal submission. The dominant role the Church played in the delivery of social services and its virtual monopoly on education lasted well into the 1940s, when the state started to reclaim some of these functions. The main arguments found in Father Beausoleil's book met the approval of Father Mailloux, who was the director of the Institute of Psychology at the Université de Montréal, where he had developed courses on delinquency and its psychology in the early 1940s and supervised a number of PhD students on related subjects (Szabo 1977; Hamelin 1986). Meanwhile, at McGill University, Dr. Cormier established in 1955 the legal psychiatry clinic at the Faculty of Medicine, which had close links with the St. Vincent de Paul penitentiary, where counselling services were offered to inmates (Poupart 2004). Schools of social work at McGill, Université Laval, and the Université de Montréal also had an interest in criminology through courses on the treatment of young offenders from the 1940s onward. All of these precursors held the common belief that "criminals" suffered from various forms of moral and psychological deficiencies that could be alleviated by a scientific treatment based on the medical professional model (for a more detailed discussion of the criminological promises made by early criminologists, see Hogeveen, this volume). Finally, in 1958, Abbot Lacoste, from the Université de Montréal's sociology department, lured a young Hungarian sociologist whose academic future in France seemed uncertain and persuaded him to teach criminal sociology in Quebec (Fournier 1998). Denis Szabo would be the catalyst for the development of criminology as a separate entity within the university administrative structure.

## CRIMINOLOGY AS ENTREPRENEURSHIP

Denis Szabo, in his own words, explained that Quebec and criminology proved an attractive option for someone whose ambitions could not be fulfilled in the fossilized European sociological landscape (Fournier 1998). His organizing energies were immediately deployed to exploit institutional opportunities that called for the development of criminological knowledge, and which he transformed into the initial investments of what Latour and Woolgar (1979) describe as the scientific capitalism circle. First, in 1938, the Royal Commission to Investigate the Penal System of Canada introduced the concept of rehabilitation in Canada and made numerous recommendations that were ignored for the next couple of decades – among them, the need to appoint a psychiatrist for each penitentiary and the need to have parolees supervised by trained social workers (Archambault 1938). Twenty years later, the Fauteux report presented the results of the investigation conducted by the committee appointed to inquire into the principles and procedures followed in the Remission Service of the Department of Justice of Canada, reiterating the rehabilitation ideal, whose implementation required the improvement of prison officers' training by the creation of university programs where criminology would play a key role (Fauteux 1956). The creation of a National Parole Board three years later placed the other forty-three recommendations of the committee under very favourable auspices. Simultaneously, the Quebec sections of several social work and corrections learned societies adopted much earlier than their Canadian counterparts the criminology label. In 1956, the fusion of the Canadian Penal Association and the Division de la délinquance et du crime du Conseil canadien du bien-être (Delinquency and Crime Division of the Canadian Welfare Council) gave birth to the Canadian Corrections Association, whose French name read the "Canadian

Society of Criminology." Similarly, the *Canadian Journal of Corrections*, first published in 1958, bore in French a different title: *Canadian Journal of Criminology* (Poupart 2004). These nuances reflected the evolving status of criminology in Canada: although the discipline had gained control of the associated fields of practice in Quebec, competing claims were still being made in the rest of Canada by social workers and psychologists (Grygier 1962; Bertrand 1964). Finally, at the international level, Father Mailloux became the national delegate of the International Society of Criminology in 1950 and its vice-president in 1962, reinforcing the legitimacy of criminology in Quebec academic circles.

These converging possibilities collided with the personal and professional ambition of Denis Szabo, who was put in charge of a master's program in criminology launched by the sociology department in 1960, the same year Cambridge and Berkeley universities started their own criminology programs. Two years later, the administrative burden on the program proved unbearable for the chair of the sociology department, who supported the creation of a separate criminology entity.[5] A PhD program was added in 1965, and a bachelor of arts in criminology was offered starting in 1967 (Poupart 2004). The teaching route was preferred over a more research-oriented outfit because it was believed that "research within universities is a perishable good, whereas a grade, a label, a diploma make you virtually irremovable" (Fournier 1998, 100). To minimize the reluctance and opposition to the new department, Szabo hired its first professors from among the students of his potential competitors (the "founding fathers") and was careful to maintain a balance between the disciplines that could lay claim to the new department (psychology, psychiatry, criminal law, and forensics). The decision to create a PhD program very early was dictated in part by the need to train and retain the brightest students in order to reinforce the faculty with young professors loyal to the emerging discipline (Szabo 1977). The "criminology transplant" faced several objections: the first dealt with the unbounded nature of criminology and the concern that its interdisciplinary approach would attract academic laggards who would downgrade the already precarious reputation of the social sciences. The response was, as we have seen above, to enrol directly or indirectly the support of names bearing the stamp of credibility in their respective disciplines. A second objection was that there was no need to create a new department that had no equivalent anywhere else in the world and which could be, for that matter, administered by a range of existing administrative units. Criminologists replied that disciplinary divides were creating blind spots and preventing a more integrated study of the crime phenomenon, and that only a "synthetic science" (Carroll and Pinatel 1956, cited in Poupart 2004, 90) or a "complex science" (Ellenberger 1969) could overcome this hurdle. Of course, the intellectual project advanced here is not to unite all sciences but to design a new one that would specify its own categories (Laplante 1994). The third, more pragmatic, concern had to do with the student demand for such courses and programs. As it happens, the Quiet Revolution led to a democratization of higher education, and the number of social sciences students in the province swelled from 7,817 in 1961 to 20,010 in 1975, benefiting in part the new department. The reform of post-secondary education implemented by the Quebec government in 1967 also strengthened the new undergraduate program. Finally, the professionalization of the criminal justice sector provided numerous employment opportunities for the new criminology graduates. In 1969, the Quebec probation service required its employees to obtain a university degree, preferably in criminology or social work, and the School of Criminology's 1973 yearbook stated that there were not enough graduates to fill all the available positions on the job market (Poupart 2004).

In 1966 and 1967, Szabo grew restless and secured funding from the Ford Foundation (along with the University of Toronto and nine American universities), which supported travel grants for European academics and expanded his international network. The following years, the US government, the Canadian government, and the Quebec government provided ongoing funding, justifying the ICCC creation in 1969. A satellite institute of criminology was opened in the Ivory Coast with the support of the Canadian International Development Agency, and a privileged relationship was developed with the National University of Zulia in Venezuela in order to "evangelize" Latin America (Fournier 1998). By the end of the 1970s, the institutionalization of criminology at the Université de Montréal was complete: more than 120 students were graduating every year, finding work inside the criminal justice system, and climbing through the ranks, to the point where a number of ministers and police and prison commissioners were alumni of the department. New professors whose allegiances to criminology were unquestionable had been recruited and were generously funded to conduct research, the results of which could be published in the peer-reviewed journal *Criminologie* or presented at the biennial conferences of the Quebec Criminology Society. Finally, public inquiries on the criminal justice system systematically called on their expertise.

However, this ambitious project – and its "demiurge"– was confronted by internal dissent as it grew in scope and its future became unproblematic. A second generation of criminologists, equipped with strong sociological credentials, engaged its predecessors with a critical theoretical framework that drew its inspiration from Berkeley's radical School of Criminology (Bertrand 1986, 102), the Frankfurt School, and Michel Foucault's work (Brodeur 1993). Their engaged research sought to deconstruct the perceived naive analysis of "crime" and its social control mechanisms and to further the rights of "oppressed" groups such as women, visible minorities, and inmates (Landreville 1986). This critical criminology backlash of the 1970s and the 1980s found a perfect target in someone who had openly and relentlessly pursued the development of the school through contacts with the establishment, in Canada, and abroad (Fournier 1998). Despite this rejection of criminology as they found it and vigorous debates with their positivist counterparts on the direction the school should take, the Montreal critical criminologists never threatened its strong clinical orientation. Instead, they suggested that clinical criminologists take advantage of the few "bubbles of freedom" left in the criminal justice system to provide "psychosocial" help to individuals caught in its web, while being careful not to legitimize the system, whose decay was inevitable anyway (Landreville 1986, 29).

## THE QUESTIONABLE RELEVANCE OF A DUAL MODEL

The acute strategic instinct Szabo displayed in the initial phases of the history of the Université de Montréal's criminology department (which became a professional school in 1972) and the ICCC placed the emphasis on accommodating and cajoling potential enemies. This was done mainly by taking care to maintain a balance between the two professional models between which criminology swayed. The first one, ingrained into the founding fathers' philosophy, drew its inspiration from the medical profession, with its treatment function. The context of authority that characterizes the treatment of offenders obviously introduced variations to this model, which were the subject of some soul-searching from clinicians who had to reconcile their humanist ideal with the fact that the very institutions that provided them their patients sometimes aggravated their patient's condition (Laplante 1994). The second model was more analytical and research-oriented, focused on the social dimensions of crime and deviance, and the underlying factors that influence them and shape their representations. It reflected more Szabo's initial training in sociology and the idea of criminology as a new science that he was promoting. Many theoretical frameworks were eventually embraced (and discarded) within this model, from both ends of the ideological spectrum, depending on the conceptual trends of the time (Cordeau 1986). This equilibrium proved both beneficial and problematic in the long run: beneficial because the power-sharing arrangements ensured that no internal crisis could derail the institutional development of the department and undermine the credibility of its members, despite the occasional robust exchanges of views or tensions generated by the recruitment of a new colleague, yet problematic because it never addressed the identity crisis that resurfaced at regular intervals and subsists to this day. The discipline in which each professor's PhD was awarded can be used as a very rough and imperfect proxy of his or her affinities with either the clinical model or the analytical one. Rather unsurprisingly, two groups emerge from the current pool of twenty-three appointed professors: the first group is made up of criminologists by training, representing 52 percent of the faculty (n = 12); a second homogenous group of psychologists account for one-quarter of the teaching body (n = 6). Finally, a residual cluster of five professors (21 percent) originate in cognate disciplines such as sociology, political science, law, and philosophy where the analytical posture prevails. This dichotomy is reflected in the curriculum, which is heavily influenced by the clinical group at the undergraduate level, whereas postgraduate studies place more emphasis on analytical approaches. If it has served the Quebec academic criminology community well for the past forty years, this duopoly does not necessarily foster endogenous innovation, and its ability to confront the challenges that new fields and universities are launching will soon be tested.

In 1999, the School of Criminology launched an undergraduate program in security and policing studies that responded to the increasing levels of qualification required from public and private security workers (Hébert, Dupont, and Cusson 2004). The expectations of the new student clientele proved slightly different from the more familiar criminology students: the new cohort – whose average entrance scores were lower than their counterparts – openly resisted teaching materials that were not practically connected to their chosen career, in line with the broader trend toward applied criminology programs described by Laura Huey in Chapter 3. They made it explicit by assessing poorly the professors who did not modify their course content accordingly and complained to the school's chair. Since students'

evaluations are taken into consideration by tenure and promotion committees, a vote was soon taken at a faculty meeting that let professors opt out of
teaching commitments in the new programs if they so desired (Brodeur 2005).
To this day, very few professors – besides the three explicitly recruited to
develop the new program – are teaching to the security and policing students.
Hands-on courses have so far been restricted to clinical interactions, and the
introduction of what has been perceived as an encroachment on both teaching philosophies (analytical and clinical) has generated fierce resistance from
both sides of an established binary professional model that has formed the
backbone of criminology at the Université de Montréal for the past decades.

For most of this period, the School of Criminology and the ICCC have
benefited from a virtual monopoly on criminology teaching and research at
the provincial level. So much so that other departments that have manifested
an early interest in criminology dropped their offerings in that domain when
the founding fathers retired in the late 1970s and early 1980s (Laplante 1994).
However, a recent assessment of the university landscape unveiled developments strongly supporting John Braithwaite's intuition that the demise of
the Keynesian state and a shift toward a regulatory state will also mark the
decline of criminology as we know it (Braithwaite 2000). The withdrawal of
the state from its welfare functions and its transformation into a steering
instrument harnessing the rowing power of community organizations and
private business is very well reflected in the new courses and programs offered
by innovative post-disciplinary universities and departments. No less than
six programs (from undergraduate certificates to master's concentration) are
offered in the field of drug addiction by health sciences, medicine, and social
work departments. Université Laval's School of Social Work, which offers
several criminology courses, lets its students choose an "entrepreneurial" or
an "international" track, with corresponding curriculum adjustments. Two
business schools are offering postgraduate certificates in forensic accounting
and financial crimes enforcement, explicitly marketed to businesses that must
comply with the Sarbanes-Oxley Act passed by the US Congress in 2002 in
order to improve corporate accountability following the WorldCom and
Enron scandals. The lead taken by business schools to deliver such courses
seems to confirm criminology's lack of interest for corporate crimes and financial fraud, as James Williams highlights in Chapter 4. Moreover, five
universities offer bachelor's degrees in "psychoeducation," which emphasizes child development and early intervention as a way of preventing youth

offending. Finally, a business school and an engineering school have launched two postgraduate degrees in the information security area: one deals with the governance, audit, and security of information technologies, leading to a professional risk management certification, while the other offers cyberinvestigation courses, including subjects such as the psychopathology of cybercriminals and the prevention of cybercrimes.

If the School of Criminology and ICCC can still claim a provincial monopoly on the "criminology" label and the features that usually define an autonomous discipline, the list of programs (and their associated research undertakings) enumerated above underscores the reordering of jurisdiction occurring in the fields of crime, security, and regulation (Ericson 2003). The boundaries that Quebec criminology maintained successfully for the past forty years around the study of crime and deviance seem to be dissolving, reflecting a broader shift "away from the two power/knowledge axes that had long distinguished the discipline" (Haggerty 2004, 217). It is still too early to predict whether it will change the balance of power for the long term or accelerate the emergence of new interdisciplinary arrangements. But if academic criminologists do not seem overly concerned by this evolution, practitioners have adopted a more aggressive stance in order to defend their professional domain against perceived threats to its integrity.

## From Theory to Practice: Achieving the Status of a Profession

As mentioned earlier, the criminology department at the Université de Montréal became a professional school in 1972, in order to strengthen the ties with its graduates' potential employers by sending them the signal that they would be hiring specialists rather than theoreticians. Another indirect objective was to reassure potential students that the burgeoning discipline could provide them with good employment prospects (Poupart 2004). Compulsory field placements were soon built into the undergraduate curriculum, and a professional association of Quebec criminologists – whose membership was exclusively accessible to graduates of the school – sought to build coalitions with other "helping" professionals such as social workers, guidance counsellors, psychologists, and child development workers. This process did not go as smoothly as expected. First, the questions of identity and professional ethics became a major barrier, and most of the discussions with other professional associations never went beyond very practical organizational considerations. Second, a love-hate relationship quickly erupted between the school's professors and their former students, who were themselves asserting their autonomy over what it meant to be "doing" criminology in practice (Rizkalla 1977). Lacking financial resources and following a loss of interest from its members, the association stopped its activities toward the end of the 1980s.

In 2000, the Quebec government set up a committee to examine the state of professions in the health and human relations sector. The report this committee published (known as the Bernier report) made recommendations on twenty-five of the forty-five existing professional corporations (Groupe de travail ministériel sur les professions de la santé et des relations humaines 2002). As a result, the professional corporation law was amended to create exclusive fields of practice (that is, "clinical activities in direct contact with patients") and activities (that is, "assess[ing] the psychological state or personality disorders of patients") instead of relying solely on a monopoly over professional titles that did not offer sufficient protection to the public and could be circumvented by a proliferation of labels (Lafortune and Lusignan 2004). The Bernier report also noted that criminologists – whose activities contribute to the enforcement of laws – could hardly continue to operate outside the provincial system of professions because of the harm they can potentially cause. This report could be defined as an "external source of disturbance" that led to the enlargement of the existing system by opening a "task area" to a new entrant (Abbott 1988, 117). A working group of criminologists, including practitioners, professors, and students, was established. Its first decision was to administer a survey to former students of the school to discover where they worked, what their daily activities were, and what risks they thought their practice involved for their clients or society.

Three hundred and twenty respondents replied to the survey, with a response rate of 15 percent.[6] In terms of practice, 79 percent stated that they worked in a clinical environment, whereas 21 percent worked in policy or administrative functions. The average number of regular professional activities they declared was four (out of a range of 1 to 12), the five most frequently cited being assessment, counselling, and recommendation (58.6 percent); individual helping relationship (48.5 percent); crisis situation intervention (44.1 percent); supervision in a context of authority (43.8 percent); and networked intervention such as reference or cooperation (30 percent). Besides the ambiguities inherent in the provision of help in a context of authority where legal and organizational contingencies are compounded by the resistance of subjects, respondents identified several harmful consequences associated with criminological activities. By decreasing order, they are the incorrect evaluation of a subject's dangerousness and his or her recidivism probability, particularly in the case of violent offenders (10.3 percent); breach of confidentiality and sale of personal data (9 percent); abuse of power (8.5 percent); wrong diagnosis and improper treatment (7.8 percent); excessive restriction imposed on freedom or unjustified privileges granted (7.5 percent); and lack of respect for an individual's rights and self-respect (6.8 percent). Contrary to most other professions, these prejudices are not limited to the individual being diagnosed or treated but extend to his or her family and friends, victims, and the community as a whole.

In response to meetings with the working group, a follow-up report of Quebec's Office of the Professions (the Trudeau report) recommended in November 2005 that criminology be granted the status of a profession (Trudeau et al. 2005). One of the main arguments was the overlap with activities undertaken by other professions in the mental health and human relations field and the benefits that could result from interdisciplinary interventions. A definition of criminology's field of exercise was given as "the assessment of criminogenic factors and delinquent behaviours of individuals, as well as the effects of crimes on victims, in order to determine a plan of intervention and to implement it. It also involves supporting and restoring the social capacities of offenders and victims in order to foster their reintegration in society as human beings interacting fully with their environment" (ibid., 79).[7] Nine exclusive activities linked to the field defined above are listed. They focus on the assessment of persons suffering from mental and personality disorders, of youth offenders at risk of offending or in need of protection, and of inmates applying for parole or probation, as well as on the decision to impose restraining or isolation orders. It is still too early to interpret the significance of these recommendations, as the corresponding bill had still not been tabled in parliament by April 2010. However, one cannot help from noticing that sex therapists are the only other group the Trudeau report recommends for integration into the system of professions. The negotiations that have transpired so far suggest that criminologists and sex therapists will have to share the same professional corporation, since no other profession seems willing to co-opt them. This stratification and the compromises it entails for a junior profession with limited political leverage is perceived as the price to pay in order to achieve professional legitimacy (reinforced by mandatory continuing education and a code of ethics) and, for a minority of practitioners, to extract some autonomy from their employers. This development is unlikely to reconcile the clinical and analytical models discussed in the previous section of this chapter: some professors of the school have voiced concerns about whether they would qualify to join the corporation, having never diagnosed or treated a young or adult offender in their career. The future of students who specialize in policy evaluation, crime prevention, industrial security, and white-collar crime is also uncertain. More than anything else, the bureaucratic enclosure of a profession that has so far thrived on the idea of interdisciplinarity seems counterintuitive to many. It reduces professional work to a mere competition for jurisdiction, whose outcomes are decided behind the scene after lengthy bargaining and settlements that feel more like concessions (Abbott 1988) – not necessarily a euphoric thought for a discipline that originally displayed so much ambition.

## Conclusion

I would like to end this chapter with an anecdote Denis Szabo related in his memoirs. Michel Foucault was in Montreal to finish the manuscript of *Discipline and Punish,* and Szabo took him out a couple of times for lunch and dinner around the university campus. The ever talkative Szabo apparently commented on Foucault's work and was providing him with his views on the state of criminological research when Foucault interrupted him:

> Listen, I enjoy listening to you, talking to you, but if you don't
> mind, let's stop here. I am here to finish my book. My time is extremely limited, and above all, I want to prove a thesis. Listening
> to you, I will never complete my work because there is this, there
> is that, and there is something else. I don't have time to "chase all
> these hares," I don't have time to check all of that. I want to stay in
> a state of creative ignorance, and with you around, I see it will not
> be possible. (Fournier 1998, 156-57)[8]

They never met again, and the rest is history. In a sense, it does not matter whether this discussion is apocryphal or actually took place. It serves as a reminder that the greatest books of our discipline are not written by disembodied demigods but by human beings embedded in a complex system dedicated to the fabrication of scientific facts and controversies (Latour 1987).

This does not diminish in any way their theoretical and empirical contributions, but these contributions should be understood as also being the result of linguistic, disciplinary, and institutional contingencies that are too often swept dismissively under the carpet. In this chapter, through a very personal interpretation influenced by my institutional affiliation, I have attempted to provide some idea of what these contingencies might look and feel like for Quebec criminologists. The need to operate in different academic markets, the historical status of the discipline and its institutional position, as well as the professionalization of criminology in a broader system of expertise, are powerful influences that partly explain the lack of connections between Canadian criminology and its Quebec counterpart. One can regret it, as I hope to have explicitly or implicitly identified the benefits that a closer relationship could bring to both parties. However, the dilemmas that I have outlined here are characterized by their lack of determinism, and, to push the market metaphor to the brink of bankruptcy, all it might take for a new cycle of growth to start is a little bit of venture capital.

## ACKNOWLEDGMENTS
I am grateful to Jean-Paul Brodeur and Guy Lemire for their insightful comments on an earlier draft of this chapter.

## NOTES

1 French criminology in Canada is not limited to Quebec: the University of Ottawa, for example, maintains a large bilingual criminology department.

2 One could also include in the local French market the French articles published by the *Canadian Journal of Criminology and Criminal Justice,* whose effective readership is arguably minuscule outside Quebec.

3 The other criteria assessed were theoretical perspective (3.07), new data (3.11), style (3.12), and reference (3.16).

4 For an overview of the first twenty-five years of criminology, and the intellectual climate at the school in the mid-1980s, see, for example, the special issue of *Criminologie* (Landreville and Normandeau 1986).

5 Ericson (2003) notes how criminology has been organized in various universities by different departments, attesting to its multidisciplinary nature and to the opportunism of those departments.

6 This paragraph summarizes the results of the survey that are presented in Lafortune and Lusignan (2004).

7 Translation by the author.

8 The same anecdote was cited in Brodeur (2004).

## REFERENCES

Abbott, A. 1988. *The System of Professions: An Essay on the Division of Expert Labor*. Chicago: University of Chicago Press.

Archambault, J. 1938. *Report of the Royal Commission to Investigate the Penal System of Canada*. Ottawa: J.O. Patenaude.

Bertrand, M.-A. 1964. Les programmes de formation du personnel dans le domaine criminologique au Canada. *Canadian Journal of Corrections* 6(3): 308-19.

–. 1986. Perspectives traditionnelles et perspectives critiques en criminologie. *Criminologie* 19(1): 97-111.

Bourdieu, P. 1986. The Forms of Capital. In *Handbook of Theory and Research for the Sociology of Education*, ed. J. Richardson, 241-58. New York: Greenwood Press.

–. 1993. *Sociology in Question*. London: Sage.

Braithwaite, J. 2000. The New Regulatory State and the Transformation of Criminology. *British Journal of Criminology* 40(2): 222-38.

Brodeur, J.-P. 1993. Éditorial to the Special Issue on Michel Foucault and (Post)Modernity. *Criminologie* 26(1): 3-11.

–. 2004. Lacan, Foucault et la criminologie. *La Célibataire* 9: 153-63.

–. 2005. Police Studies Past and Present: A Reaction to the Articles Presented by Thomas Feltes, Larry T. Hoover, Peter K. Manning, and Kam Wong. *Police Quarterly* 1(8): 44-56.

Carrol, D., and J. Pinatel. 1956. Rapport general sur l'enseignement de la criminologie. In *Les sciences sociales dans l'enseignement supérieur*, ed. UNESCO, 9-55. Paris: UNESCO.

Cordeau, G. 1986. Entrevue avec José Rico. In *Penser la criminologie: Propos recueillis sur 25 ans de criminologie au Quebec*, ed. M.-E. LeBeuf and D. Gauthier, 15-27. Montreal: École de Criminologie.

Ellenberger, H. 1969. *Criminologie du présent et du passé*. Montreal: Les Presses de l'Université de Montréal.

Ericson, R. 2003. The Culture and Power of Criminological Research. In *The Criminological Foundations of Penal Policy: Essays in Honour of Roger Hood*, ed. L. Zedner and A. Ashworth, 31-78. Oxford: Oxford University Press.

Fauteux, G. 1956. *Report of a Committee Appointed to Enquire into the Principles and Procedures Followed in the Remission Service of the Department of Justice of Canada*. Ottawa: Queen's Printer.

Fournier, M. 1998. *Entretiens avec Denis Szabo: Fondation et fondements de la criminologie*. Montreal: Liber.

Gannon, M., K. Mihorean, K. Beattie, A. Taylor-Butts, and R. Kong. 2005. *Criminal Justice Indicators, 2005*. Ottawa: Statistics Canada.

Garfield, E., and A. Welljams-Dorof. 1990. Language Use in International Research: A Citation Analysis. *Annals of the American Academy of Political and Social Sciences* 511(1): 10-24.

Godin, B. 1996. Parle, parle, jase, jase: L'utilisation du français dans les communications scientifiques. In *Le français et les langues scientifiques de demain*, ed. Conseil de la Langue Française, 55-68. Montreal: Conseil de la Langue Française.

–. 2002. Les pratiques de publication des chercheurs: Les revues savantes québécoises entre impact national et visibilité internationale. *Recherches Sociométriques* 43(3): 465-98.

Groupe de travail ministériel sur les professions de la santé et des relations humaines. 2002. *Une vision renouvelée du système professionnel en santé et en relations humaines*. Quebec: Office des Professions du Quebec.

Grygier, T. 1962. Education for Correctional Workers: A Survey of Needs and Resources. *Canadian Journal of Corrections* 4(3): 137-51.

Haggerty, K.D. 2004. Displaced Expertise: Three Constraints on the Policy-Relevance of Criminological Thought. *Theoretical Criminology* 8(2): 211-31.

Hamelin, M. 1986. Entrevue avec le R.P. Noel Mailloux o.p. In *Penser la criminologie: Propos recueillis sur 25 ans de criminologie au Québec*, ed. M.-E. Lebeuf and D. Gauthier, 39-46. Montreal: École de Criminologie.

Hébert, L., B. Dupont, and M. Cusson. 2004. *Document de réflexion sur le livre blanc: La sécurité privée partenaire de la sécurité intérieure*. Submitted to the parliamentary committee on the reform of the private security bill in Quebec by the Université de Montréal.

Lafortune, D., and R. Lusignan. 2004. La criminologie québécoise à l'heure du rapport Bernier: Vers une professionnalisation? *Criminologie* 37(2): 177-96.

Lahire, B. 1999. Champ, hors-champ, contrechamp. In *Le travail sociologique de Pierre Bourdieu*, ed. B. Lahire, 23-57. Paris: La Découverte.

Laplante, J. 1994. La criminologie québécoise, 1940-1991. In *Traité de criminologie empirique deuxième édition*, ed. D. Szabo and M. LeBlanc, 351-84. Montreal: Les Presses de l'Université de Montréal.

Landreville, P. 1986. Évolution théorique en criminologie: L'histoire d'un cheminement. *Criminologie* 19(1): 11-31.

–, and A. Normandeau. 1986. *Politiques et pratiques pénales, special issue of Criminologie*. Montreal: Les Presses de l'Université de Montréal.

Latour, B. 1987. *Science in Action*. Cambridge, MA: Harvard University Press.

–, and S. Woolgar. 1979. *Laboratory Life: The Construction of Scientific Facts*. Thousand Oaks, CA: Sage.

Mackey, W. 1983. La mortalité des langues et le bilinguisme des peuples. *Anthropologie et Société* 7(3): 3-23.

Martel, A. 2001. When Does Knowledge Have a National Language? Language Policy-Making for Science and Technology. In *The Dominance of English as a Language of Science*, ed. U. Ammon, 27-57. Berlin: Walter de Gruyter.

Mucchielli, L. 2004. L'impossible constitution d'une discipline criminologique en France. *Criminologie* 37(1): 13-42.

Office québécois de la langue française. 2005. *Les caractéristiques linguistiques de la population du Quebec: Profils et tendances 1991-2001*. Quebec: Office Québécois de Langue Française.

Popper, K. 1959. *The Logic of Scientific Discovery*. Toronto: University of Toronto Press.

Poupart, J. 2004. L'institutionnalisation de la criminology au Quebec: Une lecture socio-historique. *Criminologie* 37(1): 71-105.

Rizkalla, S. 1977. L'Association professionnelle des criminologues du Quebec dix ans après. *Criminologie* 10(2): 62-63.

Statistics Canada. 2003. *Language Use at Work: Highlight Tables, 2001 Census*. Ottawa: Statistics Canada.

Stefanéscu, A., and P. Georgeault. 2005. *Le français au Québec: Les nouveaux défis*. Montreal: Fides.

Szabo, D. 1977. Histoire d'une expérience québécoise qui aurait pu mal tourner. *Criminologie* 10(2): 5-38.

Trudeau, J.-B., M. Caron, C. Demers, A. Dion, A. Dubois, H. Joncas, F. Laflamme, and G. Rondeau. 2005. *Partageons nos compétences: Modernisation de la pratique professionnelle en santé mentale et en relations humaines*. Quebec: Office des Professions du Québec.

Tsunoda, M. 1983. International Languages in Scientific and Technical Publications. *Sophia Linguistica* 13: 69-79.

Van Leeuwen, T.N., H.F. Moed, R.J.W. Tijssen, M.S. Visser, and A.F.J. Van Raan. 2001. Language Biases in the Coverage of the *Science Citation Index* and Its Consequences for International Comparisons of National Research Performance. *Scientometrics* 51(1): 335-46.

Whitley, R. 1984. *The Intellectual and Social Organization of the Sciences*. Oxford: Clarendon Press.

## 2
# Reconciling Spectres: Promises of Criminology

*Bryan R. Hogeveen*

> Critique of what we are is at one and the same time the historical
> analysis of the limits impressed on us and an experiment with the
> possibility of going beyond them.
>
> ＞ – Michel Foucault, "What Is Enlightenment?"

## Introduction

William Kerrigan (1999) claims that keeping a promise is one of humanity's most enduring and attractive tests of virtue. At first blush, this weighty axiom certainly seems tenable. We take oaths of office, vow to be faithful in marriage, and swear to repay student loans. "Do you promise?" is a familiar childhood refrain. Any pledge to silence concerning particular inconvenient content could easily be forfeited through crossed fingers. For their part, inaugural Canadian criminologists (such as John L. Edwards, Tadeusz Grygier, and Denis Szabo) made promises to governments, university officials, and criminal justice practitioners – although I do not believe these were delivered with fingers crossed – to contribute to effective crime control through relevant research, teaching, and advice to politicians and administrators.[1] In concert with state and criminal justice officials, criminologists determined what counted (and continues to count) as relevant research about crime. Criminological promises, then, as they inhabited the consciousness in question, were curtailed and structured by perceptions about what scholarly work would be valued as relevant to legislators and administrators.

The potential for the criminological promise to turn back against itself, for what was once considered the best turning out to be the worst, forms a significant part of my deconstructive reading of criminological promising and criminology as a promise. Before arriving at this discussion, I examine the promises made during the 1960s when Canadian criminology was a burgeoning discipline. My purpose is not to sully the early criminological project or to ossify its discourse but to examine it from various meaning horizons and inquire as to whether there are spirits that perhaps may be (re)-affirmed. As such, this chapter intimates a sense of mourning and affirms an emancipatory ideal that steps outside the bulwark of a priori truth(s) and is inspired by the faces of tyranny and oppression.

## The Structure of a Promise: Initiating Promises

Frank Potts (1963, 10), director of psychology at the Provincial Department of Reform Institutions, stated plainly enough: "To study criminology is to study one of mankind's oldest and most stubborn problems. If progress is to be accelerated, we must pool our brains and our resources in such a way that ignorance will be replaced by knowledge. This is what a Canadian institute of criminology would do." Potts's words allow us to experience the criminological promise cognitively and intuitively. We experience it through his profession to decipher an ancient relic and thereby substitute "ignorance" with "knowledge." Until this point, it seems, crime had denied scholars theoretical insight into its essence. Early Canadian criminologists were convinced that such stubborn "ignorance" could be vanquished by employing the theoretical and methodological perfection offered by the mathematical natural sciences. Criminologists – not only in this country but throughout the West – busied themselves establishing criminology as the *scientific* discipline par excellence where valid, reliable, and objective knowledge about the "stubborn" problem of crime would be realized and disseminated. E.R. Markson and V. Hartman (1963, 19), for their part, were convinced that a "better understanding and control of crime and criminal behaviour" required an "attempt to collect, correlate, and unify the basic materials of criminology, and to extract from these data general principles." John L. Edwards (1961-62, 200), a pioneer of Canadian criminology and the first director of the Centre of Criminology at the University of Toronto, was of the opinion that criminologists should be "dedicated to the pursuit of truth and with no suspicion of bias attaching to their opinions." Indeed, Edwards's concern with the pursuit of truth without prejudice is intertwined with the "universalist bias" of modern science, which holds that so long as it is objective and reliable – extracted from the world of being and existence – *scientific* cognitive activity is universally valid (Weber 2000). We can further link this universality to *truth* as the essence of knowledge, which Potts (1963) imagined to be ignorance's antithesis. Indeed, "untrue knowledge is an oxymoron," given how spuriousness would be disavowed as such (Weber 2000). Truth and knowledge (even though they are etymologically irreducible) are taken to be homogenous in the scientific discourse of inaugural criminologists such as Potts, Hartman, and Edwards.

Rationality for conjoining truth/knowledge in counter-indication to ignorance was embedded within the discourse of science.[2] Tadeusz Grygier, one of the first to champion Canadian criminology, argued that "the main problem, both theoretical and practical, is the *scientific* control of criminal behaviour. Such control must entail the ability to foresee the consequences of our actions; and this, in turn, requires not only vision, but also prediction methodology, careful experimentation, and statistical analysis" (1963, 42, emphasis added). Early criminologists thus cloaked themselves in the cold comfort that "science" furnished. In this quotation, Grygier articulates the essence of modern science as prediction through experimentation and statistical analysis. Markson and Hartman (1963, 17) held the similar view that, "because he is scientifically trained, [the criminologist] can contribute more objectively to legal and penal reforms." Thus, prediction via instruments of science sanctioned criminological investigation as the essence of a messianic promise aimed at effective crime control.

Embedding criminology within the scientific aesthetic can certainly be taken as a proactive attempt to establish the budding discipline on secure footing. Claiming scientific pedigree, if not status, a priori confirms its legitimacy. Authenticating studies of crime and crime control in the language and practices of science, however, puts criminology in a precarious place. It forces its adherents to justify their work as science or to provide an alibi for any seeming departure from Truth. Debating whether criminology is a science, or whether its scholars should strive toward this measure, is not my intention here. Rather, I am attempting to situate early Canadian criminologists within a context whereby the discipline was sanctioned through and by science.[3] For their part, Grygier and his contemporaries were haunted by the spectres of science. They abhorred losing cachet with governments and universities, among others, if their claims about crime were exposed as fallacious or irrelevant. Heidegger was aware of how such claims to mirror the theoretical perfection of the mathematical sciences could both bolster and undermine influence and reputation. He claimed that "not to be a science is taken as a failing which is equivalent to being unscientific" (1977a, 194). Indeed, if there is a single truth about crime and criminality – and criminologists, through the application of the scientific method, are the only ones acquainted with it – then scientific dominion over truth goes unquestioned. However, if the elements that encourage the kind of foresight Grygier delighted in are not transcendental but are instead discovered to be culturally relative, then the status of criminology as science is "fatally undermined" (Fox-Keller 1987, 45).

As one suspects after reading Grygier's commentary, the bulwark of scientific knowledge, as far as criminologists are concerned, was intimately connected with its propensity to establish immutable and predictive sequences. As such, scholarly investigation was oriented toward the past only so far as it was prognostic of the future. Through cultivating outcomes derived from "careful experimentation" and "statistical analysis," criminologists affirmed mastery over a previously uncertain future. Charles Hendry (1963, 5), director of the School of Social Work at the University of Toronto, recited a well-worn refrain that, through science, criminologists would be "responsible for formulating suggestions for social policy ... and social action." The promise of criminology, then, was to progressively master and curtail uncertainties through "scientific control" and investigation. According to Markson and Hartman (1963, 17), criminological inquiry should entail a "systematic study of all the measures to be taken in the spheres of prevention and other methods of treatment ... to rob it of this practical function is to divorce criminology from reality and render it sterile." These criminologists laboured within an ontological framework wherein demonstrating the linkages between their scholarship and the criminological promise of relevance to government(s) and the criminal justice state rebuffed charges of epistemological irrelevance – honoured now by some critical scholars as much in the breach as in observance.

Claiming responsibility for an (un)certain future imputes an obligation to revere the contents of the promise. But, in what ways and through what means were these early scholars to realize their obligations? Irwin Haskett, the Ontario Minister of Reform Institutions, in 1962 argued that

> crime is costing Canadians millions and millions of dollars annu-
> ally, whilst the wastage in human life and happiness is beyond
> computing. No adequate effort has been made to pool our brains
> and resources in tackling this problem ... this department feels
> that the goal is a university centred institute of criminology that
> could have a three fold function: to conduct research, to teach and
> to act as consultant to legislators and administrators. (cited in
> Potts 1963, 7)

The growing size and urgency of the crime problem, then, underscored the need for a science of crime and scholars responsible for its control.

Frank Potts (1963, 7) reiterated Haskett's sentiments when he claimed that a Canadian institute of criminology would have a threefold function: "to conduct research, to teach and to act in a consultant capacity to legislators and administrators." Potts's contemporaries, it seems, embraced this threefold promise made for them, on their behalf, before them. Hendry (1963, 6, emphasis added), for his part, was convinced this scholarly initiative "holds great *promise*." These additional promises do not challenge the logic of an anterior promise to control crime, belie science, or traverse its practical function. These are, rather, ancillary obligations that buoy the crime control promise and bolster criminologists' affirmation of relevance. That is, through promises of applicable research, teaching, and advice to politicians concerning crime, inaugural criminologists excavated what was, and in many ways is still, considered the discipline's relevant content and epistemology.

Let us now examine these threefold promises in greater detail. First, the *promise of relevant research*. Criminologists, much like today, were expected to conduct both theoretical and operational research, with a decided emphasis on the latter, situated and conducted in "appropriate field settings" (Potts 1963, 8). Although it is axiomatic to suggest that academic criminologists today possess relative autonomy to decide on what substantive elements will be engaged through their scholarship, research problems for early criminologists were somewhat decided for them. Potts explains that "the problem for research usually is one that has been identified by, or in consultation, with, the policy maker, the administrator or the practitioner in the field" (ibid.). Research was and is predicated on its relevance.

Second, the *promise of relevant teaching*. The promise of teaching was intimately intertwined with the anterior criminological promise of crime control. Again, with this promise, early scholars were convinced that pedagogy should be stimulated by and relevant to the "field." Many of the scholars and government officials campaigning for Canadian criminology and criminological institutes championed teaching of not only or merely undergraduates or graduate students but also government officials. Involvement in the training and disciplining of future and contemporary practitioners meant research findings would be disseminated beyond the confines of academic debate. Markson and Hartman (1963, 15) made the case that "criminology can further the efforts of corrections by providing its practitioners with the results of competent basic research regarding crime." Schooling in criminological knowledge derived from scientific research that pried "true" laws and precepts loose from the field of crime prepared the next generation of frontline workers. As a "science" and through research, criminology promised the competency practitioners evidently lacked. On this point, John L. Edwards (1961-62, 200) lamented: "It is still possible for a lawyer fairly well versed in criminal law to become a member of the judiciary with next to no knowledge of the origins or nature of criminal behaviour and with no practical acquaintance either with the regimes operating in penal institution[s] or with other methods for the treatment of offenders." Moreover, a 1956 report on corrections (the Fauteux report) agitated for "professional education and research on crime and on the programs which seek to control crime, because without development in these fields Canadian efforts will lack professional understanding and direction" (Committee Appointed to Inquire 1956, 85). Before the 1960s, then, there existed a perceived lack, a nothing, a dearth in scientific knowledge/truth about crime and its control, which criminologists, through legitimacy acquired from science, promised to bridge.

Last, the *promise of relevant consultation with legislators and administrators.* "What could a government department expect," Potts (1963, 9) queried rhetorically, from an institute of criminology? He answers that they would profit (1) by being kept informed about world research and the institute's research findings; (2) by having research carried out in its own departments; (3) through staff training without additional costs; and (4) through its consultant capacity. As far as the state was concerned, this epistemo-juridical creation and dissemination of a regime of knowledge/truth concerning crime constituted criminology's essence.

Underlying and informing criminologists' pledge to control crime was a "will to truth" that, as Foucault has famously articulated, induces power. Thus, the question is not what is true or false or how did governments recognize hypotheses about crime as scientific, but rather, how was the harmony between truth and its utility qualified? "Truth," as Foucault (1994, 427) observes, is centred "on the form of scientific discourse and the institutions that produce it." Moreover, as he also claimed, the *reason of state* supplied the subjects to which relevant research must be directed). That is, truth does not have a certain need for discovery heterogeneous to, or at odds with, a will to power. It is, rather, caught up in the rise of disciplines such as criminology, whose scientific investigations ensnared subjects in relations of power as objects requiring correction, discipline, and assimilation.[4]

## The Structure of a Promise: Traces and Iterability

It is impossible to read these early texts without experiencing the exhilarating feeling inspired by a firm promise and a commitment to labour toward its fulfillment. My interest in dredging up the past is not to vet the entire scholarly enterprise or to slag its early practitioners. Indeed, below I attempt a restructuring of a certain spirit of criminology. Why, then, am I concerned with promises made a half century ago? It is for many reasons, but primarily because scholars today are haunted by its spectres. Its interpellative condition is experienced when the media calls, anxious to sort out the "cause" of youth crime, or when crime scholars are put on display in community talks. A promise signals a future event that seems on first impression plausible; it pledges beyond its author, without certainty of what or whom is spoken for or about (Derrida 1998). Indeed, Grygier, Hartman, Edwards, and others pledged responsibility to control crime through the instruments of a scientific discipline called criminology. This promise does not end with the subject but bleeds out and transcends him or her, affecting the work and expectations made of present-day criminologists. Assurances exceed their authors, such that they function in absence and circulate so long as the promise remains unrealized (Burns 2001, 49). One need only open a Canadian criminology textbook to evidence how these promises have become the orthodoxy (still) disseminated to the scholars of tomorrow.

Because (im)possible promises were made in the name of an institute of criminology and for the discipline, they have transcended generations such that they are inherited by present and future scholars writing or subsumed under this rubric. Many writing under criminology's banner, or forced under its umbrella for bureaucratic or disciplinary convenience, are still held to account for it. They perhaps feel the tug of relevance and science when filling out applications to the Social Sciences and Humanities Research Council or fashioning a paper for the discipline's hegemonic journals (that is, *Criminology*). Even when not outwardly assuming responsibility and allegiance to the criminological promise, such allegiance is often attributed to one by the media, administrators, reviewers, and politicians, among others.

For example, I was working in my office the morning after the rather appalling murder of a university-aged youth in Edmonton when the phone rang. I held my breath and answered the call, certain of who, or rather what, was on the other end. The reporter – I was right – inquired whether I could explain to her why violent crime was increasing in Edmonton. After informing her that in fact the latest police statistics confirmed the opposite, she bellowed: "You're the criminologist; explain to me why we keep seeing these violent crimes then." To which I replied, "Because you keep reporting them." She hung up. This is a scene that is repeated time and again across this country as reporters require an "expert" on crime (a criminologist, no doubt) to buttress their stories' angles. Often we oblige – albeit grudgingly. In these instances, we are interpellated as criminologists. We come to embody the role promised by the founding fathers to be experts on the causes, trends, and maybe even "solutions" to the crime problem. The write-up in the newspaper or the tag line on the local news broadcast (Dr. Bryan Hogeveen, *Criminologist*) confirms our allegiance and fidelity to criminology, whether or not we indeed experience it as such.

Let us pause for a moment before moving on and consider what would conjugating criminological promises with the present convey? What if the promise of crime control was perfectly actualized? If we concede that the structure of the promise contains a trace of perversion, we must also make allowances that the realization of the promise – to constitute it in presence, in the present – means perfect actualization. During the 1960s, criminological promise(s) announced relevant foundational content (to teach, to research, to advise, to control), which are not (yet) fulfilled. It is not my contention that all scholars have given up the ghost – many continue to be encouraged by the promise and its future possibility. Let us put aside for a moment the feasibility of this (im)possibility and follow the significance of the criminological pledge. From the outset, criminology was caught up in a power/ knowledge nexus wherein its promise was intimately tied to correcting deviant subjectivities. Abrogating crime was the essence of the criminological promise through which the discipline constituted itself as a science – a science dedicated to marshalling the criminal Other. The criminologist self, then, implies and requires otherness to such an intimate extent that it is impossible to think of that self without reference to a deviant Other. Instead, in quite Hegelian terms, one passes into and through the Other. Successful realization of the criminological promise through absolute control of crime and the assimilation of difference requires the death of both the discipline and its deviant Other.

Categorizing the Other as criminal or the negation of the good shored up disciplinary boundaries and contains the insidious beginnings of exclusionary practices that disavow, rather than welcome, wider and more inclusive patterns of harmony (Pavlich 2004, Hogeveen 2005). Readers should not take my critique as an "obituary" written during criminology's slow death (Sumner 1994). Instead, I want to suggest that instead of scholarly work (r)ejecting the Other from society through a coercive and intrusive criminological praxis that has taken many forms – from diversion (read "widening the net") to reformed court practices to its latest incarnations – it should embrace a restructured criminological promise of emancipation(s) offered in a context of post-disciplinarity.

Canadian criminologists of the past saturated our present time with a promise that we did not sign, did not endorse, did not give a "yes" to. I am fully cognizant of how many contemporary scholars have turned away from this messianic and perhaps dangerous promise of a future to come. Indeed, many who are reading this will argue that it is the very negation of *this* promise that informs their work. I too fit into this category. My work interdicts the original promises of criminology and, as such, is haunted rather than inhabited by a certain criminological spirit. It suggests a restructured praxis, which solicits responsibility aimed not at controlling the Other but at reneging on the inaugural promise of relevance (read "greater and more intrusive state control") in the interests of emancipation(s). But, as such, it does not escape inaugural criminological promises. In its resistance to inaugural criminological promises, this chapter depends and is imprisoned by them.

## The Structure of a Promise: Reconciling Spectres

Melancholy and disenchantment hang like an ominous haze over criminology, especially over its critical element. Although I sense this malaise, a certain criminological spirit perhaps may be retained – in radically altered form, of course. In his engagement with Marx's ghost, Derrida (1994) suggests that one never inherits without reconciling some spectre – and in the case of criminology, more than one ghost. The preceding discussion has assuaged several of criminology's ghosts, but because spectres are revenant – they begin by coming back – we can never fully disburden ourselves of their weight. Thus, as opposed to fighting against it, to speaking against it – so doing means fighting a losing battle against an apparition that cannot be easily defeated – scholars may embrace and speak with certain elements of this ghost – not on its terms, but on those set by the (critical) writers of today. In Jean-Paul Sartre's words, it is to "make something of what we were made into." Instead of cursing the criminological destiny, can a restructured criminological promise be located and discerned that negates the appropriation and manipulation of the Other for the purposes of self- and disciplinary promotion? If we are to speak and write with the spectres of criminology, what essence – in revised form, of course – perhaps may be preserved?

In the remainder of this chapter, I suggest how two elements of the criminological promise may be reclaimed. However, they become (almost) unrecognizable in the form and under the conditions I suggest. First, today there is a need for inverted and restructured criminological promises that open up to, instead of closing down around, alterity and possibility. Second, such a project requires a radical opening and reworking of disciplinary borders to the scholarship of "other" disciplines. Taking inspiration from a certain spirit of criminology would be to keep faith with that which has always made it in principle interdisciplinary, specifically as a host to "others" attracted to the study of crime. The group of 1960s academics who contributed to criminological epistemology was interdisciplinary, if such a thing ever existed. The disciplines represented among those lobbying for an institute of criminology included, but were not limited to, law, forensic psychiatry, social work, psychology, psychoanalysis, and theology. The only seeming requirement for membership was to submit to "a common desire for the advancement of [relevant] criminological knowledge" (Markson and Hartman 1963, 11). Crime scholars such as Frank Potts (1963, 7) were convinced that a multi-disciplinary faculty was required to cut the Gordian knot that is criminologists' subject matter. More to the point, criminological problems were thought to be of such complexity that they required sophisticated methodologies and epistemologies that no single discipline could profess.

Such an approach to the study and control of crime was not, however, without its potential problems. Denis Szabo (1963, 31), one of Canada's first criminologists, was concerned about the "imperialist tendencies" of law and psychiatry. A 1957 UNESCO (1957, 55) report boasted a familiar refrain: "The pre-eminence of a single discipline ultimately retards the whole field's development." Despite imperialist markings, most advocates favoured the department approach, whereby criminology would become host to scholars of various stripes who studied crime, the criminal, and his/her control. Markson and Hartman (1963, 16), believed "that the programme should be established as an autonomous unit within the university, employing its own staff, and calling upon the staff of other university departments to contribute to its activities ... Cross fertilization of this kind is required in order to further the development of criminology and its basic disciplines." John L. Edwards (1961-62, 199) opined that "the teaching and research staff of such an institute must be drawn, on as broad a basis as possible, from the various disciplines

concerned with different aspects of criminology." Today, the spectre of interdisciplinarity casts a long shadow over the discipline. Indeed, criminological
textbooks almost invariably define criminology along these lines. Larry Siegel
and Chris McCormick in *Criminology in Canada* (2006, 5-6) argue that "an
essential part of criminology is the fact that it is an interdisciplinary science
... an integrated approach to the study of criminal behaviour. Criminology
combines elements from many other fields."

Early Canadian criminologists seemed intent on welcoming scholars
from disparate disciplines into their combined interest. Recently, however,
and under disciplinary, institutional, and political pressure, the discipline
has become progressively myopic (Menzies and Chunn 1999). In increasing
numbers, critical scholars are leaving the rubric that has hosted them for
decades, declaring the host hostile. After a combined six decades publishing
and teaching under the criminology marquee, iconic scholars Dorothy Chunn
and Bob Menzies (2006), for example, have recently migrated away from the
discipline. In a rather sobering review, the authors charge that "critical scholarship about crime is coming to be pursued and practiced less and less under
the official imprimatur of 'criminology' and more and more within the more
inviting [and, ironically, increasingly interdisciplinary] scholarly environments of sociology and anthropology departments, law faculties, law and
society schools, women's studies, history, political science and humanities
units." Indeed, a discipline that initially boasted openness to "other" scholarship has seemingly closed down on itself – especially as it relates to
critical inquiry (see also Dupont, this volume).[5]

This condition was forecast over three decades ago by Robert Ratner
(1971), who made the point that "isolating the subject in one departmental
discipline ... can only stultify the growth of knowledge and research appropriate to the study of criminological problems." His point was that when disparate and distinct fields of inquiry are subsumed under the name of the host,
the Other becomes something other to itself. But this should come as no
surprise. John L. Edwards (1961-62, 199) argued that there are many "advantages which ensue from the creation of some form of organization with responsibility for *unifying* the present limited and dispersed efforts of
sociologists, lawyers, psychiatrists, and anthropologists, to mention only
some." Criminology, according to Edwards, would become a consolidating
force that would gather others into itself. By muscling "crime" away from
dispersed disciplines and anchoring it as an unambiguous scientific endeavour, criminology scholars declared their sovereignty. However, instead of

encouraging wider engagement with crime in all of its manifestations, this cannibalistic tendency has seemingly stifled creativity and openness. Heidegger (1977a, 195) claims that such names (that is, criminology) "begin to flourish only when original thinking comes to an end." Thinking, which pushes the limits of "truth" and ontology becomes circumscribed when situated under the demands placed upon it by such rubrics. But there can be no substituting a name, a concept, a foundation for another. No, the "new" that will perhaps emerge will be radically Other. Can there be a critical criminology to come, a criminological promise, which may come, which is open to "other" disciplinary scholarship without effacement and collapse? Perhaps.

What I have in mind is an open scholarship, which remains unfettered by promises set out by disciplinary forerunners, where nothing lies beyond question, critique, and deconstruction. This requires an expanded scholarly space that recalibrates the content that intrinsically inhabits the perception of what currently counts as criminological relevance. It will not be circumscribed by a tradition of promises, the vows of administrative and governmental relevance, or the limits hollowed out by early protagonists. This criminology "to come" will cross disciplinary boundaries or efface them altogether without being lumped into what is now called interdisciplinarity. Basically, it could, perhaps, take the form of post-disciplinarity, which is dissociated from disciplinary sovereignty and is, rather, open to independence of thought (Derrida 2002b).

Second, and coincident with an opening of disciplinary barriers, is a restructuring of the criminological promises along emancipatory lines. Even though there is an imminent possibility of even the most well-intentioned promise morphing into a threat, of the best turning into the worst, I am not prepared to recede into the relativist and nihilistic dogma that "we" should never promise anything. In the first instance, this experience is simply not possible. Even when academics intimate that they promise nothing at all, such is still a promise – a promise of nothing. Rather, this section calls for a restructured criminological promise of emancipation(s) to come. Restructuring the promise thus inverts the criminological relation to otherness. In the place of exclusion and intrusion into the lives of Others, a restructured promise that opens up to, and is responsible to, otherness is gathered. Instead, then, of closing down upon otherness in the name of and as "justice" (read "retribution"), emancipation(s) opens out to alterity. This is a promise made in the memory of capitalism, colonialism, racism, and tyranny both past and present. Walter Benjamin (1968, 254, emphasis in original) implores that "like every generation which preceded us, we have been endowed with a *weak* messianic force to which the past has a claim." Benjamin here allies a history and present, in particular of those rejected by history, with a promise of emancipation to come. Motivation to continue or commence political struggles against subjugation and tyranny, whatever the case may be, buoys this assumption.

Emancipatory promises for a future to come bind us to the dead and obligate us as much as to future generations (Fritsch 2002). No emancipation(s), as Derrida (1994, xix) claims, is possible or indeed thinkable for those who "are not yet born or who are already dead, be they victims of wars, political or other kinds of violence, nationalist, racist, colonialist, sexist, or other kinds of exterminations, victims of the oppressions of capitalist imperialism or any of the forms of totalitarianism" without *responsibility* to the messianicity of this promise. *This* criminological promise overflows its limits – we can never be responsible enough or labour hard enough toward it. Responsibility is the essence of this promise knotted with emancipation(s). Because it is anchored in the faces that surround me here and now (the gross overincarceration of Aboriginal youth, nefarious rates of homeless and poverty in light of affluence, genocide, misogyny, and – but certainly not limited to – the atrocities of Abu Ghraib), the call provoking the promise of emancipation(s), and my responsibility for meeting this call, cannot be deferred. It is imminent.

To be certain, emancipation(s) exceeds conceptualization. Derrida issues the following caution to anyone intent on setting out a priori foundations. Left unattended and allowed to close down on itself, seemingly emancipatory programs are "always very close to the bad, even to the worst[,] for it can always be reappropriated by the most perverse calculation. It's always possible" (Derrida 1990, 971). Indeed, such politics, ethics, and promises must remain in the realm of the future *(avenir)*. Once it has taken on substance and limits placed upon it, the emancipatory ideal becomes lifeless. It has been achieved – or so it seems. Politicization of domestic violence through law, for example, has certainly drawn considerable attention to wife assault and misogyny. Many more women are alive today as a result of feminist interventions. But, can we say that law has set women free of the bondage that is domestic violence? That justice for victims of domestic violence has been realized? Of course not. Indeed, many feminist scholars contend that counter-charging and insensitivity to women's needs have perverted the domestic violence court's vision of justice for female victims (Snider 1994; Minaker 2001). Joanne Minaker and Laureen Snider (2006) make the case that the domestic violence court's ameliorative promise has recently been denigrated through the commonsense dogma that spousal assault is experienced in gender-neutral ways. The conjugation of the promise to create laws and a court to protect women from domestic violence has been turned back against itself and the disadvantaged women in whose name such battles were fought. As Minaker and Snider (ibid., 770) state:

> The invention and celebration of "husband abuse" makes it more difficult to deal with real power imbalances between male and female partners, and easier to ignore or explain away empirical evidence showing that family violence usually means wife abuse. For men and men's groups, if women are really "just as bad as men" it becomes acceptable – even legitimate – to avoid dealing with the causes and consequences of the still ubiquitous reality of male violence against women. When policy makers take husband abuse claims at face value, resources allocated to rape crisis centres, shelters and services for battered women can be reduced or eliminated.

But evidence such as this does not necessarily condition nihilism – quite the contrary. In "Force of Law," Derrida (1990, 971) states that "nothing seems to me less outdated than the classical emancipatory ideal." Criminologists should insist and demand it, especially as we continue to witness the violent fallout from neo-liberal politics. However, there can be no precedent for this promise of an emancipation "to come," and I do not intend to provide such a foundation here. The "to come" of emancipation(s) implies a non-contemporaniety with the present and appeals to a constant reworking and refusal of established limits.[6]

Whatever messianic element or condition may arrive through such a criminological promise, it should nevertheless be considered interminable. Such a critical project, however, does not locate its essence in antithesis or foundational judgment (Pavlich 2000). The criminological promise should therefore not yoke itself to a manner of critique that simply negates the present. In attempting to transcend established limits, this form of critique fixes the scholar within the foundations that inspired the critique in the first instance. Indeed, even revolutionary movements, as George Pavlich (2000) suggests and history confirms, become slaves to the ontic that inspired the event in the first instance – especially after fighting has subsided and calm has returned. Confronted by a cold void once occupied by the state and capital, leaders of the revolt almost invariably fall back into the familiar instead of forging ahead into the experience of the outside – which is "afloat, foreign, exterior to our interior" (Foucault 1994, 426). The outside is perhaps a dangerous place of the "Nothing" that lacks the familiarity and aegis of a priori truths (Heidegger 1977b).

It is, however, exceptionally difficult to locate a purely reflexive discourse that bellows an affirmative "yes" to the outside and does not wholly lead this thought back to the complacency of what came before (the ontological inside). Such an experience of critique risks "setting down readymade meanings that stitch the old fabric of interiority back together" with the new emancipatory project (Foucault 1994, 427). A restructured criminological promise and the critique it engenders is directed toward the outside, where it must be contented to push into the void. This promise that welcomes the outside it addresses is not a hope for an open future that unfolds in the wait. Waiting, as Foucault observes, is unsatisfactory given how "any object that could gratify it would only efface it" (ibid.).

Nietzsche (1998, 7) queries in *Beyond Good and Evil*: "Who is willing to worry about such dangerous Perhapses?" Although he responds that we must wait for these enterprising philosophers of the dangerous perhaps to arrive, he sees them coming. Are contemporary criminologists of the ilk Nietzsche's discourse foretold? Perhaps. Whatever the case, a criminological promise of emancipation(s) must be planted firmly beyond good and evil and located in an open dialectic that eschews totality in favour of openness and possibility – the *perhaps* about which Nietzsche inquires. As such, it must master the awe inspired by the thought of the outside without erasing the alterity and heterogeneity that emerge alongside it (Derrida 1997). Without this kind of critique, the emancipation promise remains rooted in present conditions and parasitic upon the ethos it abhors. It becomes emancipatory only to the extent available within current parameters. Does this, then, mean that criminologists should cease their battle against tyranny? No, just the opposite. We should renew it again and again in a way that resists reappropriation and encourages an opening to the future. What I am insisting upon is not a quick fix for centuries of old oppressions but a laborious process of working, pushing, and exposing limits of the possible. Criminological promises should, then, embrace increasingly more emancipatory possibilities and even more dangerous perhapses that are not responsible to the state or criminal justice, but to the changing faces of tyranny mirrored in past and present injustice(s).

## Conclusion

Ambitious programmatic statements about criminology's future(s) are not promised herein. Instead, I have followed and interrogated the grounding of criminological relevance in promises. It is not to be taken as a manifesto of the criminological nihilist caught between unqualified immersion in criminal justice ends or epistemological irrelevance. Rather, I am calling for a criminology of possibility (Hogeveen and Woolford 2006). Or, perhaps not necessarily a *criminology* of possibility, but an anarchic essence that perpetually escapes codifications and prowls behind, beside, and within our factual experience. The unfettered disciplinary scholarship I have in mind – the very motive of identification and cataloguing becomes problematic in this instance – dissolves part of its critical essence the moment it submits to bureaucratic convenience (Allen 2006).

Derrida (2002b, 141) describes the contemporary university system as a techno-scientific institution whose products can be employed by "multinational military industrial complexes or techno-economic networks." Similarly, criminology's products have been placed on the global market in the forms of zero tolerance, restorative justice, and broken windows (Wacquant 2001). Moreover, criminology, as Huey (this volume) maintains, has become a discipline that propagates the status quo: where "tell me what I need to know to get a job" has become the student's rallying cry. Even when students are enticed to think critically about their space, their time, and their tolerance(s), it seems that would-be dissidents are as quickly assimilated into the established order – an ethos they never opposed in the first instance. Many may despise what is being done to their fellow humans throughout the globe; but they *desire* what that world offers them.

Ends-oriented inquiry and pedagogy proceeds to the extent that its ground remains unquestioned. Criminology heretofore has remained firmly ensconced within the epistemological cycle of manifesting tighter controls over the structurally disadvantaged and producing bodies capable of controlling the Other, while leaving the a priori structural conditions of criminality largely unscathed. Thus, the triple vision of end-oriented scholarship (relevant research, advice, and teaching) is maintained only to the extent that it loses sight of the very "ends of its own ends" (Derrida 2004, 141). The discipline remains controlled and governed by the field it examines: readily observable in the categories and rhetoric employed (crime, victim, cause, criminal, and so on). It is the responsibility of an "open" criminology to trouble the most conservative forces of the criminal justice system with discourses not easily accommodated in its economy and ecology (Derrida 2004). Such scholarship must assume responsibility for entering into a tireless negotiation with its own heteronomy from the insidious domination of the poor so as to maintain the possibility of welcoming a future beyond tyranny and (r)ejection of alterity.

Derrida (2002a, 4) argues that "a philosopher is always someone for whom philosophy is not given, someone who in essence must question the self about the essence and destination of philosophy. And who reinvents it." The same holds for *possible* criminology: what is meant and intended by criminology must be rethought – an infinite task. This rethinking must also unmask the promises that silently buttress it while obfuscating the structural inequalities that produce its subject. I am not here pitting theory against methods or critical against mainstream scholarship. Rather, this chapter has suggested the necessity of moving beyond such clichéd dichotomies – there is value and reason in both – toward praxis that calls criminology's tacit and expressed discourse(s) to account. Criminology of *possibility*, beyond criminology, would be agreeable to all manner of research, scholarship, and discourse, but would not be content thus. It is not simply a manner of submitting criminology to critique, as I am doing here, but of transforming its discourse, pedagogy, and affiliation with "other" disciplines and to the university. It seems that those who venture along this path should not set themselves in opposition to criminology, nor should they give way to polemics to establish their ends. Rather, scholarly responsibility must challenge the conservative forces of criminal justice and governance strategies that conceal tyranny, along with the scholarly promises that serve as alibis.

## ACKNOWLEDGMENTS

I thank George Pavlich, Joanne Minaker, and the editors for their helpful suggestions.

## NOTES

1 "Canadian" criminology was not an insulated epistemological entity. Rather, it was influenced by American and (especially) British developments in scholarship (for example, Leon Radzinowicz's work) and disciplinary organization.

2 The genealogy of the academic study of crime and its control in Canada predates the establishment of disciplinary criminology in the 1960s. Throughout the late nineteenth and early twentieth centuries, humanitarian, philanthropic, political, and scholarly groups coalesced around the problem of deviance. For example, although most well known for his study of the Dionne quintuplets, W.E. Blatz, a

University of Chicago-trained psychologist, took a keen interest in juvenile delinquency. In addition, eugenicists such as C.K. Clarke and the philanthropic elite
such as W.L. Scott often clashed over what was the most effective means through
which to govern deviance (Hogeveen 2002, 2005).

3   Today, many criminologists delight in distancing themselves from these ostensible
    fetters. See for discussion Hogeveen, Martel, and Woolford (2006).

4   One immediate consequence of this or that claim to embody, realize, or conjugate
    the criminological promise, to constitute it as presence, in the present, is locating
    the scholar on the side of suppression of alterity.

5   See also Robert Ratner's (2006) retrospective account of his attempt to establish
    critical criminology in Canada and the resistance(s) he encountered.

6   See also Pavlich (2000); Hogeveen and Woolford (2006); and Woolford and
    Ratner (2003).

## REFERENCES

Allen, G. 2006. What Kind of Body Is Speaking Here? The Pupils of the University.
    *Parallax* 12(3): 1-7.

Benjamin, W. 1968. On the Concept of History. In *Illuminations*, ed. Hannah Arendt,
    253-64. New York: Fontana.

Burns, L. 2001. Derrida and the Promise of Community. *Philosophy and Social Criticism*
    27(6): 43-53.

Chunn, D.E., and R. Menzies. 2006. So What Does All of This Have to Do with Crim-
    inology? Surviving the Restructuring of the Discipline in the Twenty-First Century.
    *Canadian Journal of Criminology and Criminal Justice* 48(5): 663-80.

Committee Appointed to Inquire into the Principles and Procedures Followed in the
    Remission Service (Fauteux Report). 1956. *Report.* Ottawa: Queen's Printer.

Derrida, J. 1990. Force of Law. *Cardozo Law Review* 11: 919-1126.

–. 1994. *Specters of Marx: The State of the Debt, the Work of Mourning and the New Inter-
    national.* London: Routledge.

–. 1997. Perhaps or Maybe. *PLI: The Warwick Journal of Philosophy* 6(2): 1-18.

–. 1998. *Monolingualism of the Other, or, The Prosthesis of Origin.* Stanford, CA: Stanford
    University Press.

–. 2002a. The Right to Philosophy from the Cosmopolitical Point of View. In *Ethics,
    Institutions and the Right to Philosophy,* translated by Peter Trifonas, 1-18. New York:
    Rowan and Littlefield.

–. 2002b. The University without Condition. In *Without Alibi,* translated by Peggy Kamuf,
    202-80. Stanford: Stanford University Press.

–. 2004. The Principle of Reason: The University in the Eyes of Its Pupils. *Eyes of the
    University: Right to Philosophy* 2. Trans. Jan Plug. Stanford: Stanford University
    Press.

Edwards, J.L. 1961-62. Canadian Teaching and Research in Criminology. *Criminal Law Quarterly* 4(1): 171-201.

Foucault, M. 1994. The Thought of the Outside. In *The Essential Foucault*, ed. P. Rabinow and N. Rose, 423-41. New York: New Press.

Fox-Keller, E. 1987. The Gender/Science System: Or, Is Sex to Gender as Nature Is to Science? *Hypatia* 2(3): 45-63.

Fritsch, M. 2002. Derrida's Democracy to Come. *Constellations* 9(4): 574-97.

Grygier, T. 1963. Dimensions of Criminology. *Canadian Journal of Criminology and Corrections* 5(1): 40-46.

Heidegger, M. 1977a. Letter on Humanism. In *Martin Heidegger: Basic Writings*, 1st ed., ed. D.F. Krell, 213-66. San Francisco: HarperCollins.

–. 1977b. On the Essence of Truth. In *Martin Heidegger: Basic Writings*, 1st ed., ed. D.F. Krell, 111-38. San Francisco: HarperCollins.

Hendry, C. 1963. Toward Collaboration in the Study of Crime and Corrections. *Canadian Journal of Criminology and Corrections* 5(1): 1-6.

Hogeveen, B. 2002. Mentally Defective and Feeble-Minded Juvenile Offenders: Psychiatric Discourse and the Toronto Juvenile Court 1910-1930. *Canadian Bulletin of Medical History* 20(1): 43-74.

–. 2005. Toward "Safer" and "Better" Communities? Canada's Youth Criminal Justice Act, Aboriginal Youth and the Processes of Exclusion. *Critical Criminology* 13(3): 287-305.

–, J. Martel, and A. Woolford, eds. 2006. Law, Society and Critique in Canada. *Canadian Journal of Criminology and Criminal Justice* 48(5): 633-46.

Hogeveen, B., and A. Woolford. 2006. Critical Criminology and Possibility in the Neoliberal Ethos. *Canadian Journal of Criminology and Criminal Justice* 48(5): 681-701.

Kerrigan, W. 1999. An Anatomy of Promising. *Raritan* 19(2): 27-41.

Markson, E.R., and V. Hartman. 1963. Function and Organization of a Model Institute of Criminology. *Canadian Journal of Criminology and Corrections* 5(1): 11-27.

Menzies, B., and D. Chunn. 1999. Discipline in Dissent: Canadian Academic Criminology at the Millennium. *Canadian Journal of Criminology* 41(3): 285-97.

Minaker, J. 2001. Evaluating Criminal Justice Responses to Intimate Abuse through the Lens of Women's Needs. *Canadian Journal of Women and the Law* 13(1): 74-91.

–, and L. Snider. 2006. Husband Abuse: Equality with a Vengeance? *Canadian Journal of Criminology and Criminal Justice* 48(5): 753-80.

Nietzsche, F. 1998. *Beyond Good and Evil: Prelude to a Philosophy of the Future*. Oxford World Classics. Trans. Marion Faber. London: Oxford University Press.

Pavlich, G. 2000. Nietzsche, Critique and the Promise of Not Being Thus ... *International Journal for the Semiotics of Law* 13(3): 357-75.

–. 2004. Restorative Justice's Community: Promise and Peril. In *Critical Issues in Restorative Justice*, ed. B. Toews and H. Zehr. New York: Criminal Justice Press.

Potts, F. 1963. Institute of Criminology. *Canadian Journal of Criminology and Corrections* 5(1): 7-10.

Ratner, R.S. 1971. Criminology in Canada: Conflicting Objectives. Working paper. Copy in possesssion of the author.

–. 2006. Pioneering Critical Criminology in Canada. *Canadian Journal of Criminology and Criminal Justice* 48(5): 647-63.

Siegel, L., and C. McCormick. 2006. *Criminology in Canada: Theories, Patterns and Typologies*. Toronto: Nelson.

Snider, L. 1994. Feminism, Punishment and the Potential of Empowerment. *Canadian Journal of Law and Society* 9(1): 75-104.

Sumner, C. 1994. *The Sociology of Deviance: An Obituary*. Buckingham: Open University Press.

Szabo, D. 1963. Criminology and Criminologist: A New Discipline and a New Profession. *Canadian Journal of Criminology and Corrections* 5(1): 28-39.

UNESCO. 1957. *Teaching Social Sciences: Criminology*. Paris: UNESCO.

Wacquant, L. 2001. The Penalisation of Poverty and the Rise of Neoliberalism. *European Journal on Criminal Policy and Research* 9(4): 401-12.

Weber, S. 2000. The Future of the Humanities: Experimenting. *Culture Machine* 2, http://www.culturemachine.net/index.php/cm/article/view/311/296.

Woolford, A., and R.S. Ratner. 2003. Nomadic Justice? Restorative Justice on the Margins of Law. *Social Justice* 30(1): 177-94.

# 3
# Commodifying Canadian Criminology: Applied Criminology Programs and the Future of the Discipline

*Laura Huey*

> The reality is that the modern state-supported university is, by turns, a corporate-sponsored research wing, a quasi-parental holding tank for late adolescents, and a training institution for the ambitious.
>
> – Mark Kingwell, *Nothing for Granted*

Of the university functions that Mark Kingwell sardonically enumerates in the quotation that opens this chapter, my own particular interest is in the university as training institute. As I discuss in the pages that follow, over the past few years, criminologists have witnessed a notable increase in the number of Canadian colleges and universities offering applied criminology in the form of programs and courses that appear to offer little more than vocational training for entry into the "exciting field of criminal justice." My present concern is that this academic discipline appears to be morphing into little more than a consumable product.

In this chapter, I trace the contours of this shift through an analysis of larger patterns of corporatization within higher learning and with reference to schisms within the discipline of criminology. In doing so, I advance two arguments. First, that the increasing corporatization of criminology represents a significant threat to the teaching of criminology: the present overemphasis on applied methods and technologies within programs and curricula within the discipline impairs a principle function of both academia generally and criminology specifically – namely, our ability to influence the development of critical reasoning skills, including teaching students to grasp, apply, and develop theoretical models in the pursuit of understanding phenomena within the social world. My second concern is the direct impact that the marketing of these programs has on student expectations. Looking at recent employment trends, I contend that for students who have been targeted by university and college marketing campaigns extolling the benefits of entering criminal justice as a "growth field" and offering means of success in the form of "practical skills," there is instead a harsh reality: the bulk of job creation appears to be in low-paying jobs within the private sector. Further, even with increased demands from the private sector for "trained graduates," it remains unclear as to whether employment creation will ultimately be able to keep pace with student demands for jobs.

## Commodified Knowledge(s): The Corporatization of Higher Education

> Education can be regarded as a variable commodity, a "quality" product which can be purchased in order to ensure social and cultural reproduction.
>
> – Leslie Pugsley, "Throwing Your Brains at It"

Western universities have long embodied two sets of educational goals that are often treated as dichotomous: the acquisition of knowledge and the reproduction of professionals (Bradney 1992). The origins of the Western university system lie in the second of these goals; early universities functioned primarily as training centres for lawyers, clergy, physicians, and other professional groups (ibid.; Ash 1991). From its inception, the intrinsic value of this form of higher education was held to lie in its use value – that is, in the ability of universities to create trained specialists to "enter the key professions on which the wealth of the nation and the quality of life ultimately depends" (Ash 1991, 6).

It is important to note, as both Dupont and Hogeveen detail in this volume, that use value was deemed critical to the development and subsequent rise of criminology. Indeed, Hogeveen, in particular, demonstrates how early criminologists viewed their fledgling discipline in light of its ability to be relevant to practical criminological matters, including the ability to instruct government officials and field workers in the "science" of crime control – that is, these early scholars treated criminology largely as an academic enterprise for churning out. I draw attention to this historical fact because subsequent developments within the discipline and within academia generally gave rise to alternative visions of both the "criminological promise" and the larger "academic promise."

What happened was, simply put, that the primacy of the use-value goal within academia did not go uncontested. As Bradney (1992) notes, in the mid-1800s, educators' views as to the primary purpose of a university education underwent a moderate shift with the infusion of liberal doctrine into academia. At this moment, the newly emerging "liberal university saw its responsibility as to reproduce professions, but professions defined as much by social custom as by technological requirements, and to transmit cultural capital in its broadest and most metaphorical sense" (Scott 1984, 30). Today, the liberal view of universities as centres of knowledge production and transmission remains central to how many university educators see themselves and their work. For example, in his defence of the liberal tradition within the Canadian university system, Neil Tudiver (1999, 155) asserts that "the traditional university produces knowledge through research, and distributes it freely in the public domain through teaching, publication, and community service."[1]

Since the 1990s, the historic tension between these two educational values has increased steadily as a direct result of the promotion of use value as *the* central goal of university programs and curricula in the West. The dominance of the use-value goal within the Canadian university system has been linked to at least three significant social, political, and economic factors that operate variously at the level of the university, the provincial and federal governments, and globally. These often interrelated factors are (1) reductions in government funding of higher education, (2) the rise of the knowledge economy, (3) and the influence of the public managerial model (Miller 1998; Tudiver 1999).

Provincial funding of higher education has the most direct influence on university practices. As Miller (1998, 19) notes, "there is a connection between the structures and political pressures at the provincial, state, [and] federal level[s], the economy at regional or national and international level[s], and the practices of university presidents and the creation and transmission of cultures within universities' managements." From the 1980s onward, Canadian universities have witnessed declines in provincial funding levels, with the result that university managers have had to turn to other revenue sources to offset budget shortfalls (Tudiver 1999). Encouraging private-sector investment has been one of the primary strategies employed, increasing student tuitions another. The removal of provincial caps on tuition fees has facilitated this second process.

To continue attracting and retaining students in the face of increasing fees, universities have had to develop means of appealing to students' self-interests. One of the most prominent means utilized is the linking of higher education with increased job prospects in promotional literature, so that higher education becomes seen not as a right and thus something one expects as an entitlement of citizenship but, rather, as an investment for which one willingly pays, with the reasonable hope of future returns. To this end, we find universities scrambling to enter into partnerships with the private sector, developing new undergraduate and graduate applied programs, and revising curricula to include increased emphasis on so-called professional training.

The current trend toward treating higher education centres as professional training facilities is not unique to Canada. Thus, we find Stanley Aronowitz (2000, 158) lamenting an American academic system that "has fudged the distinctions between training, education, and learning," with the result that many colleges and universities "have thrust training to the fore and called it education." The rise of training as education represents a key characteristic of the new global knowledge economy (Bell 1973; Schiller 1981; Castells 1989). Based on neo-liberal principles of the Chicago School, and drawing particular inspiration from human capital theory (Becker 1994), the knowledge economy model posits that there is an education-economy nexus whereby investment in education is rewarded by improved opportunities in the labour market (Shacklock, Hattam, and Smyth 2000). The model assumes that "the skills, attitudes and competencies acquired in education are transferable to the workplace and technology requires a higher level of skilling of workers" (Blackmore 1990, 180).

The American variant of neo-liberalism upon which the knowledge economy is founded is grounded in a particular view of the relationship between the social and the economic that profoundly alters the way in which education is viewed: the social sphere is treated as part of the economic sphere rather than as a separate domain (Lemke 2001). The social is thus rendered a function of the economic, and all human activities – including education – become subservient to the dictates of the marketplace. Reflecting on the impact of neo-liberal knowledge economy-based policies on higher education centres in Australia, Bullen, Robb, and Kenway (2004, 8) point to a central concern that this shift has engendered more generally:

Current knowledge economy policy in Australia works to intensify the already pervasive view of a dichotomy between learning for its own intrinsic pleasure and learning which is vocationally, commercially, scientifically and technologically oriented ... Within institutions of higher education, learning for its own sake has become a luxury that increasingly few students can afford, and disciplines in the humanities and creative arts are increasingly unable to provide.

The result of this shift, these scholars argue, is that the "knowledge that matters in a knowledge-based economy thus theorized is technological knowledge" (ibid.).

Because the primary goal of education under this model is to serve the market, not surprisingly we find the rise of public managerialism among institutes of higher education. "Public managerialism" is the term commonly used to describe various techniques and strategies aimed at "reforming" public-sector institutions and agencies so that they perform according to business principles found within the private sector (Deem 1998; Miller 1998; Rose 1999). Under "managerialism," public entities are expected to implement policies and procedures that emphasize fiscal responsibility, accountability, standardization of processes, performance measures, and competitiveness (Miller 1998). And, to the extent that the public sector is expected to "replicate the 'realities' of the market in some idealized private sector free market," universities and other private institutions compete with each other for students, utilizing aggressive marketing campaigns to target potential "customers" (ibid., 3). As Deem (1998, 47) suggests, this transformation of university management goals has entailed profoundly altered relations within university systems:

> Until quite recently, the notion that the activities and cultures of universities either required managing or were, in any meaningful sense, "managed," would have been regarded as heretical. Universities were perceived as communities of scholars researching and teaching together in collegial ways; those running universities were regarded as academic leaders rather than as managers or chief executives.

With a new private-sector customer ethos influencing universities, and particularly their marketing and recruitment drives, today's potential students are no longer viewed as applicants seeking selection for university and college places but as potential consumers of the university's products and services (Ka-ho 1997). To encourage these potential customers, university recruitment becomes increasingly geared toward offering students not simply an education but also "convenience, service, lifestyle, and reputation" (Tudiver 1999, 160), with curriculum choices that encompass "cores and options from which students, as customers, can choose" (Ka-ho 1997, 4).

One of the most desirable of consumer choices now available from the corporate university is the ability to access applied programs to enhance professional training. Courses and programs are tailored to the perceived needs of both the marketplace and those seeking to enter it as professionals (Miller 1998). Once largely academic disciplines now offer courses that are variously taught by "professionals in the field," emphasize "practical skills," include role-playing exercises to help students gain experience in particular professional situations, and include fieldwork exercises that may involve external evaluation of student performance. An increasing number of programs also facilitate direct student access to the market through student practicums and private-sector internships. Although none of these options is inherently bad or problematic in and of itself, as we shall see in relation to the teaching of criminology as an applied field, the move toward valuing education solely according to extrinsic values presents significant concerns.

## The Rise of Applied Criminology Programs in Canada

Attention: Criminology Students
Are you interested in exploring different strategies for interacting with people in a criminal justice context? [Our criminology course] will introduce approaches to crisis management, negotiation, conflict de-escalation, and decision-making. Professionals from a variety of backgrounds in the criminal justice system will discuss and demonstrate related skill sets throughout the semester. Challenges with difficult client groups and situations will be addressed and interventions surveyed.

– sign posted in the hallway of a Canadian college

Of particular interest in this chapter is the rise of applied criminology within the Canadian context. This branch of criminology is perhaps more commonly known, certainly within US schools, as criminal justice studies. At its core, this field is properly understood as an approach that treats criminology as a practical matter. Braithwaite (1993, 387), for example, describes applied criminology as an art form that affords the criminologist the ability to "multiple theoretical significances in a practical problem, thus bringing the practitioner to a differentiated understanding of the problem."

Despite Braithwaite's conceptualization of applied criminology as bounded by theoretical significances, in practice and in the classroom this form is easily distinguishable from what is often termed "academic criminology" on the ground that the former is concerned with the transmission of practical knowledge, whereas the latter is conceptualized as a scholarly pursuit centred on "deepening our understanding of the complexities of social phenomena such as crime and criminality" (Frauley 2005, 250). Ericson and Carriere (1994, 90) also make this distinction:

> Driven by practical questions, practices and power relations of those working within the criminal law institution, [Applied] Criminology begins with questions of reform and improvement – what is faulty? How can it be corrected? How can it be made more efficient? – rather than questions arising from problems and academic puzzles derived from scholarly literature.

To add to any possible confusion, in Canada, applied and academic criminology are also found subsumed within distinct categories that highlight their differences. Applied criminology is frequently conceptualized as a form of "protective service" – clearly, a practical set of concerns – whereas academic criminology is treated as a category of sociology and thus as a social science with both theoretical and grounded concerns.[2]

Although it is beyond the scope of this chapter to provide a comprehensive review of the various applied criminology programs and courses on offer at universities and colleges across Canada, a brief examination of a few of these should suffice to illustrate the increasing breadth and scope of choices available. For example, many undergraduate criminology programs today offer applied courses for students seeking careers in policing, corrections, and juvenile justice, as court workers, in restorative justice, and in other related areas. One community college offers applied criminology courses in its correctional worker program. Students are advised that they will be expected to "apply their acquired knowledge and skills of crime definitions, crime statistics and the causes of crime (from Introduction to Criminology) to a variety of contemporary criminal justice issues." "The focus of inquiry," students are further told, "will be on practical application."[3] Other approaches to the study of applied criminology are exemplified by undergraduate programs offering specialized training in "security and policing," or bachelor of general studies' programs that offer "police studies options." Students of one such police Studies program are able to take courses in "managerial control" and "criminal intelligence and crime analysis" at the Pacific Region Training Centre of the RCMP.[4]

There are also an increasing number of applied programs and courses available to graduate students. One eastern Canadian university offers graduate students an opportunity to participate in one of its two masters-level programs, which include a standard MA in criminology (with emphasis on theoretical criminology and research methods) and a non-research-based MA in applied criminology for students pursuing "careers in correctional services, the administration of justice, or in a field related to justice based interventions at the individual social level." Another school in the west that has been solidifying its applied approach to both teaching and research over the past few years has moved even further in that direction. Presently, both undergraduates and graduates of this school are able to work within the private sector as part of accredited coursework in field practicums after completing coursework on "professionalism in criminal justice."

The emergent rise in applied criminology offerings reflects two very different processes that have converged. The first of these is perhaps the most apparent to those outside the field: the commodification of higher education and, in particular, the prioritization of use value among university administrators. As discussed above, the dominance of use value has impacted Western academia generally, thus it would be tremendously naive to assume that somehow criminology would remain untouched by this larger transformation. For those within the field there is another likely factor also at play: the fragmentation of criminology and the lack of a unitary disciplinary focus (Clear 2000).

From its inception, criminology has been "highly differentiated in its theoretical, methodological, and empirical concerns" (Garland 2002, 15). Thus, as an umbrella discipline, it encompasses a wide range of academic and practical pursuits that have as their central focus the problem of crime and its treatment. This lack of a unitary focus leads to often disparate views as to how criminologists should view their discipline and what is an appropriate endeavour within their field. For example, Roberta Bisi (1999, 109) views the discipline thus:

Criminology not only deals with the causative studies of the criminal phenomenon and the study of crime as a social phenomenon.
It also aims to train workers in aiding the prevention and suppression of crime so as to ensure greater personal and public safety.
This effort can find reason of being only by attempting to transform Criminology courses within universities into even more
developed schools of method, able to underline the sense of
problems, stimulate reflections and generate more doubts than
certainties, instead of using a teaching method based exclusively
on the sole transmission of a great quantity of information that
lacks notions.

For Bisi, the supposed strength of criminology lies in its ability to operate as
a practical field and not simply as a site of pure study and knowledge reproduction. Critical criminologists Robert Menzies and Dorothy Chunn (1999,
287) survey the landscape of criminology and take away a different impression, one that clearly reflects a view of the discipline as holding both transformative and transgressive potentials not currently being realized:

Criminology is possibly the most modernist of all the social "sciences"; replete with ontological hierarchies, ideological choices,
moral dichotomies, binary thought forms, and fictive divisions between the sinners and the virtuous, the authors and their subjects,
the knowers and the known. As Foucault ... writes, it originated as
– and arguably remains as its core – a repressive penal enterprise
aimed at subjugating through science the human will to innovate
and resist. A few hours spent reading the standard journals, or a
couple of days devoted to random sampling of American Society
of Criminology sessions at the annual meetings, will acutely if
depressingly bear out this unflattering depiction of the discipline.

The two views highlighted above fall within what are often termed the
"positivist" and "critical/reformist" camps respectively; the division they reflect
is widely held to be *the* primary schism within the field. However, criminology is significantly more fractured than this simple split would suggest.
Divisions also exist within subfields of both major streams, as well as within
institutions and at personal and professional levels. Menzies and Chunn
(1999, 291) make this point, for example, in relation to critical criminology,

noting that this community has also been "beset by its own disciplinary struggles, internal divisions, competing allegiances, and the familiar irritations of departmental and personal politics."

In a penetrating analysis of the fragmentation of criminology, Ericson and Carriere (1994, 105) suggest that we need to approach this phenomenon in light of "what it is" – "the inevitable result of academic and institutional change in risk society." These authors contend that as societies become increasingly consumed by questions of risk and safety, demands for institutional responses are generated. The role of criminologists therefore becomes to "help myriad institutions construct suitable enemies, control the irrational by rational means, and apply insurance-formatted technologies" (ibid.). In doing so, criminologists necessarily "contribute to an increasingly destructured, fragmented, and reflexive existence" that necessarily mirrors the myriad interests within societies (ibid.). The perceived needs that the increased emphasis on personal and other forms of risk create find expression in market-based demands on universities and colleges to reproduce trained professionals to deal with crime problems "on the ground," demands that are threatening to profoundly alter the teaching of criminology.

## Pedagogical Issues: Generating 'Use Value'or Serving Up 'McCriminology'?

> Closer to home, administrators of the new corporate university have been abetting the aims of "Applied" Criminology by promoting the institutionalist ideals of accountability, employability, practical knowledge, and technical innovation. Translated, these discourses threaten to (re)construct academic criminologists as service providers who are responsible for giving student consumers what they apparently demand – namely, concrete "marketable" skills – in the most "accessible" and inexpensive manner possible.
>
> – Robert Menzies and Dorothy E. Chunn, "Discipline in Dissent"

The potential effects of corporatization that Menzies and Chunn discuss in the quotation that opens this section are already being felt within the discipline of criminology and particularly in relation to the manner in which it is being taught. In talking with other criminologists, it is clear that they are feeling pressure to teach criminology courses in applied forms and that this pressure is coming largely from students, who are increasingly being led through university and college marketing claims to believe that the primary, if not sole, purpose of teaching criminology is to provide them with job skills training. I too have felt this pressure. As someone who has taught criminology courses at a liberal arts college, I have experienced the disappointed looks of students who discover that their "policing instructor" is not a police officer and, worse still, has absolutely no intention of discussing the fine art of "busting perps." I recall one course evaluation where in response to the statement: "our instructor explains/demonstrates/illustrates the subject well," a disappointed student wrote: "but she's not a cop ☹." Although I might not offer the technical and experience-based knowledge of a police officer, what I do offer is a critical perspective on the police institution based on both my own research and that of other scholars in the field – that is, I teach criminology as a traditional academic discipline. My results are mixed: some students leave my courses feeling that they have learned something worthwhile – I derive this view from positive evaluations, personal comments, and the fact that I get a fair amount of repeat business and referrals – whereas one or two students each term sit at the back of the class, arms crossed, wearing disgusted looks as I critically deconstruct police culture and policing tactics.

I am hardly the first criminology instructor to complain of the pressure from students to transform my pedagogy into a style that can be more readily digested as job training. Mathieu Deflem (2002, 3), many of whose experiences in the classroom eerily echo mine, notes that in teaching a course on criminal justice, "there was even downright resentment from some students against my instruction as a direct result of the fact that the course adopted a sociological approach to Criminal Justice." Similarly, readers will recall from an earlier chapter in this book Benoît Dupont's discussion of the outright resentment experienced by professors teaching in the applied policing program, following its introduction at the School of Criminology at the Université de Montréal. As Dupont notes, professors who did not modify their course content to placate the demands for lectures and materials deemed "practically connected" to the policing field faced poor evaluations. The situation, which must have been intolerable for those young faculty members approaching tenure decisions, was only resolved through a departmental bifurcation.

What these students are primarily objecting to is the insertion of theoretical models and abstract forms of thinking into what they perceive as their technical training. This perspective, encouraged by marketing schemes emphasizing criminology as vocation, clearly wars with an alternative view of the discipline as a social science, and thus as a space for the development of analytical skills. As Frauley (2005, 253-54) notes, the latter approach demands a "concomitant pedagogy ... concerned with the fostering of theoretical thinking and analytical abilities that would be widely transferable rather than with only the imparting of technical information or specialised skills for routinised labour."

Some proponents of applied programs would be likely to disagree with the view that vocation-oriented training discourages the development of students' critical reasoning skills. Indeed, in searching the Internet for discussions of applied criminology, I happened across the following comments offered by a faculty member at a school that offers one such program: "We want our students here to graduate with a critical eye not necessarily so that they will ill-fit the job that they take, but so they can better fit, be better informed and make decisions based on sound critical thinking and research as opposed to, necessarily at times, political motives" (cited in McMahon n.d.). This is an entirely commendable view. However, it does raise an interesting question. Given that, if they are able to secure work in their field, most graduates of bachelor of arts or criminal justice diploma programs will enter the market at lower levels within the criminal justice system, are critical-thinking skills necessary or even desirable for such lower-end jobs? Probably not. And thus, to the extent that the market is permitted to dictate course curricula and its teaching, we can expect not only pressure from students to dispense with theory but also pressure from external market forces to fashion teaching approaches that de-emphasize analytical reasoning in favour of basic training.

Further, it is clear that despite the best intentions of administrators of applied criminology programs, the disproportionate emphasis placed on "practical skills" within course curricula and marketing literature has an effect that undermines the message that theory and critical-thinking skills are important for students. Let's take the importance of criminological theory as an example. Every term I explain to my own students that each of us has ideas as to why the world works in particular ways, and many of us call our ideas theories. Social science theory grounds attempts at explaining social relationships in empirically tested data. Unlike someone's personal musings as to, for example, "why idiots are able to get driver's licenses" or "why all politicians are crooked," social science theory relies on rigorous processes that adhere to the twin concerns of validity and reliability. In my own experience, when this is explained to students, much nodding of heads occurs. However, before too long groaning and whining about the lack of relevance or importance of theory begins to percolate. Theory is not about the real world, I am told. Unnithan (1999, 104) reports similar views expressed by students in response to theory-based courses: "Criminology was about 'theory' and other courses were about 'reality'; the latter, [students] protested, were based on 'common sense.'" Such views are lent credence by university and college literature that tell students that "practical," skills-oriented coursework will enhance their ability to secure employment opportunities in criminal justice.

Some readers might suggest that if replacing theory with training is what both the market and students are demanding, we ought to deliver and keep our "customers" satisfied. But I'm not convinced that sacrificing the development of skills and abilities that will provide students lifetime benefits over their personal and professional careers in the interest of achieving short-term goals is really in anyone's best interest. As Williams and Robinson (2004, 373) sagely note, "without the explanatory power of general theoretical principles, criminal justice educators are limited to subjectively describing the structure and function of our systems of criminal justice rather than explaining why these systems behave the way they do." Frauley (2005, 249) places one of the negative consequences of the training approach into sharper focus: "Without a methodological and pedagogical concern for a practice of theory or to foster thinking theoretically among students, 'justice,' for instance, will continue to be held to be transparent, to refer only to fairness and effectiveness in the administration of the criminal law, or to be an epiphenomenon of administrative practice."

Contemporary liberal arts education demands pedagogy that inculcates within students the ability to think critically, creatively, and reflexively (Williams and Robinson 2004). Such education is seen as fostering the development of informed and engaged citizens, individuals who are necessary to the healthy functioning of society. When criminology students are not provided opportunities to develop means of thinking outside the box, including critically engaging with their own beliefs, as well as with the ideologies of others, they are moreover ill-equipped to confront the challenges they may face working within a criminal justice system that deals in complex social problems. To effect meaningful solutions within the system, encouraging myopia is clearly not the answer. In discussing this problem within the US context, Williams and Robinson (2004, 387) point to what ought to also be seen as a central concern for Canadian criminologists: "Lacking a pedagogical model that seeks to fulfill liberal arts goals, criminal justice educators are relegating themselves to second-class status and limiting the potential of their graduates to that of maintaining the status quo of criminal justice rather than developing the intellectual skills to evaluate and improve it." Ultimately, to the extent that Canadian criminology schools continue transforming their pedagogy to keep up with demands for courses, course materials, and programs that emphasize use value at the expense of theory and critical reasoning, we risk dumbing down the discipline and scaring away those students we most hope to attract – the best and the brightest who are attracted to the discipline's promise but prefer to develop their knowledge and critical skills rather than becoming cop wannabes, as criminology students are all too often viewed as outside the discipline (Deflem 2002).

## Potential Impacts of "Pumping Them Out": Surplus Labour Population or Expanding Penal Systems?

> Every year, I open a large introductory course by asking the cliché question of philosophy, Why are you here? The answers always range from the pious to the pragmatic, but I have noticed lately a funny trend: the answer is foreign sports cars, German for preference ... This year, a student told the class she was there because she wanted "an Audi" ... rare is the student who arrives at university with a clear sense of higher education's independent value.
>
> – Mark Kingwell, *Nothing for Granted*

As much as one might be inclined to condemn students for seeing education largely, if not solely, in economic terms, it is rather difficult to blame them when institutions of higher education actively encourage the development of such attitudes. Within my own field, current and potential students are increasingly bombarded with a plethora of university advertisements promising them any number of potential benefits upon entering the "criminal justice market." For example, I discovered this message contained not on a matchbook cover but on a poster in a hallway of a local college:

Discover a rewarding career in
- policing
- community corrections
- victim-offender mediation programs
- restorative justice programs

- community crime prevention programs
- other community-based programs

Apply Now!

Other schools offer similarly enticing promises: criminal justice not only offers a "rewarding career" but also "is an exciting and diverse field that offers a variety of challenging career avenues and opportunities for specialized research and study ... we can help you prepare to launch or advance your career."

Now, whether criminal justice is a truly exciting field is perhaps debatable, but what is not debatable is the problematic nature of the underlying premise of these promises, or of the explicit claim made to students that criminal justice is an emergent employment growth market with the potential to offer decent wages, good benefits, and job security. Take, for example, this claim from a school, one that was made in various guises by several others: "Labour market predictions for criminal justice and related areas are very favourable, as demographic trends and public safety and security concerns have increased demand for criminal justice professionals." The source of the data used to support this claim is never cited, so we have no means of directly verifying the veracity of claimants' sources. The only potential source that I could locate that might offer support for such a contention is the Job Futures (Government of Canada) website, which, utilizing data from the National Graduates Survey of 1995, describes job prospects for police officers as "good." Other schools justify their contention of increasing job growth in the criminal justice field by pointing to the impending retirement of the baby boomer generation. "In the near future," one university claims, "there will be a large number of retirements in the public sector, including areas which require or would value a background in Criminology." Similarly, students are advised that "the strong demand" in criminal justice "is the result of impending significant retirements as well as the expected continued increasing demand for criminal justice workers with university degrees." Leaving aside the potential impacts on the employment market of repeals of mandatory retirement, a subject currently under discussion in several employment sectors, it is worth briefly exploring the question of how the so-called criminal justice employment market is actually performing in light of claims that it is generating high demand for qualified students.

To test these claims, I draw on two sets of figures. The first of these I have extracted from the Canadian Centre for Justice Statistics (2002), which utilizes census data. There is one limitation in using this source, and it is the

TABLE 3.1

**Canadian criminal justice employment**

| Branch | 1994-95 | 2000-01 |
|---|---|---|
| Police | 75,351 | 75,863 |
| Courts | 12,074 | 11,901 |
| Adult corrections | 27,103 | 32,607 |
| Prosecutions | 3,199 | 3,609 |

NOTE: These employment figures include both federal and provincial workers (all jobs).
SOURCE: Canadian Centre for Justice Statistics 2002, 17.

same limitation that befuddles those criminology departments making labour market predictions: the most recent census figures are from 2000, and thus we have no means of assessing current market conditions beyond cobbling together figures from other sources or through sheer speculation. Canadian census data do, however, permit a means of highlighting historical employment trends across four of the major branches of criminal justice. What these figures reveal is that employment in this field has remained remarkably stable through the late 1990s into the year 2000.

As the figures in Table 3.1 demonstrate, the number of jobs in the four major branches of Canadian criminal justice in the public sector posted, at best, very moderate increases over a six-year period, with the largest growth occurring in the field of adult corrections (approximately 5,500 jobs). Indeed, we discover that from 1994 to 2001, the total number of public policing jobs increased by only 0.67 percent, prosecutions by 11 percent, and there was a marginal decline in the number of court workers (-1.43 percent).

The second data source that I consulted was Job Futures Canada's website (2005), which posts both information and predictions on employment prospects. In looking at Job Future's market predictions, one finds that employment opportunities appear to fall short of what criminology students might reasonably expect their employment outcomes to be. For example, of graduates of "protection and correction services" programs, 28 percent found employment as police officers or firefighters, 20 percent became security guards, 12 percent worked in "other occupations in protective service," 4 percent became paralegal or social service workers, and 4 percent entered fields related to travel and recreation. These results lead Job Futures to conclude that with a diploma from an applied criminology program, "you'll have a better chance of finding work as a police officer or firefighter" – clearly an incorrect interpretation of the data. Actually, graduates had a better (at 82 percent) chance of finding "other work" as neither a police officer nor firefighter. Further, once all "protection"-oriented jobs are accounted for, recent graduates have a 40 percent chance of finding work entirely unrelated to the "protection" field (ibid.).[5]

But what of graduates of degree programs – do they fare better? The National Graduates Survey of 2000 similarly places applied criminology students under the category of "security and protective services" (Allen and Vaillancourt 2004). Of the 3,400 graduates of college programs in this field, 2,300 were able to secure full-time employment within two years of graduation (approximately 67 percent).[6] Of these 2,300 former students, 83 percent were engaged in full-time work in 2002. I note that the study does not provide data on the number of graduates who were able to secure employment within the criminal justice field, nor do we know the relative degree of job satisfaction experienced. What we do know is that the median income earned by new college graduates of applied criminology programs is approximately $33,300 per annum.[7] In my own highly unscientific poll, I asked four classes of undergraduate criminology students (approximately 120 of them) as to whether they would be satisfied with a starting salary of $33,300 per annum upon completion of a criminology degree or a criminal justice diploma. The results were an unequivocal "No."[8]

The available data on graduates of applied programs at the bachelor of arts level is more difficult to interpret in their scarcity. Of the three hundred graduates of bachelor of arts programs in "personal, protective and transportation services," the number of people in full- or part-time employment is not supplied (Allen and Vaillancourt 2004). Similarly, data on income levels for this group of graduates are not provided. Thus, we have little means of knowing exactly how this group of graduates is performing in the marketplace. One might reasonably speculate that BA graduates fared slightly better in the criminal justice jobs sweepstakes than those with only diplomas or certificates, simply as a consequence of higher levels of education being of higher value within the knowledge economy. However, it is also unlikely that all or perhaps even the majority of BA graduates were able to find jobs, or at least public-sector jobs, within their major field. I make this claim in light of the well-known system capacity limits of the criminal justice system (Garland 1996). There can never be enough available jobs within the system for all those who want them or even for all those who have their degrees or diplomas in hand, because there is always an end limit to what the public is willing to pay for public services.

Although there is much we do not know about student performance in the marketplace, what we do know from the 1997 National Graduates Survey is that 20 percent of graduates of "protection and correction services" programs entered the private security field. This result is not surprising given that much of the unprecedented growth in criminal justice that university and college administrators have been hawking has actually been in the private sector. Undoubtedly, if the numbers were available, we would similarly find that a good proportion of graduates from the 2000 cohort also entered the private security field as part of a continuing labour market trend since the early 1990s: the number of people employed by the private security industry increased by 69 percent between 1991 and 2001 alone (Sanders 2005, 178). The most recent figures available reveal that in 2001 there were some seventy-three thousand individuals employed as security guards (Canadian Centre for Justice Statistics 2004).

The number of private security guards employed is comparable to the number of public police officers, but these two occupations are hardly comparable in terms of salary and benefits: in 2000, the average annual employment income for police officers was approximately sixty thousand dollars ($59,888), whereas security guards averaged twenty-seven thousand per annum ($27,369) (ibid., 15). As Stanley Aronowitz (2000, 16) sagely notes of the shift toward emphasizing educational use value:

> This mad race toward occupational education, and to the intellec-
> tual bottom, comes at a time when good jobs are disappearing
> and competition is sharper than at any time since the Great De-
> pression. For the truth is that, despite glowing reports of economic
> boom, there are fewer good jobs, if by a "job" we designate work
> that provides health and pension benefits, offers long-term con-
> tinuity with a single employer, and income commensurate with
> qualifications.

I am more than a little inclined to view Aronowitz's point as particularly salient when discussing the career employment prospects of criminology undergraduates, many of whom have been misled to believe that a simple piece of paper will guarantee them entree to excellent positions in the criminal justice marketplace.[9]

I want to end the discussion by sounding one further warning bell. Writing of the French student protests in May 1968 that marked a seminal point for many academics, Pierre Bourdieu (1999, 27) ascribes what he perceives to have been the central cause of student unrest: the "overproduction and devaluation of diplomas." Within Canadian criminology, we are rapidly approaching a similar crisis point. With an expanding number of programs promising skills that will assure a swift and profitable entry into the Canadian "criminal justice market," numbers of students with specialized training are increasing each year. However, as we have seen, the "market" is unlikely to be able to bear their numbers or the weight of students' expectations about employment opportunities, decent wages and working conditions, good benefits, and job security.

The cynically pragmatic among us might note that there is one means available for accommodating growing student demand for entry into the criminal justice market: Canadians could always expand their existing penal-welfare complex. Although such an option is morally repugnant to me and to many other criminologists who abhor any efforts that result in further net widening, I note that others have cheerfully interpreted such activities as potential windfall opportunities for student employment. Indeed, in advertising the benefits of its criminology program, one eastern Canadian university notes on its website that "in the public sector, there continues to be strong commitment by governments to provide job opportunities in Criminology-related fields, as evidenced by the plans to build a major new corrections facility in the Greater Toronto Area." It would not be an overstatement to suggest that this text contains within it a distinctly odious notion: that governments would, indeed should, use incarceration and other penal measures to foster employment and economic opportunities. Is this really a belief that criminologists want to inculcate within students and promote within the public sphere?

I would suggest that when considering the use of punishment as a means of facilitating graduate employment, even the most cynical of us ought to first consider the advice of Nils Christie (2004, 108): "Economic gains must be seen in relation to penal costs." The appropriate job of the criminologist is to factor into our gross calculations not only the social pain and suffering caused by the criminal act but also the pain and suffering caused by society's response (ibid.). Without this calculation, criminologists, who already "have an extraordinary potential for being dangerous people," cast themselves and their students as "technicians in pain delivery of a magnitude and scale in sharp contrast to central values" (116). In short, encouraging students in the belief that there are personal and social economic incentives to furthering the number of people who fall within the domain of the criminal justice system is *contra* to the critical, indeed socially pragmatic, attitudes that we ought to be promoting.

## Conclusion

> It seems that criminologists have not made any collective effort to come to terms with the organizational, political, economic and ethical consequences of increased emphasis on commercial activities.
>
> – Mark Israel, "The Commercialisation of University-Based Criminological Research in Australia"

I began this article with a central question: What does the proliferation of applied criminology programs mean for the discipline's future? I'm afraid that at the moment the answer seems rather grim. This grimness has to do in large part with the concern articulated by Mark Israel in the quotation that opens this section: criminologists have clearly not begun to really address the changes that are taking place within our discipline as it increasingly turns itself over to the interests of the marketplace. In this chapter, I identify two particular concerns that I see as arising from one of the symptoms of this transformation – the proliferation of applied criminology programs in Canada. These concerns are (1) curricula and pedagogy that emphasize use value at the expense of students learning theory and developing critical-thinking skills, and (2) the likelihood that we are creating more criminology students than the "criminal justice job market" can actually bear. In relation to the second of these concerns, I highlight another problem for further consideration: that Canadian criminologists' treatment of the criminal justice system as a marketplace is having a negative impact on how we view the system and our relation to it. Indeed, I suggest that we pay attention to the fact that by promoting entry into the system for ever increasing numbers of students what we risk doing is altering the system's shape by creating demands for jobs that can be filled only by an expanding penal complex.

Clearly, as scholars and educators, we need to begin by asking ourselves what we see as the ultimate goal of our pedagogy. Is our purpose simply to reproduce credentialed individuals for the criminal justice industry, or is it something more, something deeper? Do we continue fragmenting criminology along existing lines, or do we try to develop some set of cohesive and coherent guidelines to help us shape our discipline's future, as opposed to simply letting the future overtake us? These are good starting questions for a long, complex set of debates that Canadian criminologists clearly need to have and which appear to be already overdue. In considering our fate, we might also ponder Neil Postman's (1995, 31) wise admonition: "Any education that is mainly about economic utility is far too limited to be useful, and in any case, so diminishes the world that it mocks one's humanity."

## NOTES

1   Tudiver's (1999) comment that the "traditional university" embodies the liberal view can be regarded somewhat ironically given that the traditional purpose of university was not the production and dissemination of "pure" knowledge – that is, knowledge for its own sake – but rather knowledge in support of the professions and thus ultimately the economy.

2   For example, the 2000 National Graduates Survey (NGS) subsumes applied criminology programs under the category of "personal, protective and transportation services" (see, for example, Allen and Vaillancourt 2004). Job Futures (Service Canada) (2005), which utilizes the 1997 NGS data to provide a resource website for students on employment issues, designates applied criminology programs under the category of "protection and correction services."

3   Throughout the chapter, the reader will note that I quote from various unnamed sources in order to demonstrate various points about the marketing of applied criminology programs. The sources upon which I am drawing are materials produced by various Canadian colleges and universities that I have chosen not to publicly identify.

4   This particular program provides an excellent example of the increasing involvement of external agencies, including both public and private sector organizations, in the provision of courses tailored to their identified human resource needs.

5   The single largest employer of police officers, the RCMP, states that of the approximately eight thousand applications it receives each year to join the force as regular members, only one thousand are accepted into its training academy – that is, applicants have, at best, a one-in-eight chance of success (RCMP 2005). These are numbers most students are likely not aware of.

Some critics might note in response the RCMP plan to double its recruitment intake for 2006 – a recruitment class of approximately 1,600 cadets. This appears to be a one-time-only measure to combat staff losses because of retirements.

6　The actual number of graduates in full-time employment as a portion of the whole is not explicitly provided in the study. To find this number, I had to extrapolate from the fact that 3,400 is the total number of graduates on page 26 of the report (Table A-2), and that 2,300 is the number of graduates listed under 'labour force activity' (Table A-4) on page 29.

7　The NGS also reveals that $26,000 is the annual income for those at the twenty-fifth percentile, and that 75 percent of graduates earn $40,600 per annum or less. No mean is provided.

8　The students I polled live in British Columbia, which has a higher cost of living than many other provinces. Students in other provinces might find $33,300 a desirable starting salary. On average, students felt that a more appropriate minimum starting salary for a graduate of such a diploma program would be approximately $40,000 per annum.

9　Particularly telling are the examples of students who assure me that grades are irrelevant because future employers aren't "going to ask for my transcripts" – in other words, they naively view the diploma or the degree as an automatic right of entry into the marketplace.

## REFERENCES

Allen, M., and C. Vaillancourt. 2004. Class of 2000: Profile of Postsecondary Graduates and Student Debt. In *Statistics Canada Report*. Culture, Tourism and the Centre for Education Statistics Division, catalogue no. 81-595-MIE, no. 016.

Aronowitz, S. 2000. *The Knowledge Factory: Dismantling the Corporate University and Creating True Higher Learning*. Boston: Beacon Press.

Ash, E. 1991. *Towards the 21st Century: A Prospectus for UK Universities*. London: CVCP.

Becker, G. 1994. *Human Capital: A Theoretical and Empirical Analysis with Special Reference to Education*. Chicago: University of Chicago Press.

Bell, D. 1973. *The Coming of Post-Industrial Society: A Venture in Social Forecasting*. New York: Basic Books.

Bisi, R. 1999. Teaching and Professional Training in Criminology. *European Journal of Crime, Criminal Law and Criminal Justice* 7(2): 103-29.

Blackmore, J. 1990. The Text and Context of Vocationalism: Issues in Post-Compulsory Curriculum in Australia since 1970. *Journal of Curriculum Studies* 22(2): 177-84.

Bourdieu, P. 1999. *Practical Reason: On the Theory of Action*. Stanford, CA: Stanford University Press.

Bradney, A. 1992. Ivory Towers and Satanic Mills: Choices for University Law Schools. *Studies in Higher Education* 17(1): 5-21.

Braithwaite, J. 1993. Beyond Positivism: Learning from Contextual Integrated Strategies. *Journal of Research in Crime and Delinquency* 30(4): 383-99.

Bullen, E., S. Robb, and J. Kenway. 2004. "Creative Destruction": Knowledge Economy Policy and the Future of the Arts and Humanities in the Academy. *Journal of Education Policy* 19(1): 3-22.

Canadian Centre for Justice Statistics. 2002. Justice Spending in Canada, 2000/1. In Statistics Canada, catalogue no. 85-002-XIE (Juristat).

–. 2004. Private Security and Public Policing in Canada, 2001. In Statistics Canada, catalogue no. 85-002-XIE.

Castells, M. 1989. *The Informational City: Information Technology, Economic Restructuring and the Urban-Regional Process*. Oxford: Blackwell.

Christie, N. 2004. *A Suitable Amount of Crime*. London: Routledge.

Clear, T.R. 2000. Has Academic Criminal Justice Come of Age? Presidential address at the meeting of the Academy of Criminal Justice Sciences, Washington, DC.

Deem, R. 1998. "New Managerialism" and Higher Education: The Management of Performances and Cultures in the United Kingdom. *International Studies in Sociology of Education* 8(1): 47-70.

Deflem, M. 2002. Teaching Criminal Justice in Liberal Arts Education: A Sociologist's Confessions. *ACJS Today* 22(2): 1, 3-5.

Ericson, R.V., and K. Carriere. 1994. The Fragmentation of Criminology. In *The Futures of Criminology*, ed. D. Nelkin, 89-109. London: Sage.

Frauley, J. 2005. Representing Theory and Theorising in Criminal Justice Studies: Practising Theory Considered. *Critical Criminology* 13(3): 245-65.

Garland, D. 1996. The Limits of the Sovereign State: Strategies of Crime Control in Contemporary Society. *British Journal of Criminology* 36(4): 445-67.

–. 2002. Of Crimes and Criminals: The Development of Criminology in Britain. In *The Oxford Handbook of Criminology*, 3rd ed., ed. M. Maguire, R. Morgan, and R. Reiner, 7-50. Oxford: Oxford University Press.

Israel, M. 2000. The Commercialisation of University-Based Criminological Research in Australia. *Australian and New Zealand Journal of Criminology* 33(1): 1-20.

Job Futures (Service Canada). 2005. Protection and Correction Services. Service Canada, http://www.jobfutures.ca/.

Ka-ho, M. 1997. The Cost of Managerialism: The Implications for the "McDonaldisation" of Higher Education in Hong Kong. Public and Social Administration Working Paper Series, City University of Hong Kong.

Kingwell, M. 2005. *Nothing for Granted: Tales of War, Philosophy, and Why the Right Was Mostly Wrong*. Toronto: University of Toronto Press.

Lemke, T. 2001. The Birth of Bio-Politics: Michel Foucault's Lecture at the College de France on Neo-Liberal Governmentality. *Economy and Society* 30(2): 214-29.

McMahon, M. N.d. Control as Enterprise: Reflections on Privatization and Criminal Justice, http://www.stthomasu.ca/.

Menzies, R., and D.E. Chunn. 1999. Discipline in Dissent: Canadian Academic Criminology at the Millennium. *Canadian Journal of Criminology* 41(2): 285-97.

Miller, H. 1998. Managing Academics in Canada and the United Kingdom. *International Studies in Sociology of Education* 8(1): 3-24.

Postman, N. 1995. *The End of Education: Redefining the Value of School.* New York: Vintage Books.

Pugsley, L. 1998. Throwing Your Brains at It: Higher Education, Markets and Choice. *International Studies in Sociology of Education* 8(1): 71-92.

Rose, N. 1999. *Powers of Freedom: Reframing Political Thought.* Cambridge, UK: Polity Press.

Royal Canadian Mounted Police (RCMP). 2005. RCMP Recruiting website, http://www.rcmp-grc.gc.ca/.

Sanders, T. 2005. Rise of the Rent-a-Cop: Private Security in Canada, 1991-2001. *Canadian Journal of Criminology and Criminal Justice* 47(1): 175-90.

Schiller, H.I. 1981. *Who Knows: Information in the Age of the Fortune 500.* Norwood, NJ: Ablex.

Scott, P. 1984. *The Crisis of the University.* Beckenham, UK: Croom Helm.

Shacklock, G., R. Hattam, and J. Smyth. 2000. Enterprising Education and Teachers' Work: Exploring the Links. *Journal of Education and Work* 13(1): 41-60.

Tudiver, N. 1999. *Universities for Sale: Resisting Corporate Control over Canadian Higher Education.* Toronto: James Lorimer.

Unnithan, N.P. 1999. Criminological Theory and Criminal Justice Policy: In Search of Pedagogical Connections. *Journal of Criminal Justice Education* 10(1): 101-10.

Williams, E.J., and M. Robinson. 2004. Ideology and Criminal Justice: Suggestions for a Pedagogical Model. *Criminal Justice Periodicals* 15(2): 373-92.

# Expanding the Criminological Focus . . . . . . . . .

Contemporary criminology is an interdisciplinary endeavour, one that involves diverse orientations and methodologies. Nonetheless, a core set of agendas, frameworks, and political orientations have tended to dominate. In Part 2, James Williams, Andrew Woolford, Diana Young, and Stacey Hannem propose different ways to expand the discipline to incorporate a broader range of substantive foci. Their chapters exemplify the rich scholarly insights that can derive from such efforts while also revealing novel opportunities for political practice.

Criminologists routinely assert that it is important to study corporate crime. At least part of the motivation for encouraging such research stems from a belief that studying corporate criminality is a political intervention that confronts the assumptions of research that is narrowly focused on a limited array of street crimes. That said, few scholars have taken up the challenge to actually study corporate criminality. The subfield of corporate crime research has consequently always been comparatively marginal, a situation that has become more pronounced in recent years. This increased marginalization is typically attributed to factors external to the discipline, such as declining research funding and a reduced number of case studies available for analysis (itself a function of the trend toward greater financial deregulation).

In his analysis of the field of corporate criminality, James Williams eschews this externalist orientation in favour of examining how five assumptions internal to criminology have helped straitjacket the study of financial wrongdoing. The first limitation concerns the tendency for criminologists to accentuate the wide array of social and material harms produced by corporate wrongdoing and then to try to reconceptualize those harms as crimes. This strategy helps reveal the limitations of conventional definitions of crime while also stigmatizing corporate wrongdoing. Although this stance can be politically powerful, it can also be faulted for substituting a realist definition of crime with a realist definition of harm, in the process ignoring how harms are themselves subject to competing attributions and interpretations. Williams is not suggesting that corporate activities are not harmful but, rather, that these harms are themselves subject to a process of interpretation and attribution rather than being given, self-evident, and incontrovertible. The second limitation is methodological and pertains to the centrality of case studies as the preferred method of analysis. This reliance has put academics at the mercy of the knowledge production work and interpretative frameworks of the official bodies responsible for investigating cases of corporate wrongdoing. One result has been a literature dominated by horror stories of corporate excess that fosters a partial and distorted view of financial crime.

The third limitation of existing criminological scholarship concerns the range and scope of theoretical approaches. In particular, corporate wrongdoing tends to be explained as a function of personal or organizational greed. This approach disproportionately emphasizes economic and financial motivations for corporate wrongdoing and tends to draw too sharp a contrast between financial and non-financial motivations. It also imputes an excessive instrumentality and singularity to corporate actors.

The fourth problematic factor concerns assumptions about the dynamics of regulation, in particular, the common theme that state regulatory efforts are inadequate. One limitation of this orientation is that it pits the state against business interests, simplifying the complex relationships between these actors while missing how states constitute both corporations and markets. In the process, it also tends to ignore, downplay, or dismiss the regulatory efforts of other extra-state bodies and simplifies the considerable complexity of regulatory actors and knowledges. Finally, existing scholarship tends to approach the economic and financial field as exotic and foreign territory, a stance that contributes to a characteristic lack of identification with economic wrongdoers and a neglect of how conflict and contingency can operate in this field.

The latter half of Williams's chapter outlines how analysts might proceed beyond these self-imposed analytical limitations. His research on securities fraud in Canada exemplifies the need to problematize the aims and dynamics of regulation, something that necessitates scrutinizing what regulation actually entails. As he notes, markets are themselves social and cultural constructions, and part of those constructions include discourses about regulation, a major component of which involves efforts to design these activities as crimes – or to resist such typifications. In the day-to-day operation of regulation, however, formal law plays a secondary role, typically arriving late in the process. Financial actors are first defined as problematic for reasons that can be highly case specific, and the law is applied after the fact to accomplish assorted ends. These efforts are undertaken by regulators who police the boundaries of legitimate and illegitimate financial actors in a process that involves contradictory regulatory mandates. Recognizing the sheer complexity of financial regulation (which is not a single phenomenon but a process that involves a multitude of different players operating with different understandings of security) suggests that approaching regulation as a field is a fruitful way forward.

Despite the problems characteristic of contemporary criminological approaches to corporate wrongdoing, Williams does not fault the discipline. Instead, he suggests that criminology is a more ambitious and ambiguous enterprise than is apparent in the often essentialist depictions of criminology presented by the discipline's detractors. Criminology is still relevant to the study of financial wrongdoing, providing that analysts expand their parameters and abandon realist ontologies of crime and harm in order to concentrate on processes of control, ordering, and governance. Such inquiries will be all the more insightful to the extent that they are informed by a broad array of disciplines, including criminology.

One social scientific discipline that has been only minimally embraced by criminologists is the nascent field of genocide studies. Andrew Woolford encourages criminologists to rectify this situation but cautions that such inquiries must be highly reflexive to ensure that we are sensitive to the discipline's legacy. Otherwise, we risk engaging in a simple disciplinary expansion that ignores questionable assumptions about the criminological enterprise. The study of genocide therefore presents an opportunity to learn from criminology's more unpalatable legacies, including how it has played a role in domination, traded in essentializing categories, and helped to criminalize stigmatized groups. An additional acute concern for Canadian scholars of genocide should be to examine Canada's colonial history as a means to rectify the totalizing and essentializing thought that often occurs in the analysis of genocide.

In recent years, greater attention has been paid to the question of why, to date, there has not been a criminology of genocide. Proposed answers include because criminology has been biased toward easily quantifiable phenomena, because analysts have structured their inquiries in light of national interests, and because there is a fear among researchers of morally charged topics. Woolford, however, provocatively asks why we might assume that there *should* be a criminology of genocide. Although he ultimately believes that a particular version of criminology of genocide might be appropriate, he is concerned that the emerging criminological move to embrace studies of genocide might amount to a self-interested attempt to render criminology more profound and to provide its practitioners with the sense of distinction that can come from studying horrible acts.

Woolford is suspicious of all five of the most prominent arguments that have been advanced for why we should develop a criminology of genocide. The first is that the deadly scope of the crime justifies such inquiries. However, this justification involves employing a questionable hierarchal ranking of harms while ignoring a host of other dangers. It also risks downplaying serious harms of genocide, such as forced expulsion, rape, and cultural loss, which might be placed further down the ranking of social harms. Second, some have argued that a criminology of genocide is warranted because criminology has a history of *objectively* analyzing horrible crimes. This justification entirely misses the point that genocide is an inherently normative category and ignores how comparable claims to neutrality or objectivity have themselves played a role in genocidal practices. A third argument is that the discipline of criminology can benefit from the study of genocide. Although this is undoubtedly true, such inquiries are purely redemptive if they leave the discipline's foundational assumptions unaddressed. A fourth prominent justification for a criminology of genocide is that it will help foster an awareness of genocide. One obvious question that arises, however, is whether the public is actually unaware of genocides. It also relies on a naive assumption that with greater knowledge of genocide will come a greater willingness to stop such acts. In fact, many genocides have been perpetrated with the full awareness of global publics and politicians. The final argument is that a criminology of genocide is warranted by the simple fact that genocide is a crime, and criminology is the study of criminal behaviour. Woolford is uncomfortable with such a justification because the category of genocide is itself a historical accident of state labelling practices. Our studies cannot be justified simply on the basis of statist legal definitions. This is a particularly pressing limitation given that the harms of genocide can be legal (according to state law) when they occur. Moreover, it presents the unpalatable scenarios of criminologists arriving very late to an active intellectual field to claim it as our own, rather than humbly entering into an existing multidisciplinary debate.

There are, therefore, several reasons to be suspicious of what criminology, as traditionally constituted, might bring to the study of genocide. This is particularly important given that rather than being a bulwark against extermination, criminology has played a prominent role in genocidal practices. In Nazi Germany, for example, the entire discipline became subservient to Nazi rule as criminologists sought state support for their biological and eugenic research. Criminology has also traditionally been bound by an atomizing framework that conceptualizes victims and perpetrators as mutually exclusive categories, something that has inherent limitations when studying genocide where all parties might be guilty of atrocious acts.

For Woolford, the criminology of genocide must begin with a reflexive and responsible critique of the discipline. This is imperative if we are going to allow the particularity of genocidal crimes to reformulate our thinking rather than simply imposing our existing categories on such acts. In Canada, this requires confronting our colonial history and ongoing relations with Aboriginal peoples. It involves being attentive to Aboriginal voices and fostering an approach that tackles the continuation of colonial legacies.

Woolford therefore concludes by using the experience of Aboriginal Canadians to accentuate some of the central dilemmas in contemporary formulations of "genocide," revealing many of these assumptions to be poorly suited for understanding Aboriginal Canadians' historical experience of colonialism. So, for example, while the definition of genocide enshrined in the 1948 UN genocide convention contains some conception of cultural genocide, it appears as a lower form of harm than "traditional" genocide. Such a formulation is inherently problematic for Aboriginal Canadians who have experienced the cultural violence of colonialism, most notoriously in the residential school system. A second issue concerns the formal assumption that in order for acts to be deemed genocide there must be genocidal intent. Such a formulation appears to ignore actions that have genocidal consequences, irrespective of intent. This understanding is particularly problematic in the Canadian context where Aboriginal peoples were subjected to an array of practices, some of which entailed genocidal intent, but also others that were characterized by a form of deadly neglect. The convention is limited too by virtue of how it is situated in Western notions of what constitutes harm. This orientation ignores how harms are identified and experienced differently by different groups. Woolford proposes that we must conceptualize harms and losses from the standpoint of the victimized groups themselves. Finally, he addresses the issue of how one is to identify a group for the purpose of understanding the victims of genocide. This is a central concern in relation to Canadian Aboriginals, whose history accentuates the fact that groups are not natural pre-given entitles. Instead, questions always remain about the parameters of a group and who gets to make such determinations – questions intimately connected to practices of power. In Canada, the very notion of an Aboriginal people (or peoples) was a colonial invention created for administrative purposes. Hence, it is simply inadequate to embrace the definition of "groupness" employed by the perpetrator. Instead, one needs to concentrate on the victims' understandings of their situation.

Diana Young examines how community-based alternatives to prison are expanding and teases out the implications of this development for our under-standing of power, governance, and resistance. Typically associated with re-storative justice, community-based corrections are often contrasted with formal law and legal doctrine. This stark dichotomy ultimately misses the complex networks of power in which such developments should be situated. Rather than a distinct set of practices, community-based alternatives present a malleable political concept, one that appears in different guises that, for different reasons, appeal to groups at both ends of the political spectrum. Fiscal conservatives are drawn to the prospect that community-based initia-tives will reduce prison costs. Progressive groups, in contrast, embrace the notions of accessibility and inclusiveness that inform community-based developments and are also drawn to the critique of formal legal practices espoused by community advocates. Liberals often embrace the greater infor-mality of such measures, a development that is more worrying to legal profes-sionals, who worry that informality can decrease due process protections.

Part of the difficulty in analyzing community-based initiatives is concep-tual. Advocates of such programs typically rely on a questionable distinction between community and the state, while admitting that it can be impossible to precisely articulate what a community entails. Although community has an appealing and almost mythical quality, when these qualities must be translated into concrete, real-world initiatives, they can result in policies and programs that belie the inclusive and democratic rhetoric central to their initial rationale. Critics underscore how community-based programs have, in practice, amounted to yet another expansion of the state apparatus of control. Although Young suggests that it is fair to characterize such initiatives as community-based, one must recognize that this does not entail the ideal-ized mythical notion of community but instead refers to a form of governance that operates in the name of community and that is operationalized toward particular ends.

In unpacking the actual dynamics of governance inherent in community-based initiatives, Young makes an important contribution to our understand-ing of the relationship between law and governance. She notes that law, rather than being a self-contained sphere of social activity, itself depends on a host of extra-legal forms of governance, such as experts, codes of conduct, and notions of reasonableness. Basic legal concepts draw on wider social norms, suggesting an interdependency between forms of governance that are often treated as distinct. Hence, law is contingent on other practices of power, such as classification and evaluation, many of which are intensified in community-based initiatives.

One novel dimension of these developments concerns their starkly utilitarian aspects. These became pronounced in a context of increased demands for alternatives to costly and ineffectual prisons. At the same time, one of the central paradoxes in community alternatives is that they have been directed at a larger set of problematic offenders. The new populations of individuals enrolled in such programs have been disproportionately drawn from those committing offences that have traditionally been seen as minor but which have received heightened attention through a reinvigorated punitive "law and order" politics. Despite this punitive rhetoric, these individuals are typically spared the harshest end of the criminal justice system and diverted to programs that are ostensibly more humane.

Young is ambivalent about the desirability of such developments. She is concerned about how the courts appear to be using community sanctions to generate new and more detailed knowledge of offenders. Such policies also mask hegemonic practices, most notably in how they use extra-legal mechanics of governance to ensure conformity. There are also questions about the degree to which community agencies are autonomous, as they must ultimately be subservient to the ultimate goal of the criminal justice system, which is to produce law-abiding citizens. So, for example, although community alternatives have embraced harm reduction policies, these have typically operated by establishing a series of goals for a participant, including enhancing their health or occupational status. However, when institutionalized in the legal system, people who accomplish such goals can still be seen as failures if they do not abstain from alcohol or drugs.

Young, though, recognizes that community governance can have multiple social consequences, some of which offer the prospect for unanticipated progressive possibilities. For example, the discourse of addiction that permeates community alternatives entails possibilities for transformation and empowerment. There are also novel possibilities in a community context to resist oppressive forms of power. At the most basic level, that community alternatives are presented to offenders as a "voluntary" program means that participants in such programs can resist by simply withdrawing from such programs. This suggests that community programs must be minimally responsive to the needs and demands of offenders or risk unmasking the naked exercise of power.

Stacey Hannem seeks to expand the criminological focus in another way, by drawing attention to the situation of the family members of incarcerated persons, a population profoundly affected by correctional practices but which has received little academic attention and few governmental resources. Although in recent years the traditional criminological focus on offenders has been augmented by studies of victims, Canadian criminologists have not yet examined the situation of the families of incarcerated persons. Many of the family burdens pertaining to incarceration fall typically on women, given the gender profile of the incarcerated population, which consists of an overwhelmingly high proportion of men. Furthermore, women are more likely to stay in a relationship with their incarcerated male partners, compared with men who are partners of incarcerated women. Although feminist criminologists have pushed criminology to examine the gendered social relations affecting women as offenders and victims of crime, there has been relatively little corresponding attention to the female partners of prisoners. These women's lives are also affected in profoundly gendered ways. Hannem reports findings of a pioneering empirical study she has conducted on the experiences of families of incarcerated men in Canada, based on interviews with twenty-eight family members of male prisoners, along with nine service providers. Theoretically, Hannem is interested in stigma, how it is institutionalized, its relationship to marginalization, and how it is gendered. Hannem views the marginalization of prisoners' families and the hardships they experience as, in part, the outcome of a "sticky" stigma transferred from the prisoner to his family. This stigma apparently helps justify the social neglect of prisoners' families and their financial, emotional, and social needs. Her chapter displays the gendered nature of sticky stigma, shown in how patriarchal understandings of family relationships allow stigma to be most easily transferred from men to their female partners and families.

At a substantive level, it is the first Canadian study of its kind. Hannem has examined the uniquely Canadian aspects of the families' experiences, for example, the consequences of the geographic dispersal of Canadian penitentiaries over great distances and the distinctly Canadian practice of the use of private family visits within prisons.

Up until now, what we knew about the situation of family members was derived from a relatively small number of studies from other countries. Some common themes emerge from that previous work. Ever since the first studies in the United States in the 1920s revealed a concern for the difficulty that female family members were having in making ends meet while their partners were incarcerated, the financial hardship of women with partners in prisons has been a key theme that emerges again and again in this field. Later studies accentuated the broad range of problems women face while their partners are incarcerated. These included not only financial hardships but also problems managing children, loneliness, isolation and feeling ostracized, distrust of authorities, and unawareness of what few services might be available to them.

Hannem's research identifies four key areas of concern for Canadian families affected by incarceration: financial and practical difficulties; emotional hardships; social stigma; and institutionalized, structured stigma. She highlights the iatrogenic effects of incarceration on families. In addition to loss of income and other costs associated with incarceration – for example, huge phone bills because of collect calls made from inside prison – there are other practical difficulties, including lengthy distances to travel, a problem exacerbated in Canada where prisons are far-flung. The women face difficulties maintaining relationships and with the loss of the father's involvement in child rearing. They are often stigmatized and isolated from the community because of their association with a convicted man. Families are also victimized institutionally as a result of their being officially perceived as being a greater risk simply by virtue of having an incarcerated partner. They face a form of structured stigma that targets them for scrutiny as "risky," for example, routine screening for drugs by an ion scanner that is prone to false positive findings. This institutionalized stigma is shown to exacerbate the experiential difficulties of coping with involuntary separation from a loved one and negotiating the maintenance of family relationships throughout incarceration. Hannem concludes with a series of suggestions for change, provided by the participants in her study.

# 4

# Corporate and White-Collar Crime: The Study of Financial Wrongdoing in the Era of Neo-Liberalism

*James W. Williams*

For even the most optimistic of scholars, the perusal of recent work on corporate and white-collar crime is bound to leave one somewhat disheartened. Since the halcyon days of the 1970s, the number of publications in this area has declined dramatically, with fewer scholars actively engaged in this field of research (Lynch, McGurrin, and Fenwick 2004). On one level, this is nothing new, as the study of corporate wrongdoing has long occupied a marginal position in the criminological tent, representing more of a freakish side show than the main event. And yet, it would appear that things have become even more desperate of late. The culprit this time is neither benign neglect nor open hostility but, rather, a far more profound and disturbing evisceration of the conditions of knowledgeability upon which the study of corporate and white-collar crime depends.

Spurred by neo-liberalism and the siren calls of privatization and deregulation, this decline is manifested in two related developments. First, the deregulatory impetus has produced extensive cutbacks to the budgets and legal authority of a whole host of regulatory agencies, thus reducing the number of documented cases of corporate wrongdoing. Given that criminologists rely on this case-processing capacity, opportunities for research have been seriously affected (Snider 2000). Second, the corollary of this is both a growing hostility toward corporate crime research in general, as revealed in the erosion of financial and institutional support for these types of studies, and greater difficulties in securing access to relevant research sites (Tombs and Whyte 2003). With the fuse essentially lit at both ends, a number of commentators have been moved to pronounce the death of corporate crime, lamenting its disappearance from the legal and political landscape and its increasing "invisibility" to researchers and the public alike (Snider 2000; Tombs and Whyte 2003; Tombs and Hillyard 2004). Neo-liberalism has thus not only undermined the enforcement of corporate and white-collar crime, it has generated a very real crisis of knowledgeability.

Interestingly, one of the responses to this rather bleak state of affairs has been to call into question the relevance of criminology to the study of corporate and white-collar crime. Hillyard et al. (2004), among others, have exhorted us to move "beyond criminology" and its thoroughly conventional constructions of law and crime and to focus instead on the societal harms produced by corporate activity: "Criminology is to be abandoned since its focus upon crime, law, and criminal justice has always been inadequate" (ibid., 27). Even those working from very different theoretical camps have argued that criminology is increasingly irrelevant to the study of corporate crime, chiding the discipline for its theoretical shallowness and placing their bets instead with related disciplines such as the sociology of law (Pearce and Tombs 1999, 2004; Braithwaite 2000; see also Parker and Braithwaite 2003). Criminology's promise in this area would thus appear to be rather dim, with serious questions being asked about the discipline's ability to come to terms with the harms perpetrated by corporations and other financial actors, and to engage with the theoretical questions these activities raise. That the largest wave of corporate scandal in recent US history has barely registered on the criminological radar, let alone resulted in any meaningful research, speaks volumes to this rather sad state of affairs.[1]

Resisting the temptation to simply pull up stakes and move on to more hospitable climes, this chapter actively engages with this state of despair. However, rather than offering yet another post-mortem on the corporate and white-collar crime literature, one that places the cause of death squarely at the feet of external causes such as deregulation, the objective here is to probe the entrails of the literature and to examine the extent to which the stagnation of corporate crime scholarship in recent years is attributable, at least in part, to internal factors – namely a series of self-imposed assumptions and theoretical postures that have straightjacketed the literature and curtailed the range and scope of its engagements with corporate criminality. The analysis of these various assumptions, five in total, is the task in the first section of the chapter. Having documented these internal limits, I then turn to the question of where do we go from here and offer several possibilities based on complementary literatures that are directly relevant to the study of corporate and white-collar crime yet which have been largely overlooked. The fruits of this cross-pollination are then examined with reference to a specific substantive context: the policing of financial markets in Canada. The subject of an extensive study I conducted, the field of securities regulation offers interesting insights that are useful in contextualizing and transcending the identified limits of the existing literature and thus setting a course for renewal. These possibilities are explored in the conclusion of the chapter, which restores a certain promise to criminology. With these objectives in hand, we begin by looking inward.

## Looking Inward

Despite its enduring marginality and pronounced deterioration over the past twenty years, there has been a surprising lack of internal criticism and self-reflection in the corporate and white-collar crime literature. This is not to suggest that the literature has been completely devoid of critique. There have, in fact, been a series of fairly high-profile skirmishes and internal debates. However, these have been primarily taxonomic, rather than diagnostic, in nature. That is, they have involved debates over the appropriate definitions of core terms such as "white-collar" and "corporate" crime, and the extent to which these definitions should reflect the characteristics of offenders versus the nature of the offence. The result is a veritable dog's breakfast of competing terms and categories, most of which overlap and few of which are really analytically useful. Eschewing this largely semantic struggle, the following discussion presses the literature on its more foundational claims and assumptions – particularly within its "critical" stream.[2] This effort may thus be described, albeit rather loosely, as primarily archaeological in nature, focusing on the discursive boundaries of the field, boundaries that are germane to its present form yet which are taken for granted and thus remain largely overlooked. This critical assessment hinges on five core analytical tendencies and points of critique: (1) the definition of corporate crime, (2) methodological limits, (3) theoretical range and scope, (4) the dilemmas of regulation, and (5) the nature of the financial field.

### "LET'S TALK ABOUT REAL CRIME"

From its inception in the work of Sutherland in the 1930s, the study of corporate and white-collar crime has had as its primary mandate the search for "real" crime. This follows from the insight that many of the most harmful and socially injurious activities are neglected by criminologists and the public given the domination of a decidedly narrow, legalistic view that limits "crime" to the violation of criminal law. Although the various forms of corporate wrongdoing documented by Sutherland (1983) were both socially injurious and legally prohibited, they were spared criminalization by virtue of this somewhat suspect juridical distinction. It is this very sensibility that has guided the literature ever since as corporate and white-collar crime scholars have endeavoured to expose the material harms associated with corporate and financial activities and to then use these harms, reconceived as "crimes" and juxtaposed with established constructions of criminality, to reveal the limitations of conventional definitions of crime and the short-sightedness of mainstream criminology.

Despite its value as critical fodder and its role in revealing the social and historical roots of extant criminal categories, this search for "real crime" has not been without its costs. Most notably, it is couched in a realist ontology, not of crime per se but, rather, of harm. Most corporate crime scholars explicitly reject the notion that crime in general has an essential and unmediated reality, its definition shaped by myriad social, political, and economic forces. And yet, much of their work is premised on the notion that (1) certain forms of corporate activity are *inherently* harmful, thus making them candidates for criminalization, and (2) these harms are *self-evident* and *incontrovertible* and can be identified through objective and disinterested inquiry. It is, of course, impossible to deny the harms associated with an investor losing millions of dollars because of a phantom gold deposit (for example, Bre-X), or an employee being killed in an explosion resulting from senior management's failure to abide by health and safety regulations (for example, Westray), and I have no interest in doing so. However, the difficulty with this approach, and the realist ontology that underlies it, is that it overlooks the extent to which designations of "harm" are themselves not only ambiguous but also subject to competing interpretations and attributions. This may not be the case in the above examples, but harms are seldom so cut and dried. Most are routine, inscribed within daily operations, and rooted in activities whose nature and effects are unclear.[3] By focusing on the more extreme cases, we run the danger of scanting these subtleties and thus missing more entrenched, yet less visible, forms of harm. Departing from this approach does not require that we abandon our critical sensibilities but, rather, that we devote more attention to the logics and practices through which corporate harms are defined and problematized. To be clear, it is the self-evident nature of "harm" as an ontological category and unassailable referent for criminological inquiry that is being challenged here, rather than the harmfulness of corporate activities.

## EXPLORING THE LITTLE SHOP OF HORRORS

The second cornerstone of the corporate and white-collar crime literature hinges on the question of method or, more specifically, a particular mode of analysis: the case study. In surveying the established literature, one is no doubt struck by the heavy reliance on individual case studies of corporate wrong-doing, with key details gleaned from a combination of media reports, legal proceedings, and journalistic accounts. In contrast, interviews and first-hand observational research are quite rare. In many respects, this reliance on case studies is perfectly understandable given the methodological challenges and barriers involved in the study of corporate and white-collar crime (Snider 2003; Tombs and Whyte 2003) – the most obvious of which is the unwilling-ness of most, if not all, companies to provide access to researchers whose declared interest is documenting the scale and causes of corporate illegality. Nevertheless, the result of this overreliance on case studies is that the corpor-ate crime literature has come to resemble a catalogue of corporate horrors, a showcase in which various forms of licentious greed and callous disregard are put on display. Moving through this little shop of horrors, we can see the Ford Pinto, the Dalkon Shield, and, more recently, the tobacco industry and Firestone tires.

Although effective in substantiating the harms caused by corporations, this reliance on the case study method has invariably generated a distorted and somewhat partial view of corporate wrongdoing. There are several con-siderations here. First, given the selection criteria – that is, instances of cor-porate offending that either have received media attention or have been the subject of regulatory or legal proceedings – the cases that are typically made available for analysis tend to be the most egregious and feature the most discernable forms of harm. Given this element of atypicality, it is problematic to generalize from these incidents to corporate practices more generally.

Second, information on these cases is limited to specific institutional sources, such as the media, government reports, and legal proceedings, and is thus produced and crafted from a particular point of view. These primary definers may omit relevant details and will most certainly present a take on corporate crime that best suits their own institutional interests. Third, in relying on the work product of other agencies and institutions, criminologists are inevitably held hostage to not only the vicissitudes of shifting mandates and priorities but also the vagaries of funding. Thus, the fruits of this meth-odology have become quite rare in recent years as the aforementioned forces of deregulation and decriminalization have produced fewer and fewer cases of corporate wrongdoing on which to feast.[4] Finally, this methodological approach is consistent with, and actually encourages, the realist ontology of crime and its related difficulties. Specifically, by focusing on clear and unmediated cases of corporate harm – the very cases that are likely to be deemed worthy of regulatory action and media attention – corporate crime scholars are once again bound to essentialized and reified views of harm that overlook more subtle and complex manifestations of corporate criminality. The ontological limits are, in this respect, artifacts of methodology.

## "THOSE GREEDY BASTARDS"

Moving beyond questions of ontology and method, the third cornerstone of the corporate and white-collar crime literature hinges on theory and, more specifically, on the theoretical assumptions and frameworks brought to bear in accounting for corporate wrongdoing. Despite its varied manifestations and discursive subtleties, one single factor repeatedly figures in theoretical accounts of corporate offending: the pragmatics of greed. This is the belief that the primary driver and motivation for corporate crime, in its various forms and guises, is the rational, calculated pursuit of financial self-interest. Of course, "greed" is seldom directly cited in these aetiologies, with scholars relying on more sophisticated language, for example, "the profit motive" and the pursuit of specific corporate objectives such as growth, productivity, and a high stock price. Likewise, in most theoretical accounts, greed and the pursuit of profit is far from the only, or even the most central, explanatory factor. Much of the corporate and white-collar crime literature is concerned with identifying how organizational and environmental variables create opportunities for greed to be manifested in corporate wrongdoing. For the more critical scholars, whose work is informed by Marxist or neo-Marxist sensibilities, emphasis is placed instead on the structural determinants of greed. Here greed and the pursuit of profit are tied to the structural features of the capitalist political economy whose primary drivers – the realization of value through the exploitation of labour and the externalization of production costs – are conceived as inherently criminogenic. Nevertheless, despite these very real departures in theoretical assumptions and directions, these accounts remain rooted in a decidedly visceral conception of greed and a related sense of normative outrage.

There are two notable problems with this approach. First, it places far too much emphasis on the economic and financial motivations of corporate and other financial actors. To be sure, the primary mandate and raison d'être of the corporation is to generate a profit and to produce strong returns on shareholder investments. However, this is not the only objective that guides companies. Other considerations, such as safety records, legal liabilities, and the development of new technologies, emerge as competing objectives that must be balanced with strong financial returns. Moreover, scholars have been prone to exaggerate the degree to which financial and non-financial objectives, such as health and safety, are counterpoised and are thus mutually exclusive. Rather than a simple dichotomy, a complex balance often ensues between these competing objectives, a balance further complicated by the fact that these goals are themselves unclear and are mediated through various constructions of cost, risk, probability, and liability. Recognizing this is not to be naive but, rather, to recognize the complexity of modern corporations. Closely related to this, the emphasis on greed imputes an excessive rationality and intentionality to corporate actors and activities. Although profit may be the goal, the means of achieving financial objectives are not always clear, thus making strategic action – the very type of action associated with legal violations – problematic. Ultimately then, to present corporations as single-minded, rational calculators imparts a degree of rationality and a singularity of purpose that is contradicted by organizational research that reveals modern corporations to be very good at projecting appearances of rational decision making while, in reality, being beset by ambiguity, uncertainty and internal politicking (see, for example, Meyer and Rowan 1977).

This limited understanding of, and engagement with, the complexities of modern organizations speaks to a second, more general problem with the corporate and white-collar crime literature and the analytic of greed: its theoretical narrowness and its failure to dialogue with related bodies of research and scholarship. For the most part, theories of corporate and white-collar crime are borrowed, with minor adjustments and modifications, from criminology more generally. The literature thus abounds with references to the organizational manifestations of strain, the impact of social learning and differential association, and, of course, rational choice and deterrence. Given this lineage, it should come as no surprise that its theoretical vision is myopic and fails to adequately reflect the practical realities of organizations, professions, and economies – all substantive domains that strike at the heart of corporate and white-collar crime yet are overlooked because of the short-sightedness of the literature. The paucity of theory is aptly noted by Stanley (1994, 233) who, in a decidedly pessimistic tone, asserts that the "attempt at theoretical explanation is woefully inadequate." To overcome these limits and develop a more sophisticated theoretical account of corporate offending, we need to "sweep across the disciplines" (Braithwaite 2000, 235) and engage more dialogically with traditions such as socio-legal studies, economic sociology, organizational theory, and sociology of the professions, as well as with disciplines such as philosophy and political science. What is needed in the field of corporate crime, more so than any other area of criminology, is thus a "radical opening and reworking of disciplinary borders to the scholarship of 'other' disciplines" (Hogeveen, this volume). Pursuing these ties is the best opportunity for overcoming the narrowness and sense of isolationism that currently haunts the literature.

## PUTTING THE FOX IN CHARGE OF THE HENHOUSE

There is one long-established truism held by most corporate and white-collar crime scholars: that existing systems of regulation and enforcement are inadequate and ineffective, and are unable to contend with the sheer scale of corporate illegalities. The diagnosis of this regulatory anemia varies. Some focus on the ability of corporations, through their legal and professional intermediaries, to undermine and dilute legislative initiatives and to subvert the intent, if not necessarily the letter, of the law, thus eviscerating the implementation and intended effects of legal standards and regulations. Others have drawn attention to the inflexibility of the large bureaucracies tasked with the enforcement of these regulations, as well as a paucity of funding and resources. Regardless of the specific cause, there is a sense that things have only gotten worse under the mantra of neo-liberalism as regulatory budgets have been further decimated and regulatory initiatives have been off-loaded to self-regulatory bodies whose mandates are seen to run counter to the public interest. Although some have argued that self-regulation, particularly if backed up by the threat of state enforcement for non-compliers, is potentially effective (for example, Ayres and Braithwaite 1992), most have equated these self-regulatory initiatives with an absence of regulation (for example, Snider 2000). The sense is that corporations are now freer than ever, and that self-regulation, given the input of corporations into the design and administration of regulatory regimes, is commensurate with putting the fox in charge of the henhouse. This is held to be true regardless of the delegated role of the state in steering these systems of self-regulation – with the state, more often than not, relegated to the position of passenger being steered and rowed by other parties.

Setting aside the question of whether this portrayal is accurate – that is, whether self-regulatory regimes are actually (in)effective in practice – there are two related difficulties with this general account of state versus self-regulation and the assertion that corporations now rule the roost. First, it is premised upon a dichotomized view of regulation in which states, as fonts of regulatory authority and ambition, are juxtaposed with corporations seeking to flout the law. Regulation is thus conceived as an exogenous force exercised through the formal auspices of the state and its various satellite agencies, and directed toward corporate actors who invariably attempt to counter and resist these unwanted regulatory intrusions through various strategies of resistance, circumvention, and co-option: "Regulation is presented as something imposed externally on regulatees (most commonly by state agents in the 'public interest') and naturally resisted, either by subversion or by avoidance" (Stenning et al. 1990, 93). The problem is that this presumes that states and markets are fundamentally distinct and neglects the extent to which state regulation is actually constitutive of corporations and markets. The state performs this function by (1) crafting essential legal categories, (2) guaranteeing the enforceability of contracts, and (3) offering financial support when companies and economies fall on hard times. Moreover, rather than oppositional forces of encroachment and resistance, relationships between states, law, and corporations are both complex and multidirectional, as corporations strive to influence and selectively interpret the law, whereas legal provisions are used by the state to shape and constitute corporations and their environments. By dichotomizing states and markets, this complexity is overlooked.

A second difficulty follows closely from the first. In asserting that states and markets are fundamentally opposed and that, as the role of the state is diminished, the autonomy and influence of corporations is enhanced, corporate and white-collar crime scholars presume that the only meaningful form of regulation is provided by, and through, the state. To the extent that state activities are limited or undermined, so the reasoning goes, regulation is bound to be ineffective. However, this overlooks the regulatory functions performed by a whole host of quasi-public and private organizations and agencies working within what can best be described as a regulatory patchwork. This includes not only formal organizations and associations whose regulatory mandates are defined and delegated by the state but also a diverse cadre of professional and occupational groups whose labour is central to both the practical mobilization of these various regulatory regimes and the design of initiatives that are ultimately governmental in their nature and effects yet are wholly removed from the formally designated regulatory system (Dezalay 1996; Schmidt 2005; Williams 2006). Here we can point to the contributions of lawyers, forensic accountants, compliance and risk managers, private investigators, and computer specialists, groups whose professional visions and self-interests betray any simplistic alliance with either the state or private corporations. They are regulatory wild cards, enhancing the power of business in some contexts while undermining and subverting it in others. These emerging forms of financial governance are not only exercised through non-state institutions and agencies; they also rely on rather unconventional tactics and forms of authority. These include various forms of civil liability, as well as informal sources of pressure and coercion that are manifestly non-legal yet unfold in the "shadow of the law" (Mnookin and Kornhauser 1978), backed by the threat of legal force. Without question, the standard response to these types of regulatory arrangements is that they are bound to be ineffective and are thus dismissed as largely symbolic and chimerical attempts to manage corporate reputations and reassure the public. This may in fact be the case. However, before we arrive at this conclusion, we must first recognize the complexity of contemporary modes of financial governance and, having jettisoned caricatured portraits of non-state regulation, critically assess the extent to which they are effective in accomplishing specific regulatory objectives. The questions of effectiveness and adequacy must thus be examined, rather than simply assumed.

## WHERE THE WILD THINGS ARE

The final cornerstone of the corporate and white-collar crime literature involves a tendency to conceive of the economic and financial field as a natural and somewhat wild space. By natural, I certainly do not mean inevitable nor wholly removed from social, political, and economic influence. Rather, it refers to the portrayal of the financial field as one of untrammelled ambition in which the drive for economic gain trumps all else and the various players struggle for competitive advantage freed of legal constraints and the hindrances of regulatory oversight. This is, in many respects, consistent with a view of regulation as a means of controlling the corporate beast, of saving society from its natural drives and instincts, and of civilizing its atavistic tendencies. What is interesting is that, in many accounts, this sense of wildness translates into a depiction of the financial field as exotic and quite foreign.

This is particularly evident in the treatment of corporate executives and managers, who are caricatured in a way that reveals a true absence of identification. They are portrayed as especially callous and uncaring in their valorization of profit and disregard for the harms they cause to employees, consumers, and the environment. They are also conceived as a largely homogenous group, moved by a singularity of interests, as reflected in terms such as "the elite" or the "power block." Ironically, all of this is indicative of a form of othering that resonates quite strongly with the depiction of conventional forms of criminality in the mainstream criminological literature. However, rather than the marginalized street offender predisposed to acts of violence, here attention is directed toward corporate executives similarly inclined toward wrongdoing, not because of intrinsic biological and psychological deficiencies and abnormalities but, rather, because of the imperatives of the profit motive and a criminogenic political economy. In each case, there is a lack of identification, a reification of motives and interests, and an expression of moral opprobrium, all of which belie the complexities of these activities and fail to distinguish between different actors who are all painted with the same broad strokes.

One of the key by-products of this particular rendition of the business world, and the related attributes of wildness, foreignness, and homogeneity, is that it actually contributes to the naturalization and rationalization of the financial field. By subscribing to this view of markets as homogenous and rational spaces, corporate and white-collar crime scholars neglect not only the vagaries of conflict and contingency but also the extent to which the financial field is itself socially constituted, the historical product of political struggle and discursive labour, rather than pre-given and legitimate in and of itself. This applies to finance, business, and markets, as general fields of activity, as well as to specific products such as stocks, bonds, and derivatives. This very point is made by de Goede (2005, xxv) who, in proffering a Foucauldian archaeology of financial markets, notes that "many authors assume finance to be an autonomous sphere with clearly defined boundaries and take for granted the unproblematic existence of money, banknotes, credit, financial instruments, etc. as a material starting point to their inquiries." This, of course, "assumes the incontestable economic reality of globalizing capital flows and powerful markets and leaves questions concerning the representation of financial and economic reality unanswered" (5). It is this failure to question the self-evident nature of the financial field, to probe its social and historical roots and the discursive labours that sustain it, that represents a key lacunae of the corporate and white-collar crime literature. Here these more nuanced and contextualized forms of inquiry are impeded by the implicit othering of financial actors, by caricaturized attributions of wild economic aggression, and by the homogenization and naturalization of the financial field. Within this analytical stance, we can once again see the outlines of the ontology of "real harm" and "real crime."

By way of summary, what emerges from this review is the notion that the existing corporate and white-collar crime literature is tethered to very specific lines of ontological, methodological, and theoretical inquiry that limit and restrain its scope and analytical range. These limits are self-inscribed. They are not solely attributable to the usual suspects of regulatory ineffectiveness or political resistance but, rather, follow from a view, developed within, of the corporate and financial world as a wild and exotic domain in which natural forms of greed and avarice manifest themselves in the single-minded, rational pursuit of wealth, profit, and competitive advantage. Accordingly, emphasis is placed on the production of "real harms" – forms of readily identifiable criminality that are allowed to flourish within a regulatory system that is decidedly hands-off and in which corporations, through their professional agents and intermediaries, are obliged to regulate themselves. Faced with this situation, the best that corporate and white-collar crime scholars can hope for is to catalogue these harms, putting corporate monsters on display in the hopes of capturing the attention of a seemingly despondent public and moving politicians to take action. Unfortunately, this has culminated in a style of analysis that is both theoretically narrow and conceptually broad, and which attributes a rather simplistic and highly rationalized set of motivations to financial actors while overlooking the political conflicts and struggles, and forms of discursive labour, that in reality underlie the financial field. This situation is made worse by the failure to engage with related literatures that would help corporate and white-collar crime scholars to see beyond these self-inscribed limits and allow them to enjoy the fruits of theoretical and empirical cross-fertilization. Faced with this rather desperate state of affairs, the question inevitably arises: Where do we go from here?

## Where Do We Go from Here?

The answer to this question, and the future of corporate and white-collar crime scholarship, hinges on a broader discussion of the relevance of criminology to the study of corporate and financial wrongdoing. On the one hand, there are those who would argue that the advancement of the literature requires that we abandon criminology as an orienting framework and pursue alternative theoretical paradigms. Thus, for authors such as Pearce and Tombs (2004, 372), the abandonment of criminology would appear to be a foregone conclusion given that it "has been constructed in a way that does not lend itself easily to addressing organization (corporate or state) crime." Although agreeing with the substance of their criticism, I would opt for a less radical course. This hinges, first, on the recognition that criminology as a discipline is itself quite ambiguous and, in fact, has long extended beyond simplistic ontologies of "crime" and "criminal justice" and included more general forms and dynamics of social ordering, governance, and control. I would thus agree with Shearing (1989, 178) that "ordering is now, and has always been, our proper focus." This recognition of the breadth of criminology is an important first step. However, the question remains: If criminology is defined so broadly that it encompasses general forms of ordering and control, what distinguishes it from neighbouring disciplines – for example, sociologies of law and governance? In other words, is there something unique to criminology that preserves its relevance to the study of corporate and white-collar crime, or should we agree that much of the work on corporate wrongdoing already occurs in socio-legal and regulatory literatures and simply move on?

My position is that criminology remains relevant as a disciplinary site given that much of what is most central to the study of corporate wrongdoing involves examining how these illegalities are framed and problematized in a way that allows them to be defined as non-criminal. That is, considerations of criminality remain relevant to understanding legal and societal reactions to corporate and white-collar crime and to the continued juxtaposition of crime in the suites with crime on the streets. Moreover, "crime" continues to be valuable as a juridical and bureaucratic category, as a particular designation of wrongdoing that is one of the key stakes in the practical processing of cases by various regulatory agents. Thus, the possibility that a given transgression may be reframed as a "crime" is often essential in shaping informal negotiations and interactions between regulators and suspect companies – designations of criminality are strategically invoked and resisted on a regular basis, even if these infrequently result in the actual production of so-called corporate crimes. In this respect, corporate crime, and criminology more generally, are useful in designating a field of legal processing and consumption, rather than a clearly identifiable form of conduct differentiated on the basis of its inherent attributes and characteristics – that is, its "real harms."

With these arguments in hand, rather than abandoning criminology, I would urge corporate and white-collar crime scholars to instead focus on expanding the range and scope of the literature by engaging more directly and conscientiously with complementary bodies of research and scholarship. Examples of literatures that would be helpful in revitalizing the study of corporate crime while maintaining a foothold in the criminological domain include recent work in socio-legal and regulatory studies, which explicitly recognizes the diversity of financial governance and economic regulation and has gone to great lengths to examine the extent to which regulation is enacted through complex intersections and interrelationships involving a series of public, quasi-public, and private entities (see Parker and Braithwaite 2003). Referred to as "decentred regulation" or "regulatory pluralism" (Black 2001; Scott 2001), this body of work takes non-state forms of regulation seriously rather than simply dismissing them. It also focuses attention on the diversity and complexity of law and, in particular, on the notion that regulatory objectives are often accomplished through informal or non-legal strategies and tactics that nevertheless draw on law's legitimacy and its existence as a potential course of action and form of redress should informal solutions fail to bear fruit.

Valuable contributions may also be solicited from literatures on organizations and professions. Despite a central concern with organizational forms and contexts of wrongdoing, corporate and white-collar crime scholars tend to ascribe to a very limited understanding of organizations. More often than not, they are reduced to either localized opportunity structures that restrain or enable individualized expressions of greed or instruments through which broader economic and political logics find their practical realization. A more sophisticated understanding of organizations as semi-autonomous social, economic, and political contexts characterized by strategy and uncertainty, consensus and conflict, and attempts to demonstrate competencies in ways that satisfy external stakeholders yet fail to be reflected in everyday practice is key in advancing the corporate crime literature. This focus is particularly important given that organizations actively participate in the enactment of law and the construction of regulatory meanings through various forms of negotiation, struggle, and compromise (McBarnet 1994; Edelman and Suchman 1997). Here they depend on a variety of professionals, including lawyers, accountants, and insurance agents, who sell along with their expertise their "regulatory capital" (Reichman 1992), a form of recognized and legitimate authority that lends credence and credibility to corporate interpretations of the law. Often it is professionals, through their expertise and interpretive labour, that mediate relationships between law, corporations, and markets, and thus mobilize not only the law, but also distinct regulatory regimes (Dezalay and Garth 1996; Ericson, Doyle, and Barry 2003; Williams 2005, 2006). Given this central role, not only organizations but also professionals must be taken more seriously.

The study of corporate criminality would also benefit from a more active engagement with a variety of theoretical traditions. This includes the work of Foucault (1989, 1991) and the tradition of governmentality studies (for example, Rose 1999), which have provided important insights into the nature and operation of neo-liberal forms of governance – in particular, the role of expertise and related calculative devices in translating broader governmental programs into more localized strategies, tactics, and technologies of rule. It is somewhat strange, given the huge theoretical dividends paid by this perspective in accounting for more general forms of social ordering, that these insights have not been applied to the study of corporations and governance within a financial context. Future research should explore this possibility. Valuable insights may also be gleaned from the work of Pierre Bourdieu (1987, 1993) and his concepts of social field and symbolic capital. These may be helpful in overcoming the unidimensionality and homogeneity imputed to the financial field, and in recognizing the dynamics of internal conflict and competition as various players struggle for competitive advantage and control over the economic and symbolic resources at stake in that field. This same analytic may be fruitfully applied to the regulatory arena, which is similarly organized in terms of competing yet unequal positions involving a variety of players – including public agencies, quasi-public and private organizations, and professional groups.

Having positioned ourselves on the boundaries of criminology, we must proceed by expanding the range and scope of the corporate and white-collar crime literature along the lines suggested above. We need to take seriously the contributions of scholars working in related fields, such as socio-legal studies, organizational studies, and the sociology of the professions, and recognize that, although corporate crime may have disappeared, it has since reappeared in other places and in different forms – in civil lawsuits, in the bylaws of professional associations and self-regulatory bodies, and in the interpretive labours of accountants and lawyers. We must suspend our search for "real harm" and instead come to terms with the complexity of the regulatory field and its enactment through a range of intermediaries and forms of discursive labour. And yet, pursuing these more expansive lines of inquiry does not require that we abandon criminology, but that we continue to use the analytic of "crime" as a point of juxtaposition, a juridical, bureaucratic, and social category in relation to which regulatory meanings are crafted and responses to corporate illegalities may be framed and weighed – all the while recognizing that "crime" is part of the micro-politics of governance and is itself constitutive of the outer limits of the regulatory field. These are the advantages of taking up a position on the boundaries of criminology, of acknowledging the marginality of "corporate crime," and of recognizing that disciplinary cross-fertilization represents the best opportunity for the advancement of the existing literature. To offer a brief glimpse of what this type of dialogical future might look like, the remainder of this chapter takes up my own research on the governance of financial markets.

## Financial Governance and the Regulation of Financial Markets

Although it may be true that corporate and white-collar crime have been rendered increasingly invisible under the weight of neo-liberalism, the bankruptcies of former Wall Street darlings Enron and WorldCom no doubt offer an exception to this trend. Whether because of the sheer scale of the losses involved, or the roots of the scandals in systemic conflicts of interest and persistent regulatory lapses, these scandals precipitated a sustained public, legal, and legislative reaction culminating in the passage of the Sarbanes-Oxley Act in July of 2002. And yet, despite the appearance of an earnest attempt to crack down on financial fraud, these reforms have been met with considerable skepticism, if not outright disdain, by critics who have dismissed them as political supplications and/or symbolic hedges against future scandals rather than serious attempts at long-term reform. In the words of Laureen Snider (2004, 18), one of the more vocal Canadian critics: "While some new laws and standards have been adopted and some maximum penalties increased, the key question remains: will the new measures deter and sanction financial crime more effectively than in the past?"

The critics may well be right. However, what is troubling about this critical stance is that it hinges on a particular notion of effectiveness that is neither clearly stated nor seriously examined. Here once again we can see the spectre of the aforementioned limits of the literature, as the reforms are deemed ineffective given their failure to curtail the aggressive pursuit of profit by self-interested executives, obvious in cases such as Enron and WorldCom, and the inability of regulators to tame the wild forces of the market given their continued reliance on regimes that are decidedly self-regulatory in nature. The problem with this view is that it limits our understanding of regulation, and regulatory (in)effectiveness, to the presence versus absence of manifest harm and the failures versus successes of formally designated state agencies. This neglects the extent to which regulatory outcomes are ambiguous, and regulation is itself constituted in situ through complex intersections involving a host of regulatory players – all of which seek to problematize and govern market activities based on their own unique mandates, logics, and strategies. Whether these activities are ultimately (in)effective is secondary. First we need a sophisticated understanding of exactly what is entailed in the practice of financial governance.

It was this very interest that motivated my own study of securities fraud in Canada, which sought to examine the question of regulatory effectiveness by first coming to terms with the complexities of the regulatory field and the reality that securities regulation in Canada is a product of intersections between a range of public, quasi-public, and private players. Here I was interested in moving beyond existing research on securities regulation and its focus on individual regulatory agencies understood in isolation (Shapiro 1984; Condon 1998) and/or violations of specific laws such as insider trading (Reichman 1993). Similarly, I wanted to avoid simply searching for "real crimes" – cases of financial greed that could be added to the catalogue of corporate horrors and used as evidence of increasing corporate control over financial regulation as fated by the natural inclinations and savage instincts of financial markets. In charting this somewhat novel analytical course, I drew upon three key conceptual elements that, in combination, helped to transcend the self-inscribed limits of the literature and provide a more nuanced and sophisticated starting point from which to examine the governance of financial markets in Canada, as well as corporate misconduct more generally.

## THE NATURE OF FINANCIAL MARKETS

The first of these three elements has to do with the nature of financial markets. That is, their characteristics, properties, and organizing logics. Unfortunately, most studies of financial regulation tend to scant this question, taking as their starting point existing legal provisions and requirements – as embodied in securities legislation – and then proceeding to examine the extent to which market participants conform to, or deviate from, these regulations. This then sets the stage for their more central concern with the ability of regulatory agencies to detect, identify, and remedy these legal breaches. However, in casting the analytical net so narrowly and pegging it so firmly to the terrain of law, these contributions have failed to systematically address the broader issue of exactly what is being regulated. Moreover, in so doing, they have inadvertently embraced a rather limited and somewhat caricatured view of financial markets as naturalized and highly rational spaces constituted in terms of informationally mediated transactional flows involving a range of buyers, sellers, enablers, and intermediaries. Markets are thus taken for granted and reduced to a unidimensional expression of financial interest.

What is omitted from these accounts is the fact that financial markets are themselves social and cultural constructions. They are creatures of economic discourse, the products of a historical labour through which they have been endowed with the very attributes of permanence, solidity, and naturalness that are subsequently taken for granted.[5] Moreover, "regulation" is itself part of this discursive fabric. The activities, public statements, programs, and mandates of regulators are central to the imagined regulatability and orderliness of markets – hence the importance of not dismissing statements about market integrity and investor confidence as disingenuous or illusory, but taking them seriously and examining how they figure as discursive and representational devices that have a very real impact on markets themselves. All of this is to suggest that regulation is far more complex than simply detecting violations of legal rules and sanctioning offenders. The study of regulation and regulatory practice must reflect this.

## THE PROBLEMATIZATION OF MARKETS AND THE PRODUCTION OF FINANCIAL DISORDER

The second core element guiding the research follows closely on the heels of the first and involves a particular take on the nature, not of markets, but of economic wrongdoing and financial disorder. As noted above, the existing literature on securities regulation has been geared primarily to the analysis of violations of specific legal rules and procedures, and a critical assessment of the nature and adequacy of the regulatory response. More often than not, these analyses are rooted in specific types or categories of legal violation, such as "insider trading" or "inadequate disclosure." My approach was somewhat different. Rather than focusing on pre-established and preconstituted categories or designations of illegality, I was interested in probing the more subtle and inchoate sets of logics, frames, and tactics through which market activities and market actors are defined and constituted as problematic. Of course, the law most certainly comes into play here. It defines the field of activity and the parameters of regulatory practice. However, regulatory activities are seldom informed directly by legal prohibitions. Rather, they reflect localized decisions that certain practices and players are problematic and disorderly – with the law then used to codify these disorders and render them amenable to official and authorized regulatory action. My interest was thus not in financial crime per se, nor extant legal prohibitions but, rather, in a particular mode of problematization, a cluster of visions, frames, and logics through which financial disorder is defined and constituted, and subsequently made subject to various paths of legal consumption. Here the analysis once again drew its inspiration from Foucault (1989, 1991) and, in particular, the notion that governance is constituted through, and is contingent upon, a dynamic of discursive problematization – that is, the identification of certain practices, identities, and relations as problems requiring intervention and corrective action. Following from this, the issue is not the isolation of "real harms" and "real crimes" as pre-existing objects, but the analysis of how specific types of financial activity are deemed problematic, and the extent to which this mode of problematization is ultimately constitutive of certain financial truths – the most central of which is the truth of the market itself.

When applied to the specific context of securities regulation in Canada, there are numerous considerations that guide and inform the problematization of market activity. First, the problematization of the market is invariably shaped and informed by the contradictory mandate of regulators. On the one hand, regulators are tasked with preserving investor confidence and trust through the design and implementation of effective regulatory regimes. Yet, on the other hand, these same agencies are required to attract capital investment by ensuring that markets are efficient and fluid – which typically means limiting the intrusiveness, if not necessarily the scope, of regulation. These contradictory mandates play a critical role in shaping regulatory initiatives and, in particular, the types of actors and activities that are likely to be defined as problematic and targeted for regulatory intervention.

Second, much of what passes for regulation – and thus problematic market activity – involves the policing of the boundaries or borders between legitimate and illegitimate financial actors and activities (see Williams 2008). In this respect, the primary concern on the part of agencies such as the Ontario Securities Commission (OSC) is not financial misconduct in and of itself but the purchase and sale of securities by marginal or peripheral players that either fail to play by the rules of the game – such as confining market manipulation to certain acceptable limits – or which undermine the interests of legitimate players. For example, the OSC has expended significant effort putting penny stock dealers out of business, as well as monitoring the involvement of organized crime figures in the markets. Interestingly, this identification of egregious conduct perpetrated at the margins of the legitimate market has the effect of normalizing what might otherwise be considered questionable or damaging activities. Examples include hedge funds that issue negative and damaging reports on public companies to profit from shorted stock;[6] the ability of large, institutional investors to move markets in ways that disadvantage smaller participants; and improper disclosure by listed companies. The effect of this juxtaposition is not only a deceptively bright line between true misconduct and normal market activity but also the legitimation of the market more generally, as the calling out of patent wrongdoing sends the message that all is well with the market as a whole.

### THE DIVERSITY OF THE REGULATORY FIELD AND THE POLITICS OF REGULATORY SPACE

The third and final element that guided my research involves an explicit recognition of the complexity of regulation and, in particular, the diversity of the regulatory field. In contrast with most forms of street crime, which are governed through a single legal regime and a dedicated regulatory agency, financial markets are subject to a range of regulatory players, logics, and interests. This stems in large part from the complexity of markets themselves, which encompass distinct lines of activity – from the buying and selling of stock to the disclosure of information to the investing public – and are dependent upon several actors, each bound to a unique regulatory regime. The various actors include (1) individual brokers and brokerage firms responsible for buying and selling securities, as well as writing research reports and providing recommendations on specific stocks; (2) issuers, the companies whose stocks are listed on public exchanges; (3) the investment bankers and underwriters who assist with public offerings of stock; (4) professional accountants and lawyers responsible for ensuring compliance with securities laws; and (5) market participants themselves. The varying involvement of these players in market activity requires distinct forms of regulatory scrutiny. For example, a large part of securities regulation involves monitoring issuers and ensuring the adequate disclosure of material changes in their operations. Similarly, the monitoring and oversight of brokers is required to ensure that they effectively and faithfully represent the interests of their clients in recommending stocks and executing trades. These trades are themselves objects of regulation, as assurances need to be provided that the ongoing stream of buying and selling is a reflection of fair and transparent market practices and has not been unduly influenced by distortions such as insider trading or market manipulation schemes.

This complex mixture of market players and activities has spurred an equally diverse regulatory field consisting of various agencies and stakeholders that may be situated, albeit rather loosely, on a continuum of public to private. These include (1) the RCMP and its integrated market enforcement teams – specialized white-collar crime units formed in 2003 to tackle serious securities frauds (Williams 2008); (2) securities commissions in each of Canada's thirteen provinces and territories; (3) self-regulatory organizations – such as the Investment Dealers Association, the Mutual Fund Dealers Association, and Market Regulation Services Inc. – tasked with regulating the sale of financial products and the daily trading of securities; and (4) private regulators, such as shareholder advocacy groups that use their financial and legal capital to influence corporate practices through share ownership and voting rights, civil lawsuits, and public pressure.

Given the range and variety of regulatory actors, it is far more appropriate to conceive of regulation, and financial governance more generally, in terms of a field. Borrowing once again from Bourdieu (1987, 1993), this allows for the recognition that regulation is a product of relationships and interactions between a range of regulatory players that occupy different positions – the public versus private status of the regulator being only one consideration here – and that are able to mobilize different forms and types of regulatory authority. These interrelationships are made more complex by the reality of overlapping mandates and shared jurisdictions, as well as by the ambiguous legal status of many of the activities these agencies are tasked with regulating. A case of insider trading may be classified as a regulatory breach of the Securities Act under the aegis of the OSC or a violation of the Criminal Code best left to the RCMP. Politicking is thus the norm as jurisdictions and investigative rights are debated, and cases are allocated based on strategic decisions rather than the best course of regulatory action. All of this suggests that in order to understand the regulation of financial markets, we first need to come to terms with the complexities and politics of the regulatory field itself.

## Conclusion: Advancing the Front

Several implications follow from this brief sketch of the governance of financial markets in Canada – each of which serves to further illuminate the identified limitations of the corporate and white-collar crime literature and to reveal potential lines of development, revitalization, and renewal. First, in conceptualizing corporate wrongdoing, it is helpful to suspend the search for "real harm" and "real crime" and to focus instead on the more Foucauldian question of how notions of order and disorder are crafted within markets as discursive formations. This allows for a focus on *how* conceptions of disorder and crime are created and mobilized, and to what effect, rather than the standard preoccupation with *why* real crimes are neglected or ignored. Moreover, this emphasis on modes of problematization, and not manifest forms of criminality, is itself dependent upon the notion that markets and market activities are socially, politically, and economically conditioned, rather than mere manifestations of a natural, foreign, and exotic financial sphere. They are themselves constituted through regulation, not simply subject to it. Thus, what is at stake in the analysis of corporate and white-collar crime is not merely revealing the reality, the truth, behind corporate practices and identifying "real" forms of disorder but examining how representations of disorder are constituted and accepted as true. The shift away from a realist ontology and the embrace of a constitutive and discursive approach to both governance and the objects of governance are important ingredients of this alternative approach.

Second, to the extent that it is feasible, studies of corporate and white-collar crime should move beyond the case study method and attempt to incorporate a range of methodologies – in particular, interviews and participant observation. Corporate crime researchers are masters of documentary research. However, this inevitably limits the range and scope of their analysis. Many of the insights that have emerged from the reported research on securities regulation have relied on interviews as well as attendance at industry and professional conferences. These have afforded opportunities to assess and contextualize the stated mandates of regulatory agencies and to examine more contextually the extent to which regulatory programs are actually translated into practice. Given the key links between theory and method, this expanded methodological approach is essential to moving beyond simplistic attributions of greed and avarice as driving forces behind corporate wrongdoing and mobilizing broader theoretical frameworks, insights, and possibilities. Abandoning the search for "real harm" and "real crime" is an important first step in moving beyond the proverbial little shop of horrors.

Third, while it may be true that the regulation of corporate crime has undergone a significant transformation under neo-liberalism and that, more than ever, regulatory responsibilities have been delegated to non-state agencies, this does not necessarily invariably translate into a regulatory vacuum, with corporations in the driver's seat. The complexity of evolving regulatory arrangements, or networks, is clearly apparent in the financial field, where securities regulation most certainly meets the definition of decentred regulation or regulatory pluralism. Financial governance is effected by various agencies through a range of techniques, strategies, and technologies and is directed toward myriad players, activities, and transactions. On its surface, it would appear that this is a clear example of neo-liberal regulatory arrangements, with the markets essentially left to their own devices. And yet, market actors and transactions are clearly subject to a range of restrictions, prohibitions, and requirements that circumscribe and limit their activities in very real ways. These modes of governance do not follow a single logic or set of interests, and they are likely to have different effects depending on the position of regulatory objects within financial space. Ultimately, this regulatory network may be judged to be inadequate and ineffective. However, this is a matter of empirical inquiry, rather than logical assumption, an inquiry that depends upon a more radical questioning of categories such as "crime" and "harm," as well as evaluative judgments of "effectiveness" and "adequacy." This requires that we move beyond the self-inscribed limits of the corporate and white-collar crime literature and engage with a broader theoretical and methodological universe.

In conclusion, having covered a great deal of territory and provided at least one indication of how core issues relating to corporate criminality may be rethought and reframed, the question posed at the outset of this chapter remains: Is criminology relevant to the study of corporate and white-collar crime, or should we move beyond criminology? The answer to this question depends, in part, on one's view of the discipline. If criminology is equated with a narrow administrative tradition bound to the ontology of crime and the search for causes and solutions to conventional forms of criminal behaviour, then the answer is most certainly no. However, if criminology is defined in much broader, less disciplinary terms, if it is freed from the realist ontologies of crime and harm, and if it is explicitly situated in relation to broader questions of control, ordering, and governance, then the prospects appear much brighter. This no doubt requires that we continue to work on the margins or boundaries of criminology, drawing inspiration from adjoining theoretical and disciplinary frameworks, and recognizing that "crime" represents a particular bureaucratic and political framing of trouble, disorder, and contravention, rather than an essential reality. It is in this respect, as a point on a continuum of social ordering, a bureaucratic and social category that may be juxtaposed with other organizational and professional designations, that "crime" remains most useful. Beyond these theoretical and conceptual issues, the ongoing engagement with criminology is also useful given the critical sensibility that runs throughout the work of most corporate crime scholars, one that is directly informed by questions of social (in)justice and that is built upon a strong appreciation for the links between crime, law, and power. It is this critical sensibility, a sense of righteous indignation, tempered with careful analysis and reflection and situated in relation to a much broader theoretical universe, that holds the greatest promise for criminology and preserves its relevance to the study of corporate and white-collar crime.

## ACKNOWLEDGMENTS

Research for this chapter was made possible by a grant from the Social Sciences and Humanities Research Council. I would also like to thank the editors, as well as the three anonymous reviewers, for their helpful comments and valuable feedback on earlier drafts of the chapter.

## NOTES

1   The reference here is primarily to the collapse of dot-com darlings Enron and WorldCom, although the more recent crisis in the subprime mortgage sector provides an equally fitting case in point.

2   The "critical" stream within the literature refers to authors who are expressly critical of "corporate crime" as a legal and institutional category, and who draw on Marxist, neo-Marxist, and Foucauldian sensibilities in locating corporate misconduct within its broader socio-political and socio-economic context. This can be contrasted with the more conventional end of the literature where authors tend to rely on more narrowly legalistic definitions of corporate crime and to explain this activity using theoretical frameworks imported, with limited modifications, from criminology more generally. Interestingly, these fractures follow national lines as Canadian and British scholars, such as Frank Pearce, Laureen Snider, Harry Glasbeek, and Steve Tombs, tend to reside within the critical camp, whereas their American counterparts, with the exception of David Friedrichs, Ron Kramer, and Ray Michalowski, are largely aligned with the conventional camp. The analyses presented in this chapter are geared more toward the former than the latter and seek to recognize the strengths of the critical stream while overcoming its internal limits.

3   This is especially the case for financial crimes such as insider trading, which is not only shrouded in legal ambiguity but is also subject to principled disagreements as to its very harmfulness – it is decried by some as a parasitic activity yielding unfair advantages for those in the know, yet lauded by others as a sign and symptom of efficient markets.

4   This is further exacerbated by the reliance on settlement agreements, in which the details of alleged offences are sealed and not disclosed to the public, as well as the increasing use of non-prosecution agreements in which corporations consent to specific behavioural and operational changes in return for the guarantee that they will not be prosecuted.

5   As de Goede (2005) notes, a key component of this historical and discursive labour hinged upon the development of indices such as the Dow Jones Industrial Average, the stock ticker, and the *Wall Street Journal* in the late 1800s. These endowed the markets with a seemingly natural calculability and were instrumental in severing the link between financial speculation and gambling that had prevailed in public discourse throughout the nineteenth and early twentieth centuries.

6   Shorting stock refers to the practice of borrowing shares of a company and then selling those borrowed shares at the current market price. The hope is that the stock price will fall over time so that the stock can be repurchased at a lower price with the investor profiting from the difference.

## REFERENCES

Ayres, I., and J. Braithwaite. 1992. *Responsive Regulation: Transcending the Deregulation Debate.* New York: Oxford University Press.

Black, J. 2001. Decentring Regulation: Understanding the Role of Regulation and Self-Regulation in a "Post-Regulatory" World. *Current Legal Problems* 54: 103-46.

Bourdieu, P. 1987. The Force of Law: Toward a Sociology of the Juridical Field. *Hastings Law Journal* 38: 805-53.

–. 1993. *Sociology in Question.* London: Sage.

Braithwaite, J. 2000. The New Regulatory State and the Transformation of Criminology. *British Journal of Criminology* 40(2): 222-38.

Condon, M. 1998. *Making Disclosure: Ideas and Interests in Ontario Securities Regulation.* Toronto: University of Toronto Press.

de Goede, M. 2005. *Virtue, Fortune, and Faith: A Genealogy of Finance.* Minneapolis: University of Minnesota Press.

Dezalay, Y. 1996. Between the State, Law, and the Market: The Social and Professional Stakes in the Construction and Definition of a Regulatory Arena. In *International Regulatory Competition and Coordination: Perspectives on Economic Regulation in Europe and the United States,* ed. W. Bratton, J. McCahery, S. Picciotto, and C. Scott, 59-88. Oxford: Clarendon Press.

Dezalay, Y., and B.G. Garth. 1996. *Dealing in Virtue: International Commercial Arbitration and the Construction of a Transnational Legal Order*. Chicago: University of Chicago Press.

Edelman, L.B., and M.S. Suchman. 1997. The Legal Environments of Organizations. *Annual Review of Sociology* 23: 479-515.

Ericson, R.V., A. Doyle, and D. Barry. 2003. *Insurance as Governance*. Toronto: University of Toronto Press.

Foucault, M. 1989. *The Archaeology of Knowledge*. London: Routledge.

–. 1991. Governmentality. In *The Foucault Effect: Studies in Governmentality*, ed. G. Burchell, C. Gordon, and P. Miller, 87-104. Chicago: University of Chicago Press.

Hillyard, P., C. Pantazis, S. Tombs, and D. Gordon. 2004. *Beyond Criminology: Taking Harm Seriously*. Halifax: Fernwood.

Lynch, M.J., D. McGurrin, and M. Fenwick. 2004. Disappearing Act: The Representation of Corporate Crime Research in Criminological Literature. *Journal of Criminal Justice* 32(5): 389-98.

McBarnet, D. 1994. Legal Creativity: Law, Capital, and Legal Avoidance. In *Lawyers in a Postmodern World: Translation and Transgression*, ed. M. Cain and C.B. Harrington, 73-84. New York: New York University Press.

Meyer, J.W., and B. Rowan. 1977. Institutionalized Organizations: Formal Structure as Myth and Ceremony. *American Journal of Sociology* 83(2): 340-63.

Mnookin, R.H., and L. Kornhauser. 1978. Bargaining in the Shadow of the Law: The Case of Divorce. *Yale Law Journal* 88: 950-97.

Parker, C., and J. Braithwaite. 2003. Regulation. In *The Oxford Handbook of Legal Studies*, ed. P. Cane and M. Tushnet, 119-45. New York: Oxford University Press.

Pearce, F., and S. Tombs. 1999. *Toxic Capitalism: Corporate Crime and the Chemical Industry*. Toronto: Canadian Scholars' Press.

–. 2004. Dance Your Anger and Your Joys: Multinational Corporations, Power, Crime. In *The Blackwell Companion to Criminology*, ed. C. Sumner, 359-76. Malden, MA: Blackwell.

Reichman, N. 1992. Moving Backstage: Uncovering the Role of Compliance Practices in Shaping Regulatory Policy. In *White-Collar Crime Reconsidered*, ed. K. Schlegel and D. Weisburd, 244-68. Boston: Northeastern University Press.

–. 1993. Insider Trading. In *Beyond the Law: Crime in Complex Organizations*, ed. M. Tonry and A. Reiss, 55-96. Chicago: University of Chicago Press.

Rose, N. 1999. *Powers of Freedom: Reframing Political Thought*. New York: Cambridge University Press.

Schmidt, P. 2005. *Lawyers and Regulation: The Politics of the Administrative Process*. Cambridge: Cambridge University Press.

Scott, C. 2001. Analyzing Regulatory Space: Fragmented Resources and Institutional Design. *Public Law* 2001: 329-53.

Shapiro, S.P. 1984. *Wayward Capitalists: Target of the Securities and Exchange Commission.* New Haven, CT: Yale University Press.

Shearing, C.C. 1989. Decriminalizing Criminology. *Canadian Journal of Criminology* 31(2): 169-78.

Snider, L. 2000. The Sociology of Corporate Crime: An Obituary (or Whose Knowledge Claims Have Legs?) *Theoretical Criminology* 4(2): 169-206.

–. 2003. Researching Corporate Crime. In *Unmasking Crimes of the Powerful: Scrutinizing States and Corporations,* ed. S. Tombs and D. Whyte, 49-69. London: Peter Lang.

–. 2004. *This Time We Really Mean It! Cracking Down on Stockmarket Fraud.* Paper presented at "Governing the Corporation: Mapping the Loci of Power in Corporate Governance Design," international colloquium of the Institute of Governance, Public Policy and Social Research, Belfast.

Stanley, C.C. 1994. Speculators: Culture, Economy, and the Legitimation of Deviance. *Crime, Law, and Social Change* 21(3): 229-51.

Stenning, P., C. Shearing, S. Addario, and M. Condon. 1990. Controlling Interests: Two Conceptions of Order in Regulating a Financial Market. In *Securing Compliance: Seven Case Studies,* ed. M.L. Friedland, 88-119. Toronto: University of Toronto Press.

Sutherland, E.H. 1983. *White-Collar Crime: The Uncut Version.* New Haven, CT: Yale University Press.

Tombs, S., and P. Hillyard. 2004. Towards a Political Economy of Harm: States, Corporations, and the Production of Inequality. In *Beyond Criminology: Taking Harm Seriously,* ed. P. Hillyard, 30-54. Halifax: Fernwood.

Tombs, S., and D. Whyte. 2003. Scrutinizing the Powerful: Crime, Contemporary Political Economy, and Critical Social Research. In *Unmasking Crimes of the Powerful: Scrutinizing States and Corporations,* ed. S. Tombs and D. Whyte, 3-48. New York: Peter Lang.

Williams, J.W. 2005. Reflections on the Private versus Public Policing of Economic Crime. *British Journal of Criminology* 45(3): 316-39.

–. 2006. Private Legal Orders: Professional Markets and the Commodification of Financial Governance. *Social and Legal Studies* 15(2): 209-35.

–. 2008. Out of Place, Out of Line: Positioning the Police in the Regulation of Financial Markets. *Law and Policy* 30(3): 306-35.

# 5
# Criminological Nightmares: A Canadian Criminology of Genocide

*Andrew Woolford*

Like many disciplines, criminology is susceptible to the imperial dream of expanding its epistemological domain to include topics heretofore unexplored through the criminological spyglass. However, as Marlowe discovered, sometimes adventures into the exotic unknown reveal most clearly the horror that lies within one's heart of darkness (Conrad [ca. 1899] 2003). Such is the potential of the recent criminological foray into the field of genocide studies: it might reveal the dark side of criminology. But this is not an outcome that we should fear; instead, it is an opportunity for criminology to interrogate and learn from its past. For example, criminology has been a "discipline of difference" (Hinton 2002, 12) and purveyed logics of social division and exclusion. Criminology has traded in totalizations and essentializations, thereby offering states a semblance of intellectual legitimacy for destructive projects of social engineering. Criminology has also helped criminalize and stigmatize already despised individuals and groups. These criminological nightmares rest just below the surface of our disciplinary dreamscape, threatening to emerge and disrupt our best intentions. Without critical and reflexive engagement with these subterranean currents, we risk a return of the repressed – a criminology that contributes to, rather than counters, genocidal logics. We also risk a criminology that imposes concepts of crime and punishment on genocidal contexts that are too complex for this reductive language, while providing redemptive and self-serving benefits to the discipline by overwriting the exclusionary moments of its past. In this chapter, I argue for a criminology of genocide that is sensitive to the discipline's legacy and that takes unveiling this past (and its present manifestations) as a starting point for a reflexive and responsible encounter with the topic of genocide. In addition, I argue for a *Canadian* criminology of genocide, which would entail a critical confrontation with Canada's colonial history as a means to reveal the Eurocentric thinking that too often takes root in discussions on genocide.

## Why a Criminology of Genocide?

Recently, concern has been expressed over criminology's failure to tackle the problem of genocide (see Brannigan 1998; Laufer 1999; Day and Vandiver 2000; Friedrichs 2000; Yacoubian 2000; Alvarez 2001; Hagan and Greer 2002; Morrison 2003).[1] Some ask how it is that a discipline that takes the study of crime as its main objective can overlook what is widely considered to be the most terrible of crimes. In engaging this question, criminologists have pointed to key disciplinary barriers that serve to limit the study of genocide. Friedrichs (2000) and Alvarez (2001) note criminology's methodological biases toward topics that are more readily quantified, that research funding within the discipline is typically directed toward subjects of national interest, and the wariness of criminologists to engage in research that is morally charged and threatens to remove their "safe," "scientific" distance. Hagan and Greer (2002) add that political contexts can influence the choice of research topics in criminology. They argue that the Cold War played an important role in distracting criminological attention from genocide, as the post-Nuremberg controversy over who had the right to apply laws of genocide and war crimes discouraged criminologists from examining issues of international law.

There is a question, however, that comes before that of why criminologists have failed to examine genocide, and this is why should there be a criminology of genocide? Before we address this matter, we might first examine potential problems that may arise with the application of a conventional criminological perspective to genocide. For example, the atomizing language of criminology – in particular, terms such as "victim" and "perpetrator" – may be wholly inappropriate in genocidal contexts where "victims become killers" (Mamdani 2001); that is, where identities of victim and perpetrator are fluid and not easily cast. Criminology's traditional terminology may provide little purchase in situations, such as those still unfolding in East Africa, where Tutsi-perpetrated mass killings in Burundi sent Hutu refugees across the Rwandan border to later join the cadres of the infamous Interahamwe, one of the primary killing forces within the Rwandan genocide. Further adding to the complexity of this situation, after the Tutsi-led Rwandan Patriotic Front (the RPF, itself not innocent of human rights violations) "ended" the Rwandan genocide, the Hutu genocidaires became refugees in neighbouring nations, including the Democratic Republic of the Congo (DRC), bringing with them the violence of the "machete season" (Hatzfeld 2005). This was followed by a RPF incursion into the DRC that culminated in Rwandan forces occupying Kinshasa. How does one transport conventional criminological theories

designed to understand street crime into such an inter-regional, deeply historical, and dangerously political situation without engaging in gross simplification? How does one employ conceptual tools that assume distinct victims
and perpetrators when these identities overlap and intersect? Yet, conventional criminology has been undeterred by these difficulties. Sykes and
Matza's techniques of neutralization (Day and Vandiver 2000), manifestations
of Turk's non-partisan conflict theory (ibid.), and Hirschi's control theory
(Brannigan 1998; Brannigan and Hardwick 2003) have all been spotted in
the hills of Rwanda.

The atomizing language of criminology, not to mention the Western legal
tradition, also threatens to concentrate attention on individual acts rather
than on structural problems. This tendency is evidenced in the quasi-legal
South African Truth and Reconciliation Commission (TRC), which took as
its focus "gross human rights violations" (see Minow 1999), ignoring a long
history of colonial relations during which black South Africans were denied
opportunity, education, training, and general economic equality. As Mahmood
Mamdani (2000) notes, the TRC examined relations between perpetrators
and victims only, not those between beneficiaries and the disadvantaged. The
language of law, and by association the language of more legalistic forms of
criminology, thus played a limiting and reductive role in attempts to repair
the "crime" of apartheid (Christodoulidis 2000), and left much harm unaddressed in the new South Africa.

Here we confront the problem that conventional criminology takes as
its object something called crime, which refers to officially designated wrongs.
But can we, as Hannah Arendt (1963, 291-92) asks, "apply the same principle
that is applied to a governmental apparatus in which crime and violence are
exceptions and borderline cases to a political order in which crime is legal
and the rule?" Although we have the 1948 United Nations Convention on
the Prevention and Punishment of the Crime of Genocide (UNCG), national
laws prohibiting genocide, as well as a framework of laws on torture and
other international harms, we also face situations in which harms are legal
according to the laws of oppressive regimes. Mamdani (2000) illustrates this
conundrum with the examples of the apartheid land laws and the Group
Areas Act, which together led to the forcible displacement of 3.5 million
people from their homes and livelihoods. Legalized displacement and other
harms often accompany genocide, ethnic cleansing, and mass violence, but
a narrow focus on what is "criminal" distracts from the true scope of damage

and destruction wrought by these events. In other words, as James Williams (this volume) suggests with respect to white-collar crime, a focus on extreme harmful action, and subsequent attempts to criminalize this action, can lead one to overlook "more entrenched, yet less visible, forms of harm."

The expansion of criminology's domain should not be undertaken lightly, as criminological methods and epistemology are by no means neutral when it comes to issues of genocide and mass violence. Indeed, a brief examination of the work of criminological scholars *during* periods of genocide illustrates that criminology was anything but a bulwark against extermination. For example, criminologists who took a stand against Nazi racist criminalizations were a minority, outnumbered by their Lombrosian counterparts, who produced criminological research indirectly supportive of the project of elimination. As Wetzell (2000) demonstrates, it is a mistake to think that criminology under the Nazis was simply a corrupt science perverted by the ideology of racial hatred. Relative to criminological developments in other countries at the time, and growing out of the criminology of the Weimar Republic, criminology under the Nazis showed increasing methodological and conceptual sophistication. Despite this sophistication, criminologists crucially failed on two counts under Nazi rule. First, many criminologists opportunistically courted the Nazi leadership to gain political and financial support for their existing criminal-biological and eugenics-based research (ibid.). Second, criminological thinkers, including those who were suspicious of criminal sterilization policies, and even those who favoured sociological over biological approaches, generally treated criminological categorizations such as "social" versus "asocial" and "corrigible" versus "incorrigible" as unproblematic (ibid.).

Under Nazi rule, criminology operated largely as a dominated and subservient discipline, beholden to state-defined notions of criminology rather than engaging in an autonomous evaluation of the social world. Criminology did not exhibit a disciplinary ethics that would embolden its stance against the state's exclusionary and eliminationist intentions. Instead, the discipline fell to an instrumental careerism that made it complicit in what has been called the "crime of the century" (Friedrichs 2000). Criminology has therefore not proven itself an antidote to the poison of genocidal thinking. So why then a criminology of genocide?

To date, criminologists studying genocide have offered various answers to this question: (1) the *deadly scope* of the crime of genocide demands criminological attention; (2) criminologists are accustomed to studying tragic and terrible circumstances and therefore can maintain *objectivity* when studying the horrors of genocide; (3) criminology, as a discipline, *can benefit* from an engagement with genocide; and (4) according to international legal and quasi-legal documents such as the UNCG, *genocide is a crime*, making it an appropriate object of criminological inquiry. None of these, however, is sufficient reason for launching a criminology of genocide.

## DEADLY SCOPE

The argument appealing to the *deadly scope* of genocide is often enhanced by the suggestion that deaths caused by genocide in the twentieth century have far outstripped those caused by street crime and present perhaps the twenty-first century's greatest danger (Friedrichs 2000; Yacoubian 2001). Unfortunately, by participating in a competition of the hierarchy of global suffering, we run the risk of minimizing other threats to human existence, such as environmental destruction, precarious living conditions, disease, and famine. If criminology is truly to be based on the deadly scope of human suffering, it will need to amplify its scholarly focus to include all such harms. But this amplification of criminology should not be automatic, since no matter how detrimental these phenomena may be, we still need to assess whether there is a qualitative difference between these vast and often global harms and the conventional fodder of criminology. Given the atomizing tendencies of conventional criminology discussed earlier in this chapter, it is fair to suggest that traditional criminology may not be ideally suited for the examination of complex global dangers. Thus, for criminologists to play a part in studying these broader harms, they will need to avoid simply transposing the mainstream criminological canon onto topics such as genocide; rather, they will need to devise a different criminology that is sensitive to the specificity of destructive global contexts.

It is worth noting that the *deadly scope* argument tends to give inordinate attention to deaths, which can result in a disregard for other forms of harm that are also significant parts of genocide. Criminologists studying genocide must acknowledge the many attendant harms of genocide: forced expulsion, rape, cultural loss, mass theft, and torture, to name but a few. Although killing is certainly a primary component of most definitions of genocide (see, for example, Lemkin 1944; Fein 2002), these other harms often precede genocidal killings, have lingering effects that continue to trouble societies in their post-genocide years, and contribute to the perpetuation of cycles of violence (see Minow 1999). In this sense, just as a narrow emphasis on crime can result in inattention to more subtle forms of harm, so too can a fixation on the deadly scope of genocide.

## CRIMINOLOGICAL OBJECTIVITY

The second rationale suggests that criminologists are ideally suited to research genocide because we are familiar with the study of horrible crimes. That is, we have stood before murderers, rapists, and other feared groups, *objectively* gathered our empirical data, and generated concepts to help explain their harmful behaviour (Day and Vandiver 2000; Yacoubian 2000). This argument alludes to the criminologist's supposed ability to remain neutral when confronting deviant activities that often cause a great deal of public turmoil. However, as Freeman (1991, 194) notes, "genocide is an inescapably normative concept; there cannot be a justified genocide. It is not killing but murder. The definition of 'genocide,' therefore, presupposes a normative theory which distinguishes justified killing from murder." Thus, the term "genocide" (much like the concept of crime) implies normative engagement. Therefore, any notion of objectivity employed should not be so detached from the subjective context that it threatens to diminish solidarity with genocide's casualties. As demonstrated in several studies of genocide and war crimes (for example, Milgram 1974; Bauman 1989; Kelman and Hamilton 1989), the ideal of a pure scientific neutrality has, in many cases, been an important component of the conduct of genocide, as it allows participants to separate themselves from the consequences (that is, the victims) of their actions. Clearly, there is a performative contradiction in emulating the very stance we are critiquing.

Moreover, criminology must address its internal relationship to genocide. Broadly, it is no longer tenable to imagine criminology in a space outside the social world, as suggested in the assumptions of objectivity expressed in the existing conventional criminology of genocide literature. Criminology cannot sustain the image that it watches social action as a disinterested spectator because criminology is itself implicated in the universe of crime. As others have observed, through its analysis and study of crime, criminology often constitutes the very objects (so-called criminal events) it chooses to examine (Steinart 1998) and too often takes for granted state definitions of crime, thus reinforcing prevailing exclusionary biases. The notion of objectivity ignores how criminology has been complicit in mobilizing these exclusionary biases in genocidal contexts. Indeed, a facile notion of objectivity allows the discipline to remain existentially safe from genocide's horrors, and allows it to comfortably launch a criminology *of* genocide with little concern for the fate of criminology *in* genocide. For example, contemporary criminologists when venturing into the field of genocide studies too often overlook research conducted by previous purveyors of criminological exclusion. This is unfortunate, since there is an important negative lesson to be learned from the likes of Robert Ritter, a German researcher of juvenile delinquency who because of his radical racialist views rose to be head of Germany's Criminal Biological Institute of the Security Police. Ritter employed his own brand of "objective" criminological science to gather biopolitical data to help legitimize the Nazi assault on the Roma and Sinti peoples. Caught up in a narrow vision of modern science, Ritter allowed himself to become a tool of Nazi extermination.

## CRIMINOLOGY CAN BENEFIT

The third rationale claims that criminology can benefit from a scholarly engagement with genocide. This argument is correct to the extent that criminologists need to reflect on and reform their discipline in light of world-historic events such as genocide, as is suggested in this chapter (see also Morrison 2007). But this rationale takes a redemptive turn when it leaves foundational criminological assumptions unaddressed. Along these lines, Day and Vandiver (2000, 56) write: "We strongly disagree with the notion that [genocide] should be placed beyond the boundary conditions of our field. To do so results in lost opportunities to test the generalisability of our concepts and lost opportunities to integrate concepts from other disciplines." This positivist and instrumentalist argument turns criminological genocide studies toward the mundane tasks of testing theories and expanding criminological discourses, rather than critically evaluating these activities in light of genocidal events. Others hope that criminology will become "more profound" (Friedrichs 2000, 21) by bringing genocide into its disciplinary boundaries. In both examples, the benefits accruing to criminology are redemptive because the disciplinary reforms they promote are superficial to the extent that they leave the discipline's baseline assumptions unchallenged. In this sense, the benefits do not incite a reimagining of criminology; instead, they reaffirm the core of criminological study and redeem it in the shadow of its previous failings.

Alvarez's (2001, 2) contention that criminology should "assist in the process of shaping understanding and increasing awareness of genocidal crimes" also falls prey to the temptation of criminological redemption. He suggests that academics have a responsibility to refuse silence and to make the horrors of genocide widely known so that people no longer stand idly by in the face of mass slaughter. Although we may debate the efficacy of scholarly study as a vehicle for spreading such a message, this nonetheless appears an admirable goal. However, is it true that Western societies lack an awareness of genocide? Each month, publishers release several new genocide- or Holocaust-related books. Mainstream films on the Rwandan genocide augment those on Nazi Germany, Bosnia-Herzegovina, Cambodia, and so on. Indeed, one could argue there is a surfeit of genocide consciousness, especially a Holocaust consciousness that has arisen through the proliferation of Holocaust museums (including several located in North America, well away from the gas chambers of Europe) and films such as *Schindler's List* and *Life Is Beautiful*. This awareness did not exist immediately following the Second World War but has become familiar within modern Western cultures since the 1970s (Novick 1999). Sadly, this heightened awareness has done little to prevent genocides in Iraq, Cambodia, Bosnia, and Rwanda (Power 2002). As Cohen (2001, xii) eloquently posits, "our touching faith in 'if only they knew' underestimates the willfulness of denial in the face of knowledge."

To some extent, the excess of genocide information illustrates that the field of genocide studies has become a market for generating academic status. Friedrich's (2000, 21) aforementioned desire to make criminology "more profound" through the study of the Holocaust hints at the collective profits potentially available to the discipline, but individual criminologists can also benefit from teaching and researching genocide – the unquestioned nobility of the cause of repairing and preventing genocide casts an aura of seriousness upon the criminologist. In addition, it is not uncommon for academics of all stripes to seek the distinction that comes with expanding their respective fields in new and important directions. This colonizing mentality is an expected outcome of the competitive nature of academic markets, but we must understand and critically examine the workings of our marketplace to ensure that our research is motivated by something beyond self-interest. As Bourdieu (2001, 113) reminds us, "good causes" are no substitute for epistemological justifications and do not allow one to dispense with the reflexive analysis that sometimes leads to the discovery that the propriety of "good intentions" does not necessarily exclude an interest in the profits associated with fighting a "good fight." As criminologists studying genocide, our good intentions too often mask our self-interested engagement with this topic and provide us with the conceit that we are simply messengers – uninvolved mediating parties responsible for the objective delivery of information about genocide to the masses. This ignores that genocide is not only a criminal phenomena open to study but that it is also a criminalizing process in which criminological categorizations may be complicit.

## GENOCIDE IS A CRIME

The final argument for a criminology of genocide is the most basic. It states that the international community has identified genocide as a crime (and the same is true for many national criminal codes); therefore, criminologists, as scholars of crime, should be interested in this topic. Yacoubian (2000), for example, emphasizes the criminal nature of genocide and puzzles over criminology's failure to examine this "crime." But it is an unconvincing argument that because criminology is the study of crime it ought to study this most deadly of crimes. We cannot base our study of genocide solely on historically contingent state (and United Nations) decisions to legally identify this form of harm, especially considering that it was only in 1948, through the signing of the UNCG, that genocide officially became a "crime." This designation came after the Holocaust, the Armenian genocide, the German slaughter of the Herero, the colonial assault on indigenous peoples, and countless other paradigmatic examples of genocide. Therefore, instead of resting our study on legal definitions, we have to ask what exactly a criminological perspective might contribute to the study of genocide.

Also, although it is true that genocide is now defined as a crime under international law (though the UNCG has been rarely enforced), there is a danger that overemphasizing criminal codification might result in an attempt to "discipline" genocide, privileging criminological inquiry because criminology is, of course, *the* study of crime and, as William S. Laufer (1999, 73) notes, "genocide is a crime without a criminology." To date, the study of genocide has had the benefit of diverse voices, ranging from journalists and historians to anthropologists and philosophers, to name only a few. Criminologists must not simply come late to the field and claim this to be rightfully their territory. Instead, criminologists must join the multidisciplinary debate and open themselves to theories, concepts, and methodological tools produced in other fields. In other words, we must be somewhat "undisciplined" in our approach. Or, as Bryan Hogeveen (this volume; see also Williams, this volume) suggests, we could embrace a form of post-disciplinarity, since criminology's engagement with diverse traditions should do much to shake (and perhaps even transform) any sense of disciplinary certainty. Moreover, there is a need to take an internationalist perspective toward criminological research on topics such as genocide and mass violence. Most North American and western European criminological discussions of genocide fail to incorporate the work of authors living in areas where mass violence is more prominent (for example, Nikolić-Ristanović 1998; van Zyl Smit 1998). Regionalism has for too long been the trend in criminology, as local issues remain our primary sphere of interest despite the growing globalization of crime.

Most criminologists studying genocide acknowledge the need for multidisciplinarity; however, they have also been too eager to demonstrate the applicability of the Western criminological canon to genocide. In so doing, they too often take an "add criminology and stir" approach to genocide studies by mechanistically applying the discipline's mainstream theories to various genocides. Many of these theories were developed with respect to male youth and street crimes and are often dumb to the radical and "transgressive" (Stone 2004) social contexts within which genocide occurs. This is not to say that it is impossible to successfully draw on elements of criminological theory and redevelop them to work within the broader context of genocide research, but one's priority should be the extent to which the theory allows for a better understanding of genocidal social worlds rather than a mere demonstration of the elasticity of criminological thought. Only through a critical expansiveness is a criminology of genocide possible. Otherwise, criminologists will find themselves engaged in a futile project to forcibly contain within a criminological paradigm a subject matter that defies all attempts at constraint.

## A REFLEXIVE AND RESPONSIBLE CRIMINOLOGY OF GENOCIDE

For these and other reasons (see Jamieson 1998; Morrison 2003, 2007; Woolford 2006), we need to interrogate the limits and limitations of conventional criminological thought before imposing this framework on a new research object. Consequently, a criminology of genocide begins with a reflexive critique of criminology, reawakening our criminological nightmares in the hopes that we might prevent them from recurring. Through a deep exploration of our foundations and assumptions we can begin the project of criminological transformation required to responsibly tackle the subject of genocide. The word "responsibly" is used here to suggest that we must not simply force our conceptual tools on situations about which we know too little. A responsible criminology of genocide would instead allow the particularity of the genocidal context to serve as an opportunity to reformulate criminological thought. As well, this would require reconsideration of those elements of criminological thought that are inadmissible on moral grounds. on the basis that they obstruct solidarity with the dead, with survivors, and with the families and descendants of both groups. This is a move away from a redemptive criminology of genocide, which reflects a conservative and selective reading of the criminological past. It forges solidarity with those who suffer and have suffered under exclusionary modes of thought and action. Following this approach, criminology can contribute to the field of genocide studies by subjecting itself to a rigorous critique informed by the problem of genocide and thereby uncovering criminological forms of logic and reasoning consistent with those that help make genocide thinkable (Mamdani 2001).

This reflexive project does not end at our disciplinary doorstep, however; it also requires consideration of other components of our identities, such as our national backgrounds. For Canadian criminologists, this reflexivity begins not only with a confrontation with mainstream criminology but also with Canadian colonial history. Our contribution can be derived from critically engaging the totalizing, essentializing, and Eurocentric aspects of our relations with Aboriginal peoples within Canada. In the next section, I argue that being attentive to the exclusion of Aboriginal voices and of the specificity of various colonial-Aboriginal interactions creates space for a Canadian criminology of genocide that tackles the continuation of colonial logics in contemporary thinking about Aboriginal genocides.

## Why a Canadian Criminology of Genocide?

The colonization of Canada occurred not only through the force of arms but also (if not primarily) through the force of law. This is not to suggest that federal and provincial colonial governments necessarily acted "legally" in their dealings with Aboriginal peoples. Indeed, these governments often operated beyond law, calling upon states of exception that allowed them to ignore their legal requirement to negotiate treaties with Aboriginal groups in some regions (for example, British Columbia and the Yukon), to violate the terms of the treaties that they did sign, and to disregard the societal structures and the very humanity of Aboriginal peoples (Agamben 2005). Nonetheless, governments did implement legal tools aimed at assimilating Aboriginal groups, including such notably biopolitical policies as the Indian Act (1876), which is still in place today and has served to regulate nearly all aspects of Aboriginal lives, from governance to education to economy.[2] Given the use of law in attempts to destroy Aboriginal communities, the study of

Aboriginal genocides requires a critical standpoint toward interpretations and definitions based in the Western legal tradition and other forms of Euro-centric thinking. This standpoint can be enhanced by giving weight to Ab-original understandings of colonial harms so that the question of genocide is informed by Aboriginal experiences of destruction.

Indeed, these Aboriginal experiences and understandings of colonialism are important to the primary question of genocide research, the definition of genocide. Genocide scholars can draw on both legal and analytical defin-itions of genocide. The key legal definition, which serves as a basis for do-mestic and international legal definitions of genocide, is the 1948 UNCG. Article 2 of this convention reads:

> In the present Convention, genocide means any of the following acts committed with intent to destroy, in whole or in part, a na-tional, ethnical, racial or religious group as such:
>
> a Killing members of the group;
> b Causing serious bodily or mental harm to members of the group;
> c Deliberately inflicting on the group conditions of life calculated to bring about its physical destruction in whole or in part;
> d Imposing measures intended to prevent births within the group;
> e Forcibly transferring children of the group to another group.

Scholars have debated whether this definition is too broad or narrow for analytical purposes. Those who see it as too narrow are most concerned by the exclusion of political groups, since, they argue, these groups can be as persistent and as central to identity formation as the ethnic, racial, or religious categorizations included in the convention (see Kuper 1981; Letgers 1984). For those who charge that the definition is too broad, the convention is criticized for conflating genocide, in terms of the physical extermination of groups, with what might otherwise be referred to as "ethnocide" or "cul-tural genocide" (Chalk and Jonassohn 1990; Totten, Parsons, and Hitchcock 2002). Following this latter interpretation, although the terms of the UNCG allow for an argument that Canadian genocides occurred, Aboriginal experi-ences of Canadian colonialism are often described as instances of cultural genocide where the objective was the cultural, not the physical, elimination of Aboriginal peoples (Ponting and Gibbons 1980; Wotherspoon and Satze-wich 2000). This has resulted in the Canadian case being excluded from much comparative research on genocide (see Bischoping and Fingerhut 1996).[3] The qualifier "cultural" apparently places "cultural genocide" one step below "real" genocide in the hierarchy of harms. It suggests a different form of genocidal *intent*, one that seeks to *destroy* the *group* not as a physical entity but, rather, as a cultural formation. However, there are several Euro-centric assumptions at work in qualifying Canadian colonialism as cultural genocide that Canadian criminologists of genocide must critically address.

## GENOCIDAL INTENT?

Notions of genocidal intent are often interpreted in a manner favourable to the so-called good intentions that guided liberal idealism in its encounters with Aboriginal peoples, no matter how damaging the consequences of this idealism. More generally, Moses (2002) identifies a debate between liberals and post-liberals over the question of intention within the UNCG and sub-sequent attempts to define genocide. For Moses, the former overemphasize the question of agency and thereby focus too heavily on state intention as a measuring rod for defining genocide. In contrast, post-liberals overemphasize structural determinants of genocide by examining, for example, how the rul-ing relations of colonialism inevitably led to the elimination of indigenous cultures and/or peoples (see, for example, Barta 1987). Moses seeks to over-come this problematic binary in genocide studies by treating genocide as a dynamic process in which structural patterns of modernization and nation building are, under specific conditions, fashioned into murderous ideologies directed toward a despised group. Genocide, here, is no longer understood as a linear process that begins with intent and ends in elimination, nor as the mechanical result of structural determinations. In his earlier work, Moses (2000) also identifies genocidal "moments" that arise when, for example, developmental or colonizing activities with non-genocidal objectives meet with Aboriginal resistance and shift into periods of intentional genocidal action. Other scholars have also developed process-oriented models for understanding genocide that have been particularly useful in terms of under-standing the specificity and dynamism of genocidal atrocities (see Lemkin 1944; Arendt 1973; Levene 2000; Mann 2005) and for moving us beyond both a teleology of intent and structural determinism.

One problem these scholars help to address concerns how our search to identify intent often reads back upon accepted cases of genocide, imposing a linear path from intent to elimination. However, in most cases, the path to destruction is uneven and circuitous, and intent emerges at specific points in the face of specific challenges (see Schleunes 1990; Browning 2004). In this sense, the notion of intent is too often imbued with a positivistic sensibility that presupposes that exterminatory projects are guided from start to finish by an almost scientific rationality. Attempts are then made to isolate those moments in which a genocidal intent seems clear and to build a metanarrative of destruction that explains the genocide. However, in genocidal contexts there are usually multiple competing intentions, operating alongside habituated and doxic patterns of existence.

Claims to genocidal intent are also often interpreted in a manner consistent with how intent is understood for individual crimes. But in cases where multiple actors form and negotiate their collective existence, and, in so doing, devise exclusionary, assimilationist, and exterminationist policies, intent is more likely to be multiple and complex. Thus, a fetishization of intent risks essentializing perpetrators around a coherent *logos* of extermination when, in actual fact, the unity of the perpetrating group is more difficultly achieved. Such simplification can usefully reduce genocidal actors to fully evil and calculating monsters, but it is seldom historically accurate.

In the Canadian context, the problem of intent is evident in debates about the role of disease in Aboriginal destruction, as well as in discussions about residential schooling. Until recently, genocide scholars had paid scant attention to deaths caused by famine, disease, and other harms that have been categorized as natural phenomena. To justify this oversight, they have argued that genocide involves only social and intentional means of destruction, like the calculated murders in Rwanda, Nazi Germany, and elsewhere. But a modernist assumption lies nested in this division between the natural and the intentional. We can separate only hybridic and networked phenomena such as disease and famine into the category of nature (as distinct from culture or society) because we adhere to an intellectual orientation that holds nature and culture to be mutually distinct and uncoupled, despite their clear interconnections (Latour 1993). This separation is a convenience for those who claim colonial innocence in the aftermath of the destruction wrought by European-spread diseases, but it requires that we overlook several moments where natural and cultural processes combine or overlap.

Indeed, it was not merely the force of European trade and military might that allowed for the so-called New World to be colonized. There is also the matter of what Mann (2005) refers to as biological power – the diseases the newcomers brought with them and for which Aboriginal people had not developed resistances (see also Diamond 1997). The traders and missionaries who penetrated further into Aboriginal societies carried epidemics such as small pox with them. In other cases, the diseases spread from colonial entry points through Aboriginal networks, reaching even those groups that had not yet experienced European contact. In these latter cases, the diseases acted as a pre-emptive form of ethnic cleansing, allowing Europeans to declare Aboriginal lands *terra nullius* upon reaching the decimated communities (Clayton 2000). But when disease came directly through explorers and missionaries, Aboriginal peoples often found themselves unable to evict these people from their midst, as they were likely to be economically punished for such action (see Trigger 1985). Thus, a specific set of colonial relations exacerbated disease spread among Aboriginal communities. Fully calculated moments of purposeful infection, such as through the "pestilence blankets" sent into Aboriginal communities, were indeed part of the settlement of North America (see Fenn 2000; Finzsch 2008). However, in other cases, a more subtle intent – one produced through assumptions of cultural superiority, a willingness to view Aboriginal deaths as both natural and destined, and a general disregard for the Other – was at work in the Canadian landscape. Such was the case when it was noticed in 1862 that Aboriginal persons gathered around Fort Victoria in British Columbia were suffering from small pox. After making minimal efforts to vaccinate the stricken, and some political debate on whether to create facilities to treat the sick, the colonial authorities sent British gunboats to escort the sick back to their home communities, thus ensuring the further spread of disease. Knowledge of, and indifference to, the potential deadly consequences of these actions is evident in a June 1862 issue of the *Daily British Colonist* newspaper, where it was noted that the infected were "proceeding northward, bearing with them the seeds of a loathsome disease that will take root and bring both a plentiful crop of ruin and destruction to the friends who have remained at home. At the present rate of mortality, not many months can elapse 'ere the Northern Indians of this coast will exist only in story" (cited in Lange 2003).

Intention is also complexly located in Canada's residential schooling system. In these schools, death was also common. Over half of the students at certain schools succumbed to early deaths caused by unchecked disease, poor nutrition, and a lack of proper clothing and shelter (Milloy 1999). Add to these the deaths brought on through physical and sexual assaults and the suicides that, at times, followed these attacks, and one gains a sense of the deadly nature of this "civilizing" project. It has been noted that it was the "progressives" of the time who sought to redeem Aboriginal peoples by incorporating them into colonial society (Cairns 2000). For this reason, charges of presentism are often made against those who are insensitive to the ethical milieu of government and residential school workers. Indeed, in the words of Reverend Wilson of the Shingwauk, residential schools appear benign:

> [The Indian child] must be taught many things which come to the white child without the schoolmaster's aid. From the days of its birth, the child of civilized parents is constantly in contact with the modes of civilized life, of action, thought, speech and dress; and is surrounded by a thousand beneficient influences ... He [the Indian child] must be led out from the conditions of ... birth, in his early years, into the environment of civilized domestic life; and he must be thus led by his teacher. (cited in Milloy 1999, 33-34)

However, the aim of breaching the child-parent bond and to disconnect the Aboriginal child from his or her collectivity is much more blatant in the words of former deputy superintendent of Indian affairs, Duncan Campbell Scott: "I want to get rid of the Indian problem ... Our objective is to continue until there is not a single Indian in Canada that has not been absorbed into the body politic, and there is no Indian question, and no Indian Department" (cited in Milloy 1999; see also Titley 1986; Neu and Therrien 2002). Those who seek a teleology of intent are likely to identify this latter statement as the point of origin of the Canadian genocidal process, but we must not fall into this trap and should instead try to understand the networked destruction wrought by residential schools in Canada, as they destroyed not just lives but also generations of lives by disrupting cultural patterns of parenting and knowledge transmission. In this sense, the schools reflect an all-out assault on Aboriginal ontologies, as Milloy (1999, 37) writes:

> The child, parent, and community exist in a landscape – a culture's translation of environment into a "meaning"-filled place. Parts of the programme of studies would disorient children and then attempt to re-orient them in a place filled with European

"meaning." This "programme" intersected with other parts of the Canadian colonial enterprise to drastically alter the path of Aboriginal cultural production and reproduction.

Under a Eurocentric logic, assimilatory intent combines with habituated assumptions about child rearing, racist disregard for the nutritional and health needs of Aboriginal children, and the isolation and incompetence of some of the residential school instructors. It would be a disservice to attempt to boil these deadly choices and assumptions down to a single order or policy from which we could build a metanarrative of intent. Thus, we are left with the difficult historical work of pulling apart various levels of intention and deadly inattention (based on a will to totality that disregarded all Aboriginal cultural understandings) that arise in particular circumstances, or genocidal moments, when colonial ambitions are confronted with Aboriginal resistances (Moses 2002).

WHAT IS DESTRUCTION?

Genocide carries with it notions of groupness and harm that are artifacts of a specific (in particular, modernist) viewpoint and may not reflect how group identity or harm are experienced or understood by differing collectives. As discussed above, the modern "constitution" separates the poles of nature and culture, while allowing for the proliferation of hybrids, or quasi-objects and quasi-subjects, that are amalgamations of nature and culture networked together in a complex interface (Latour 1993). This act of purification allows moderns to stack the deck in their favour, designating events and objects to either the nature or culture pole depending on which better suits their interests. Taking Latour's argument out of its science studies context, one can examine how practices of purification operate within debates about what is and what is not genocide, as the hybridity of destructive processes – for example, the slow genocide of HIV/AIDS spread through rapes or the destruction caused by (fully or partially) orchestrated famines designed to punish rebellious collectives – often complicates the picture as to what is and is not a part of a genocidal action. To deal with the hybridic nature of destruction, decisions are often made according to Eurocentric notions of what constitutes harm, ignoring that collectives might have different understandings of their suffering and potential destruction.

The UNCG exists to protect groups, and one assumes that what is considered worth protecting is group difference. Indeed, the architects of the

UNCG, including Raphael Lemkin (1944), who coined the word "genocide," intended it to protect "national" groups whose cultural difference was viewed to enrich the world community. This creates the problem of essentialism that I address below. It also has too often led to a practice whereby the difference of the Other is assessed and measured against the European self, since evaluations of cultural contributions to the world community are typically measured against the presumed beneficial offerings of Western nations. For this reason, I suggest that what needs protection is better described as singularity – a specificity that is not referenced to a privileged collective or set of collectives (see Nancy 2000; Hardt and Negri 2004). Following this notion of singularity, one would assume that what it means to *destroy* a group depends to some extent on how the group defines itself and its world (that is, its originary power). Clearly, most groups would not survive the mass killing of their members, since it is those members who construct and negotiate the meaning and identity of their group. But loss of human lives alone does not adequately describe the many possible ways in which a collective can be destroyed. It is for this reason that the UNCG acknowledges several forms of "destruction" that catalogue the potential devastating harms of mental trauma, difficult life conditions, prevention of reproduction, and the forced assimilation of children. However, some genocide scholars disagree with the UNCG's broad cataloguing of the means of destruction and argue that these harms are of a qualitatively different nature than harms that take place through mass killings (for example, Chalk and Jonassohn 1990). But this stance is problematic because it assumes that there is only one measure of destruction and that it cannot hold culturally specific meanings. For example, given the primacy of land and the physical environs within the cosmology of some First Nations, the removal of land can be experienced very much like the removal or elimination of human members of the group (Bischoping and Fingerhut 1996); that is, it can be extremely traumatic and destructive.

To illustrate this point, one need only look at the reserve system that was imposed in British Columbia and which denied Aboriginal peoples nearly all of their territories, as well as traditional hunting, fishing, and governance practices. As Harris (2002, 291) notes,

> from the late 1860s, Native leaders had protested their small reserves in every way they could, claiming, fundamentally, that their people would not have enough food and that their progeny had no prospects. In retrospect, they were right. The spaces assigned

to Native people did not support them, although the mixed economies they cobbled together, the revised diets they ate, and the
accommodations and settlements they lived in had allowed some
of them to survive.

The destructive force of colonial land appropriation is evident in the
experiences of the Tsawwassen First Nation. Located in the lower mainland
of British Columbia, their reserve was wedged between a ferry terminal, a
coal port, and a highway. The coal port and the ferry terminal destroyed all
of the shellfish and the fishing areas along the Tsawwassen beachfront. Their
longhouse was destroyed to make way for the highway. Such practices, and
their equivalents throughout British Columbia and Canada, had nearly catastrophic consequences, making it difficult to reproduce not only culturally
but also physically.[4] However, to understand this harm, and to address the
question of whether they can be considered part of something termed "genocide," one must first consider the centrality of land and resources in specific
Aboriginal lifeworlds so as to gain an adequate sense of the violence of their
removal. It is not simply an issue of the Tsawwassen losing their traditional
food supports and their longhouse; the whittling down of their reserve and
destruction of their socio-cultural environment placed severe restrictions on
how they could imagine themselves as a people in relation with, and as part
of, their physical surroundings.

## WHAT IS A GROUP?

Discussions of a Canadian genocide often assume that there is *a* Canadian
Aboriginal *people* who collectively were or were not the subjects of genocidal
actions. This ignores that it was only when the colonial powers happened
upon the so-called New World that they began a process of constructing an
"Indian" people by forcibly collectivizing distinct cultural entities. In colonies
such as Canada, this enabled the better management of a diversity of peoples,
many of whom resisted processes of colonization and assimilation. Thus,
the Indian Act (1876) operates as an administrative tool of cultural elimination. It defines the "Indian" so as to subject this person to a battery of
legal controls and restrictions and writes over cultural and tribal differences
in order to manufacture a governable Indian identity.[5] Given this history of
imposed sameness, genocide scholars should ask whether specific Aboriginal collectives have been subjected to genocide within the processes of
Canadian colonization (Bischoping and Fingerhut 1996; Moses 2002). It is

irresponsible and quintessentially colonial to assess the destruction of a people based on how we define them rather than on their self-definitions.

This raises the question of who defines the group that is the target of genocidal destruction. Moreover, what is a group? Within some analytic definitions of genocide, such as that forwarded by Chalk and Jonassohn (1990), all that matters for identifying an instance of genocide is that the perpetrator categorizes a particular set of actors as a group in racial, ethnic, religious, or political terms. This model has the advantage of allowing us to consider attempted eliminations of groups that exist solely in the imagination of the perpetrator, such as Stalin's kulaks and "wreckers." It also appears to avoid essentializing groups, since it no longer assumes or requires the existence of a fixed group worth protecting. This said, doing away with essentialized notions of the group does not necessitate a descent into individualism, a concept that is rife with assumptions that are equally troubling for the study of genocide (see Jamieson 1998). Since the concept of genocide seeks to protect collectivities and therefore assumes that collectivities have a value in and of themselves, group self-definition becomes important. We must assume that there is something about a group that deserves saving beyond the individual lives of its members (or imagined members).

The value of groups, as suggested above, is their singularity – their continuing and open efforts of collective identity formation and self-definition. Thus, to determine genocide solely through the lens of the perpetrator's imposed definition of groupness contradicts the valuation of groups inherent in the term "genocide." Moreover, it reinforces the perpetrator's power to define the Other, fixing the target group's origin, an act that is a potential stage in the genocidal process. The perpetrator often engages in efforts to totalize the group, to reduce them to a self-same, inhuman mass (see Kelman and Hamilton 1989), ignoring group processes of collective identity formation, identity confusion, and issues of hybridity (see Pieterse 2001). In this sense, we need an appreciation of genocide that moves from protecting "groups" to protecting the processes and dynamics of group existence.

In addition, even when we agree to look at specific Aboriginal groups within Canada, our notion of what constitutes a group that deserves protection is conditioned by Eurocentric standards. Despite Lemkin's (1944) efforts to examine the long history of genocide, his ideas about group cultures are still clearly shaped by a Westphalian conceptualization of the nation-state. For most subsequent genocide scholars, what is taken to be most destructive to these so-called national groups are the wars and killings that threaten the close quarters and relatively urbanized space of the European order of nation-states. This does not fit an Aboriginal cosmology with more fluid notions of groupness and less rigid territorial boundaries. For some Aboriginal groups in British Columbia, such as the Tsleil-Waututh in North Vancouver, intermarriages allowed cultural groups to meld and form relationships with neighbouring groups, and notions of shared territory fostered cooperative use of the land and its resources (Tsleil-Waututh First Nation 2000; see also Woolford 2005). In such a situation, it is not just war or calculated mass murder that is potentially destructive of the group in question. It is also the fixing of Aboriginal identities and the transformation of land into a strictly demarcated and bounded region. Somewhat ironically, these latter acts disrupt the ability of the group to reproduce itself as a group by imposing a rigid notion of what it means to be a group.

## Conclusion

By reflecting on the Canadian colonial past, a Canadian criminology of genocide continues its reflexive and non-redemptive project because it refuses nationalist narratives that paint Canada as a kinder, gentler nation and directly confronts the manner in which our frameworks of meaning and rationales operate to deny Aboriginal claims of destruction. Notions of genocide based too strongly on modernist and Eurocentric understandings of group identity, destruction, and intent fail to capture the attempts at destruction Aboriginal peoples faced. Just as our disciplinary identity was at risk in confronting our past, so too our national identity is put at risk, again in the hopes of opening it to cultural differences and culturally specific experiences of destruction. Such engagement can only expand the Canadian worldview and contribute to new, less Eurocentric and less totalizing forms of national identification. Thus, the proposed Canadian criminology of genocide is not "Canadian" because Canada's value system somehow positions it for a broader perspective on intergroup conflict, nor is it a "criminology" because criminological science provides a needed lens on genocide. Instead, it is a "Canadian criminology" in the sense that it hopes to transform the unsavoury elements of criminological and Canadian identities by seriously engaging with the issue of genocide.

## NOTES

1 Some do, however, acknowledge early criminological considerations of genocide, such as in the work of Christie (2000) and Sumner (1982, 1993, and 1997).

2 It is a testament to the resilience of Aboriginal peoples that they have, in more recent years, been able to use this oppressive legislation to preserve elements of their collective identities, such as in their opposition to the 1969 federal White Paper, which sought to construct a universal equality that would override specific Aboriginal rights. In this instance, the Indian Act was defended by Aboriginal peoples, since, despite its history as a tool of domination, it at least recognizes minimal land, political, and cultural rights. As Hall (2003) notes, the deadly and culturally destructive forces of colonialism have not gone unchallenged. Indeed, Aboriginal peoples have used, and continue to use, strategies such as constitutional law and political protest to fight for acknowledgment of their rights and title.

3 Books by Davis and Zannis (1973), Churchill (1997, 2000), and Neu and Therrien (2002) are obvious exceptions to this tendency. However, in contrast to the current analysis, these authors, although critical of the limits of the UNCG, still seek to fit Aboriginal genocide claims within its frame, thereby reinforcing its hegemony and failing to fully address its Eurocentric presuppositions.

4 Whereas the Canadian government signed treaties with several Aboriginal groups between 1850 and 1921, some regions of the country did not feature these agreements (for example, British Columbia, Yukon, and parts of Quebec). However, even those Aboriginal groups that did sign treaties found themselves facing unexpected assaults on their territory and their traditional land-based practices as these agreements were violated or manipulated (see Ray, Miller, and Tough 2000).

5 McGregor (2004) suggests that, for this reason, colonial assaults on Aboriginal peoples are better understood as governance rather than genocide. However, if my arguments above have any merit, this would be a false separation, since impositions of governance could indeed be part of a genocidal network.

## REFERENCES

Agamben, G. 2005. *State of Exception*. Chicago: University of Chicago Press.

Alvarez, A. 2001. *Governments, Citizens and Genocide: A Comparative and Interdisciplinary Approach*. Indianapolis: University of Indiana Press.

Arendt, H. 1963. *Eichman in Jerusalem: A Report on the Banality of Evil*. New York: Viking.

–. 1973. *The Origins of Totalitarianism*. San Diego: Harcourt.

Barta, T. 1987. Relations of Genocide: Land and Lives in the Colonization of Australia. In *Genocide and the Modern Age: Etiology and Case Studies of Mass Death*, ed. I. Wallimann and M.N. Dobkowski, 237-52. Syracuse, NY: Syracuse University Press.

Bauman, Z. 1989. *Modernity and the Holocaust*. Ithaca, NY: Cornell University Press.

Bischoping, K., and N. Fingerhut. 1996. Border Lines: Indigenous Peoples in Genocide Studies. *Canadian Review of Sociology and Anthropology* 33(4): 481-506.

Bourdieu, P. 2001. *Masculine Domination*. Stanford, CA: Stanford University Press.

Brannigan, A. 1998. Criminology and the Holocaust: Xenophobia, Evolution, and Genocide. *Crime and Delinquency* 44(2): 257-76.

–, and K.H. Hardwick. 2003. Genocide and General Theory. In *Control Theories of Crime and Delinquency*. Vol. 12 of *Advances in Criminological Theory*, ed. C.L. Britt and M. Gottfredson, 109-32. New Brunswick, NJ: Transaction Books.

Browning, C.R. 2004. *The Origins of the Final Solution: The Evolution of Nazi Jewish Policy, September 1939-March 1942*. With contributions by J. Matthäus. Lincoln, NB: University of Nebraska Press and Yad Vashem, Jerusalem.

Cairns, A.C. 2000. *Citizens Plus: Aboriginal Peoples and the Canadian State*. Vancouver: UBC Press.

Chalk, F., and K. Jonassohn. 1990. *The History and Sociology of Genocide: Analyses and Case Studies*. New Haven, CT: Yale University Press.

Christie, N. 2000. *Crime Control as Industry: Towards Gulags Western Style*. 3rd ed. London: Routledge.

Christodoulidis, E.A. 2000. "Truth and Reconciliation" as Risks. *Social and Legal Studies* 9(2): 179-204.

Churchill, W. 1997. *A Little Matter of Genocide*. San Francisco: City Lights Books.

–. 2000. Forbidding the "G-Word": Holocaust Denial as Judicial Doctrine in Canada. *Other Voices* 2(1), http://www.othervoices.org/2.1/churchill/denial.html.

Clayton, D.W. 2000. *Islands of Truth: The Imperial Fashioning of Vancouver Island*. Vancouver: UBC Press.

Cohen, S. 2001. *States of Denial: Knowing about Atrocities and Suffering*. Cambridge, UK: Polity Press.

Conrad, J. (ca. 1899) 2003. *Heart of Darkness and Other Tales*. New York: Oxford University Press.

Davis, R., and M. Zannis. 1973. *The Genocide Machine in Canada: The Pacification of the North*. Montreal: Black Rose Books.

Day, L.E., and M. Vandiver. 2000. Criminology and Genocide Studies: Notes on What Might Have Been and What Still Could Be. *Crime, Law and Social Change* 34(1): 43-59.

Diamond, J. 1997. *Guns, Germs, and Steel: The Fates of Human Societies*. New York: W.W. Norton.

Fein, H. 2002. Genocide: A Sociological Perspective. In *Genocide: An Anthropological Reader*, ed. A.L. Hinton, 74-90. Malden, MA: Blackwell.

Fenn, E.A. 2000. Biological Warfare in Eighteenth-Century North America: Beyond Jeffrey Amherst. *Journal of American History* 86(4): 1552-80.

Finzsch, N. 2008. "[...] Extirpate or Remove That Vermine": Genocide, Biological Warfare, and Settler Imperialism in the Eighteenth and Early Nineteenth Century. *Journal of Genocide Research* 10(2): 215-32.

Freeman, M. 1991. The Theory and Prevention of Genocide. *Holocaust and Genocide Studies* 6(2): 185-99.

Friedrichs, D.O. 2000. The Crime of the Century? The Case for the Holocaust. *Crime, Law and Social Change* 34(1): 21-41.

Hagan, J., and S. Greer. 2002. Making War Criminal. *Criminology* 40(2): 231-64.

Hall, A. 2003. *The American Empire and the Fourth World: The Bowl with One Spoon,* Part 1. Montreal and Kingston, ON: McGill-Queen's Press.

Hardt, M., and A. Negri. 2004. *Multitude: War and Democracy in the Age of Empire.* New York: Penguin.

Harris, C. 2002. *Making Native Space: Colonialism, Resistance and Reserves in British Columbia.* Vancouver: UBC Press.

Hatzfeld, J. 2005. *The Machete Season: The Killers in Rwanda Speak.* New York: Farrar, Straus and Giroux.

Hinton, A.L. 2002. The Dark Side of Modernity: Toward an Anthropology of Genocide. In *Annihilating Difference: The Anthropology of Genocide,* ed. A.L. Hinton, 1-40. Berkeley: University of California Press.

Jamieson, R. 1998. Towards a Criminology of War in Europe. In *The New European Criminology: Crime and Social Order in Europe,* ed. V. Ruggiero, N. South, and I. Taylor, 480-506. London: Routledge.

Kelman, H.C., and V.L. Hamilton. 1989. *Crimes of Obedience: Toward a Social Psychology of Authority and Responsibility.* New Haven, CT: Yale University Press.

Kuper, L. 1981. *Genocide: Its Political Use in the Twentieth Century.* New Haven, CT: Yale University Press.

Lange, G. 2003. Smallpox Epidemic of 1862 among Northwest Coast and Puget Sound Indians. HistoryLink.org, http://www.historylink.org/.

Latour, B. 1993. *We Have Never Been Modern.* Cambridge, MA: Harvard University Press.

Laufer, W.S. 1999. The Forgotten Criminology of Genocide. In *The Criminology of Criminal Law.* Vol. 8 of *Advances in Criminological Theory,* ed. W.S. Laufer and F. Adler, 71-82. New Brunswick, NJ: Transaction.

Legters, L. 1984. The Soviet Gulag: Is It Genocidal? In *Toward The Understanding and Prevention of Genocide: Proceedings of the International Conference on the Holocaust and Genocide,* ed. I.W. Charny, 60-66. Boulder, CO: Westview Press.

Lemkin, R. 1944. *Axis Rule in Occupied Europe.* Washington, DC: Carnegie Endowment for International Peace.

Levene, M. 2000. Why Is the Twentieth Century the Century of Genocide? *Journal of World History* 11(2): 305-36.

Mamdani, M. 2000. The Truth According to the TRC. In *The Politics of Memory: Truth, Healing, and Social Justice*, ed. I. Amadiume and A. An-Na'im, 176-83. London: Zed Books.

–. 2001. *When Victims Become Killers: Colonialism, Nativism, and the Genocide in Rwanda*. Princeton, NJ: Princeton University Press.

Mann, M. 2005. *The Dark Side of Democracy: Explaining Ethnic Cleansing*. Cambridge: Cambridge University Press.

McGregor, R. 2004. Governance, Not Genocide: Aboriginal Assimilation in the Postwar Era. In *Genocide and Settler Society: Frontier Violence and Stolen Indigenous Children in Australian History*, ed. A.D. Moses, 290-311. New York: Berghan Books.

Milgram, S. 1974. *Obedience to Authority*. New York: Harper Torchbooks.

Milloy, J.S. 1999. *A National Crime: The Canadian Government and the Residential School System, 1879 to 1986*. Winnipeg: University of Manitoba Press.

Minow, M. 1999. *Between Vengeance and Forgiveness: Facing Genocide and Mass Violence*. Boston: Beacon Press.

Morrison, W. 2003. Criminology, Genocide, and Modernity: Remarks on the Companion That Criminology Ignored. In *The Blackwell Companion to Criminology*, ed. C. Sumner, 68-88. London: Blackwell, http://www.blackwellreference.com/.

–. 2007. *Criminology and the New World Order*. London: Glasshouse.

Moses, A.D. 2000. An Antipodean Genocide? The Origins of the Genocidal Moment in the Colonization of Australia. *Journal of Genocide Research* 2(1): 89-106.

–. 2002. Conceptual Blockages and Definitional Dilemmas in the "Racial Century": Genocides of Indigenous Peoples and the Holocaust. *Patterns of Prejudice* 36(4): 7-36.

Nancy, J.-L. 2000. *Being Singular Plural*. Stanford, CA: Stanford University Press.

Neu, D., and R. Therrien. 2002. *Accounting for Genocide: Canada's Bureaucratic Assault on Aboriginal People*. Black Point, NS: Fernwood/Zed Books.

Nikolić-Ristanović, V. 1998. War and Crime in the Former Yugoslavia. In *The New European Criminology: Crime and Social Order in Europe*, ed. V. Ruggiero, N. South, and I. Taylor, 462-79. London: Routledge.

Novick, P. 1999. *The Holocaust in American Life*. Boston: Houghton-Mifflin.

Pieterse, J.N. 2001. Hybridity, So What? The Anti-Hybridity Backlash and the Riddles of Recognition. *Theory, Culture and Society* 18(2): 219-45.

Ponting, J.R., and R. Gibbons. 1980. *Out of Irrelevance: A Sociopolitical Introduction to Indian Affairs in Canada*. Toronto: Butterworth.

Power, S. 2002. *"A Problem from Hell": America and the Age of Genocide*. New York: Basic Books.

Ray, A.J., J. Miller, and F. Tough. 2000. *Bounty and Benevolence: A History of Saskatchewan Treaties*. Montreal and Kingston, ON: McGill-Queen's University Press.

Schleunes, K.A. 1990. *The Twisted Road to Auschwitz: Nazi Policy toward German Jews, 1933-1939*. Champaign: University of Illinois Press.

Steinart, H. 1998. Ideology with Human Victims: The Institution of "Crime and Punishment" between Social Control and Social Exclusion: Historical and Theoretical Issues. In *The New European Criminology: Crime and Social Order in Europe*, ed. V. Ruggiero, N. South, and I. Taylor, 405-24. London: Routledge.

Stone, D. 2004. Genocide as Transgression. *European Journal of Social Theory* 7(1): 45-65.

Sumner, C., ed. 1982. *Crime, Justice and Underdevelopment*. London: Heinemann.

–. 1993. *The Sociology of Deviance: An Obituary*. London: Taylor and Francis.

–, ed. 1997. *Violence, Culture and Censure*. London: Taylor and Francis.

Titley, E.B. 1986. *A Narrow Vision: Duncan Campbell Scott and the Administration of Indian Affairs in Canada*. Vancouver: UBC Press.

Totten, S., W.S. Parsons, and R.K. Hitchcock. 2002. Confronting Genocide and Ethnocide of Indigenous Peoples: An Interdisciplinary Approach to Definition, Intervention, Prevention, and Advocacy. In *Annihilating Difference: The Anthropology of Genocide*, ed. A.L. Hinton, 54-91. Berkeley: University of California Press.

Trigger, B.G. 1985. *Natives and Newcomers: Canada's "Historic Age" Reconsidered*. Montreal and Kingston, ON: McGill-Queen's University Press.

Tsleil-Waututh First Nation. 2000. *Our Land to Share: A Future for the People of the Inlet; A Comprehensive Approach to Settling an Urban First Nation Treaty in British Columbia*. Vancouver: Tsleil-Waututh First Nation.

van Zyl Smit, D. 1998. Criminological Ideas and South African Transition. *British Journal of Criminology* 39(2): 198-215.

Wetzell, R.F. 2000. *Inventing the Criminal: A History of German Criminology, 1880-1945*. Chapel Hill: University of North Carolina Press.

Woolford, A. 2005. *Between Justice and Certainty: Treaty Making in British Columbia*. Vancouver: UBC Press.

–. 2006. Making Genocide Unthinkable: Three Guidelines for a Critical Criminology of Genocide. *Critical Criminology* 14(1): 87-106.

Wotherspoon, T., and V. Satzewich. 2000. *First Nations: Race, Class and Gender Relations*. Toronto: Nelson.

Yacoubian, G.S. 2000. The (In)Significance of Genocidal Behavior to the Discipline of Criminology. *Crime, Law and Social Change* 34(1): 7-19.

–. 2001. Evaluating the Efficacy of the International Criminal Tribunals for Rwanda and the Former Yugoslavia: Implications for Criminology and International Criminal Law. *International Journal of Comparative Criminology* 1(2): 132-43.

# 6
# Power and Resistance in Community-Based Sentencing

*Diana Young*

In recent years there has been a surge of interest in new sentencing practices, specifically, community-based sentences. Community-based sentencing is difficult to define in any precise way. Generally, it is seen as a move to encourage sentencing judges to explore alternatives to imprisonment by using community resources as a means of achieving the security and supervision afforded by imprisonment, while avoiding many of the pitfalls of incarceration. It is often associated with restorative justice – restorative alternatives, insofar as they claim to restore harmony to parties to a dispute and to the community by addressing underlying causes of crime, help to alleviate those concerns about public safety that would otherwise be dealt with through imprisonment or other criminal justice processes. Keeping the offender in the community is seen as essential for restorative processes to take place. Thus, even fairly punitive forms of community-based sentences – conditional sentences, for example – are often seen as useful for their restorative potential as well.[1]

This notion of community is a contentious one. It is sometimes seen as an inclusive, democratic alternative to the exercise of power in repressive and essentializing criminal justice processes. However, for some critics the benevolent image of community in "community justice" masks the hegemonic nature of criminal law. Community-based sentencing does not represent a withdrawal of the repressive power of the criminal justice system but, rather, its extension, as these sentencing alternatives provide new mechanisms of individualized control.

Such controversies may fail to recognize the extent to which criminal law already depends on the production of knowledges from extra-legal sources for its content. Community can be understood as a multiplicity of modes of governance that provide this content; such modes of governance can be not only oppressive but also empowering, even for marginalized groups.

If community-based sentencing practices can be seen as a form of knowledge seeking by the criminal justice system, it is because more traditional forms have proven deficient in achieving the goal of crime reduction. The criminal justice system's dependence on extra-legal sources of knowledge, and the potential for resistance by the populations sought to be managed, suggest a more complex picture of power relationships that is not captured by the image of the hegemonic criminal justice system. It also may provide insight into the nature of the law in the face of Foucauldian conceptions of governance and the challenges such conceptions pose to the notion of legal power. An alternative to the traditional understanding of law as an autonomous, top-down form of power emanating from the state – one that conceives of law as embedded in and dependent on multiple sites of governance – may be more in keeping with contemporary realities.

## Law and Concepts of Power

A great deal of legal theory focuses on the law's power to coerce and, by extension, is concerned with the various protections from coercion afforded by the law and the process of legal reasoning. In contrast, Foucault raised questions concerning the role of law as a function of power in society, by suggesting that modern society is regulated not by a top-down model of sovereign power but, rather, through modes of governance where power is productive and exercised through, rather than upon, individuals (Rose 2008, 86). This suggests that law – particularly criminal law and its heavy association with repressive, centralized power – is not particularly useful as a site for the study of social control. The focus for the study of power ought not to be on the sovereign juridical model but on the "techniques and tactics" of domination (Foucault 1980, 102). As a result, legal theorists' preoccupation with law as the primary site of power in society – in terms of its ability to both shape society along the lines prescribed by particular ideological values and provide protection from the use of power by according individuals various rights – is destabilized.

Some social theorists have attempted to define scope for law and legal theory in the face of Foucauldian challenges to the concept of juridical power in modern society (Hunt 1992; also Hunt and Wickham 1994; Munro 2001; Wickham 2006). One may recognize that law has social effects and, by extension, that legal reform might not be a pointless exercise, without according the concept of juridical power any particular privilege within the range of power relationships we observe in society in general. Hunt (1992), for example, suggests that law does not govern the social, but might be seen as one mode of governance interacting with many others. A sociology of law, rather than denying law's social effects, should recast law as part of a larger network of relationships of power and resistance.

These observations implicate the potential interaction between some of the social theory that often informs critical criminology scholarship and legal theory and doctrine. Although in some ways legal theorists seek to identify an autonomous, closed system of reasoning that counts as legal, law does in fact depend on knowledges produced in the social sphere. Miller and Rose (2008, 62), for example, suggest that without social sciences to govern the social there would be no discernable objects for legal regulation.

> The theories of the social sciences, of economics, of sociology and of psychology, thus provide a kind of *intellectual machinery* for government, in the form of procedures for rendering the world thinkable, taming its intractable reality by subjecting it to the disciplined analyses of thought. (See also Hunt and Wickham 1994, 108-9)

In addition, many legal concepts articulated in legislation such as the Criminal Code and elsewhere derive their content from non-legal sites of knowledge.

Community-based sentencing provides an example of the interdependency between law and other modes of governance. This has a lot to tell us about the ways in which power is negotiated in criminal justice processes and the position of law as a discourse within that negotiation. The purpose of this inquiry is not to regret the demotion of the law, to valorize it, or to condemn it as repressive. Rather, it is to situate law as a mode of governance among others operating within the criminal justice system. The examination of recent developments in community-based sentencing shows not only that the normative discourse of law absorbs meaning and content from extrajuridical sites of knowledge production but also that it circulates within these sites. We see that the interaction between the law and the social has many different and often contradictory effects. It may transform the social even as it is transformed by it. But the discourses of right emerging from the law as an institution also give rise to possibilities of resistance and, ironically, the flourishing of subordinated discourses.

## What Is the Community?

Community-based, restorative justice has proven to be a politically malleable concept. Early proponents tended to be associated with the political left (Morris 2000; also Zehr 1990). But they have also been adopted in the service of a more law-and-order perspective associated with the political right. This perspective often makes appeals to "victims' rights" to legitimate a fairly punitive approach to criminal justice, but it also values fiscal restraint. Thus, community-based alternatives to prison have sometimes been justified by the political right as an economically efficient means of punishing offenders and meeting the needs of victims, and proponents have often followed suit by adopting economic efficiency arguments as a means of justifying their own projects (Bentley 2000).

When people say that they want to explore "community-based" alternatives to imprisonment, the expression often evokes images of progressive, compassionate approaches to justice that are favourably contrasted to the more brutal, alienating, and essentializing processes of criminal justice; in particular, community justice is seen as having a democratic and inclusive effect. Accessible and inclusive in its informality, it considers the individual needs of both the offender and the community, engaging communities in their own security, increasing awareness of the causes of crime and disorder, and ensuring that the aspirations of the community will be met.

These accessibility and inclusiveness claims may suggest a rejection of some of the claims made by the criminal justice system. Criminal justice officials see their functions largely in terms of protecting the interests of both the public and justice, guided by legislation created under conditions of democracy. Much of the rhetoric concerning the legitimization of law in liberal societies suggests that it is inclusive in the theoretically abstract nature of the legal subject and in the distance it creates between its own processes and the particularities of individuals and communities. It is that very abstraction that gives the law its public quality. Thus, there are parallels between the community justice movement and critiques in legal theory concerning the failures of the law to take account of difference, and the ultimate exclusionary effects of these claims to universality (Benhabib 1987; Young 1987). In general, many contemporary critiques of the criminal justice system evince a rejection of universal justice claims that are often associated with criminal law as a way of understanding wrongs and relationships between individuals and communities (Pavlich 1996). In the community justice discourses, the claims that criminal law makes to inclusiveness are seen as the very source of its alienating effect, its failure to attend to the real-life needs of individuals and their networks of relationships, its perceived brutality to marginalized members of society, and its lack of concern for the underlying deprivations that léad to criminality. Community-based resolution is offered up as an antidote to the unitary use of state power. So, for example, although the lack of uniformity that characterizes community-based resolutions is sometimes criticized on the grounds of due process and parity concerns, proponents make a virtue of diversity. There are many differences between individual offenders and individual victims, and attending to their individual needs will invariably result in very different dispositions.[2]

Many critics have challenged some of the claims made by community justice proponents by disputing their rather binary conception of the state and community. The terms "community" and "state" are sometimes used as if it were self-evident that society could be divided into two such discrete and monolithic entities. The two entities engage in a constant struggle for power, with the state posing an ever present threat of encroachment on autonomy of the community. Although references to the virtues of the community give a great deal of force to the appeal of community-based sentences, even proponents have been unable to articulate with any specificity what a community actually is (Pavlich 1996; also Abel 1982; Baskin 1988; Matthews 1988; Fitzpatrick 1992; Lacey and Zedner 1995; Anderson 1999). Some commentators suggest that the power of community lies not in its concrete reality but, rather, in its mythic or symbolic character (Fitzpatrick 1992; Lacey and Zedner 1995). Its very lack of specificity is actually essential to its imaginary status as counterpoint to hegemonic state power. But community justice initiatives require, as a practical matter, that the myth of community takes a concrete form. And some critiques suggest that the ways in which the "community" is represented in these initiatives belie the claims of inclusion and democracy that their proponents make.

Many of the earlier critiques focus on informal justice processes that parties agreed to participate in to avoid having to go through court processes – for example, community mediation services offered as an alternative to civil actions for minor disputes, and diversion programs as a means of dealing with minor offences that can be adequately resolved outside the criminal courts. Neighbourhood justice committees, for example, have always dealt with minor matters that would otherwise be settled in civil courts. And even community alternatives to criminal justice processes have usually been restricted to minor offences that could be subjects of diversion. So, for example, family group conferencing has generally been applied to youth who commit minor offences and who are dealt with extra-judicially. Informal justice mechanisms of these types are often presented as autonomous and distinct from the criminal justice system. However, many critiques suggest that these alternative dispute resolution processes actually end up reproducing those forms of state power, becoming in effect an apparatus of the state and ultimately legitimizing state power.

Such critiques often draw on Foucault's ideas about the ubiquitous nature of power; power relationships are diffuse and constantly reproduced throughout society, therefore one does not escape them simply by seeking alternatives to forms of direct state coercion found in the courtroom (Pavlich 1996; also Lacey and Zedner 1995; Anderson 1999). This suggests that the only way to give content to the myth of community is to select alternative modes of governance that are thought, for various reasons, to be more effective than mainstream legal processes as a means of producing law-abiding individuals. The paradox of the mythical image of community is that, as an ungoverned space, it is unknowable. To make community play an institutional role is to define it and thus deprive it of its ungoverned status.

Therefore, it is argued that community dispute resolution, although much of its appeal lies in the belief that it represents a withdrawal of state power from the lives of individuals, is actually an expansion of that power (Abel 1982; also Baskin 1988; Matthews 1988). Community-based justice, far from fulfilling its egalitarian and democratic promises, simply employs different means of governance, which may follow pastoral or disciplinary models. Mediators, therapists, and community elders are all invested with the kind of individualized power that characterizes modern society, through which they achieve a degree of surveillance that the more mainstream justice processes cannot.

This is suggested in the concept of community invoked by Nikolas Rose. He suggests that community has undergone a transformation from an image invoking resistance and the empowerment of the marginalized to a largely technical concept operating as a mechanism for the governance of populations. By this account, the social has given way to a multiplicity of communities, to which individuals owe bonds of responsibility and allegiance (Miller and Rose 2008, 92-93). The governance of individuals is achieved through such communities.

It does seem clear that when we speak of "community-based" alternatives to criminal justice processes what we are really talking about is not justice meted out by the community but the selection of a particular mode of governance that is thought to be effective in achieving certain goals of criminal justice. And the range of mechanisms employed by community-based sentencing initiatives shows that community does not function as a unitary space beyond the scope of governance but as a multiplicity of governance techniques. In family group conferences, for example, the people involved are said to constitute a "community of interest" (Braithwaite 1989, 173). Since family group conferences are most commonly used when a young person has committed a crime, this community of care will involve family members of the offender and the victim, and also sometimes members of institutions such as the offender's school or church. All of these constitute extra-legal forms of governance – the family, the school. These mechanisms are not seen to provide a more effective means on their own of dealing with anti-social behaviour; otherwise there would be no need for criminal justice involvement at all. But they are seen as a complement to the criminal justice system that can provide a better way of ensuring certain goals are met – the offender's taking of responsibility and subsequent rehabilitation, victim satisfaction and recognition, and perhaps the opportunity to expose the "roots" of crime and encourage community involvement in eradicating social problems that lead to youth criminality.

That community-based sentencing involves a selection of alternative modes of governance doesn't necessarily mean that the expression "community-based sentencing" is in itself misleading. If the modern concept of community conceives it as a multi-faceted sector to be identified and subject to a variety of modes of governance, it is perfectly accurate to understand such modes as manifestations of community for the purpose of community-based sentencing. But it does belie the mythic image of community, and many of the egalitarian and democratic claims made by proponents of community-based alternatives.

Seeing the community as a complex network of various modes of governance doesn't necessarily condemn us all to inescapable oppression. Virtually any social organization will have many norms that are reproduced in various ways and to some extent internalized by the members of the society. Modes of governance and ways in which power is distributed throughout society are seen as productive and can be empowering even for marginalized populations. The ways in which the concept of addiction plays out might be an example of this. When a person is defined as an addict, it no doubt has a stigmatizing and disempowering effect. But people who describe themselves as addicts often do so because they see it as a means of self-empowerment. Defining oneself as an addict might carry with it the possibility of trans- formation; it provides individuals with access to a variety of mechanisms that help them change patterns of conduct that they see as self-destructive. This may also result in access to various benefits that society may offer acceptably disciplined individuals – employment, status, freedom from criminal pros- ecution, and the like. And it has a certain distancing effect. The explanatory power of addiction discourses suggests that recovery is a means for individ- uals to separate themselves from regrettable things they may have done. The extent to which individuals see the definition as a source of empowerment will no doubt turn to a large degree on the extent to which they see themselves as agents of their own self-definitions. This includes not only the decision to understand themselves as addicts but also the selection of techniques to manage that condition. These techniques may be historically and culturally contingent – today's therapy might have been yesterday's religious conversion – but they nonetheless may be quite effective in allowing individuals to achieve certain aims.[3]

Individuals may also employ various forms of governance as a means of resisting power that they find oppressive. An example of this is found in the realm of identity politics. Individuals may find themselves subject to oppres- sive power through association with a marginalized group – for example, homosexuals. People have succeeded in resisting such oppression not by distancing themselves from membership in the group but by embracing the identity imposed on them as a group that espouses certain common values and aspirations. The group is reconstituted and provides a discourse that allows it to be understood in positive rather than negative terms. In this way, power that is experienced as oppressive is successfully resisted through the use of alternative techniques of the self. That the constitution of the group in the first place relied on rather debatable assumptions about the nature of sexuality does not make it any the less effective as a strategy of resistance (Foucault 1978).

The use of community justice alternatives to criminal justice processes raises some concerns, however. If the reality of individual agency in employing techniques of resistance assuages concerns about authoritarianism and exclu- sivity in the use of power, the connection of modes of governance to senten- cing practices raises concerns about the hegemonic tendencies associated with the criminal justice system. And critics of community sentencing do suggest, with some justification, that because the mythology of an autonomous community largely masks those hegemonic tendencies they are rendered more insidious, as they are less visible.

## Criminal Law and Knowledge Seeking

In a general sense, there is not anything novel about the criminal justice system's use of extra-legal mechanisms of governance. It is, for example, a long-standing practice for defence lawyers, when trying to get an accused out on bail or a sentence of probation rather than imprisonment, to refer to these extra-criminal justice mechanisms as a means of satisfying the courts that the accused's conduct can be managed without the need for incarceration. So, for example, it is a lot easier to keep an accused out of prison if that person has close connections to a supportive and non-criminal family, access to employment, an investment in some sort of educational facility, or even a commitment to pursuing some program of therapy designed to control addiction or manage anger. These are all examples of modes of governance through a community conceived as a multitude of allegiances and commitments through which the individual defines him- or herself. An accused who has such allegiances has long been considered a better candidate for pretrial release from custody, for probation, and for parole (Silverstein 2001). And, in fact, there is familiar research into the roots of crime suggesting that people who have commitments to these kinds of extra-legal mechanisms of governance are not only less likely to recidivate but also less likely to commit crimes in the first place. So there is already a connection between criminal justice processes and extra-legal modes of governance.

However, recent trends in community sentencing differ to some extent from both these more traditional ways in which the criminal justice system uses extra-legal forms of discipline and the diversion model mentioned above. Community-based sentencing is seen not only as a restorative alternative but also as having a utilitarian aspect: high incarceration rates, and the expense and perceived ineffectiveness of imprisonment as a means of creating law-abiding subjects, results in a desire to find alternatives to imprisonment. That community-based sentences are seen in this way has implications for their status in the community justice movement.

Community justice alternatives have traditionally been viewed as an adjunct to formal legal processes that were applied to disputes seen as too minor to merit the involvement of formal legal processes. More recent community justice innovations, however, are directed toward offenders who are seen as more problematic. This is essential if community alternatives are to afford a solution to the problem of incarceration. Increasingly, judges are seeking community-based alternatives for offenders who would otherwise receive sentences of imprisonment. Although the large number of such offenders is sometimes posited as a reality to which the criminal justice system must respond, the fact is that they have, as a group, been created by the criminal justice process itself. Decisions to focus policing efforts on drug users, street prostitutes, schoolyard bullies, and the like depend to a large degree on various concerns that draw a great deal of attention from time to time. And making a decision, at the policy level, to turn the attention of criminal justice officials to the arrest and prosecution of such people implies a decision that, for whatever reason, other means of governance are inadequate. Thus, it is ironic that, having made a policy decision to deal with certain kinds of crimes through criminal justice processes, there is now so much interest in employing community-based approaches to discipline.[4]

Nonetheless, it is largely as a result of the perceived crisis of overcrowded prisons and heavy caseloads that community-based sentences are now being explored as a means of dealing with offenders who are chosen *because* it is considered appropriate to deal with them using criminal justice interventions. For this reason, community-based approaches can no longer be regarded as adjuncts to the formal system but as integral to it. As a result, much of the talk concerning community-based sentencing now revolves around the establishment of links between community services and the criminal justice system (Bentley 2000; also LaPrairie et al. 2002; Harris et al. 2004; Moore 2007a). To a large degree, these links offer a conduit of knowledge that provide the court with a more detailed understanding of an offender and the various services that might be available to "meet his or her needs" – or, rather, to ensure that the person does not reoffend. The courts use this information to craft a sentence that will both avoid imprisonment and ensure that other criminal justice goals, such as the protection of society and the rehabilitation of the offender, are met.

For example, drug treatment courts make use of experts in the "psy" disciplines, such as liaison officers, who form part of the "team" of therapeutic and criminal justice officials that crafts strategies to transform the offender and who also regularly appear in open court to provide information as to the progress made by client/offenders.[5] The new Youth Criminal Justice Act contains provisions for the constitution of youth criminal justice committees and for conferencing, which is designed to a large extent to provide the sentencing judge with information about the offender and the availability of community services that can be used to craft non-custodial dispositions.[6] Sentencing circles conducted in the presence of a judge provide useful information about the viability of plans to rehabilitate and reintegrate the offender, drawing to some extent on the allegiances the offender has or is willing to cultivate in a community that has political, geographical, and/or cultural dimensions.

The establishment of linkages often also provides information that has temporal continuity. When a judge sentences an offender to imprisonment, for example, he or she is responding to directives contained in the Criminal Code, usually focusing on retributive notions of the need for punitive action but also with a view to making the individual into a law-abiding subject through deterrence, the acceptance of individual responsibility, and rehabilitation. But the content of these kinds of decisions is severely limited by the judge's lack of information on how the offender will actually experience imprisonment. Once the moment of decision making has passed, authority over the offender is transferred to corrections officials. Corrections officials represent one aspect of the criminal justice system, but they make decisions – what institution the offender is to be committed to, what kinds of rehabilitative programs will be made available to him or her, what forms of punitive discipline he or she might be subjected to – that are beyond the knowledge or control of the sentencing judge. In contrast, community-based sentences often now require the participation of sentencing judges beyond the moment of imposing punishment; they may require, for example, repeated appearances by the offender before the judge, who is thus able to monitor the offender's progress.

All of this makes the claims of community justice as being autonomous from the criminal justice system, whatever its force when applied to minor disputes, much less persuasive when used for serious criminal offences. An alternative to this picture of autonomy, however, could be community-based sentencing as a form of knowledge seeking by the criminal justice system. In view of the above discussion about the community, it's apparent that it isn't just any kind of information that the criminal justice system is seeking from these extra-legal sources. What we are really talking about is the seeking of knowledges produced by particular processes of governance. The kinds of knowledges so produced will depend largely on the nature of the "community" selected for this purpose.

## Institutional Encroachments

The dependence of the criminal justice system on knowledges from extra-legal sources leads to concerns about institutional encroachments from both sides. The first concern relates to the hegemonic tendencies of criminal law. The use by criminal justice processes of other sites of governance in the community raises the possibility, as noted above, that community sentencing is not so much a withdrawal of the criminal justice system from the field of rehabilitating offenders as an extension of its reach into the community services it is integrating. It can be assumed not only that the criminal justice system will select sources that provide the kind of information that suits its own purposes but also that these knowledge-producing communities will themselves be reconstituted in order to meet the needs of the criminal justice system. The goals of the criminal justice system – which are assumed to be the creation of law-abiding subjects – must then become the orientation of the community service provider (Moore 2007b). Communities constituted by the psy disciplines may provide an example of this. The goals of therapy are diverse and may include crafting a law-abiding subject, but many other things as well. The law already has a tradition of relying on knowledge generated by experts in the psy disciplines; however, when a therapeutic expert testifies or produces a report for courtroom use, no one really cares whether the offender is happy, has found an inspiring project for his or her life, has formed satisfying relationships, or has a new-found ability to engage in political activism. These kinds of considerations are relevant only insofar as they demonstrate that the offender will not recidivate.

So a central question about community-based sentences becomes how, exactly, are the communities involved constituted – or, perhaps, how does the involvement of such communities in the criminal justice system cause them to be reconstituted in such a way as to produce the kind of knowledge that meets the needs of the criminal justice system?

The Toronto Drug Treatment Court and the way in which it deals with harm reduction as a treatment option provides an example. Harm reduction as an approach to dealing with addiction has, over the course of the last twenty years or so, gained some legitimacy among drug treatment professionals. Addicts themselves have long employed harm-reduction techniques, such as using clean needles, avoiding certain kinds of drugs thought to carry particular risks, and cultivating relationships with suppliers who can be relied on to provide good-quality products. Many harm-reduction approaches start with the proposition that drug use is a fact in society and that it often provides people with a necessary means of dealing with other problems in their lives. As a mode of governance, it differs from other forms of addiction treatment in that it focuses not on abstinence but on strategies that will maintain the drug user's health and well-being (Marlatt 1998, 7-8). Harm reduction could be seen as a means of resistance to dominant forms of addiction treatment in that it refuses to cast the individuals as helpless victims of the disease of addiction but instead characterizes them as persons who, though addicted to narcotics, are capable of agency and of making realistic decisions that will have a positive impact on their lives. It sometimes happens that over time subordinated discourses gain a certain legitimacy and recognition – in the case of harm reduction, this seems to have occurred through its acceptance by some professionals in the drug treatment disciplines as a viable treatment alternative.

In the Toronto Drug Treatment Court, officials often use the language of harm reduction in explaining their own treatment approaches. But we can see that in criminal justice processes the meaning of this term has connotations that relate specifically to the goals of the criminal justice system (LaPrairie et al. 2002). In drug treatment court, it is assumed that people with addictions will inevitably relapse from time to time on their way to complete recovery; it is therefore the court's policy to tolerate some drug use by client/offenders. But harm reduction is not seen as a long-term solution – regardless of the client's state of health or emotional well-being, graduation from the program requires complete abstinence. Failure to achieve this goal within a certain time frame – usually about a year – will result in expulsion from the program and, for those who have already pleaded guilty to the offence that brought them before the Drug Treatment Court in the first place, punishment according to the usual practices of sentencing.

This is not surprising, given that the Drug Treatment Court is part of the criminal justice system and, as such, its primary goal is not so much the well-being of the offender but making the offender into a law-abiding productive member of society. It does, however, demonstrate that when the Drug Treatment Court incorporates psy disciplines into its own processes it is really employing a therapeutic community that is constituted in particular ways. Those communities that gain recognition by the court (and, incidentally, have access to the funding that such recognition generates) will invariably have to conform their own practices to the requirements of the criminal justice system.

At the same time, people often raise concerns about the tendency of community-based sentencing to encroach on criminal justice. These concerns are often expressed in terms of the possibility that some community-based sentencing practices may undermine such dearly held legal principles as due process, the rule of law, and parity. Many forms of community-based justice require that the offender forego his or her right to a trial on the question of legal guilt in order to participate in a community-based program that might seem, at the outset, a more attractive alternative to prison. The non-adversarial nature of community-based sentences raises concerns that the offender's rights and interests will not be adequately defended and that the offender might wind up being subjected to restrictive and punitive measures far beyond anything that a sentencing judge would have imposed.

Some perspective on this issue might be gained by bearing in mind the ways in which the criminal justice system is inherently deeply dependent on extra-legal forms of governance. Although it is sometimes seen as a rather unitary, top-down, and authoritarian form of social control, the criminal justice system functions not only through the operation of law but also through reliance on many processes, means of governance, and ways of understanding and defining things. The obvious example of this is in the increasing use of experts in various fields – particularly the mental health field. We can also see it in the decision-making practices of police, Crowns, and judges, all of whom employ specific types of knowledges as criteria in determining questions of credibility, dangerousness, and the like. Criminal justice officials are also governed by understandings – formal ones contained in policy manuals and codes of conduct and also informal ones concerning professional practices and norms. None of these can be found in the Criminal Code, and they go far beyond bare questions of legality.

On a deeper level, these forms of extra-legal governance are often implicated in legal rules themselves. The very fundamental notion of a free, and therefore criminally responsible, subject sometimes is assessed as a function of expectations about the disciplined and therefore empowered subject. Thus, such defences as necessity or duress are understood as conditions that would overbear the will of the reasonable person. The image of the reasonable person itself has attributes that cannot be found in any piece of legislation. It is really a vessel whose content is given by assumptions that adjudicators make about the appropriately well-disciplined individual. At present, for example, the reasonable person does not abuse narcotics, does not subscribe to extreme or marginal religious beliefs, has faith in medical professionals, but may be a person in an abusive relationship who uses violence in self-defence.[7] The issue of provocation, both as a partial excuse (*Criminal Code*, s. 232) and as a mitigating factor in sentencing, requires some understanding of normal power relationships in society. Is there legally relevant provocation in a racial slur, a wife threatening to leave her husband, or a homosexual advance? Trust relationships, which are a relevant factor in sentencing (*Criminal Code*, s. 718.2(a)(iii)) and in the definition of some sex offences (*Criminal Code*, s. 153) presuppose a particular relationship of power that carries certain obligations to avoid acts of self-interest. In addition, most of the goals of sentencing set out in the Criminal Code – separation, deterrence, rehabilitation, individual responsibility – are vague terms that can be given content only through the use of extra-legal norms to determine the extent to which the offender is or can be made to be a disciplined subject. Even the purely retributivist aspects of sentencing, which are, at least theoretically, grounded in justice rather than crime control concerns, must draw on expectations about the normal uses of power in order to assess the gravity of a particular offence. Thus, the "black letter law," by itself an abstraction, often relies on social practices of power to derive its content.

So the image of criminal justice as a distinct social entity is perhaps misleading not only because it fails to recognize the ways in which criminal justice norms are incorporated into power relations generally but also because it fails to recognize the degree to which criminal justice is embedded in social practices of governance, and in many cases relies on them for its doctrinal coherence. Therefore, although much of the contemporary literature on community-based sentencing stresses the need to strengthen the links between the criminal justice system and social service providers, this may not be as extreme a qualitative change as it may first appear.

## Resistance and Modes of Governance in Criminal Justice

Another way of seeing the due process kinds of concerns mentioned above is to consider the scope afforded by the criminal justice processes for employing techniques of resisting power. Power in Foucauldian terms is not a static phenomenon but is constantly being renegotiated by individuals who find means of resisting oppression and demanding inclusion. By this account, whatever freedom the individual enjoys is a form of activity, and inclusion is not assured by institutional structures but by the dynamics of power and resistance (Foucault 1978, 95; Foucault 1982, 219-22). The obvious example of resistance within traditional criminal justice practices is an accused's capacity to plead not guilty and resist attempts by the Crown to prove guilt. And even at the sentencing stage, there is some scope for argument about the appropriate measure of punishment. Although whatever arguments or defences raised on behalf of the accused must conform to certain parameters established by criminal law and procedure, this form of resistance is not only real but also necessary if the criminal justice system is to maintain its legitimacy.

Now, one might argue that since criminal law is embedded in a network of modes of governance that give content to its rules and guide the decisions that judges make, as in society at large, these modes are subject to a degree of negotiation and resistance. A simple example might be found in the way that family relationships are constituted as modes of governance that suggest a subject who may be unlikely to commit crimes. Previous generations of defence lawyers might have been loathe to mention an offender's involvement in a committed same-sex relationship as an indication of reliability, as such relationships were more likely to be conceived as evidence of deviance; however, various processes have to some extent legitimized same-sex relationships, and now such a relationship could easily be configured as an indicator of positive forms of extra-legal governance. One could see in this an example of the criminal justice system simply passively absorbing wider patterns of resistance and legitimation, but resistance can actually occur within the bounds of courtroom processes themselves. For example, images of dangerousness contained in evidence of professionals such as probation officers and psy experts are sometimes successfully resisted through cross-examination, often by invoking competing images that might emerge from alternative modes of discipline.

This suggests that governance in criminal justice processes might turn out, surprisingly, to be more amenable to negotiation and resistance than the community-based alternatives that are mythologized as more inclusive and accessible.

One could argue that in many community-based sentences the limited scope for resistance available through criminal justice processes evaporates. In many cases, this evaporation of forms of resistance occurs through the language of voluntarism. Many forms of community-based sentencing require, at the outset, the offender's agreement to forego the ordinary processes of the criminal justice system and to submit to the practices of the selected community. The validity of this agreement often includes formal requirements, such as the provision of legal advice. This voluntarism may delegitimize any subsequent attempts by the offender to resist the modes of power exercised by the psy experts. Such resistance is likely to be cast in terms of the offender's failure to accept responsibility for his or her own rehabilitation and expulsion from the community-based program.

However, it is possible that such concerns fail to appreciate the extent to which the criminal justice system is dependent on extra-legal forms of governance for its legitimacy and relevance. The linkages that sentencing courts using community-based alternatives seek to forge suggest a need by the criminal justice system to absorb additional kinds of knowledge apart from what is already endemic to it. This knowledge seeking suggests a desire to give more or different kinds of content to the legal rules. This may be construed as an effort to expand the scope of coercive criminal law power and to use ever more effective means of suppressing resistance. Concerns about the hegemonic tendencies of the criminal justice system should not be ignored; however, it is easy to exaggerate this danger in considering the knowledge-seeking function of community-based alternatives if we forget the extent to which the criminal justice system is dependent on extra-legal forms of knowledge.

It is not irrelevant that criminal justice officials who employ community-based alternatives do not, by and large, see what they are doing in terms of seeking hegemonic power; they seem, rather, to believe that they are using knowledge as a means of responding creatively to the perceived deficiencies of more traditional criminal justice practices. These perceived deficiencies are numerous, but from a criminal law perspective they are widely seen in terms of the failure of more traditional sentencing practices to reduce crime.

The aspirations of the criminal justice system, and its dependence on extra-legal forms of governance, suggest that there is, even in community-based sentencing alternatives, scope for effective resistance. Offenders who participate in such alternatives do, in fact, resist the modes of discipline they employ, simply by withdrawal from the program or by refusing to cooperate, resulting in expulsion. This may seem to be something of a Hobson's choice from the offender's point of view; the alternative to compliance is subjection to ordinary criminal law processes and often imprisonment. But high attrition rates, for example, in the Toronto Drug Treatment Court (almost 85 percent of all offender/clients withdraw or are expelled) suggest that this resistance is real.

The undeniably punitive response to such resistance may suggest that the interaction of the criminal justice system and aspects of community governance is essentially an attempt to use the violently coercive mechanisms available in the criminal sphere to force compliance to other, more invasive forms of individualized control. It is easy to see in this a rather grim picture of community-based sentencing as inevitably setting up offenders for subjection, one way or another, to authoritarian, top-down forms of oppression. But it should be borne in mind that resort to sentencing practices that have already been designated as inadequate for many purposes is hardly a triumph for criminal justice officials either. It is, in other words, not for no reason that the criminal justice system has sought increased access to extra-legal modes of governance. They mean to use these modes as a means of reducing crime.[8] Their continued viability – particularly in terms of their access to funding and support – is likely to depend on their success in creating acceptably disciplined subjects without resort to imprisonment. In this way we can see how the need for violent suppression really does signify the failure of the liberal state.

So if these disciplinary communities are, to a large degree, constituted by the requirements of the criminal justice system, it should be recognized that they will fail to meet these requirements unless they achieve a significant degree of buy-in from the individuals whom they seek to discipline, which will require a degree of accommodation of demands for inclusion coming from the bottom up.

This suggests that the processes going on in community-based sentences cannot be understood in simple terms of social control but as a complex interaction of power relationships and resistance. Its continued viability as a method of reducing crime depends on its ability to accommodate the aspirations of the offenders who will be subjected to governance. Therefore, the idea of community-based sentencing as signifying a withdrawal of the state, or as the subordination of extra-legal modes of governance in the interests of exercising control over the individual, may fail to recognize the very real ways in which the criminal justice system is dependent on both. Thus, while the mythologizing of the concept of community may result in an uncritical glorification of community-based sentencing alternatives, an overly pessimistic view of the hegemonic potential of the criminal justice system may lead to an ultimately unproductive rejection of all efforts for reform (McMahon 1990, 1992). There does seem to be scope for resistance in community sentencing processes, but it is not through the identification of one just or true form of governance, be it the law or something else. The scope for resistance seems to lie in the interdependence of the law with the sources of knowledge on which it relies – the complex interaction of modes of governance and the way in which individuals deploy them.

## NOTES

1   *R. v. Proulx*, [2000] 1 S.C.R. 61, 140 C.C.C. (3d) 449, 30 C.R. (5th) 1.

2   *R. v. Moses* (1992), 71 C.C.C. (3d) 124 (Y. Terr. Ct.).

3   For example, Marianna Valverde (1998, 205) suggests that self-help groups might offer alternatives – and a means of resistance to – the various discourses that medicalize drinking or drug-taking habits.

4   Lacey and Zedner (1995, 305) point out the disjuncture between the rise in community-based criminal justice initiatives and the destruction of "the very infrastructures which might be thought to make references to the community meaningful" during the Thatcher years in England and the Reagan years in the United States (see also Hillian, Reitsma-Street, and Hackler 2004, 361).

5   The Toronto Drug Treatment Court refers to offenders as "clients."

6   These provisions are found in ss. 18, 19, and 41.

7   *R. v. Creighton*, [1993] 3 S.C.R. 3, 83 C.C.C. (3d) 346, 23 C.R. (4th) 189; *R. v. Lavallee*, [1990] 1 S.C.R. 852, 55 C.C.C. (3d) 97, 76 C.R. (3d) 97; *R. v. Naglik*, [1993] 3 S.C.R. 122, 83 C.C.C. (3d) 526, 23 C.R. (4th) 335; *R. v. Tutton and Tutton*, [1989] 1 S.C.R. 1392, 48 C.C.C. (3d) 129, 69 C.R. (3d) 289.

8   This statement should, perhaps, be heavily qualified. It often happens that resort to criminal measures are taken for reasons having nothing to do with public safety or crime reduction, even though they are often justified by reference to their efficacy in this respect. A recent example of this might be the calls from three political parties in the last election for increased mandatory minimum sentences for gun-related offences as a means of dealing with the perceived "epidemic" of firearms in Toronto and other Canadian cities. There is, of course, no evidence that mandatory minimum sentences will have any deterrent effect. This suggests that the rationale for such measures is really more for their symbolic, rather than utilitarian, value. Nonetheless, it does seem to me that if community-based sentencing initiatives are going to become more than a marginal aspect of the criminal justice system, they will have to justify continued support and funding by reference to success rates.

## REFERENCES

Abel, R. 1982. Introduction to *The Politics of Informal Justice: The American Experience*, ed. R. Abel, 1-13. New York: Academic Press.

Anderson, C. 1999. Governing Aboriginal Justice in Canada: Constructing Responsible Individuals and Communities through Tradition. *Crime, Law and Social Change* 31(4): 303-26.

Baskin, D. 1988. Community Mediation and the Public/Private Problem. *Social Justice* 15(1): 98.

Benhabib, S. 1987. The Generalized and the Concrete Other. In *Feminism as Critique: On the Politics of Gender,* ed. S. Benhabib and D. Cornell, 77-95. Minneapolis: University of Minnesota Press.

Bentley, P. 2000. Canada's First Drug Treatment Court. 2000 31 C.R. (5th) 257-74.

Braithwaite, J. 1989. *Crime, Shame and Reintegration.* New York: Cambridge University Press.

Fitzpatrick, P. 1992. The Impossibility of Popular Justice. *Social and Legal Studies* 1(2): 199-215.

Foucault, M. 1978. *History of Sexuality.* New York: Pantheon Books.

–. 1980. Two Lectures. In *Power/Knowledge,* ed. C. Gordon, 78-108. New York: Pantheon Books.

–. 1982. The Subject and Power. In *Michel Foucault: Beyond Structuralism and Hermeneutics,* ed. H.L. Dreyfuss and P. Rabinow, 208-26. Chicago: Chicago University Press.

Harris, P., B. Weagant, D. Cole, and F. Wienper. 2004. Working in the Trenches with the YCJA. *Canadian Journal of Criminology and Criminal Justice* 46(3): 367-89.

Hillian, D., M. Reitsma-Street, and J. Hackler. 2004. Conferencing in the Youth Criminal Justice Act of Canada: Policy Developments in British Columbia. *Canadian Journal of Criminology and Criminal Justice* 46(3): 343-66.

Hunt, A. 1992. Foucault's Expulsion of Law: Toward a Retrieval. *Law and Social Inquiry* 17(1): 1-38.

–, and G. Wickham. 1994. *Foucault and Law: Towards a Sociology of Law as Governance.* London: Pluto Press.

Lacey, N., and L. Zedner. 1995. Discourses of Community in Criminal Justice. *Journal of Law and Society* 22(3): 301-25.

LaPrairie, C., L. Gliksman, P.G. Erickson, R. Wall, and B. Newton-Taylor. 2002. Drug Treatment Courts: A Viable Option for Canada? *Substance Use and Misuse* 37(12): 1529-66.

Marlatt, G.A. 1998. *Harm Reduction.* New York: Guilford Press.

Matthews, R. 1988. Reassessing Informal Justice. In *Informal Justice,* ed. R. Matthews, 1-24. London: Sage.

McMahon, M. 1990. "Net Widening": Vagaries in the Use of a Concept. *British Journal of Criminology* 30(2): 121-49.

–. 1992. *Persistent Prisons?* Toronto: University of Toronto Press.

Miller, P., and N. Rose. 2008. Political Power beyond the State. In *Governing the Present,* ed. P. Miller and N. Rose, 53-83. Cambridge, UK: Polity Press.

Moore, D. 2007a. *Criminal Artefacts: Governing Drugs and Users.* Vancouver: UBC Press.

–. 2007b. Translating Justice and Therapy: The Drug Treatment Court Networks. *British Journal of Criminology* 47(1): 42-60.

Morris, R. 2000. *Stories of Transformative Justice.* Toronto: Canadian Scholars' Press.

Munro, V.E. 2001. Legal Feminism and Foucault – A Critique of the Expulsion of Law. *Journal of Law and Society* 28(4): 546-67.

Pavlich, G.C. 1996. *Justice Fragmented: Mediating Community Disputes under Postmodern Conditions.* New York: Routledge.

Rose, N. 2008. The Death of the Social? In *Governing the Present,* ed. P. Miller and N. Rose, 84-113. Cambridge, UK: Polity Press.

Silverstein, M. 2001. The Ties That Bind: Family Surveillance of Canadian Parolees. *Sociological Quarterly* 42(3): 395-428.

Valverde, M. 1998. *Diseases of the Will: Alcohol and the Dilemmas of Freedom.* Cambridge: Cambridge University Press.

Wickham, G. 2006. Foucault, Law, and Power: A Reassessment. *Journal of Law and Society* 33(4): 596-614.

Young, I. 1987. Impartiality and the Civic Public: Some Implications of Feminist Critiques of Moral and Political Theory. In *Feminism as Critique: On the Politics of Gender,* ed. S. Benhabib and D. Cornell, 56-76. Minneapolis: University of Minnesota Press.

Zehr, H. 1990. *Changing Lenses: A New Focus for Crime and Justice.* Toronto: Herald Press.

# 7
# Stigma and Marginality: Gendered Experiences of Families of Male Prisoners in Canada

*Stacey Hannem*

Historically, criminologists have primarily focused their attentions on either crime and its perpetrators or the criminal justice system's response to offending. More recently, the victims of criminal acts have also entered the criminological landscape. The use of incarceration, in particular, is often discussed as though it is a punishment that affects only the offending individual. Although critical criminologists have critiqued the overuse of imprisonment as a primary response to crime, they have rarely posed any challenge to this narrow view of incarceration as affecting only the prisoner. In fact, the use of imprisonment has serious collateral effects on the families of the incarcerated: families face economic and practical difficulties related to the prisoner's incarceration, they deal with the difficult emotions that accompany involuntary separation from a loved one, and they battle the stigma of association with criminality. The intimate partners (opposite and same sex), children, parents, and siblings of the incarcerated must negotiate the policies of the criminal justice system and deal with the social reality of their connection to someone who has been convicted of an offence. Despite the profound impact incarceration has on these individuals, the experiences of the family members of prisoners are rarely considered in discussions of crime and punishment.

This chapter describes the difficulties faced by the families of incarcerated men in Canada and the marginal position of these families in relation to the criminal justice system and its policies. The findings are based on data from interviews and focus groups involving twenty-eight people who have experienced the incarceration of a male family member and nine people who provide services to the families of prisoners.[1]

Although feminist criminologists have worked hard to draw attention to women as offenders and victims of crime, the fact remains that most prisoners are male and most of their partners are female. This study focuses on the female partners of male prisoners, a large population of women whose experiences have mostly been ignored by criminology. These women's lives are, arguably, as affected by the criminal justice system as those of female offenders and victims. Indeed, I argue that the experiences of prisoners' families are highly gendered, analyzing the key role gender plays in their situations.

A brief review of existing international literature on prisoners' families provides a context for this research, showing, among other things, how themes of gender and stigma emerge.

## Review of the Literature on Prisoners' Families

Although there are several isolated studies of prisoners' families dating back to the early- and mid-twentieth century (see Bloodgood 1928; Sacks 1938; Blackwell 1959; Zalba 1964), only recently have the families of prisoners become a topic of some interest in academia and have publications on the subject begun to proliferate. Yet, considering the thousands of studies of crime, offenders, and corrections published each year, the families of these convicts are still marginalized in the social sciences. The first study of note was conducted by Pauline Morris in the United Kingdom, where she conducted in-depth interviews with 932 inmates and 676 prisoners' wives over a period of three years. Morris found that the most commonly mentioned problems faced by prisoners' wives were money (41 percent), management of children (34 percent), loneliness and sexual frustration (32 percent), and fears about what would happen when their husband was released (23 percent). To date, nearly all existing studies of prisoners' families have found that finances are a major source of worry for the families of incarcerated men.[2] From as early as R.S. Bloodgood's 1928 study to the most recent research, the incarceration of a spouse and/or parent is known to often cause financial hardship in the form of lost income and increased expenses (see, for example, Schneller 1976; Liker 1981; Curtis and Schulman 1984; Fishman 1990; Comfort 2008). The research that I discuss in this chapter concurs with these findings. Early research alluded to the gendered nature of these financial outcomes, while later research (see especially Lowenstein 1984, 1986; and Girshick 1996), including my own, engages with the impact of gender and the already marginal location of women in the job market as a key contributor to financial hardships.

Nancy Anderson (1965) completed a small study of prisoners and their families in Melbourne, Australia, aimed at determining whether community services were meeting the needs of this population. She determined that the bulk of support services offered specifically to this population took the form of financial aid and social welfare; only a few agencies offered family counselling or social programs. Anderson (1965, 1967) recommended that existing community agencies be linked with those that provide services for prisoners' families in order to coordinate their efforts and offer a wider range of services. The lack of services offered to the families of prisoners is another important theme in the literature (see Sacks 1938; Schneller 1976; Bakker, Morris, and Janus 1978; Lowenstein 1984; Fishman 1990; Withers 2003; Condry 2007).

In the 1970s, we see the first suggestions that the difficulties experienced by the families of prisoners can be considered a form of collateral punishment. Schneller (1976) argued that the imprisonment of married men violates the principle of specificity of punishment by causing hardship to the wives and children, who are legally innocent. He recommended that programs and policies to assist these families be put in place to mitigate some of the hardships caused by the incarceration of a husband and father. Bakker, Morris, and Janus (1978) concurred with Schneller and even went so far as to argue that the families of prisoners were themselves victims of the criminal justice system. The findings of this study corroborated earlier reports of financial and emotional hardships, feelings of stigmatization by criminal justice officials and individuals in the community, lack of information about the criminal justice process and incarceration, and perceptions of significant increases in stress levels and family chaos (ibid.).

Fewer studies have looked at the emotional aspect of involuntary separation because of incarceration. Those that considered this aspect of a loved one's incarceration have found that prisoners' families encounter a range of emotional turmoil, both during and following the period of incarceration. The stress and sadness do not necessarily end at warrant expiry. Many families have great difficulties adjusting to life post-incarceration and coping with the (re)negotiation of family roles (Fishman 1990).

The 1990s saw the publication of two monographs based on qualitative research on the experiences of prisoners' wives. In 1990, Laura Fishman published her ethnographic study of thirty prisoners' wives in the State of Vermont, *Women at the Wall: A Study of Prisoners' Wives Doing Time on the Outside.* Fishman interviewed the wives about their relationships with their husbands prior to incarceration and explored the women's experiences in dealing with their husbands' imprisonment and separation from the family. Financial difficulties, emotional stress, family readjustment, lack of resources, and social stigma emerged as primary themes in Fishman's research. Lori

Girshick's (1996) book *Soledad Women: Wives of Prisoners Speak Out* is unique in that Girshick herself was married to a prisoner at California's Soledad Prison (whom she met and married during his incarceration). She conducted interviews with twenty-five other women whose husbands were also incarcerated at Soledad Prison. Her findings closely mirror those of Laura Fishman but emphasize that the husband's incarceration often results in a loss of income and the exacerbation of existing financial problems, recognizing that the families of many prisoners have a lower socio-economic status (ibid.). Her feminist analysis of the issues reveals the complex intersections of gender, race, and class that impact prisoners' wives' understandings and experiences. Although Fishman and Girshick have each produced a wonderful qualitative study of the experiences of prisoners' wives, they have been criticized for failure to engage with the question of ethnicity and for under-representing minority groups in their interview samples (Comfort 2008).

The children of prisoners are thought to be particularly affected by the incarceration of a parent. The vast majority of recent studies of prisoners' families focus on the impact of parental incarceration on children, exploring the emotional and social issues that arise, including family separation, trauma, isolation, behavioural problems, and increased risk of offending behaviour (see Shaw 1992; Gabel and Johnston 1995; Seymour and Hairston 2001; Boswell and Wedge 2002; Bernstein 2005; Marstone 2005). Most of these studies are of American prisoners and their children. Given the sheer enormity of the prison-industrial complex in the United States and the fact that, at any given time, one or both of the parents of an estimated 2.3 million American children are in prison (Parke and Clarke-Stewart 2003, 191), it should come as no surprise that concern has begun to emerge for the welfare of these young victims of the criminal justice system. Increases in the numbers of incarcerated parents and spouses have led to studies of the difficulties and issues of maintaining family contact through visitation and describe the experiences of stigma, frustration, and humiliation that often accompany the family's entrance to a prison (Carlson and Cervera 1992; Arditti, Lambert-Shute and Joest 2003; Comfort 2003; Christian 2005).

Stigma emerges as an important concept in the literature. Many of the studies engage with the notion of stigma and discuss its effects on the social interactions of family members. The literature generally concurs that stigma is a problem for the families of incarcerated persons. However, the examination of stigma is conducted primarily at the symbolic and individual level. Most recently, Rachel Condry (2007) has published a study of the relatives of serious, violent, and sexual offenders in England. Her research involved in-depth interviews with thirty-two family members, focusing on the families' feelings of shame related to the offence and the impact on their identity, social interactions, and adjustment. The experience of stigmatization and the impact of the offence emerge as a primary theme in this work. Condry explores the negotiation and resistance of stigma at the individual level, describing how family members attempt to make sense of their loved one's crime and their use of strategies of resistance and stigma management to maintain a sense of identity and to cope with feelings of guilt.

Gwénola Ricordeau's (2008) study of prisoners' families in France considers the effects of incarceration on family relationships and argues that imprisonment punishes the entire family. She too found the effects of stigma to be salient for prisoners' families, often contributing to family breakdown because of the family members' desire to separate themselves from the origin of the stigma and to preserve their own identities as distinct from that of the offender.

Megan Comfort (2008) published a book based on her research on the wives and partners of prisoners at San Quentin State Prison in California. Comfort focused her study on the maintenance of intimate relationships despite the barriers of prison. She details the experiences of prison visitation, conjugal visits, and the intrusiveness of corrections on inmate-family interactions. Most surprisingly, her work also examines the prison as a site of power and control for women who are struggling to cope with difficult and sometimes abusive relationships but who wish to maintain their ties to these men. The prison is viewed as offering a reprieve from abuse and an opportunity for change.

Although Fishman (1990), Girshick (1996), Condry (2007), and Comfort (2008) all mention that family members encounter stigmatization by guards upon entering the penitentiary, none of them engages with the institutionalized nature of this stigma and how it appears to be expressed in policies that label families as risky, which form the social context in which these guards operate. Significantly, the Canadian experience is also absent from the literature.

The lack of research on the situation of Canadian prisoners and their families is a significant gap. Only one Canadian study has been undertaken, by the Canadian Families and Corrections Network in Kingston, Ontario, in cooperation with the Correctional Service of Canada, published in 2003 (see Withers 2003). The strategic policy document that resulted from this research advocated better services for prisoners' families in the context of correctional services (ibid.). Key areas of concern included the need for correctional staff who interact with family members and visitors to the institution to be properly trained and sensitive to the needs of families, the high cost of telephone calls originating in the institutions, the lack of funding for support services to prisoners' families, and the need to integrate families more fully into release and reintegration planning (ibid.). This consultation is the only published study of the effects of incarceration on Canadian families to date and, as a policy document, offers no theoretical or contextual analysis of the findings.

## Prisoners' Families and Gender

A definite gender bias exists in family members' experiences of incarceration. In fact, the lack of attention given to the families of prisoners may, in itself, be seen as resulting from the marginalized status of women in our society. Although the vast majority of incarcerated persons in Canada (and, indeed, around the world) are men, it stands to reason that many of these men are engaged in relationships with women who are deeply affected when their men are sent to prison. Although much money and effort has been invested in the study of incarcerated persons and the prison complex, the female partners of these men have been neglected or considered as appendages to their men.

As described in the literature, the problems faced by families of the incarcerated are predominantly women's problems. These difficulties are the result of a complex intersection of patriarchal norms, the gendered division of labour, and the traditional role of woman as carer. When a woman is imprisoned, it is rare that a male partner or spouse remains on the outside, maintaining the family unit and awaiting her release (Casey-Acevedo and Bakken 2002; Maidment 2006).[3] When a man is incarcerated, if he has a spouse or partner she is more likely to retain custody of any minor children and will often attempt to preserve her relationship and sustain the family unit throughout the incarceration. Girshick (1996) attributes this tendency to work to preserve the relationship to expectations that the wife will act as a caregiver and to the importance of the wife/mother role in the formation of a woman's identity. A woman's identity, in her own mind and in the perceptions of others, is often closely linked to her husband/partner and his social status, particularly if she does not have a career or social identity that is separate from her husband/partner and family. This phenomenon allows for the stigma of a husband/partner's identity as a criminal to be easily transferred to his wife/partner in her interactions with others. Although some marital relationships do break down and end in divorce because of incarceration, even these women are not immediately exempted from the impact of incarceration and the emotional, social, and financial difficulties that it poses. In fact, they are subject to the additional hardship of relinquishing the often central "wife" identity.

Women are also often financially dependent on their male partners, whether as a primary or second income earner. As I discuss below, female partners and children left behind when a man is sent to prison often suffer significant financial hardships. Although husbands, fathers, and brothers are also affected by the incarceration of a loved one (whether male or female), the impact is likely more often mitigated by a financial status that is independent of the incarcerated family member, and they may have less tendency to link their own identity with that of their incarcerated loved one. Men are more likely than women to have a social status that does not rely on marital or kinship ties, including an occupational status outside the home. This autonomous identity appears to significantly reduce the likelihood of transferred stigma as others relate to the non-deviant, established, master status. Conversely, female spouses and children who do not have an established, positive public identity that is capable of overriding the negative impact of their familial relationship to an incarcerated person are more likely to experience greater transferred stigma and to find it socially debilitating. In light of this gendered experience, my research is focused on the families of male prisoners, with particular emphasis on the hardships that female partners and children face. Many of the issues discussed in this chapter also apply to the families of female prisoners; however, the experience of a mother's imprisonment and separation from her children carries other unique implications that I do not address here and are certainly worthy of further study.

## Stigma and Marginality

According to Erving Goffman (1963, 3), stigma is "an attribute that is deeply discrediting" and that reduces the person, in the minds of others, "from a whole and usual person to a tainted, discounted one." But more than an attribute alone, stigma is more precisely understood as the "relationship between attribute and stereotype" (4). That is, a particular attribute comes to be defined as an undesirable or negative characteristic – a stereotype is associated with the attribute. Those who possess this attribute are automatically associated with the stereotype and, as a result, are subject to avoidance or discriminatory behaviours as others react to the stereotype rather than to the individual. The single, stigmatized characteristic comes to form a master status in the eyes of others, overshadowing other, positive characteristics. Discriminatory behaviour or avoidance when faced with an undesirable attribute is observable evidence of stigma.

Goffman (1963, 30) also identified that some discrediting attributes appear to have the quality of being "sticky": the negative stereotype that accompanies it is spread from the stigmatized individual to those close to him or her. That stigma is so easily transferred is reflective of our belief that the character and characteristics of an individual's companions tell us something about that person. This normative assumption is perfectly encapsulated in the adage "birds of a feather flock together." Thus, those who have a significant social relationship to a discredited or stigmatized person may be marked by association and suffer similar discrimination or avoidance. It is this sticky stigma that marks the families of incarcerated men. Many of them have never committed a criminal act or been involved in deviant lifestyles and yet are marked by association with a convicted person.

As I suggested earlier, the transference of stigma in this fashion is also highly gendered. Although this phenomenon has not been researched in great detail, there is evidence that women are more vulnerable to the effects of transferred stigma and more likely to be the targets of obvious avoidance or discrimination because of their association with a stigmatized individual (see Gray 2002; Hannem 2008; Kampf 2008; Smith, Mysak, and Michael 2008). This tendency can be traced back to patriarchal beliefs that tend to limit the identities of women to their marital and motherhood roles and thus tie their identities and fates to those of their partners or children. As such, it is likely that the female partners and mothers of male prisoners are more greatly affected by sticky stigma than other male relatives of prisoners and are more apt to suffer from social isolation. For wives or partners, this is compounded by the view that a marital or intimate relationship with a prisoner is an association rooted in choice, rather than in blood ties (Condry 2007; Hannem 2008). Thus, those who cannot be held personally responsible for the association may not be viewed to be as culpable as those who *choose* to maintain a relationship with a convicted man. A mother's culpability, on the other hand, is tied to her responsibility for child rearing (Gray 2002; Condry 2007; Hannem 2008). The crimes of the incarcerated man are believed by many to stem from his upbringing and to be a direct reflection of the quality of parenting he received (Condry 2007; Hannem 2008). Although the relationship between gender and the transference of stigma is in need of further research, there are clear indications that one's gender and social role can have a profound impact on the experience of sticky stigma.

The experience of stigmatization is made even more problematic by its frequent correlation with marginality. When we speak of stigmatized and marginalized populations, it is clear that we are often referring to the same groups of people. These individuals encounter social censure, avoidance, and discrimination as observable evidence of stigma, but they are also often marginalized, excluded from consideration in social policies, silenced politically and socially, and sometimes the victims of financial exploitation and exclusion. Drawing on the understanding that marginality is rooted in power imbalances (Cullen and Pretes 2000), and evidenced by the relative lack of social, political, and/or economic power of the stigmatized and marginalized, we can examine the dyadic nature of stigma and marginality and the ways in which they perpetuate and reinforce one another.

Much early critical criminology was influenced by, and evolved in part from, symbolic interactionism, though these roots are not always obvious. It is beyond the scope of this chapter to develop this topic here, but I argue elsewhere (Hannem 2008), following Ian Hacking (2004), that the work of Goffman can be usefully synthesized with the various work of Michel Foucault (who, of course, exerts a profound influence on current critical criminology) – for example, Foucault's various writings that deal with the theme of marginalization, as summarized by Gutting (2005). As Gutting writes, Foucault argues that the marginalized are a normal part of our society; they speak the same language, share the same cultural and social understandings, and appreciate many of the values of mainstream society. They often play essential economic or social roles in our communities, and yet they are perpetually on the borders of society for one (or both) of two reasons. Either their identity and life are perceived as being significantly defined by values that are counter to the mainstream, or they belong to a group whose welfare is systematically subordinated in favour of the welfare of the larger, mainstream group (ibid.). The families of prisoners fit into each of these categories. Marginality, then, might be conceived as often the practical outcome of stigma, which prevents marked individuals from being fully accepted in their communities. Stigma can create and perpetuate a situation of marginality by permitting the community to deny full citizenship rights to, or to turn a blind eye to, the sufferings of those who are perceived as counter to the mainstream and therefore undeserving of these considerations. The lived experiences of prisoners' family members and the difficulties they encounter may be seen as directly linked to the stigma of criminality that is attached to them by virtue of their association with a convict. Where stigma does not directly *cause* the associated difficulties, the problems are allowed to persist by virtue of a stigma that seemingly justifies social neglect.

## Financial and Practical Difficulties

The disproportionate effect of the incarceration of male partners on women is, in part, reflective of patriarchal norms in our society that expose women to financial vulnerability and greater rates of poverty (Girshick 1996). If there are young children in the household, the male may be the primary provider while the woman is the primary caregiver, and his removal from the household because of incarceration can be financially devastating to the family. Established patterns of family life will be disrupted and require the female partner to take on the role of sole parent and provider. Regardless of the family's original financial status, incarceration is likely to have a negative impact and require a change of lifestyle, and most often this difficulty is borne by women. The collateral costs of incarceration may include the loss of a second income; the cost of keeping in contact through visits, telephone calls, and relocation; the cost of providing various financial supports to the incarcerated family member (including the provision of spending money and luxury items); difficulty finding employment; and the potential impact on property values. In the interest of space, we address here only the first two, which seem to have the greatest repercussions for the families of incarcerated men.

The participants in my study came from various economic and occupational situations, ranging from unemployed and collecting disability pension to middle-class professionals and small business owners. Regardless of the family's original financial status, all families appear to experience at least some difficulties, primarily related to the loss of a second (or sole) income and the added expenses of maintaining contact with the incarcerated loved one. As one participant said,

> the financial burden of having somebody incarcerated is phenomenal. Already there's a single-income family, single-parent family, and you're adding to that travel expenses, sometimes to include car expenses, long-distance expenses – I mean, my husband is in

an institution where it's not long distance to call, but he has to call me collect and it costs me two dollars and fifty cents every time he calls. (Catharine, a prisoner's wife)

The problem of lost income has been noted repeatedly in previous studies of prisoners' families (see, for example, Morris 1965; Fishman 1990; Girshick 1996; Comfort 2008). Although just two of the women whom I spoke with reported that their husbands had been the sole earner of the family income prior to the incarceration, other studies have found many more families engaged in a traditional gendered division of labour that saw the female partner work only in the home. The imprisonment of the primary income earner poses considerable financial hardship that has lasting implications for the family:

I had one credit card, with a – well, for me, a pretty hefty amount on it – and then I started gettin' more. They'd send me something in the mail about getting a card, you're preapproved, and I got it, 'cuz they wanted to know, like, are you in the same situation, and uh, on the phone, I'd just say yes, I am, you know, they didn't specifically say financial! But you see he was here for a year and a half [before he was sentenced to prison]. Still making money. So I got as much as I could. And he went right away and got a line of credit ... This was on Wednesday that the cop came ... he by Friday had gone and gotten our line of credit increased as much as he could. And, uh, as I say, even after he left, when I got a job, it wasn't a great job, but it was a job. And I, like I was in trouble, financially – we were in debt. (Isobel, a prisoner's wife)

Although the majority of the women whom I spoke with had an independent source of income at the time of their partner's imprisonment, several made a point of mentioning how much easier life would be for them with a second income to assist in paying bills and maintaining a household. What is not often considered is that the prisoner's family is essentially a single-parent household, with all of the struggles that are commonly associated with that status (Lowenstein 1986). Although there is a second parent, the incarcerated father does not make enough money to provide the child support that a divorced woman might receive. As Anne put it:

Life goes on and you're by yourself to pay for everything. But,
there's very little support that they [the incarcerated partner] can
give you because, when you make $6 a day you can't [send money
for your family]. (Anne, a prisoner's wife)

The wives who are left behind to struggle alone with bills and child rearing
often feel resentment toward their partner, who is seemingly isolated from
financial stress by the walls of the prison. The prisoner's basic needs are provided by the correctional system, while the needs of his family are ignored.
The incarcerated partner is no longer able or expected to provide for his family,
and the women feel that they (literally) pay the price for their partners' crimes:

He doesn't have to worry about how he's gonna pay the rent,
buy groceries, pay the huge phone bill – sometimes I think he's
got it pretty easy being in there, compared to us. (Daphne, a
prisoner's wife)

This is a perfect example of what Julian Roberts (2006) described as
"collateral punishment." Although they are not the targets of the sentences
levied, the partners and children of convicted men experience the period of
incarceration as punitive, and it can have a profoundly negative effect on their
quality of life. The marginal location of women and children and the stigma
of association with criminality seemingly obscure this collateral punishment
from the view of the public and the correctional system. Either no consideration is given to the effect of imprisonment on those who are left behind, or
the difficulties faced by these families are glossed over as being the fault of
the offender, rather than the result of our choice as a society to utilize prison
sentences. From an insensitive public, one might hear: "He should have
thought about his family *before* he committed that crime!" The financial
impact of incarceration on families is not acknowledged by the public or by
the government as an area of social responsibility to be addressed.

The added expenses that are directly related to the incarceration of a
loved one exacerbate the effect of lost income. To cope with involuntary
separation from a husband, father, son, or brother, family members will often
put a great deal of money and effort into maintaining regular contact and
communication with the incarcerated man. These costs can be substantial,
yet the wives/partners of incarcerated men whom I spoke with emphasized
that the expenditures were necessary if they wanted to preserve the family

unit and to allow their children to continue a relationship with their father. Although the wives/partners and children of male prisoners are most affected by these added costs, parents and siblings will often also incur additional expenses in maintaining a relationship with an incarcerated son or brother and in supporting him throughout the period of incarceration. Elderly parents and others who are on a fixed income often find that the costs prohibit them from having as frequent communication as they may wish.

In Canada, one of the biggest complaints among the families of prisoners is the cost of telephone communication. Prisoners cannot receive inbound calls at the penitentiary, and until 2010 all outbound calls were made collect, preventing access to less expensive means of billing such as calling cards, prepaid long distance, and unlimited calling plans. Collect calls are the most expensive way of calling, and the families of prisoners often were faced with the choice to limit their telephone contact or pay exorbitant phone bills:

> My phone bills were, like, three and four hundred dollars a month! Ridiculous. And I just couldn't afford to anymore. I have bills to pay, and the kids. So now, I told him, he can only call twice a month, and I talk and the kids talk to him, but not long. If he calls more than that, then I have to say no. And I feel like shit when that happens, like, really bad. But I just can't. (Daphne, a prisoner's wife)

The Correctional Service of Canada (CSC) claimed that the use of collect phone calls was necessary in order to have a record of inmates' telephone contacts in order to protect institutional security. The needs of families are not considered and, consequently, family members considered this policy to be punitive. Although the Canadian Families and Corrections Network and the Correctional Investigator made recommendations to the CSC in 2003 to address the costs of the phone system, a less expensive phone system was not fully implemented until 2010.[4] While the new telephone system allows inmates to pay for their telephone calls using prepaid calling cards, families with incarcerated loved ones still cannot benefit from unlimited calling plans available to Canadian consumers. Further, although the calling card system was intended to place the burden of paying for phone calls onto inmates instead of families, many families provide the funds to their incarcerated loved one to pay for the phone cards! Thus, while improved and less expensive, the costs of maintaining family contact are not entirely alleviated. The new telephone system is a computerized system into which CSC must input approved numbers to allow the call to be placed. This "Millenium System" will only allow calls to land lines. This seemingly flies in the face of the fact that Canada is an increasingly wireless society, and many individuals have only a cell phone as their primary means of communication. The families of Canadian prisoners must maintain land line telephone service in order to receive calls from their incarcerated loved ones. The seeming recalcitrance of the CSC to address this problem and the long delay in making changes to the inmate telephone system is just one example of how the families of in-carcerated persons are forgotten by the system and how their quality of life is sacrificed in the name of public safety.

Visits to the incarcerated family member can also pose considerable costs. The sheer geographic size of Canada and the dispersal of federal penitentiar-ies mean that men are often incarcerated in a different city from their families and sometimes at a great distance.[5] There are no federal institutions in New-foundland and Prince Edward Island or in any of the three northern territor-ies. Convicted persons from these regions sentenced to federal time will end up far from their homes and families. More than half of the women whom I spoke with lived more than a two-hour drive from the penitentiary where their loved one was incarcerated, with the furthest a ten-hour drive. Con-sequently, families often spend a great deal of money to facilitate visits to the penitentiary, paying for gas or other travel, accommodation, and food. For some families, the cost is prohibitive:

> I didn't go to [the penitentiary] – I just didn't have the money. You
> know, if I coulda just had the money. But you have to look at it –
> do I borrow money to go? I still had kids in school, um, what do
> I do? You know, do I – and at the time air flights weren't so cheap,
> even that few months ago you didn't get cheap flights as much
> as you do now. Or at least I didn't, I wasn't aware of them. And
> I couldn't, I didn't know if I could justify it – I just didn't think I
> could justify it. (Isobel, a prisoner's wife)

Even families that live relatively close to the prison in which their loved one is incarcerated may have difficulty travelling to the institutions because they are often either not accessible via public transportation or do not co-ordinate visiting hours with public transportation schedules (Withers 2003).

Family members on a fixed income may not have access to a vehicle or be able to drive themselves and must rely on the kindness of friends for transportation to the prison or pay the cost of an expensive cab ride. Some non-profit organizations offer transportation assistance to nearby prisons. For example, the Salvation Army organizations of Toronto and Ottawa offer weekend shuttle service to prisons in the Kingston area (a two-and-a-half-hour or one-and-a-half-hour drive, respectively) for a small fee. However, many families are not aware of the available services or may find even the nominal cost to be beyond their budget. Thus, visits, for some families, can be rare and are eagerly anticipated.

When families can afford to visit, there are still pitfalls that may prevent their visit and render the expenditure a waste of funds. The institution may be locked down and visits cancelled without warning because of concern for institutional security. Several women in the sample found themselves the subjects of suspicion after testing positive for drugs on the ion scanner or being singled out by the drug dogs, although they stated that they were not carrying contraband or users of drugs themselves. Visits may be temporarily or permanently cancelled as the result of such an incident. Many families can barely afford the costs of visits, so to spend the money to travel, only to be turned away from the prison, is very frustrating. To make the visiting budget stretch, some families try to take advantage of the private family visiting program.

The private family visiting program is unique to Canada, and other studies of prisoners' families in the United States and United Kingdom have not addressed this issue. The private family visit permits family members to spend up to seventy-two hours with their loved one in a small cottage or trailer on the prison grounds. The extended length of the visit, as compared with a two- to three-hour standard contact visit in the visiting room, makes it more worthwhile for families that are travelling a long distance. The private family visit provides important bonding time for families in an environment that is unmonitored, except for scheduled inmate counts. The situation allows them to interact in a way that simulates normal family life, including cooking their own meals and eating together. When asked about the importance of private family visits, one wife and mother responded:

> Absolutely, the family visits are helpful. [The kids] would have
> no relationship with their father otherwise, right? There's only so

much you can do with phone calls, letters, and, so yeah, it's absolutely necessary to have them, I think for us as well as for him. It's
– we're his link to society. (Anne, a prisoner's wife)

Although private family visits are eagerly anticipated and provide valuable family time, they also come with additional costs. Visiting family members are responsible to provide all of the groceries for the weekend, and these
supplies cannot be brought from home. The items must be purchased from
a grocery store approved by the institutional administration and delivered
directly from the store to the prison, to be scanned for drugs and other contraband. Any leftovers at the end of the weekend must be left behind in the
visiting trailer or thrown in the garbage. Women find this particularly irritat-
ing when they purchase condiments, such as salt, pepper, and butter, knowing that they will not be fully used during the visit. However, to not purchase
these items is to risk going without if there is none in the trailer.

The women to whom I spoke also reported that their husbands/partners
or sons often request special meals that may be outside the family budget.
They may find it difficult to refuse these requests, even when they cannot
afford them, because they feel sorry for the prisoner's lack of freedom. As one
wife put it:

So, he'll ask me, "Can you order steak, or seafood?" Things that
he loves, you know, but they don't get that kinda stuff in prison.
And I'm going, "Yeah, sure, like I don't even eat those things out
here – I can't afford them!" But I save up, or I use my credit
card, because I figure he doesn't have much in there. (Megan,
a prisoner's wife)

Despite the associated costs, many of the family members whom I spoke
with made concerted efforts to visit, if not regularly, then at least as often as
possible. They considered the costs of visiting a necessary expenditure to
maintain the family relationship. In other cases, women may make the decision to move in order to ensure that they and/or their children will be able
to have regular contact with the incarcerated husband/father:

I've made the decision that if our relationship is going to work,
and it will, I believe it will in my heart, I have to be near him. And
so, I moved. I can't live in another province and see him twice a

year and expect this relationship to just flourish and be incredible.
And talk to him once a week because that's all I can afford to, so
in making the decision that our relationship is a priority to me, I
had to move. And so financially it set me back, but what that did
is then it put me in communities where I don't know anyone, and
so – I don't have a lot of social contact with people and ... yeah,
I'm pretty alone. (Brenda, a prisoner's partner)

[I take my daughter] almost every time – that was the whole idea
of us moving down here, which was that she could establish a
proper relationship with her father. That's why I quit my job with
a good salary and a company car. I could have kept my job back
home and continued coming down here every other weekend, but
it was too hard on her. I'd load her up in a car on Friday night and
drive back again on Sunday night. That is no way to build a relationship. Let's face it. Even for us, we can get to see each other
more, so that makes it nicer. (Sue, a prisoner's wife)

Moving to a new city is an expensive undertaking that can also be socially isolating. In addition to the financial costs, families are taking on social
and emotional consequences. Because of the stigma associated with criminality and its transference to the families of incarcerated men, many family
members find themselves estranged from their extended families and friends
and have difficulty building new relationships. Consequently, there is often
little support and assistance for families to draw on. This stigma and lack of
support is reflective of the larger societal (non-)response to the families of
prisoners.

## SOCIAL AND COMMUNITY RESPONSE

Social supports to aid families financially affected by incarceration are limited in Canada. Although some families may qualify for welfare or social
assistance payments, many make do with a single salary and stretch their
budget to accommodate the additional expenses of visiting, phone bills, and
supporting their incarcerated loved one. Sometimes families receive temporary assistance from churches and other charitable organizations:

There's not a lot of financial help out there for families, other than
the regular social assistance and food banks and, you know,

Christmastime, those kinds of things. The other thing that was
helpful is that Christmastime, Bridges of Canada would send gifts
and food for families, and you'd get a food box from them and
you'd get a gift or two for the child and even one for the spouse,
but mostly the children. And that was very encouraging because
Christmas is always a tough time as a single parent – I mean, I've
had to go to food banks, not very often, um, I was unemployed
for a while, so I was on UIC for a while because I just lost jobs
because of the stigma attached. (Catharine, a prisoner's wife)

The services and assistance available to prisoners' families are often piecemeal
and are not available in all communities. There is no national or government
organization in Canada that is funded to provide financial assistance to
prisoners' families, other than provincial welfare and social assistance programs that are available to all families facing economic hardship. These
programs do not take into account the additional expenses that families affected by incarceration encounter.

According to section 71(1) of the Corrections and Conditional Release
Act, which governs Canadian prisons, prisoners have the right to reasonable
contact with their families via telephone, correspondence, and visiting, subject to limitations deemed reasonable for the protection and security of the
institution and involved persons. Although families have the legal right, then,
to contact with their loved one, this right is not necessarily made affordable
or easily exercised. The families of prisoners are not guaranteed to be treated
with dignity or given the freedom to exercise their right to reasonable contact
in a way that is convenient and financially viable for them. The additional
expenses and financial costs placed on families of incarcerated men that are
directly related to imprisonment are often justified by the priority placed on
institutional security.

Societal indifference to the hardships that are created when a family
member is imprisoned is symptomatic of the marginal position of prisoners
and their families in the community. This marginality is perpetuated by the
social stigma that accompanies criminality. There is little concern to invest
public funds to ease the hardships of those who, by virtue of their association with a convict, appear less than deserving. Although imprisonment is
generally intended as a punishment that is specific to the individual who
committed the crime, alleviating the unintended consequences of imprisonment for innocent citizens whose life and family relationships are affected

by incarceration is not seen as either a social or a political priority. The welfare of these families is subordinated to the cause of the so-called war on crime, and the effects of imprisonment on families are seen as an acceptable level of collateral damage. As Foucault suggests, this is one of the hallmarks of a marginalized population: the subordination of its well-being for the convenience and security of the majority.

## Symbolic Stigma and Prisoners' Families

Beyond perpetuating financial stresses, societal indifference and stigma have significant effects on prisoners' family members. Symbolic stigma is experienced in everyday, individual interactions and is rooted in negative stereotypes. Symbolic stigma is most commonly enacted in rituals of avoidance or discrimination. For instance, the family members of prisoners often find that friends and relatives discontinue relationships, presumably in order to distance themselves from the origin of the stigma:

> When everything happened, I lost many many friends. I lost many friends after I made the decision to stay with Tom; I lost many friends the day it happened and people never bothered to phone. (Brenda, a prisoner's partner)

> I've, you know, lost job opportunities and friends – and family relationships because of this, um, the decision to plan a life with Ron and, you know. So, so that was difficult, and the people that you're closest to are the ones who are placing the stigma on you – and the rest of the community just follows suit. (Catharine, a prisoner's wife)

Similarly, the children of prisoners may find themselves ostracized from other children, particularly when their peers' parents discover the family situation. There is a great deal of incentive to manage one's identity by keeping the incarcerated family member a secret:

> Jocelyn once told friends when she was in first grade, I think. And the daycare worker grabbed me and she said, "I don't know if it's true, I don't care, but your daughter's been saying this, that her father is in prison, and just so you know, you might want to have a talk with her because some parents will pull their kids away if

they think it's true." So, I spoke with her. She ended up going back
and saying, "Oh, you believed me? That's stupid! That was a joke!"
type of thing. (Anne, a prisoner's wife)

David, my son, he was afraid of people knowing about his step-
dad because they, you know, parents wouldn't let their kids play
with him and those kind of things. That was very, very difficult.
(Catharine, a prisoner's wife)

The tendency of significant others and community members to sever ties
with families affected by incarceration can be traced to the social stigma that
accompanies criminality and the propensity for stigma to be transferred from
the convict to his family and friends. The stigma of criminality is used to
justify the social and political marginalization of prisoners' families and
enables the community to disregard the impacts of incarceration on family
members without guilt. Because having an incarcerated family member is
not a visible attribute, many prisoners' families find it easiest to cope by
keeping their situation a secret in order to avoid stigma in the community.
Goffman (1963, 42) refers to this strategy as "passing" – "the management
of undisclosed discrediting information about self"; many individuals who
possess an invisible stigmatic attribute find passing to be an effective means
of decreasing negative social interactions. All of the family members in the
sample reported at least selectively choosing to keep their situation a secret
from others, or feeling that it was not relevant information that needed to be
disclosed in many situations:

In the community that I live in now, no one knows. So, I haven't
had any repercussions that way, and I haven't felt anything socially.
(Brenda, a prisoner's wife)

Um, some people, [I tell] some people, you know, but most of the
time we sort of just, you know, well, he's out of town or whatever,
because it's easier. (Francine, a prisoner's mother)

However, the very act of keeping one's life secret can perpetuate feelings
of shame and ensure that the families of prisoners remain isolated. Consequently, these individuals often lack social support when they need it the

most. Their inability to share the details of their day-to-day lives with co-workers and acquaintances means that they often forego the possibility of supportive friendships in order to mitigate the chance of negative stigma reactions:

> It's, um, it's a very isolating thing, I think, unless you talk to other people who are in the same situation. Um, and not everybody wants to talk about it. I mean, it's not something you go around saying, "Oh! You know, my son's gone to jail!" You know, whereas if somebody has a serious illness or something like that, it's – there's not the same – stigma, I suppose you would say. Yeah. So, yeah, it's isolating. (Francine, a prisoner's mother)

The double-edged sword of identity management and selective disclosure is that it serves to perpetuate feelings of marginality and stigmatization in individuals who are unwilling to be forthcoming about their situation. Their assumption that others will react negatively to them is never challenged and is thus strengthened, ensuring that the cycle of secret keeping and isolation is continued.

## Stigma in Institutional Interactions

The social effects of stigma are most pronounced when the discreditable characteristic is a visible one that is known to others. Although having an incarcerated loved one does not leave a visible mark and can be hidden from others, there are situations in which this discreditable status becomes evident and "passing" is impossible. Not the least of these situations is a visit to an imprisoned family member. The very act of entering the institution opens one to the scrutiny and judgment of correctional staff. Nearly all of the family members (twenty-seven) in the sample had visited the prison where their loved one was incarcerated, and the vast majority reported multiple incidents of rude or demeaning treatment by correctional guards at the visitor centre. Many reported a general feeling that prisoners' family members were not respected by the corrections staff or treated courteously:

> Most of the staff see you through the same glasses as they see the offenders. They see you as the offender as well. There's very little respect given to families. And interestingly enough, the higher the

security level, the worse it gets ... I remember one time I was waiting to go into a PFV [Private Family Visit] and, um, I was signed in, and you know, most of the staff know who you are and you have no idea who they are, there's just too many of them. And one staff member, they were talking about videos and one staff member asked the other, "What are you gonna watch for videos tonight?" and he said, "Oh, I think I'll get [name of a porn video with the interviewee's first name in the title], which is a common porn video, and because of my name, my first name, um, you know, so it was directed to me. And, like, families just don't deserve, nor do they expect that kind of disrespect. (Catharine, a prisoner's wife)

They're crappy at [the prison]. Really crappy. Um, I can't tell you exactly how because it's, it's more a feeling, a condescending, patronizing type of thing than ... than anything. It's not like you can give a story and say, "Well, they did this, or they did that." Uh, it's like when we go down to [the visiting room from the prison entrance], it depends on the guard. Some of them are miserable as hell. They'll wait 'til everybody's checked in before they'll let one of us through. You know, some of them will let four at a time go. Others don't care. And that takes a good twenty minutes off your visit. (Isobel, a prisoner's wife)

Clearly, the poor treatment of prisoners' family members is not a part of CSC's official policies, which, according to its website, are based on a core value of "respecting the dignity of all persons." However, the seeming prevalence of antagonistic encounters between correctional staff and visitors at penitentiaries across Canada, occurring across various levels of security, suggests that the phenomenon may be more institutionally pervasive than merely based in the prejudices and attitudes of certain individuals. It is likely that the attitudes of the guards are reflective of a larger social stereotype of prisoners and their families as risky individuals who pose a danger to institutional security and possibly to the general public as potential perpetrators of crime. This assumption is embedded in the structure of the institution and its security policies, which appear to direct disproportionate scrutiny at visitors and family members while neglecting to inspect the behaviours of staff, volunteers, suppliers, and professionals to the same degree. Family members are keenly aware of this discrepancy and describe feeling targeted and treated "like criminals." The commissioner's directive on the searching of visitors to federal penitentiaries states that, "in all facilities except minimum security and Community Correctional Centres, there will be a routine non-intrusive search of all visitors upon entering the institution" (Correctional Service of Canada 2004b, 3). However, the precise nature and procedures for these searches are determined by the institutional head of each prison, who is required by the directive to establish an institutional search plan based on the security needs of the institution (ibid.). Likewise, although the directive states that there is also to be a protocol for searching staff upon entry to the prison, policy allows the institutional head a substantial amount of discretion in dictating the scope and types of searches. This discretion is exercised in a way that is consistent with the belief that prisoners' family members might introduce drugs into the prison, these family members being subjected to greater scrutiny than either staff or those who are designated as professional visitors or volunteers.

The ion mobility spectrometry device or ion scanner, as it is commonly referred to, is a constant source of frustration for family members who visit the prison regularly. The ion scanner was introduced to Canadian federal correctional institutions in 2004, and all but three of the interviewees had encountered the device.[6] Two of the wives specifically identified the ion scanner as having profoundly changed their experience of visiting at the prison in a negative way. They characterize its use as assuming criminal involvement where often none is present and feel that they are treated as potential, or actual, criminals:

> Then they put in that ion scanner and for the first little while they were gauging their thing and it wasn't putting up the small quantities of whatever they pick up – I wasn't ringing and in my head I was like, "Well, I don't do drugs, I'm not in contact with drugs, I'll never ring." And then all of a sudden I started. I started to ring ... But, it wasn't regular, and it wasn't like some women I know, they rang almost every week when they went. It never got like that with me. But I started to really resent the fact that I was treated like I had done something wrong when I hadn't. And – I'm so straight, it's crazy! I'm probably straighter than three-quarters of the employees

in there! I do nothing! Nothing! I sit home and take care of my
kids, I have no time to do anything else! (Anne, a prisoner's wife)

Family members who are taking prescription medications often find that
they set off the ion scanner. Three of the interviewees recounted instances
where their use of legally prescribed medications caused them difficulties and
anxiety at institutional security. These types of stories were also a common
topic of discussion during the focus groups. The staff members who operate
the ion scanner are trained to recognize the threshold variations in positive
tests for opiates and other drugs that may be caused by legal prescription
medications. However, even when legitimate prescription medications cause
a positive reading on the ion scanner and staff are informed that the individual has a medical prescription, family members are treated as suspect and
are often detained for lengthy periods while a threat risk assessment is completed to determine if the individual will be allowed to continue visiting the
institution. Family members are very aware that this process could cost them
their visiting privileges, and they perceive a palpable power imbalance between
themselves and the correctional staff. Although the correctional service's need
to prevent the transfer of drugs into the prison is legitimate, family members
who are not involved with drugs but who scan positive often feel that they
are treated in an unnecessarily harsh manner, rather than being processed in
a professional and efficient way.

Anne interpreted the correctional staff's rude treatment after scanning
positive for drugs as a form of humiliation, meant to shame her for her relationship with an incarcerated man. The lack of explanation and information
increases the anxiety and fear family members experience and results in
frustration with the correctional staff:

It's very frustrating [when you test positive on the ion scanner].
And then, if you get somebody that doesn't explain anything to
you, you go sit down and you're like, I don't understand, and then
the guard at the visit will say to you, he goes, "Oh, you rang!?
[sarcastic tone] I mean, nobody else did." Like, aahhh! Hey, listen,
I know I don't do anything! And if I can ring, that means if you
were tested, you would probably ring! You know, like, give me
some credit. But you don't get it, because you're involved with
somebody who, in their eyes, doesn't deserve it. And that gets
to be frustrating. (Anne, a prisoner's wife)

There is not a lot of education given to family members about policy or procedure in terms of corrections. They're just told what to do and if they don't do it, they get refused visits. There's no explanation as to security, security issues. Families don't know what the guys are living inside – they don't know the kinds of things – I mean, we only know what our husbands or boyfriends or sons or nephews tell us, okay, and that's their perception of things. So, we don't know what they're involved in, what they should be staying away from and perhaps are not. So, you know, there's no open communication between staff and family members, which is very, is extremely difficult. Because family members do not want to be embarrassed, they do not want to be made a spectacle of, they do not want to be punished like they're little children – and have done something wrong and they don't even know what they've done wrong. So, it's, it needs to be improved upon, the communication between staff and just, you know, families need to be respected just because they're humans. And it doesn't happen. (Catharine, a prisoner's wife)

In focus groups, the women described a general sense of being targeted and under suspicion – as being the main focus of the CSC's drug prevention policy. In fact, the guidelines for the use of the ion scanner prescribes its use for scanning only visitors to the institution, who are defined as "immediate member[s] of the family (mother, father, sister, brother, spouse or common law spouse); anyone who has been approved to visit the inmate; or any other member of the public entering the institution that is *not a CSC employee*" (Correctional Service of Canada 2004a, 2, emphasis added). There is no reference to scanning employees and contract staff on a regular basis. The institutional emphasis on visitors as a potential source of drugs seems to create a divisive in-group/out-group mindset in the correctional staff, which serves to exacerbate the stigmatic attitudes that individual staff members often present to prisoners' family members. Most of the family members emphasized that the problem is not the routine drug screening – they understand the requirements of institutional security – but the suspicion and disdainful treatment they feel they receive as a result. Family members, on the whole, do not believe that correctional staff are adequately screened for drugs and believe that undue blame is placed on visitors for the quantity of drugs available in prisons:

Well, let's get it this way – you can, a person coming in can't bring a heck of a lot in, for the amount of drugs that are in prisons. So think about it, the suppliers, the people that are bringing in the meats, that sort of thing, um, the guards. I mean in KP [Kingston Penitentiary] if you look at the thing that happened, well ten, fifteen years ago in KP where they had, um, they had massive, I think there was ten guards that were named, the two that committed suicide, whether they actually committed suicide or not, that whole thing was drug related. Um, I mean, John said himself that when he, his father died when he was in prison and one of the guards came up and gave him a drink. Actual liquor, said, "You probably need this" – it should not have been in the prison, right? ... So I mean, you're not gonna, the only way that you could have zero tolerance in a prison is that you test everybody. (Jane, an ex-prisoner's wife)

Most recently, the 2007 CSC Review Panel reported that it was informed by "staff and unions that visitors are considered one of the major sources of drugs coming into the penitentiaries" (Correctional Service of Canada Review Panel 2007, 31). Notably, the role and interest that union and staff members may have in protecting the reputation of the CSC and its employees was not questioned or remarked on, and the panel did not recommend any changes to institutional policy on the screening of correctional staff. However, it did recommend the enhancement of visitor screening and included the advice of the Canadian Centre for Abuse Awareness that "any visitor convicted of attempting to transport illicit drugs or narcotics into institutions be banned for life from entry upon CSC premises" (Canadian Centre for Abuse Awareness, as cited in ibid.). It recommended the increased use of drug dogs, ion scanners, and searches of visitors to the institutions. This narrow focus on visitors as the primary source of drugs trafficked into the prisons, which seemingly excludes CSC staff and contractors from suspicion, reflects a stigmatic view of prisoners' family members and their associates as a risk to institutional security and, by extension, to public safety. Conversely, the correctional staff are perceived to be protecting the public from the dangers related to criminality and drugs and are therefore themselves not risky or subject to suspicion. Power, then, shapes official knowledge about the sources of drugs in prison and affects institutional policy in a way that overtly blames prisoner's family members for introducing drugs into prisons, ignoring the possibility of staff involvement in the institutional drug trade.

The unfortunate reality is that the actions of a few visitors who attempt to import drugs into the prison (and sometimes succeed) affect the treatment of prisoners' families as a whole. The rude and disrespectful treatment that family members often experience does not directly contribute to institutional security, but it does serve a useful function in reinforcing the hierarchy of the institution, which places staff above visitors and inmates. The institutional policies that focus risk management disproportionately on visitors allow individual staff members to justify the stigma they place on family members and perpetuate negative interactions between family members and staff on an individual level. This intersection of institutional security policies and the treatment of visitors exemplify the complex, dyadic relationship that exists between structural and symbolic forms of stigma in which one reinforces the other in a continuous circle. It is the symbolic stigma of association with criminality that initially prompts the definition of prisoners' families as risky individuals, justifying increased surveillance and risk management responses. The risky identity and associated danger to institutional integrity that is assigned to family members then prompts the maintenance of an in-group/out-group division that allows correctional staff to deny prisoners' family members basic respect and courtesy, manifesting in increased symbolic forms of stigma at an interpersonal level. Family members rightly argue that if staff were subject to the same levels of scrutiny and suspicion upon entrance to the institution, they would be more likely to recognize that the individuals entering the prison are not uniformly "risky" and would treat visitors as individuals, reacting to risk on a case-by-case basis rather than prejudging families on the grounds of their association with a convict.

We see similar characterizations of prisoners' families as risky when we look at the few interventions that are designed to assist the families of incarcerated persons and particularly their children. For instance, children with an incarcerated parent often act out and experience difficulties in school and may find themselves involved with child welfare services, mentoring programs, and other social development programs designed to reduce the risk of future offending (see, for example, Virginia Commission on Youth 2002; House of Hope 2003; Withers 2003). Although these interventions are meant to improve the child's current and future welfare, there is no doubt a stigma attached to being singled out as a problem child or future criminal in a classroom or group of children, and interventions may exacerbate the child's acting out by causing him or her to internalize the negative label and stigma. Regardless of the child's individual temperament, behaviour, and prospects, he or she is characterized as being at risk of becoming criminal and labelled by virtue of his or her parent's status as a convicted person. Although the child is being intervened on, and provided programs to mitigate, potential criminality, the home situation, financial difficulties, separation of the family, and stigma in the community are ignored.

## Discussion and Suggestions for Change

The significant symbolic and institutionalized stigma that surrounds criminality and, by extension, prisoners' families perpetuates a social climate that permits the political neglect of these families and their needs. Although not all of the hardships encountered by the families of prisoners are a direct function of stigma or outright discrimination, the social and institutional failure to address these issues can be viewed as the outcome of complex symbolic interactions that construct these families as unworthy of assistance. Symbolic forms of stigma allow discrimination, marginality, and neglect to go unremarked upon, while structural stigma at the level of the institution both creates difficulties and perpetuates the existing symbolic stigma through techniques of risk management. The resulting marginality may not be the intended outcome of institutional policies, but the malign neglect of stigmatized populations and failure to address their needs result in marginalization and negative outcomes. Consequently, steps must be taken to normalize and demarginalize prisoners' families in order to emphasize the need for assistance and services to combat the collateral punishment that we exact through the use of imprisonment. Care should be taken to ensure that services are offered in the spirit of compassion rather than as a technique of risk management, in order to avoid the possibility that stigma will be exacerbated and perpetuated through interventions.

In Canada, we are just beginning to see the mobilization of prisoners' family members toward the creation of social change, as evidenced by the participation of family members in recent colloquia to discuss issues of imprisonment, and by the number of family members whom I spoke with who were actively involved in establishing support services or contemplating possibilities for contribution to change. The participants in my study provided a range of suggestions for services and action to combat the effects of incarceration on families. Many proposed programs and services would address not only the specific needs of families but also the needs of their incarcerated loved ones for appropriate assistance with substance abuse and mental health issues, rehabilitation, and reintegration. They reasoned that any assistance provided to their incarcerated family member would, by extension, relieve some of the concern and pressure placed on them to support and assist in the rehabilitation and re-entry process.

The need for information and to be kept informed was mentioned by almost all the participants. From the point of arrest until the completion of the sentence, family members felt that they were often floundering and were not provided with crucial information about their loved one's situation that would aid them in decision making and planning for the future. Information about everything from the availability of financial aid, to the procedures for visiting correctional institutions, to the needs of the offender upon release was sorely lacking, and family members were not made aware of available services and assistance. Family members repeatedly emphasized the need for information about the court process and the correctional system to be provided much earlier in the process and uniformly offered to the families of all accused persons. Several of the women (both wives and mothers) mentioned that they obtained information about the criminal justice process and the correctional system only through their own resourcefulness and persistence in demanding answers to their questions. They emphasized that not everyone would have the tenacity or ability to chase down the information that they need in order to obtain assistance. Families that are the most marginalized by virtue of poverty or lack of education are least likely to obtain information about much needed services.

The availability of existing services should be standardized to all federal penitentiaries and expanded to meet the needs of all families. The assistance that does exist is not uniformly available and depends on the geographic and social location of the penitentiary. Often the families that are travelling the furthest to prisons in remote or rural areas have the least access to services. The provision of financial and material support was another item on family members' wish list of services, particularly as it pertained to the costs of visiting and maintaining contact with their loved ones. There were suggestions that the CSC could provide staple groceries for the private family visiting facilities (rather than having family members provide all of their own groceries), subsidized travel to penitentiaries that are remote or inaccessible on public transportation, and subsidized or CSC-run accommodations for families that must travel long distances to visit. Even more ideally, the CSC could prioritize and expedite the transfer of prisoners who are incarcerated far from their families to ensure that the sentence is served in the closest suitable facility to the family home. This would not only decrease the cost and logistical difficulties of visiting but enable families to visit more frequently and maintain closer relationships. The cost of telephone calls from the prisons, always a point of frustration for family members, was also raised as an area in which the CSC could make changes to alleviate costs for prisoners' families. While the new phone card system is an attempt to address this issue, as I have already discussed, it is not without limitations and still poses an ongoing cost to families of incarcerated men. It is clear that further improvements could be made in this area.

Family members also mentioned the need for personal emotional support and advocacy to be provided by someone who understands the criminal justice system and its effects on prisoners and their families. The element of understanding is mentioned as a very important criterion in identifying those who are best placed to provide support to family members. At the very least, those who offer assistance to the families of prisoners must be educated about the collateral punishment of imprisonment and sensitive to the needs of these families. That is, if services to prisoners' families were to be centralized and linked to the CSC or provincial or federal justice departments, staff should be selected for their compassion toward families and their ability to separate their view of the family from the stigma of the criminal offence. Ideally, efforts for change would contribute to the ultimate goal of breaking down and delegitimizing the sticky stigma that is attached to the families of prisoners.

Prisoners' families are not the only population to be caught in the vicious cycle of stigma, marginality, risk management, and neglect. This model is theoretically useful for examining the situations of many groups that have been constructed as risky or dangerous to an institutional and/or social order. Among these, in the Western context, one might consider gays, lesbians, and transgendered persons, those who belong to marginalized ethnic or religious groups, those in marginal occupations (that is, sex work), criminalized persons, the homeless, the mentally ill, drug users, and others. Each of these populations, in its own way, has been discredited and subject to institutionalized risk management that perpetuates symbolic (and often erroneous) stereotypes and the social neglect of important issues affecting the group as a whole.

## The Promise of Criminology for Families Affected by Incarceration

In this chapter, we have taken just a brief look at the myriad effects of incarceration on families in Canada, particularly the negative financial implications of lost income and the added costs of maintaining contact with an incarcerated loved one. There are many variations on these experiences and many more issues that we do not have space to explore here.[7] I have shown that these effects are highly gendered and used my data to make an argument about the gendered nature of sticky stigma. We have also considered the impact of individualized, symbolic stigma and the larger consequences of institutionalized, structural stigma that is bound up with risk management. It is important to recognize the collateral effects of incarceration on families and the relationship between these difficulties and the stigmatic attitudes that perpetuate these issues in order to take effective steps toward breaking down stigma and demarginalizing the families of prisoners.

The focus of criminology has traditionally been narrowly centred on offending, in the search for a causal theory of crime and an understanding of the processes of regulation. Indeed, Arrigo (2000, 2001) argues that critical criminology has traditionally maintained a (misguided) focus on crime and criminality at the expense of social justice. More recently, victims and victimization have entered into the picture as an area worthy of inquiry. However, as feminists saw the need to move beyond their first-world, white, middle-class conception of liberation, so must a new generation of criminologists widen the lens of inquiry to include those who are not necessarily primary victims or offenders but are nonetheless marginalized by the processes of the criminal justice system.

The promise of criminology for the next generation is the epistemological space to explore sites of marginalization that have previously been overlooked and to engage with the iatrogenic consequences of our responses to crime and victimization. As the criminological lens widens to include broader interpretations of crime and human rights violations (see Woolford, this volume; Williams, this volume), new experiences of victimization and marginality will also emerge and seek a voice and legitimization in criminological theory and advocacy. Shifting our concern to a larger understanding of social justice opens the space in criminology to shed light on injustices and work through research and advocacy to address the pains of marginalization, such as those experienced by the families of prisoners.

## ACKNOWLEDGMENTS
I wish to acknowledge the helpful comments of Aaron Doyle, Flo Kellner, and Katharine Kelly on earlier versions of this chapter, as well as the financial support of the Social Sciences and Humanities Research Council of Canada and Carleton University.

## NOTES

1   One limitation of the first sample noted is that it included only one person who identified as Aboriginal. Further research should explore in more detail the specific effects of incarceration on the loved ones of First Nations prisoners, especially given the overrepresentation of Aboriginal people in the penal system. For a fuller discussion of the methods, sample, and process of recruiting interviewees for the research see Hannem (2008).

2   And those studies that do not make this claim (for example, Condry 2007) do not engage with the question of financial or practical difficulties.

3   Many imprisoned women are already single mothers, or existing relationships may dissolve post-incarceration. In the absence of a father, the dependent children of incarcerated women are most often sent to live with extended family or put into foster care. Thus, the burden of raising children and coping with issues of incarceration is often shifted to a female relative – the mother or sister of the incarcerated woman, for instance.

4   A pilot project allowing the use of prepaid phone cards was tested in Ontario and Quebec in late 2008 with nation-wide implementation in early 2010.

5   This problem is even greater for female inmates, given the relative paucity of correctional facilities for women (see Maidment 2006).

6   Of the three, one, a sister, had not encountered the ion scanner because she did not visit the prison, and the other two were wives who had visited the prison but whose loved ones had been released before the ion scanner was introduced in 2004.

7   For more information on families affected by incarceration in Canada, see Withers (2003) and Hannem (2008).

## REFERENCES
Anderson, N. 1965. *When Father Goes to Gaol.* Melbourne: Victorian Council of Social Service.

–. 1967. Prisoners' Families: Unmet Needs and Social Policy. *Australian Journal of Social Issues* 3(1): 9-17.

Arditti, J.A., J. Lambert-Shute, and K. Joest. 2003. Saturday Morning at the Jail: Implications of Incarceration for Families and Children. *Family Relations* 52(3): 195-204.

Arrigo, B.A. 2000. Social Justice and Critical Criminology: On Integrating Knowledge. *Contemporary Justice Review* 3(1): 7-37.

–. 2001. Critical Criminology, Existential Humanism and Social Justice: Exploring the Contours of Conceptual Integration. *Critical Criminology* 10(2): 83-95.

Bakker, L.J., B.A. Morris, and L.M. Janus. 1978. Hidden Victims of Crime. *Social Work* 23(2): 143-48.

Bernstein, N. 2005. *All Alone in the World: Children of the Incarcerated.* New York: New Press.

Blackwell, J. 1959. *The Effects of Involuntary Separation on Selected Families of Men Committed to Prison from Spokane County, Washington.* PhD diss., State College of Washington.

Bloodgood, R.S. 1928. *Welfare of Prisoners' Families in Kentucky.* US Department of Labor, Children's Bureau. Publication no. 182. Washington, DC: US Government Printing Office.

Boswell, G., and P. Wedge. 2002. *Imprisoned Fathers and Their Children.* London: Jessica Kingsley.

Carlson, B.E., and N. Cervera. 1992. *Inmates and Their Wives: Incarceration and Family Life.* Westport, CT: Greenwood Press.

Casey-Acevedo, K., and T. Bakken. 2002. Visiting Women in Prison: Who Visits and Who Cares? *Journal of Offender Rehabilitation* 34(3): 67-83.

Christian, J. 2005. Riding the Bus: Barriers to Prison Visitation and Family Management Strategies. *Journal of Contemporary Criminal Justice* 21(1): 31-48.

Comfort, M.L. 2003. In the Tube at San Quentin: The "Secondary Prisonization" of Women Visiting Inmates. *Journal of Contemporary Ethnography* 32(1): 77-107.

–. 2008. *Doing Time Together: Love and Family in the Shadow of the Prison.* Chicago: University of Chicago Press.

Condry, R. 2007. *Families Shamed: The Consequences of Crime for the Relatives of Serious Offenders.* Cullompton, UK: Willan.

Correctional Service of Canada (CSC). 2004a. *Technical Requirements for Ion Mobility Spectrometry Devices: Guidelines 566-8-2.* Ottawa: CSC, http://www.csc-scc.gc.ca/text/plcy/doc/566-8-2gl.pdf.

–. 2004b. *Use of Non-Intrusive Search Tools: Guidelines 566-8-1.* Ottawa: CSC, http://www.csc-scc.gc.ca/text/plcy/doc/566-8-1gl.pdf.

Correctional Service of Canada Review Panel. 2007. *A Roadmap to Strengthening Public Safety: Report of the Correctional Service of Canada Review Panel.* Ottawa: Minister of Public Works and Government Services Canada, http://www.publicsafety.gc.ca/csc-scc/cscrprprt-eng.pdf.

Cullen, B.T., and M. Pretes. 2000. The Meaning of Marginality: Interpretations and Perceptions in Social Science. *Social Science Journal* 37(2): 215-29.

Curtis, R.L., and S. Schulman. 1984. Ex-Offenders, Family Relations and Economic Supports: The "Significant Women" Study of the TARP Project. *Crime and Delinquency* 30(4): 507-28.

Fishman, L. 1990. *Women at the Wall: A Study of Prisoners' Wives Doing Time on the Outside.* New York: SUNY Press.

Gabel, K., and D. Johnston, eds. 1995. *Children of Incarcerated Parents.* New York: Lexington Books.

Girshick, L.B. 1996. *Soledad Women: Wives of Prisoners Speak Out.* Westport, CT: Praeger.

Goffman, E. 1963. *Stigma: Notes on the Management of Spoiled Identity.* Englewood Cliffs, NJ: Prentice Hall.

Gray, D.E. 2002. "Everybody just freezes. Everybody is just embarrassed": Felt and Enacted Stigma among Parents of Children with High-Functioning Autism. *Sociology of Health and Illness* 24(6): 734-49.

Gutting, G. 2005. *Foucault: A Very Short Introduction.* Oxford: Oxford University Press.

Hacking, I. 2004. Between Michel Foucault and Erving Goffman: Between Discourse in the Abstract and Face-to-Face Interaction. *Economy and Society* 33(3): 277-302.

Hannem, S. 2008. *Marked by Association: Stigma, Marginalisation, Gender and the Families of Male Prisoners in Canada.* Phd diss., Carleton University.

House of Hope. 2003. *Families of Offenders Awareness Campaign.* Ottawa: House of Hope and Ministry of Public Safety and Emergency Preparedness Canada.

Kampf, A. 2008. "A little world of your own": Stigma, Gender and Narratives of Venereal Disease Contact Tracing. *Health* 12(2): 233-50.

Liker, J.K. 1981. Economic Pressures on the Families of Released Prisoners: Evidence from the TARP Experiment. *Cornell Journal of Social Relations* 16(1): 11-27.

Lowenstein, A. 1984. Coping with Stress: The Case of Prisoners' Wives. *Journal of Marriage and the Family* 46(3): 699-708.

–. 1986. Temporary Single Parenthood – the Case of Prisoners' Families. *Family Relations* 35(1): 79-85.

Maidment, M.R. 2006. *Doing Time on the Outside: Deconstructing the Benevolent Community.* Toronto: University of Toronto Press.

Marstone, C. 2005. *Loving Through Bars: Children with Parents in Prison.* Santa Monica, CA: Santa Monica Press.

Morris, P. 1965. *Prisoners and Their Families.* London: George Allen and Unwin.

Parke, R.D., and K.A. Clarke-Stewart. 2003. The Effects of Parental Incarceration on Children: Perspectives, Promises, and Policies. In *Prisoners Once Removed: The Impact of Incarceration and Reentry on Children, Families and Communities*, ed. J. Travis and M. Waul, 189-232. Washington, DC: Urban Institute Press.

Ricordeau, G. 2008. *Les Détenus et leurs proches: Solidarités et sentiments à l'ombre des murs.* Paris: Éditions Autrements.

Roberts, J.V. 2006. The Ethics of Collateral Punishment. *Justice Report* 21(3): 1-3.

Sacks, J.G. 1938. *The Social and Economic Adjustments of Families of a Selected Group of Imprisoned Felons.* MA thesis, Catholic University of America.

Schneller, D.P. 1976. *The Prisoner's Family: A Study of the Effects of Imprisonment on the Families of Prisoners.* San Francisco: R. and E. Research Associates.

Seymour, C., and C.F. Hairston, eds. 2001. *Children with Parents in Prison: Child Welfare Policy, Program and Practice Issues.* New Brunswick, NJ: Transaction.

Shaw, R., ed. 1992. *Prisoners' Children: What Are the Issues?* London: Routledge.

Smith, G., K. Mysak, and S. Michael. 2008. Sexual Double Standards and Sexually Transmitted Illnesses: Social Rejection and Stigmatization of Women. *Sex Roles: A Journal of Research* 58(5-6): 391-401.

Virginia Commission on Youth. 2002. *Children of Incarcerated Parents: To the Governor and General Assembly of Virginia.* Richmond: Virginia Commission on Youth.

Withers, L. 2003. *A Strategic Approach and Policy Document to Address the Needs of Families of Offenders: Safety – Respect and Dignity – for All.* Kingston, ON: Canadian Families and Corrections Network, http://www.cfcn-rcafd.org/text/EngConsultation.pdf.

Zalba, S.R. 1964. *Women Offenders and Their Families.* Los Angeles: Delmar.

**PART 3**

# Theory and Praxis

The relationship between theory and praxis has been a central criminological concern since the early Marxist and feminist challenges to mainstream criminology. This concluding section takes up this theme in light of contemporary political projects and emerging theoretical orientations. Gillian Balfour outlines problematic attributes of contemporary critical criminological theory that become apparent when they are assessed from a critical feminist perspective. The co-authored contribution by George Rigakos and Jon Frauley argues that critical criminology would be greatly strengthened by adopting critical realist metatheory. Lisa Freeman's contribution is derived from her dual role as academic and activist, a position that provides unique opportunities to examine the dynamics of power and work for progressive social change. Kevin Walby's piece sketches the possibilities of an anarcho-abolitionist criminology.

Balfour is wary of critical feminists' embrace of governmentality and risk theory. These orientations have unmasked some of the dynamics of governmental practices, yet they appear to exclude women's voices and concerns from their analytical framework. This is particularly troubling given that governmentality approaches do not account for large-scale relations of domination or exploitation, consequently foregoing the key issue of praxis.

Balfour charts the confluence of theoretical and political factors that have culminated in this problematic situation. These can be traced to the 1970s crisis of capitalism and the attendant entrenchment of a reactionary criminal justice system and cuts in social service spending. In the face of these challenges, feminist criminologists struggled to introduce measures to improve the situation of female inmates. Their notable successes include the greater prominence given to the concerns of women in Canadian prison reforms and the emergence of domestic violence and sexual assault as official policy issues. By the mid-1990s, however, many of these promising developments started to unravel, and new political challenges began to emerge. The Arbour Commission of Inquiry into the so-called riot and cell extractions at the now defunct Prison for Women documented a long history of unequal treatment of women inmates. Highly publicized claims were advanced suggesting that men and women were equally violent. Rape shield provisions were facing persistent legal challenges. As all of this was occurring, the incarceration rate for women began to rise significantly.

A comparable series of crises emerged within critical feminist criminology. Feminists had been criticized for advancing a narrow image of women as victims of male violence, whereas race scholars called for a broader conceptual framework that would interrogate the intersections of race, class, and gender. Feminists ultimately embraced a form of identity politics that espoused an anti-essentialism and championed notions of difference. These changes in analytical orientation coincided with the emergence of neo-liberal free market policies that saw marginal and oppressed groups increasingly responsibilized and subject to risk profiling practices. Women were increasingly being incarcerated for comparatively minor offences that were themselves attributable to conditions produced by neo-liberal cuts to social service. Feminists oriented toward the cultural politics of difference were ill-equipped to deal with this rapid rise in women's incarceration. Moreover, the prominence of risk theory and a Foucauldian governmentality orientation appeared to set aside the increasingly coercive role of the state and foreclose the possibility of women's emancipation. The material conditions of criminalized women were obscured by an approach that offered few possibilities for social action. Although some risk theorists called for the engendering of the concept of risk, it remained unclear if risk theory could account for the specificity of gender. Hence, analysts were moving away from analyzing the specific situation of women at the precise moment when women were increasingly being incarcerated for offences linked to poverty, sexual exploitation, addiction, and mental health.

To rectify this situation, Balfour advocates for an explicitly critical feminist criminology, one that embraces a realist ontology that is both deeply political and theoretical. Part of this project involves a revitalized standpoint feminism. This orientation was particularly successful in engendering criminology and encouraging feminists to link theory to activism, in the process becoming more accountable for the transformative potentials of their research. It also revealed that women's law-breaking behaviour often entailed strategies to cope with highly gendered forms of marginalization and oppression. Today, a reinvigorated embrace of standpoint approaches should move toward a more complicated understanding of the political and economic contexts of women's lives in order to reveal the cultural, gendered, and class underpinnings of their experiences. Women's narratives should be repositioned as potentially subversive stories capable of revealing the connections between biography and history through personalized accounts of violence, poverty, and racism as a means to expose the brute repression of the state.

Like Balfour, George Rigakos and Jon Frauley are also concerned about the embrace of risk theory and governmentality orientations among critical criminologists. They begin their chapter with a series of questions about ontology that they argue need to be addressed in order for researchers to produce potentially progressive forms of knowledge. They contend that these questions can be addressed through the metatheory of critical realism. Rigakos and Frauley go on to demonstrate this point by challenging what they see as a popular reading of Michel Foucault's work, one they argue has culminated in researchers deploying contradictory and ultimately untenable ontological positions.

The need to address ontological issues is related to broader changes in the discipline. Where criminology was historically one component of the larger social scientific project to solve social problems, today many criminologists reject the call to rectify social problems as conceptualized through state-centred definitions of crime. Instead, these researchers aim to examine the social, political, and economic relations that support and advance distinctive visions of criminality. Such inquiries have highlighted the need to ground our theories in a sound epistemological and ontological base, yet they have also fostered passionate debates culminating in the current situation, where, Rigakos and Frauley maintain, analysts are offered the false choice between positivist scientism and a form of relativist constructionism. Rigakos and Frauley propose critical realism as a remedy for this situation, arguing that it would provide the discipline with greater ontological rigour.

Two basic and interrelated epistemological arguments characterize critical realism. The first is that reality exists independent of human beings and human understanding; reality is utterly indifferent to our endeavours. The second position is a form of fallibilism, a stance recognizing that knowledge does not necessarily accumulate over time and is always open to revision. Other attributes involve an acknowledgment that social objects are emergent and that unobserved entities can be inferred from what is seen or measured. In the social sciences, this entails a concern to recognize social action as conditioned by social structure – something that is itself alterable and continually undergoing transformation.

Although Rigakos and Frauley advocate for a form of realist science, they distinguish their work from other versions of "science" and "realism." Science is often conflated with scientism, or the appearance of doing science, a position associated with positivist metatheory. In contrast, critical realism involves a form of post-empiricist social scientific practice. It is a metatheory that can be used to craft descriptions of the world and to explain social relations. In the process it offers transcendental arguments that must be translated into workable research frameworks that involve a speculative dimension, as analysts are encouraged to contemplate and search gaps in their empirical data.

Rigakos and Frauley distinguish their "realist" position from the criminological "realism," advocated by left realists, who attempt to be "realistic" through what the authors see as surface descriptions of empirical domains. As Rigakos and Frauley note, one of the tensions inherent in left realism derives from its failure to come to grips with its undertheorized ontology or its metatheory in relation to philosophical realism.

Rigakos and Frauley argue that difficulties are particularly apparent among Foucauldian governmentality scholars, whom, they charge, engage in anti-realist posturing and then proceed to treat their objects of analysis as real. Such authors have popularized a distinctive reading of Foucault as anti-structuralist, anti-realist, and anti-criminological. In the process, Rigakos and Frauley argue, these scholars have propagated a series of misconceptions about Foucault's project and his ontology, something that has contributed to the rise of purely empirical research that is guilty of judging surface phenomena for the real. In the context of criminology, this entails overlooking how crime involves complex processes of social ordering, ultimately leaving analysts incapable of theorizing socially necessary relations. This popular relativist reading of Foucault is seen by Rigakos and Frauley to actually clash with Foucault's body of work, which contains numerous empirical studies that embrace a form of ontological realism. Indeed, Rigakos and Frauley suggest that Foucault was akin to a critical realist, as evidenced by his search for hidden attributes of social institutions and his appeal to durably underlying historical tendencies.

Rigakos and Frauley urge criminologists to "get real," which would involve undertaking research projects that seek to explore and understand the underlying causal mechanisms that produce social phenomena. For criminologists, this would involve examining how crime is related to unobservable generative processes, something that is best undertaken by using the concepts and premises furnished by critical realism.

Lisa Freeman continues exploring the theme of activism in her reflections on the prospects for progressive activists to alter dominant spatial relations. Her contribution is derived from her personal involvement in the case of *R. v. Ackerley et al.* That case resulted from a police raid on a squat in the house at 246 Gilmour Street in Ottawa. After it had been left unused for seven years, a group of activists occupied the house as a means to raise public awareness of the existing housing crisis. Ultimately, twenty-two squatters were arrested in a dramatic police raid involving tear gas and pepper spray. Five of these squatters chose to defend themselves rather than accept the

Crown's plea offer of community service. At the conclusion of the trial, the jurors were deadlocked, prompting the Crown to declare a mistrial and drop the charges. The squatters declared a victory.

Freeman interrogates this case to outline the possibilities for using legal geography to understand the constitutive role of space, law, and power and to accentuate the political importance of grassroots activism in the criminal courts. Legal geography adopts a critical orientation to the role of law, focusing on its constitutive nature. It provides theoretical tools to explore how activist legal advocacy can alter the spaces for political dissent in the courtroom. In the process, it offers other opportunities to contemplate the politics of space within institutional locations of power.

Freeman concentrates on the spatial dynamics in the case of *R. v. Ackerley et al.*, in particular on how activists interacted with and challenged the protocols surrounding the proper use of space and spatial dynamics in the courtroom. She accentuates that space is not an empty container but is instead grounded in everyday activities of social life, containing considerable diversity of conceptual objects. The structures, procedures, and sanctions of a criminal trial are one example of an absolute space – which refers to lived space, including symbolic dimensions and an assumed strict form. It takes material form in the ordering and governing of people. Within the courtroom, activists encountered a well-defined hierarchy and series of designated roles, each partially defined by their occupation of a certain space.

The activists' successes in this case can be judged along several axes. It appears that they made gains in altering the legal rights and consciousness of the public. They also may have established informal guidelines that would help future defendants secure financial support for their cases. In addition, they created new vulnerabilities in institutional power by challenging the demarcation between law and power. Such successes lead Freeman to conclude that researchers should transcend the traditional division between activism and research. Research based on activist intervention provides opportunities for scholarly research and for progressive change.

Kevin Walby's contribution also addresses anarchism, using it to critique conservative and liberal criminology. Walby draws together penal abolitionism with anarchist thought to outline what he calls anarcho-abolitionism. Conservative criminology and liberal criminology are both bound up with notions of private property, hierarchy, and authority, and with the sovereign state, he points out. Walby argues that we should think of justice beyond the criminal justice industry and think of the political beyond the state.

Walby positions anarcho-abolitionism against conservative and liberal branches of criminology and reviews various critiques of such criminology. Although there are differences in emphasis in these branches, they share a reliance on police and prison sentences – in short, on the existing criminal justice industry. Liberal realists want to reform the existing system. British left realists famously suggested that we should take crime seriously, recognizing the devastating implications of intra-class crime. Researchers working in this tradition have focused on reducing crime and violence in deprived inner-city neighbourhoods through a strong interventionist state. Although few Canadian criminologists have specifically identified as left realists, a larger number could be identified as liberal realists. They advocate short-term policy initiatives to reduce poverty and to increase integration and access to rights. Walby faults such thinkers for reifying "crime" and defining it in individual terms, and for abandoning critique. Most problematically, they appear to take for granted the need for a strong interventionist state.

Walby then goes on to outline his vision of anarcho-abolitionism. In contrast to conservative and liberal criminologies, abolitionists tend to concentrate on how social structures reproduce criminalization. They consequently advocate for forms of decentralization, decriminalization, decategorization, demedicalization, and decarceration. Walby synthesizes a form of anarcho-abolitionism that is distinctive by virtue of how it starts with the question of politics, and with a concern to reveal what has been concealed. Anarcho-abolitionists start from the position that punishment through pain is barbaric and consequently seek to abolish or reduce punitive organizations and create ways to handle conflict outside of criminal justice.

Walby notes the foundational role in critical criminology of Taylor, Walton, and Young's 1973 book *The New Criminology* and argues that, although it challenges much criminological orthodoxy, it retains fundamental difficulties concerning the role of the state. Walby situates his anarcho-abolitionism against Marxism. Like Marxists, anarchists oppose private property and the capitalist division of labour, but where Marxists may embrace a new kind of state power, anarchists see the state as something that constrains human development. Hence, they avoid the Marxist appeal to revolution in favour of a focus on ongoing processes of self-administration. Anarchists believe that power should be deployed relationally and advocate for political sociation based on voluntary non-hierarchical relations. Hence, there is a focus on self-control and self-organizing, combined with a call for smaller scale governance through local collectives.

Walby goes on to elaborate what he means by "anarcho-abolitionism." Walby argues that anarcho-abolitionism operates both as a theoretical orientation and as a practice of engaged struggle. There is a break with what Walby refers to as the "kindness towards reason" of earlier anarchists such as Proudhon and Bakunin. Walby challenges the defeatism of previous critics of community forms of dealing with confrontation, who argue that alternatives to prison will always emulate the logic of the state-driven penal system. He argues instead that we should not assume that institutions of authority will always dominate and colonize the self-organizing capacities of people. He also argues that, from the anarcho-abolitionist perspective, restorative justice will be fatally flawed if it remains parasitic on the state-based retributive justice system.

To elaborate further what is meant by "anarcho-abolitionism" and situate it in the field of critical criminology, Walby positions it against peacemaking criminology, with which it shares some commonality – for example, a focus on reducing human suffering and on advocating for non-violence. However, it does not, for example, share peacemaking's overt religious overtones; rather, it is tied more with a tradition of direct action. Walby gives examples of what he sees as already existing anarcho-abolitionism and discusses the activities of various organizations that challenge the prison-industrial complex. He makes an impassioned plea: "One could list a thousand more groups involved in struggle against the prison-industrial complex and related state agencies. The point is not to list but to get involved, to stray, as far as possible, from the label 'criminologist' and what that has traditionally meant."

# 8
# Reimagining a Feminist Criminology

*Gillian Balfour*

Like much of recent critical criminology, feminist criminology has been influenced by a "Foucault effect" (see Smart 1989; Worrall 1990; Bell 1993, 2002; Carrington 1993, 2002; Howe 1994; Razack 1998, 2002; Hannah-Moffat 2001). The appeal and promise of Foucault's lectures and essays on governmentality offer interesting possibilities for the analysis of power outside, or on the periphery of, the formal state apparatus (Pavlich 1996), the micro physics of power, and how populations are governed via techniques of self-regulation (Macleod and Durrheim 2002). In this chapter, I identify a more troubling aspect of the governmentality gaze on criminalized and imprisoned women regarding a loss of women's voices and their experiences of social exclusion, and the disappearance of praxis from critical Foucauldian-inspired feminist criminology. Specifically, I show how post-structuralist claims "that the state has no essential necessity of functionality" (Rose and Miller 1992, cited in Curtis 1995, 580) complements the current regime of neo-liberalism. Like neo-liberalism, post-structuralists, and in particular governmentality scholars, eschew causality of social problems that does not account for the large relations of exploitation and domination that underpin the changes in material conditions – the crisis of capital and the demise of welfarism – that have transformed the forms and programs of power (Curtis 1995). I question whether feminist criminologists have suitably theorized about, and advocated for, criminalized and imprisoned women when not fully acknowledging the economic and social impacts of neo-liberalism. To this end, I suggest a reimagining of a critical feminist criminology so that questions of "why?" and "what is to be done?" may be addressed.

## Losing Ground: Feminist Criminologies in Neo-Liberal Times
In the early 1970s, powerful Western economies, including the United States, Britain, and, to a lesser degree, Canada, saw a crisis of production that gave

way to a neo-liberal economic model premised on deregulation, privatization, and individualism (Ratner and McMullan 1983). Neo-liberal economics were concomitantly legitimated by a neo-conservative political ideology that further entrenched a reactionary criminal justice system (Platt 1987). Administrative criminologists such as James Q. Wilson (1983, cited in Edsall 1991, 214) in the United States argued that street crime was brought on by "the shiftless poor who were dangerous and permissive people victimizing decent citizens." Thus, neo-liberalism introduced massive cuts in spending on social services, health, and education, while neo-conservative political strategies bolstered coercive institutions such as the military, police, and prisons (Platt and Takagi 1977).

The feminist project at this time, however, shifted toward a politics of identity (Daly 1997). As Nancy Fraser (2005, 5) aptly puts it, North American feminism decoupled culture from the political economy just as neo-liberalism was on the rise: "The timing could not have been worse. The shift to a culturalized politics of recognition occurred at precisely the moment when neoliberalism was staging its spectacular comeback." In Canada during the 1980s, the politics of identity underpinned key law and policy reforms. In many ways, these were heady times for feminist criminologists in Canada as they watched decades of activism finally begin to pay off. Significant prison reforms were underway (Correctional Service of Canada 1990); women offenders were no longer "correctional afterthoughts" (Fabiano and Ross 1985); domestic violence was taken seriously by the criminal justice system (Johnson 1996); and important statutory changes to sexual assault laws were implemented (Roberts and Mohr 1994).

By the mid 1990s, however, things started to unravel. More women were being incarcerated, especially black and Native women (Snider 1994, 2003; Pollack 2000, 2004). Despite promises to the contrary, some women prisoners continued to be confined in men's maximum security prisons (Pate 2005). In 1996, a commission of inquiry headed by Madame Justice Louise Arbour was set up following the strip-searching of eight women prisoners by a male Institutional Emergency Response Team in full riot gear, followed by the involuntary transfer of six women to segregation in cells adjacent to the men's sex offender treatment unit. The Arbour report "found a culture of disrespect for the rule of law and a long history of unequal treatment of women prisoners" (Arbour 1996, 239, cited in Horii, Parkes, and Pate 2006, 307). As well, a moral panic was emerging, claiming that women were men's equals in violence (Pearson 1997; Minaker and Snider 2006). Women were increasingly charged under zero tolerance protocols for domestic violence when calling the police for protection (Snider 1994; Wood 2001). Several constitutional challenges were launched against the "rape shield provision" of the Criminal Code, threatening to dismantle hard-won protections of women's privacy (Busby 1997, 1999).[1]

Critical feminist criminology seemed to be at a crossroads. Laureen Snider (1994) questioned the feminist practice of relying on the criminal justice system and its ethic of punishment. Elizabeth Comack (1999) pointed out that feminist criminology still remained on the margins of the discipline and had constructed a narrow image of women as victims of male violence, simplifying the role of violence in women's lives. As well, critical race scholars saw white feminist criminologists engaged in ethnocentric thinking and called for a much broader conceptual framework to examine the interrelationship of race, class, and gender in historical context (Rice 1990; Crenshaw 1994). This fracturing of critical feminist criminology was taking place in a particular socio-political context of emerging "free market fundamentalism" (Fraser 2005, 299) that was to have ruinous effects on the lives of women.

The unravelling of the Keynesian welfare state under the sway of neoliberalism was symbolized in the "death of the social" (Rose 1996a) – whereby the state was no longer responsible for the security and safety of its citizens (Brodie 1995; Hudson 1998; Cossman and Fudge 2002). Within academe, Foucault's later essays on governmentality – the mentality of governance – quickly supplanted modernist criminologies with notions of rhizomatic circuits of inclusion and exclusion: a seeming archipelago of institutional responses mired in risk thinking (Rose 2000). To this end, the state functions as "a partner and animator rather than provider and manager" (ibid., 327), and individuals prudently manage their own risk of victimization via education and expert advice (O'Malley 1996).

To be sure, feminist criminologists such as Hannah-Moffat (1999, 2000, 2001, 2004) and Barbara Hudson (1998, 2002) have worked to engender the conceptualization of risk as a complex practice of power rooted in moral subjectivities, not just actuarial methods of measurement and prediction. For example, Hannah-Moffat (1999) asserts that the women-centred risk assessment technologies designed by the Correctional Service of Canada are a hybrid of subjective moralizing assessments and objective actuarial determinations. Hannah-Moffat's work reveals how the conflation of risk and gender categories allows for subjective interpretation of women's needs as risks. In more recent work, looking at the decision-making process of the

National Parole Board in cases of accelerated review for women seeking conditional release, Hannah-Moffat (2004) argues against the overdetermined fixed or static risk subject that requires actuarial justice to minimize the risk of escape or recidivism. Rather, she contends that technologies of risk assessment are designed to be dynamic and inclusive only of those needs that can be met through intervention or treatment. Hannah-Moffat (ibid., 29) asserts that such reformulation of risk allows for a renaissance of rehabilitation to supposedly meet women's needs through cognitive behavioural therapies, rather than attending to needs for employment, education, and housing. The prisoner is a "transformative subject" who must change her criminal thinking. Hannah-Moffat's research (1999, 2004) is a potent critique of the Correctional Service of Canada's women-centred correctional model, in particular, its obfuscation of the feminization of poverty, systemic racism, and patriarchal violence as legitimate risk factors.

Despite such a cogent analysis of the implications of these new politics of punishment for women, Fraser (2005, 299) points out that feminists, rather than initiating a redoubling of their analysis of the neo-liberal state, "unwittingly diverted feminist theory into culturalist channels arguing over notions of anti-essentialism and difference." Nowhere was this diversion more evident than in the words of once socialist feminist, now post-structuralist, legal scholar Carol Smart (1995, 47, cited in Snider 2003, 354), who called on feminists to denounce modernist criminology "as an endeavour inescapably bound up with greater and greater complicity with the mechanisms of discipline." It would seem, in their efforts to avoid being implicated in the disciplining of women, feminists were being encouraged to abandon the state and gender as limited conceptual tools and, in the process, have forsaken women whose lives are inextricably linked to the state (Currie 1992). This paradigm shift within feminist criminology left us ill-prepared to adequately theorize the ensuing "incarceration spiral" (Snider 2003, 354).

Despite declining crime rates, the numbers of incarcerated women have increased internationally. In the United States, between 1990 and 2000, the total number of women under correctional control increased 81 percent, whereas the number of men increased 45 percent (Bloom, Owen, and Covington 2003, 1). In Britain, the number of women prisoners increased 100 percent between 1993 and 1998, as compared with a 45-percent increase for men (Snider 2003). In Australia, female prison populations doubled between 1982 and 1998 (Grant 1999, 1). Julia Sudbury (2005, xvii) eloquently argues that this "global lockdown" of women includes immigration detention centres and psychiatric hospitals and is the manifestation of global capital-ism's prison-industrial complex, intended to "warehouse those surplus to the global economy and creating profits for private prison operators and cor-porations servicing prisons."

In Canada, Native and black poor single mothers convicted of prostitu-tion or property-related offences such as theft and fraud are greatly over-represented in the criminal justice system (Commission on Systemic Racism in the Ontario Criminal Justice System 1995; Hannah-Moffat 2000; Monture-Angus 2000; Pollack 2000).[2] The rate of women's incarceration has been steadily increasing; between 1997 and 2006, the population of federally sentenced women increased by 22 percent (Pollack 2009, 84). The number of women charged under the Criminal Code for non-violent offences has increased by 54 percent since 1977 (Finn et al. 1999, cited in Snider 2003, 370). Kim Pate (1999, 2005) argues that these data suggest the increased imprisonment of women is associated with welfare reforms, cuts to expendi-tures for social services, mental health, and education. The auditor general of Canada reports that 77 percent of Canadians accessing social service agen-cies, such as income assistance, public housing, and daycare, are women (Canada, Auditor General 2003). Thus, as neo-liberal governments claw back social services and income assistance, create new crime categories of welfare fraud, set up "snitch lines" for neighbours to report welfare recipients, legis-late expansive definitions of "spouse" that further isolate those on welfare from creating supportive relationships, and grant intrusive powers to case workers to monitor the conduct of the poor, women are increasingly vulner-able to criminalization (Chunn and Gavigan 2004).

Despite these very real effects of neo-liberal policies as gendering strat-egies, some governmentality theorists appear to set aside the increasingly coercive role of the state (see Rose and Miller 1992) and are content to theor-ize about "new technologies of freedom, [that] have been invented to govern 'at a distance'" (Rose 2000, 324). In doing so, "it is necessary to de-centre the criminal justice system – codes, courts, and constables – and to relocate the problem of crime and its control within a broader field of rationalities and technologies for the conduct of conduct" (ibid.). This position is alarmingly consistent with the ideologies and actions of representatives of neo-liberalism whereby, for instance, directors of research for the federal government's solici-tor general proclaim that factors such as race, gender, and class have very little to do with criminal behaviour and warn against getting "trapped in arguments with primary prevention advocates who believe that a society-wide focus on unemployment, sexism or racism will eliminate crime" (Andrews and Bonta 1998, 363).

For these reasons, I am concerned about the possible conflation of critical feminist criminology's drift toward governmentality with the interests of neo-liberalism. I am convinced by Fraser's (2003, 169) assertion that there has been a "return of brute repression" under the collapsing of the welfare state, which suggests that self-regulation is an insufficient analysis. I am struck by the movement of feminist criminology toward governmentality at a time when many feminist-inspired reforms to policy and law are weakening or collapsing altogether, and more women are being criminalized and incarcerated for offences that are linked to poverty, sexual exploitation, addiction, and mental illness as the "death of the social" takes hold. I am calling for a reimagining of a critical feminist criminology that is linked to a realist ontology that is deeply political and theoretical.

## Toward a Reimagining of a Feminist Criminology: Reclaiming the Standpoint of Women and Praxis

Perhaps governmentality appeals to some feminist criminologists because of the need for a new point of entry into the complex practices of carceral and regulatory power. But I am uneasy with the uncoupling of women's standpoint from theory and the erasure of political action that is apparent in governmentality literatures. Despite its rich descriptions of discipline and power, governmental scholarship offers few pragmatic possibilities for social action (Lemke 2003). For example, Steven Bittle (2002) offers a Foucauldian analysis of the neo-liberal state response: secure care for young people (girls) who are at risk for becoming involved in prostitution. Bittle (ibid., 347) cites Pat O'Malley (2000, 163-64) when he asserts: "We cannot treat [such] neo-liberal approaches as catastrophic; we must create spaces for relational hybridization and government innovation." Bittle (2002, 344) also cites Nikolas Rose (1996b, 60-61) in justifying his appreciation for government innovation when he argues that "for all the Left critiques of State and social control ... it does not yet seem to have been able to propose alternative models for regulating these citizen-shaping devices that answer to the needs of plurality." Such claims obscure the imprisonment of young girls and the gender and material relations that underpin their sexual exploitation. Governmentality's analytical tools enable us to (partially) describe how neo-liberalism governs and to ask the question of how – but without balanced attention to why and what now. It is the last point that should be of concern to critical feminists working to improve the conditions of women's lives. It is time to reposition women's narratives as potentially subversive stories (Ewick and Silbey 1995).

The intellectual history of feminist criminology reveals how women's voices are important for illuminating our analysis and strategies. Below I address the limits of standpoint as an epistemology directly, but I think it is useful to reconsider the genealogy of standpoint theory in feminist criminology at this point as we attempt to bridge the gulf between modernity's feminisms and post-structuralism. The emergence of standpoint theory and method in feminist criminology more than twenty years ago was framed by a desire to engender criminology – much like what needs to take place within the conceptual mapping of today's governmentality scholarship. Standpoint epistemology was strategic in undermining the gender neutrality of early conventional criminology. Women's experiences of oppression inform theory building in order to avoid reductionist explanations of women's lives (Hartsock 1983; Harding 1987). Starting in the 1970s and continuing into the late 1980s, feminist research challenged the gender-blind epistemology of modern criminologies. Criminalized women were too few to count (Adelberg and Currie 1987) and were simply added into the theoretical mix. To undermine the invisibility of gender, women's narratives derived from standpoint epistemology portrayed stark portraits of sexual exploitation, neglect, poverty, homelessness, and addiction (Shaw 1991; Comack 1996). These narratives of abuse generated numerous studies on the connections between victimization and criminalization. Simply put, women's law-breaking behaviour of drinking and drugging, prostitution, and violence were understood to be strategies to cope with the impact of abuse.

These early standpoint epistemologies, however, were rightly criticized for their tendency to essentialize women, to take women's experiences as self-evident and as the only basis of knowledge production (Cain 1990). In particular, women's victimization (sexual exploitation, domestic violence, rape) was viewed as a cause or pathway into violence, addiction, prostitution, or fraud (see Ritchie 1996). Margaret Shaw (1995, 448) points out that the continuum between victimization and criminalization is an essentialist understanding of women that rests upon a selective reading of women's own accounts of their lives:

> What is at issue here is not whether the women are right or wrong
> or politically correct in their judgements, but that there is in fact a

range of views, and that some of these may be antithetical to a feminist viewpoint. They do not all hate men, or see themselves as victims. The plurality of their views needs to be recognized. We need also to recognize that it is paternalistic to assume that they are necessarily "misguided," or want to have their consciousness raised.

More recent feminist scholarship has challenged the overdetermined role of abuse in women's lives, cautioning that such a strategy renders women responsible for how they cope with abuse, justifying the imprisonment of women based on their assumed need for treatment (Pollack 2000, 2004; Hannah-Moffat 2001, 2004). Julia Sudbury (2005, xv) reminds us that standpoint epistemology has followed the psychologizing and individualizing logic of the criminal justice system and, in this way, potentially "sidesteps the question of why the state responds to abused women with punishment." Although standpoint feminism engendered criminology and theorized the intersections of racism, poverty, and violence against women, it did nothing to prevent the onslaught of neo-liberalism in the 1980s and 1990s. Moreover, feminist-inspired policy reforms at that time fostered alliances between neo-conservative law and order regimes of expansive punitive responses to crime, as well as intrusion of the state into the lives of poor women and single mothers. Thus, should we contend that standpoint feminism was a failed paradigm? Possibly, but I suggest we consider the concomitant anti-feminist backlash that underpinned neo-liberalism's political and economic policies *and* the incursion of governmentality scholarship.

Despite these important criticisms of standpoint, this earlier research was instrumental in shifting feminist criminology toward imagining its own epistemology and challenging malestream criminological research. Standpoint theory made feminists accountable for the quality of the knowledge they produced and the transformative impact of their research (Cain 1990). In this way, feminist criminology was a feminist praxis that linked theory to activism on behalf of marginalized women. Standpoint epistemology was about challenging the disregard or distortion of women's gendered experiences of poverty and violence and, in doing so, advocating for meaningful social change: "Standpoint never loses sight of women as actively constructing as well as interpreting the social processes and social relations which constitute their everyday realities, and which can only be achieved through engaging directly in the intellectual and political struggle" (Harding 1987, 185).

The work of feminists such as Shoshona Pollack (2000, 2004) is clearly moving beyond the victimization-criminalization continuum, toward a more complex understanding of women's lives, paying particular attention to the political economy of punishment and the implications of engaging with the criminal justice system to ameliorate the conditions of women's lives. For example, Pollack (2004) captures the voices of black women prisoners who have been deemed resistant to treatment or out of control because of their defiance rather than dependency. We see here from a woman's standpoint the cultural, gendered, and classist underpinnings of their lives:

> So all the Black women I know are in this institution, they're here for financial gain. None of us are suffering from the norm of being a drug addict or being sexually molested by our father. We're in here purely for financial gain. We don't fit the stereotype of the "normal" inmate that is in here. We're here for financial gain.

> I am a *very* independent, resourceful person. I will do anything and everything to provide the best for my family. There are certain things I won't do, because that's not me. I'd rather go out and steal a turkey, before I'd ask a man to buy me a turkey. Because I'm in-dependent and that's the way I saw my mother, she would rather sacrifice and do it herself, than ask anybody to help her. So, I am set in my ways, kind of, because this is the way I seen it. And I've been watching it from generation to generation, right back down onto me. (a black woman prisoner cited in Pollack 2000, 76)

The criminal justice response to black women has been to punish their strategies to resist poverty (for example, fraud and prostitution) or sexual violence and to impose cognitive behavioural therapies that seek to change their criminal thinking. Pollack calls for alternative anti-oppression approaches to mental health counselling that are rooted in women's experiences of systemic, interpersonal, and structural oppressions. In this way, Pollack asserts a transformative politics rooted in the experiences of women and their capacity for agency.

Part of reimagining a feminist criminology is to reposition women's narratives as potentially subversive stories that reveal the connections between biography and history (Mills 1959), thereby "recounting particular experiences as rooted in and part of an encompassing cultural, material, and political world that extends beyond the local" (Ewick and Silbey 1995, 219). An example of repositioning women's narratives as potentially subversive stories can be seen in the recent work of equality-seeking groups such as the Native Women's Association of Canada (NWAC), the Canadian Association of Elizabeth Fry Societies (CAEFS), and the DisAbled Women's Network (DAWN). Through women prisoners' narratives of sexual harassment, neglect, and abuse, these coalition partners presented a submission to the United Nations Human Rights Committee asserting that the treatment of women prisoners by the Correctional Service of Canada violates Article 2 of the United Nations Convention on Torture (Canadian Association of Elizabeth Fry Societies 2005). Another site of political action has been the Sisters in Spirit campaign initiated by the NWAC with support from Amnesty International to document the cases of Native women who have disappeared or died a violent death, to conduct a public education and awareness campaign about violence against Native women, and to establish a toll-free hotline for the reporting of missing Native women (Amnesty International 2009). Both of these strategies of political action bring together the narratives of women's experiences of violence, poverty, and racism to expose the "brute repression" of the state as expressed through its correctional policies and policing practices. In this way, the work of the NWAC, DAWN, and CAEFS is an expression of the "power-knowledge-change-nexus" (Snider 2006, 325) that transforms women's stories into political action.

I believe it is time to reimagine a feminist criminology, as the implications of neo-liberalism for women are clear. Post-structural solutions for the harm and suffering caused by crime and imprisonment do not seem to exist. Instead, we are provided with a rich analysis of how women's lives are managed and regulated in exceedingly complex ways. Yet, we must be mindful of remaining accessible in our theoretical work. In the United States, feminist criminologist Meda Chesney-Lind (1997) suggests that one of the more troubling transformations in criminology is what she refers to as the theoretical obscurity of criminology that is "so intellectually impenetrable that it both disempowers and silences women." Post-structuralism has rendered criminology inaccessible to policy makers and "encourages us to stay off the streets [and] in front of our computers" (ibid.).

Writing of challenges confronting Canadian feminist activists and academics working on behalf of criminalized and imprisoned women, Laureen Snider (2006, 325) asserts that feminists need to produce knowledge that is heard:

Understanding how change is forged requires first and foremost, dissecting the role of experts, of expertise, and authorized knowers and knowledge claims. It is essential to examine the impact and results of feminist and non-feminist claims that have constituted woman as victim and as offender. Only by acknowledging how feminist knowledge claims and expertise become part of the knowledge-power-change nexus is there any hope (there is never any guarantee) of fashioning research and praxis with truly counter hegemonic potential.

Criminologists have the capacity to inform the public about the true fiscal and human costs of neo-liberal economics and neo-conservative crime control. Yet, subversive stories of poverty, violence, and racism are noticeably absent, and academics are less politically engaged. Just as neo-liberalism would have it.

## ACKNOWLEDGMENT

This chapter is largely based on an article that appeared in the *Canadian Journal of Criminology and Criminal Justice* in October 2006 (48[5]: 741-59) as part of a selection of writings intended to provoke discussion of the direction of a critical criminology in Canada. In that series of articles, scholars were querying how to "bring the state back in." As part of that discussion, I suggested that the influence of governmentality theorists on feminist criminologies may undermine research for, by, and about women, whom, in the wake of neo-liberalism, have become the fastest-growing prisoner population worldwide.

## NOTES

1   See *R. v. Darrach*, [2000] 2 S.C.R. 443; *R v. Ewanchuk*, [1999] 1 S.C.R. 330; *R. v. Mills*, [1999] 3 S.C.R. 668; and *R. v. O'Connor*, [1995] 4 S.C.R. 411.

2   For example, on August 9, 2001, in Sudbury, Ontario, Kimberly Rogers, a single mother who was eight months pregnant, died in her apartment, where she was confined under house arrest during a stifling heat wave. Kimberly had been convicted of welfare fraud for collecting social assistance as a full-time university student and was forced to live on a food allowance of only $18 a month (for more details on the Kimberly Rogers case see http://dawn.thot.net/Kimberly_Rogers/).

## REFERENCES

Adelberg, E., and C. Currie. 1987. *Too Few to Count: Canadian Women in Conflict with the Law*. Vancouver: Press Gang.

Amnesty International. 2009. *No More Stolen Sisters: A Need for a Comprehensive Response to Discrimination and Violence against Indigenous Women in Canada*. London, UK: Amnesty International Publications.

Andrews, D., and J. Bonta. 1998. Rev. ed. *The Psychology of Criminal Conduct*. Cincinnati: Anderson.

Arbour, the Honourable Justice Louise (commissioner). 1996. *Commission of Inquiry into Certain Events at the Prison for Women in Kingston*. Ottawa: Ministry of the Solicitor General Canada.

Bell, V. 1993. *Interrogating Incest: Feminism, Foucault, and the Law*. London: Routledge.

–. 2002. The Vigilante(e) Parent and the Paedophile: The News of the World Campaign 2000 and the Contemporary Governmentality of Child Sexual Abuse. *Feminist Theory* 3(1): 83-102.

Bittle, S. 2002. When Protection Is Punishment: Neo-liberalism and Secure Care Approaches to Youth Prostitution. *Canadian Journal of Criminology and Criminal Justice* 44(3): 317-50.

Bloom, B., B. Owen, and S. Covington. 2003. *Gender Responsive Strategies: Research, Practice, and Guiding Principles for Women Offenders*. Washington, DC: National Institute of Corrections.

Brodie, J. 1995. *Politics on the Margins: Restructuring and the Canadian Women's Movement*. Halifax: Fernwood.

Busby, K. 1997. Discriminatory Uses of Personal Records in Sexual Violence Cases. *Canadian Journal of Women and the Law* 9(1): 148-95.

–. 1999. "Not a Victim until a Conviction Is Entered": Sexual Violence Prosecutions and Legal Truth. In *Locating Law: Race/Class/Gender Connections*, ed. E. Comack, 260-87. Halifax: Fernwood.

Cain, M. 1990. Realist Philosophy and Standpoint Epistemologies of Feminist Criminology as a Successor Science. In *Feminist Perspectives in Criminology*, ed. L. Gelsthorpe and A. Morris, 124-40. London: Open University Press.

Canada, Auditor General. 2003. *Report of the Auditor General of Canada to the House of Commons*. Ottawa: Minister of Public Works and Government Services.

Canadian Association of Elizabeth Fry Societies. 2005. *Submission of the Canadian Association of Elizabeth Fry Societies to the United Nations Human Rights Committee Examining Canada's 4th and 5th Reports Regarding the Convention against Torture*, http://www.elizabethfry.ca/caefs_e.htm.

Carrington, K. 1993. *Offending Girls: Sex, Youth and Justice*. Sydney: Allen and Unwin.

–. 2002. Feminism and Critical Criminology: Confronting Geneologies. *Critical Criminology: Issues, Debates, and Challenges*, 114-42. Cullumpton, UK: Willan Publishing.

Chesney-Lind, M. 1997. Feminism and Critical Criminology: Toward a Feminist Praxis. *The Critical Criminologist* 7(3), http://www.critcrim.org/critpapers/chesney-lind1.htm.

Chunn, D., and S. Gavigan. 2004. Welfare Law, Welfare Fraud, and the Moral Regulation of the "Never Deserving" Poor. *Social and Legal Studies* 13(2): 219-43.

Comack, E. 1996. *Women in Trouble.* Halifax: Fernwood.

–. 1999. New Possibilities for a Feminism in Criminology? From Dualism to Diversity. *Canadian Journal of Criminology and Criminal Justice* 41(2): 161-71.

Commission on Systemic Racism in the Ontario Criminal Justice System. 1995. *Report of the Commission on Systemic Racism in the Ontario Criminal Justice System.* Toronto: Queen's Printer for Ontario.

Correctional Service of Canada. 1990. *Report of the Task Force on Federally Sentenced Women.* Ottawa: Ministry of the Solicitor General Canada.

Cossman, B., and J. Fudge. 2002. *Privatization, Law, and the Challenge to Feminism.* Toronto: University of Toronto Press.

Crenshaw, K. 1994. Mapping the Margins: Intersectionality, Identity Politics, and Violence against Women of Colour. In *The Public and Private Nature of Private Violence*, ed. M. Fineman and R. Mykitiuk, 93-118. New York, NY: Routledge.

Currie, D. 1992. Feminist Encounters with Postmodernism: Exploring the Impasse of Debates on Patriarchy and the Law. *Canadian Journal of Women and Law* 5(1): 63-86.

Curtis, Bruce. 1995. Taking the State Back Out: Rose and Miller on Political Power. *British Journal of Sociology* 46(4): 575-89.

Daly, K. 1997. Different Ways of Conceptualizing Sex/Gender in Feminist Theory and Their Implications for Criminology. *Theoretical Criminology* 1(1): 25-51.

Edsall, T.B., with M.D. Edsall. 1991. *Chain Reaction: The Impact of Race, Rights, and Taxes on American Politics.* New York: Free Press.

Ewick, P., and S. Silbey. 1995. Subversive Stories and Hegemonic Tales: Toward a Sociology of Narrative. *Law and Society Review* 29(2): 197-226.

Fabiano, E., and R. Ross. 1985. *Correctional Alternative Programmes for Female Offenders.* Ottawa: Programs Branch, Ministry of the Solicitor General, Canada.

Finn, A., S. Trevethan, G. Carriere, and M. Kowalski. 1999. Female Inmates, Aboriginal Inmates, and Inmates Serving Life Sentences: A One Day Snapshot. *Juristat* 19(5): 1-14.

Fraser, N. 2003. From Discipline to Flexibilization: Rereading Foucault in the Shadow of Globalization. *Constellations* 10(2): 160-72.

–. 2005. Mapping the Feminist Imagination: From Redistribution to Recognition. *Constellations* 12(3): 295-307.

Grant, A. 1999. Imprisoment of Indigenous Women in Australia 1988-1998. *Indigenous Law Bulletin* 100, 4:25.

Hannah-Moffat, K. 1999. Moral Agent or Actuarial Subject. *Theoretical Criminology* 3(1): 71-94.

–. 2000. Prisons That Empower: Neo-Liberal Governance in Canadian Women's Prisons. *British Journal of Criminology* 40(3): 510-31.

–. 2001. *Punishment in Disguise: Penal Governance and Federal Imprisonment of Women in Canada*. Toronto: University of Toronto Press.

–. 2004. Criminality Need and the Transformative Risk Subject: Hybridizations of Risk/ Need in Penality. *Punishment and Society* 7(1): 29-51.

Harding, S., ed. 1987. *Feminism and Methodology*. Milton Keynes: Open University Press.

Hartsock, N. 1983. The Feminist Standpoint: Developing the Ground for a Specifically Feminist Historical Materialism. In *Discovering Reality*, ed. S. Harding and M. Hinitikka, 283-310. Boston: D. Reidel.

Horri, G., D. Parkes, and K. Pate. 2006. Are Women's Rights Worth the Paper They Are Written On? Collaborating to Enforce the Rights of Criminalized Women. In *Criminalizing Women*, ed. G. Balfour and E. Comack, 302-22. Halifax: Fernwood.

Howe, A. 1994. *Punish and Critique: Towards a Feminist Analysis of Penality*. New York: Routledge.

Hudson, B. 1998. Punishment and Governance. *Social and Legal Studies* 7(4): 553-59.

–. 2002. Gender Issues in Penal Policy and Penal Theory. In *Women and Punishment: The Struggle for Justice*, ed. P. Carlen, 21-46. Devon, UK: Willan.

Johnson, H. 1996. *Dangerous Domain: Violence against Women in Canada*. Toronto: Harcourt Brace.

Lemke, T. 2003. Comment on Nancy Fraser: Rereading Foucault in the Shadow of Globalization. *Constellations* 10(2): 172-80.

Macleod, C., and K. Durrheim. 2002. Foucauldian Feminism: The Implications of Governmentality. *Journal for the Theory of Social Behaviour* 32(1): 41-61.

Mills, C.W. 1959. *The Sociological Imagination*. New York: Oxford University Press.

Minaker, J., and L. Snider. 2006. Husband Abuse: Equality with a Vengeance? *Canadian Journal of Criminology and Criminal Justice* 48(5): 753-80.

Monture-Angus, P. 2000. Aboriginal Women and Correctional Practice: Reflections on the Task Force on Federally Sentenced Women. In *An Ideal Prison? Critical Essays on Women's Imprisonment in Canada*, ed. K. Hannah-Moffat and M. Shaw, 52-60. Halifax: Fernwood.

O'Malley, P. 1996. Risk and Responsibility. In *Foucault and Political Reason: Liberalism, Neo-Liberalism and Rationalities of Government*, ed. A. Barry, T. Osborne, and N. Rose, 189-208. Chicago: University of Chicago Press.

–. 2000. Criminologies of Catastrophe? Understanding Criminal Justice on the Edge of the New Millennium. *Australian and New Zealand Journal of Criminology* 33(2): 153-67.

Pate, K. 1999. CSC and the 2 Per Cent Solution. *Canadian Women Studies* 19(1-2): 145-53.

–. 2005. Prisons: Canada's Default Response to Homelessness, Poverty, and Mental Illness – Especially for Women. Paper presented at the eleventh United Nations Congress on Criminal Justice and Crime Prevention conference, Bangkok, http://www.elizabethfry.ca/.

Pavlich, G. 1996. *Justice Fragmented: Mediating Community Disputes under Postmodern Conditions*. London: Routledge.

Pearson, P. 1997. *When She Was Bad: Violent Women and the Myth of Innocence*. Toronto: Random House.

Platt, T. 1987. U.S. Criminal Justice in the Regan Era: An Assessment. *Crime and Social Justice* 29: 58-69.

–, and T. Takagi. 1977. Intellectuals for Law and Order: A Critique of the New "Realists." *Crime and Social Justice* 8(Fall and Winter): 1-16.

Pollack, S. 2000. Dependency Discourse as Social Control. In *An Ideal Prison? Critical Essays on Canadian Women's Imprisonment in Canada*, ed. K. Hannah-Moffat and M. Shaw, 72-81. Halifax: Fernwood.

–. 2004. Anti-Oppressive Practice with Women in Prison: Discursive Reconstructions and Alternative Practices. *British Journal of Social Work* 34(5): 693-707.

–. 2009. "Circuits of Exclusion": Criminalized Women's Negotiation of Community. *Canadian Journal of Community Mental Health* 28(1): 83-95.

Ratner, R., and J. McMullan. 1983. Social Control and the Rise of the Exceptional State in Britain, the United States, and Canada. *Crime and Social Justice* (Summer): 31-40.

Razack, S. 1998. *Looking White People in the Eye: Gender, Race, and Culture in Courtrooms and Classrooms*. Toronto: University of Toronto Press.

–. 2002. *Race, Space, and the Law: Unmapping a White Settler Society*. Toronto: Between the Lines.

Rice, M. 1990. Challenging Orthodoxies in Feminist Theory: A Black Feminist Critique. In *Feminist Perspectives in Criminology*, ed. L. Gelsthorpe and A. Morris, 57-69. London: Open University Press.

Ritchie, B. 1996. *Compelled to Crime: The Gender Entrapment of Battered Black Women*. New York: Routledge.

Roberts, J., and R. Mohr, eds. 1994. *Confronting Sexual Assault: A Decade of Legal and Social Change*. Toronto: University of Toronto Press.

Rose, N. 1996a. The Death of the "Social"? Reconfiguring the Territory of Government. *Economy and Society* 26(4): 327-46.

–. 1996b. Governing "Advanced" Liberal Societies. In *Foucault and Political Reason: Liberalism, Neo-Liberalism and Rationalities of Government*, ed. A. Barry, T. Osborne, and N. Rose, 37-64. Chicago: University of Chicago Press.

–. 2000. Government and Control. *British Journal of Criminology* 40(2): 321-39.

Rose, N., and P. Miller. 1992. Political Power beyond the State: Problematics of Government. *British Journal of Sociology* 43(2): 172-205.

Ross, R., and E. Fabiano. 1985. *Correctional Alternatives Programmes for Female Offenders*. Ottawa: Ministry of Solicitor General Programmes Branch.

Shaw, M. 1991. *Survey of Federally Sentenced Women: Report of the Task Force on Federally Sentenced Women*. User Report 1991-94. Ottawa: Corrections Branch, Ministry of the Solicitor General Canada.

–. 1995. Conceptualizing Violence by Women. In *Gender and Crime,* ed. R.E. Dobash, R.P. Dobash, and L. Noaks, 115-31. Cardiff: University of Wales Press.

Smart, C. 1989. *Feminism and the Power of Law.* London: Routledge.

–. 1995. *Law, Crime and Sexuality.* London: Sage.

Snider, L. 1994. Feminism, Punishment and the Potential of Empowerment. *Canadian Journal of Law and Society* 9(1): 75-104.

–. 2003. Constituting the Punishable Woman: Atavistic Man Incarcerates Postmodern Woman. *British Journal of Criminology* 43(2): 354-78.

–. 2006. Making Change in Neo-Liberal Times. In *Criminalizing Women,* ed. G. Balfour and E. Comack, 323-42. Halifax: Fernwood.

Sudbury, J., ed. 2005. *Global Lockdown.* London: Routledge.

Wilson, J.Q. 1983. *American Government: Institutions and Policies.* Lexington, MA: Heath.

Wood, L. 2001. Caught in the Net of Zero-Tolerance: The Effect of the Criminal Justice Response to Partner Violence. MA thesis, University of Manitoba.

Worrall, A. 1990. *Offending Women: Female Lawbreakers and the Criminal Justice System.* New York: Routledge and Kegan Paul.

# 9
# The Promise of Critical Realism: Toward a Post-Empiricist Criminology

*George S. Rigakos and Jon Frauley*

Canadian criminology has never been more successful. In terms of enrolment, faculty hiring, and the quantity of scholarly work produced, it is at its healthiest in years. Nonetheless, criminology still remains an epistemologically and ontologically confused project lacking in theoretical depth and maturity.[1] Part of the problem is surely associated with the now common concerns Canadian criminologists raise wherever they meet: the pedagogical costs of rapid expansion; the pressure to hire academics with only a passing interest in, or even outright hostility toward, the subject of criminology; and the continued indifference by administrators who have largely viewed Canadian criminology programs as undergraduate cash cows. However, as we see it, the larger issue is far more theoretical and political. It manifests itself in various forms: the appropriation of ideological understandings of the object of criminological investigation; the ambiguity of the role of criminology and the criminologist in society; debates over what constitutes research and education; and the vast amount of empiricist research that, to our mind, threatens criminology's status as a social science. The issue, in short, has to do with how criminologists imagine scientific enquiry and whether this leads them to a total rejection of something they think constitutes science or instead leads them to embrace an equally impoverished, relativist understanding of knowledge.[2]

In what follows, we argue for post-empiricism in criminology. We take empiricism to be a concern with surface phenomena or simply the notion that anything worth knowing or which can constitute valid knowledge must be apprehendable to our senses. The adage "seeing is believing" captures the general thrust of empiricism. Of course, there are different varieties, some more sophisticated than others; we deal here only with what might be termed an ordinary empiricism of the sort that haunts criminology. We stress that we are absolutely not arguing that criminology must become less empirical.

"Empiricism" does not mean "empirical." The post-empiricist criminology we have in mind is theoretical, ontological, and empirical. It is an informed realist scientific practice influenced by the kind of analysis offered by Roy Bhaskar (1975, 1993).[3] Bhaskar and his interlocutors in the social sciences have had relatively little impact on criminology (for example, Layder 1990, 1993; Sayer 1992, 2000; Collier 1994; Archer 1995). We believe that *critical realism* holds important insights for the nature of social reality and could strengthen and enhance critical criminology, taking it beyond the mistaken impasse of quantitative-versus-qualitative enquiry.

Qualitative and quantitative, as well as critical and uncritical, criminologies might have more in common than we have traditionally been led to believe. Our task here is to present what amounts to a heterodox position, and we invite skeptics to engage fully and critically with our elaboration. First, we provide a brief discussion of the struggle for a critical criminology. Second, we distinguish scientific or critical realism from what we (and others) find to be a rather uncritical and empiricist criminological realism, setting out some differences between metatheory and substantive theory, along with basic tenets that can be utilized to inform the production of criminological knowledge. Third, we attend to anti-realism in criminology through a discussion of the appropriation of the work of the influential social theorist Michel Foucault. We illustrate that Foucault provides us with an ontology compatible with that of critical realism and argue that he is most fruitfully read as a realist and materialist. We then offer suggestions as to why he has been taken up, in the main, as if he advocated empiricism and methodological individualism for the explanation of social phenomena. We conclude with a brief discussion of the implications of "getting real" for criminological theorizing and research.

## A Critical Opening

Peter Manicas (1987, 168) offers a forceful argument as to why we should see social science primarily as a theoretical science, distinguishing it from both social research and applied social science. This distinction can be usefully thought of as the difference between the social science of criminology and the applied protective service field of criminal justice studies. Manicas defends "science," as do realists in general, as neither a positivistic nor strictly hermeneutic/phenomenological endeavour. We find this valuable, as it highlights for us not that social science should not engage with policy or the pressing problems of the day but, rather, that "science," and this is certainly the case with criminology, is often conflated with scientism. Scientism, the appearance of doing science, is often achieved by adopting something called the scientific method, which is associated with a positivist metatheory. Such a research design, however, in the end can only ever be an ideal type (Bryman 1988, chap. 2). This is most definitely not the type of science that we advocate, which is why we are being very clear that in advocating scientific or critical realism we are advocating a post-empiricist social scientific practice for criminology.

Manicas (1987) provides a general overview of the rise of the social sciences in the United States and of how universities and programs were instituted and adapted to changing economic and social factors of the early twentieth century, such as mass immigration, the rapid growth of cities, and an increase in the numbers of unemployed and homeless. The social sciences were installed in universities to help combat such social problems, and although Manicas does not discuss criminology, its development seems analogous (see Menzies and Chunn 1999; Stenning 1999). Early on, criminology was regarded as a servant of the state, a view that continued until the 1970s, when academics began to challenge this association.

Although criminology has yet to completely break free of its administrative and correctionalist roots, many scholars working in this field, some of whose work is included in this book, reject definitions of their enterprise as a call to solve social problems. Many critically minded criminologists reject a narrow and state-defined legalistic definition of crime as simply the violation of the criminal law and the criminological enterprise as merely a tool of social reform. They seek to study the social, political, and economic relations that underpin and support the production and reproduction of the categories of crime and criminality and practices of policing these boundaries (see Lacey 1994, 1995; Pearce and Snider 1995; Fattah 1997; Garland and Sparks 2000; Menzies, Chunn, and Boyd 2001). Indeed, there has been ongoing conflict over what exactly constitutes the object of criminological research and how this enquiry should be carried out (Shearing 1989; Ericson and Carriere 1994; Menzies and Chunn 1999; Rigakos 1999), preventing criminology from being the coherent and uniform discipline that many think it to be. But this tension is not new or endemic only to criminology.

Beginning in the 1970s, many criminologists and sociologists started to question their relationship with what was held to be a very conservative enterprise constrained through the discipline's traditional ties to the liberal, capitalist state (for example, McMullan and Ratner 1982; Ratner 1985, 1987;

Menzies and Chunn 1999; Stenning 1999; among others). Radical criminologies of the 1970s vociferously fought for such a space to exist (Taylor,
Walton, and Young 1973; Quinney 1974; Spitzer 1975). Recent developments
within the social sciences promise that this tension will be ongoing, while
at the same time offering a path beyond conventionalist/interpretivist and
positivistic approaches to the study of crime and justice. This, in the main,
is because of the recognition that critical inquiry requires a sound epistemological and ontological base. These developments offer the promise of a
research practice that is neither underwritten by a positivistic philosophy
of science, on the one hand, nor by the relativism of conventionalism (for
example, social constructionism, interpretivism, postmodernism), on the
other.

We believe that our research strategies shape how we think about our
objects of analysis, the research process itself, and the place and role of theorizing, and that the seeking out of alternative theoretical and methodological
resources is necessary to provide criminology with something that it is currently lacking: ontological rigour. The research strategies employed in the
production of criminological knowledge act as subtle frameworks that chan-
nel our practices and condition our understanding of the nature of crime and
its control. Critical realism holds the promise of providing a much needed
post-empiricist, alternative theoretical and methodological resource for the
renewal of criminological enquiry.

## Critical Realism Isn't Left Realism

To get at differences between critical realism and a familiar criminological
realism, it is necessary to make a distinction between different types of theory.
We can distinguish between substantive theory, descriptive theory, and
metatheory. In the realms of criminology, sociology, and legal studies, many
will be tempted to see critical realism as some variant of an existing substantive realism known as either left realism (for example, Jones, MacLean, and
Young 1986; Young 1997) or legal realism (Hunt 1978; Leiter 1996), but
such an assumption would be incorrect. These latter theories are substantive
in that they attempt to be realistic in their descriptions of the empirical domains of concern. As we will see below, critical realism holds reality to comprise more than only an empirical domain. To take only the empirical realm
to be important is, in the end, to be empiricist. This is to say that, at their
face, these substantive realisms are based on an empiricist theory of knowledge
or epistemology, which is not compatible with critical realism.

Not only does a critical realist epistemology not advocate empiricism, as a research strategy it proceeds via a retroductive mode of reasoning, which is unlike the analytic induction and deduction found in positivist and interpretivist research.[4] Indeed, a major weakness of the school of left realism is that it has never come to grips with its own problematic and undertheorized ontology and has never dealt with the wider epistemological problem of its metatheory and its relationship to issues surrounding a philosophical realism (see Menzies 1992). What we can glean from this, at the very least, is that we are talking about two very different understandings of realism, two very different levels of analysis, as well as two different modes of reasoning. Sayer (2000, 11, 70) captures this difference between substantive realism (such as left realism) and metatheoretical realism (such as critical realism) in his demarcation of "empirical realism" from critical realism: empirical realism "identifies the real with the empirical." That is, the unseen realm of tendencies and potentials that may or may not be realized is held to be equivalent "with what we experience, as if the world just happened to correspond to the range of our senses and to be identical to what we experience" (Sayer 1992, 11). In other words, that which is in fact real is greater than what human beings might be able to directly experience, including processes that have a hand in the emergence of actually existing things. Criminologists, for example, frequently speak of "power relations." These are not directly observable, but the effects of domination and subordination, wage inequality, preferential treatment, racism, and the like are experienced. We might suggest that these are embodied forms of relations of power. Analyzing the emergence of inequalities rather than the experience of inequalities themselves would take us beyond the realm of the empirical toward the realm of tendencies and potentials. This is important as the things that are of concern to social scientists are not necessarily captured, revealed, or exhausted by our experiences (including our observations).[5]

Unlike a "realistic" descriptive theory, critical realism, like that of positivism and conventionalism/phenomenology/interpretivism, is a metatheory that offers a position on the nature of knowledge and how it ought to be produced, as well as the objects that we can produce knowledge of. Metatheory underpins all descriptions and explanations of things. It operates as a research strategy that offers methodological protocols. Metatheory is often speculative and not necessarily determined by empirical data. Critical realism provides for the theorizing of what may and may not be apprehendable and what may be absent. Indeed, Bhaskar (1993) argues that a realist philosophy of science cannot proceed without fishing for these absences. As a metatheory, critical realism offers abstract arguments and concepts that must be "translated" into workable social science frameworks with specific regard to the object of investigation. This is where it can prove to be fruitful for criminological enquiry, as some have already illustrated (see Cain 1986, 1990; Woodiwiss 1990, 1998; Kerruish 1991; Norrie 1993; Pearce and Tombs 1996, 1998; Rigakos 2002, 2009; Frauley 2004, 2005, 2007a, 2007b, 2008).

## BASIC TENETS OF CRITICAL REALISM

At the epistemological level (theory of knowledge), there are at least two central and interrelated arguments made by contemporary critical realists. First, there is a world apart from human understanding that operates outside our perception, conceptual tools, and empirical comprehension. As a matter of ontology (theory of things/being), critical realists argue that the world "as we know it," or suppose it to be with some degree of "certainty," whether natural or social, remains "utterly indifferent" to our endeavours (Woodiwiss 1990, 7). Whether we privilege discursive humanism, defer to the empiricist compulsion to trust our senses, or reify our conceptual and theoretical constructs, the first tenet of realism is that *reality exists independently of human beings*. Bhaskar (1975) has offered us a model to aid in conceptualizing the nature of reality.

We have taken some liberties with this scheme, but we think this is representative of the one Bhaskar outlines in a much more thorough manner

## FIGURE 9.1

**Conceptualizing the nature of reality**

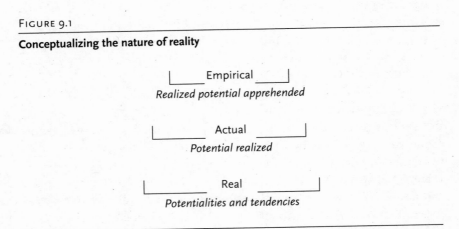

|___ Empirical ___|
*Realized potential apprehended*

|___ Actual ___|
*Potential realized*

|___ Real ___|
*Potentialities and tendencies*

SOURCE: Bhaskar 1975.

(see Figure 9.1). The *real* is the realm or domain of potentialities and tenden-cies. That is, if the conditions are right, certain things will emerge. If there is a lack of oversight in the workplace, petty theft might occur. If there is a high degree of oversight, little to no theft will occur. Because there is potential for crime does not mean that there will be crime. The second domain, the *actual*, is the realm of actualized or realized potential. Here we would move from a potential for crime or deviant conduct to its emergence and existence. But, as we well know, not all crime is known. This unknown quantity is called the "dark figure" of crime. The actual is this "dark figure." Crime exists and might be detected or become known but may not. That which does become known is an example of the third domain, the *empirical*. The empirical is the realm of sensory perception or experience. For critical realists, these three domains, or orders, are thought of as overlapping and interacting layers that together make up (social) reality. For those working from either a positivistic or a conventionalist/interpretivist approach, it is only the domain of the actual and the empirical respectively that is held to constitute the domain of theory building and science. As Sayer (2000, 12) duly notes, "in distinguishing the real, the actual and the empirical, critical realism proposes a 'stratified ontol-ogy' in contrast to other ontologies which have 'flat' ontologies populated by either the actual or the empirical, or a conflation of the two."

The second basic tenet logically follows from the first: *Realists are fal-libilists*. They believe that human beings produce knowledge and that this knowledge can be wrong. Unlike positivists, realists believe that we do not necessarily accumulate more knowledge over time. Anyone familiar with the history and development of the social sciences will know that although positivism has been a dominant metatheory for research, its idea that know-ledge is cumulative is untenable for the social sciences. We do not always, or in some linear fashion, creep closer and closer to the truth. Instead, regression – whether caused by conceptual, theoretical, or empirical errors or ideological (mis)directions and distortions – can often occur. But at any other time, and in some other area of scholarly endeavour, progress and the expansion of human knowledge can indeed occur. In fact, realists insist on the reflexive need to assess and reassess the social, historical, and political situatedness of not only concepts and ideas but also the practices that produce and reproduce them. Woodiwiss (1990, 6) summarizes the fallibility argument by high-lighting that "realists agree with the proposition that knowledge claims can never be verified or falsified" but that they "nevertheless insist that knowledge of the extra-discursive is possible" through theory and even if the results must nonetheless "be stoically accepted as necessarily never anything other than utterly fallible." Woodiwiss here is also indicating the transitive (tentative and changing) status of our knowledge. Our knowledge is open to revision, as it does not correspond exactly to our object of investigation. This raises a second issue of reference. Our categories and concepts, rather than directly corresponding to some material referent, make an always partial and fallible reference to what is a relatively enduring object. All in all, our knowledge is tentative and subject to change while our objects of study may not change or may change at a much slower (and undetectable) rate; or parts of our object may change at rates different from other parts (for example, institutions change much more slowly than human beings). Because of the difference between the state of knowledge (transitive) and the state of things we are attempting to generate knowledge about (relatively enduring), we must make a considered effort not to conflate our knowledge of things with those things themselves.

The combination of these two foundational epistemic assertions (and their implications) is what sunders misguided anti-realist approaches that are ostensibly constructionist and ontologically relativist. It also poses serious challenges to the positivist assertion that certainty is possible if the proper procedures are utilized (for example, classical experimental design). It now seems to be standard academic parlance that we should "avoid grand narratives," "conduct a more modest theoretical project," or describe our work as "neither real nor unreal." We should not only question the wisdom of these ideological pronouncements but understand that their writers almost invariably violate their shibboleths' inner logic, as they then unabashedly proceed to offer what could be viewed as a naive or empirical realist description peppered by critiques of previous theory and ending with an entreaty that "dated" approaches should be supplanted with the authors' own perspective. However, lest their critique be a self-guiding tautology of abstractions, there must be some reference to not only a discursive object (a concept) but also a material referent (the thing the concept refers to) – a thing that is beyond our constructs of it. This necessitates recognizing the non-human nature of reality, its extra-discursiveness. We will return to this issue later, but for the sake of keeping to our point, let us recap by quoting Manicas and Secord's (1983, 401) brilliantly concise distillation of this Bhaskarian argument: "One must be a realist ontologically to be a fallibilist epistemologically."

At this juncture, we should perhaps emphasize that there are subtle differences between some critical realists. The stratification of reality and its transitive and relatively enduring aspects have been a source of some conten-tion (see Harre 1986; see also Woodiwiss 1990; Harre 2001; Pearce and Woodiwiss 2001).[6] Beyond our two foundational tenets, and as López and Potter (2001, 9) have suggested, critical realism is indeed a "broad church." But there are a series of additional assertions that *most* (critical) realists can agree upon.

By way of elaborating on the tenet that reality exists independently of our knowledge of it, we point to the example of the existence of systematic inequalities within the legal-political sphere. These inequalities exist regard-less of whether or not we know of their existence. Our understanding of real-ity is always mediated through perceptual filters, so it makes little sense to hold that our knowledge corresponds exactly to what exists. Rather, as we suggest above, our categories and concepts help us to make reference to some aspect of a material referent. As our knowledge is fallible, our references will always undergo continual revision. The referent does not change but, rather, our references to it and how we make those references do.

Objects are held to belong to a stratified reality (see the discussion of real-actual-empirical above). This stratified reality is independent of our perception. Things such as "crime" or "society" can be conceptualized as the products of (at least partially) unobservable, constitutive processes and rela-tions. Social objects, then, are held to not simply exist but also to be emergent, arising from the intersection of a mass of tangled material and discursive relations. These relations require sorting out, especially in order to identify and separate the contingent relations from the necessary relations that are constitutive of the conditions under which social objects emerge and can be known by researchers. There is a concern to see empirically apprehendable phenomena as not exhaustive of that which actually exists, which means that partially obscured or unobservable entities may be inferred to exist from what can be seen or measured – investigated using the realist distinction between the empirical, the actual, and the real. By implication, this means that inher-ent to critical realism is a concern to see social action as situated activity, conditioned and shaped by social structure. Bhaskar, as well as other realists, hold to this belief. Social institutions, such as the family, religion, education, work, and law, pre-exist our birth and are relatively enduring and constrain and enable social action. Our knowledge about these, as we have indicated, is transitive. But far from reifying social structure, the latter is held to be alter-able and undergoing an incremental transformation. Social structure, it is important to note, is not simply the sum of human interaction, although it is reproduced and transformed through human interactions; it is also reproduced and transformed through non-human interactions, as well as through interactions between human and non-human entities.

As there are unobservable features of social life that can be known to some degree, our research strategies must be able to reveal and plausibly explain the existence, reproduction, and transformation of empirically apprehendable social phenomena. For example, relations of power are not directly observable but can be inferred to exist from their effects in the social world. Such effects include class conflict, gender and racial inequalities, exploitation, and domination, and any research strategy employed must be sympathetic to the status of these as outcomes or products of an intersection of different kinds of relations.

Explanation is necessarily theoretical, and theoretical work is necessary for social scientific enquiry. It is active, conceptual work that is always tethered to an empirical referent. In other words, theoretical elaboration is tethered to an ongoing concern with the thing to be described and explained. Theoretical practice, then, is integral to doing social science, including criminology. Criminology, however, suffers from indecision as to the place and role of theorizing (see Frauley 2005; Kraska 2006). This weakness pertains to the lack of attention to the crafting and operating of analytic concepts and is at least one reason for the terminological confusion over "realism" and why a critical realist-informed research practice would prove more adequate for criminology than positivism or an interpretivist/conventionalist approach.

Not only would an explicit concern with epistemology find its way into the discipline but so would a concern for ontology. Critical realism is primarily concerned with ontology, making it "thing-centred." What this means is that it begins from questions about what exists (for example, the conditions under which social objects such as "security" emerge) and then moves to questions of epistemology, concerned with the production of knowledge about what exists (for example, how can "security" be investigated). This makes it unlike either positivism or interpretivism/conventionalism in that questions of epistemology are explicitly and clearly distinguished from those of ontology.

Another way of understanding critical realism is to map its proposed possibility of knowing in comparison with other projects informed by positivism and/or conventionalism. We have illustrated this in Figure 9.2, entitled

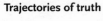

FIGURE 9.2

**Trajectories of truth**

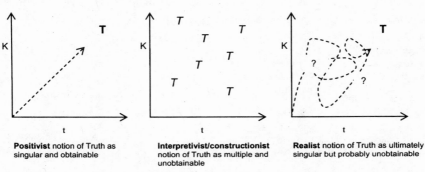

| Positivist notion of Truth as singular and obtainable | Interpretivist/constructionist notion of Truth as multiple and unobtainable | Realist notion of Truth as ultimately singular but probably unobtainable |
|---|---|---|

NOTES: T = Truth; t = time; K = Knowledge

"Trajectories of truth," borrowed and modified from Ted Palys (1989; 1992, 12, 20). These diagrams are obviously simplifications designed merely to orient the reader.

They do, however, provide us with a way to understand the differences between each metatheory's notion of truth and scientific progress, which is demonstrated here by the intersection of time and knowledge. It is also important to keep in mind that this schematic summarizes only notions of truth and knowing, which is not the same as summarizing notions of what is real, although these respective notions of truth tell us something important about how reality is conceived – that is, what it is thought to be like in order for it to be knowable or unknowable to researchers. This is because every epistemology contains within it an ontology. Positivism and interpretivism are mainly concerned with theories regarding the production of knowledge (for example, "How can we know?") and do not provide developed ontologies or concentrate on the question "What can be known?" Critical realism, on the other hand, is thing-centred. That is, it is primarily concerned with theories of things. This is why we think it would be more useful for criminology and the social sciences in general because it would begin from questions such as "What kind of a thing is 'crime'?" "What is 'regulation'?" "What is 'terrorism'?" and so on. Specifying what we know will then enable us to craft a research strategy specifically for that thing and, in the process, reveal new characteristics or qualities of that thing. The basic question not asked by most

FIGURE 9.3

**How to identify a metatheoretical position**[*]

| | Positivism | Interpretivism | Realism |
|---|---|---|---|
| *Ask yourself or the texts you are reading these questions:* | | | |

**Ontological questions**
*(What sort of thing is being investigated?)*

| | Positivism | Interpretivism | Realism |
|---|---|---|---|
| a) Does it depend on us thinking about it for its existence? | N | Y | N |
| b) Is it a material object (i.e., accessible to our senses)? | Y | N | Y |
| c) Are people the object of interest? | Y | N/Y[a] | Y/N[a] |

**Epistemological questions**
*(How should it be investigated?)*

| | Positivism | Interpretivism | Realism |
|---|---|---|---|
| a) Should one begin with observation? | Y | N | N |
| b) Should one ever reason without reference to observations? | N | Y | Y (to a degree) |
| c) Is certainty possible? | Y | Y (to a degree) | N |

**Final question**
How would you explain the links between the answers to the ontological questions and the answers to the epistemological ones?

---

a　Where double answers (for example, no/yes) are given, the first is the most common within the tradition.

*　Slightly modified from the original (Woodiwiss 2001, 136).

criminologists, and indeed sociologists, is "What must my object of study be like in order for it to be known in the way proposed?" In other words, "Why do I think I can actually attain knowledge of 'crime' by administering surveys or reading the diary of a criminal?" In both cases, we would be concerned only with what realists call the "empirical" domain of social reality, not with those things that produced this understanding. We wouldn't be able to attain knowledge of the kind of things that were at work and which impacted the author and which shaped or conditioned his or her thinking and action and which led him or her to write that diary in the way he or she did.

Woodiwiss (2001, 136) also provides a helpful schematic overview of the differences between metatheories, and we challenge our readers to take this test (see Figure 9.3).

Metatheory is not something that criminologists or sociologists have been explicitly trained to deal with, but it underpins social scientific enquiry. As such, understanding the differences between differing metatheories and thus differing social science practice allows us to be able to identify tacit assertions about the nature or objects of investigation and of social reality. Further, we can begin to formulate new lines of enquiry and new sets of questions that will help us expand our understanding and deepen our appreciation of our own practice.

## THE "FOUCAULT EFFECT" AND ANTI-REALISM

Thus far, we have argued for critical realism rather than a naive realism for criminological theory and practice. We would like to go further and take up an influential strand of criminological theorizing in order to illustrate more forcefully the terminological and theoretical confusion around "realism" in criminology. We do this by attending briefly to what we hold to be an ideologically driven realist/anti-realist debate hinging on various readings of the work of Michel Foucault.

In 1998, an interesting (albeit problematic) review of citation rates in critical criminology revealed that Michel Foucault was near the top of the list of frequently cited authors (Wright and Freidrichs 1998).[7] Most of us are well aware that Foucault has played a significant and progressive role in critical criminological theorizing and research in the last few decades (see Garland 1997). It has been Foucault's later works of the 1970s (1977, 1978) that have had the most impact, and this is likely because of direct and explicit references to themes related to crime, law, and order. Although Foucault's earlier texts (1965, 1971, 1972b) most certainly deal with themes of governance and social ordering, criminologists have largely failed to recognize this, likely because these analyses are less readily connected to the study of crime and crime control. Nonetheless, writers utilizing the concepts deployed in his later texts have often produced both empirically rich and theoretically enlightened research. Yet, an entire school of self-proclaimed Foucauldian scholars working within the ever expanding and overlapping literatures of risk and governmentality (for example, Miller and Rose 1995; Rose 1999; O'Malley 2001) maintain that Foucault's work is incompatible with a sociological or criminological project and have accepted an ideological rendering of his work as anti-structuralist, anti-realist, and anti-criminological (see also Garland 1997). O'Malley (2001, 85), for example, has argued that realism is "not consistent with governmentality's characteristic 'arealist' and anti-globalising assumptions." In part, this is likely because of a misconception of what constitutes social "science," an impoverished understanding of "realism," as well as a humanist tendency to see social structures and institutions as nothing more than a collection of individuals and their patterned activities. It is also telling that there is a failure to connect these later texts to Foucault's earlier works where his problematic is introduced and worked through, becoming developed, extended, and refined in his later texts.

Given the profound effect that Foucault's work has had on criminological theorizing, and the declarative statements of Foucauldian experts arguing his works' incompatibility with criminology (or any social scientific project) (see these pronouncements debated in Garland 1997; O'Malley, Weir, and Shearing 1997; O'Malley 2001; Rigakos 2001; Chan and Rigakos 2002), self-identified "critical" criminologists have been placed in the awkward position of either declaring their anti-realism in order to ostensibly remain consistent with one rendering of Foucault's intent or dropping Foucauldian categories from their analysis in order to get on with what resembles an "empirically realist" project. In many cases, critical criminologists have chosen to do neither and both: they make strange declarative statements about conducting an anti-realist project, avoiding grand narrative, disengaging from the search for causal mechanisms, and so on, but then proceed to treat their objects of analysis as very real indeed.

There is some confusion over what realism means and how this fits into criminological discourse. In terms of the works that borrow eclectically from Foucault, Pearce and Tombs (1998, 568) argue that certain interpretations of Foucault are "in danger of assuming the mantle of an orthodox interpretation of his work ... which in our view entails an unhelpful closure and so denial of much that his work offers to us as social scientists." We agree with this warning and would add that to employ a Foucauldian concept, attention to epistemology is necessary to understand how Foucault crafted and refined his concepts and how each is interlinked to form a system of categorization and conceptual order. But as epistemology and theorizing are largely considered to be second order to the business of "real" research, many criminologists have not grasped this. Moreover, working backwards from his work on governance and biopower toward his earlier archaeological texts provides us with an appreciation of the development and reformulation of these concepts in relation to his various substantive areas of enquiry. Foucault furnished us with not only numerous empirical studies but also an overview of how he arrived at his later positions on power and governance. Inattention to epistemological and ontological issues serves as a blockage to the development of realist metatheory for criminology and, by extension, critical practice. As critical realists suggest, we need to demarcate questions of ontology from those of epistemology. In doing so, we can also glean an understanding of how Foucault understood social institutions to be emergent structures. Importantly, this is to see in Foucault's work a form of ontological realism (see Pearce and Tombs 1999; Frauley 2007b).

Rather than simply accept the leading rendering of his work, we first argue that Foucault is best understood as resembling a scientific realist. It is important to point out that in *Discipline and Punish* (Foucault 1977), *The Birth of the Clinic* (Foucault 1973, 5), *The Archaeology of Knowledge* (Foucault 1972a, 72-74), and even in his responses to direct questions about the nature of the social, Foucault (1991, 81-82) reinforces the place and standing of real or object-like social relations, along with a concomitant depth of ontology regarding this reality (Frauley 2007b). Indeed, Foucault argues for an appreciation of durable, underlying historical tendencies (Best 1995, 99; Dean 1994, 17) and the need to carry out a "vertical investigation" of institutions, including what is "hidden," what is "released later," and even what works in opposition (Foucault 1973, 199). This is a project sympathetic to the Marxist warning that "because the bureaucracy turns its 'formal' objectives into its content, it comes into conflict everywhere with 'real' objectives" and thus both observers and technocrats can be "mutually deceived" from this "double meaning" (Marx 1978, 24).

Second, we must by extension understand that, in the main, governmentality theorists get it wrong when they declare their anti-realism and superficiality as Foucauldian (see Burchell, Gordon, and Miller 1991). Indeed, because a great many governmentalists work with a shallow, empiricist ontology of reality, the domain of enquiry is limited to what realists term "the empirical." This latter critique is best understood by attending to Rose's anti-realist proclamation, where he strangely declares: "I advocate superficiality, and empiricism of the surface, of identifying the differences in what is said, how it is said, and what allows it to be said and to have an effectivity" (Rose 1999, 56-57). We say "strangely" because the Foucauldian project was supposed to effectively challenge empiricism (a goal shared by realists). Yet, in the hands of Rose and many others, governmentality ends up merely judging the surface as the real and embracing empiricism. What Rose and many governmentalists are advocating is actually an ideological position that is anti-theoretical as well as anti-realist. To further problematize this mis-apprehension, we may point out that in the same breath as Foucault iterates his "at a distance" notion in *Birth of the Clinic* – a combination of words now turned into the canonical bedrock of governmentality research (see Rose and Miller 1992) – Foucault seems to implore analysts to go beyond surface metaphors to a "deeper level," what he calls *"a deep space, anterior to all percep-tions,"* yet nonetheless "governing them from afar" (1965, 5, emphasis added). But this is only one example among many cited by authors who have identi-fied the materialist and realist focus of Foucault's work (see Foucault 1972a, 1972b; Lecourt 1975; Arac 1980; Cavallari 1980; Sprinker 1980; Fairclough 1992; Cain 1993; Purvis and Hunt 1993; Veyne 1997; Pearce and Tombs 1998, 1999, 142-44; Pearce and Woodiwiss 2001; Rigakos and Hadden 2001; Olssen 2003; Frauley 2007b).

The implications of this misapprehension are important. Although criminologists may hold crime to be "real," when they marshal Foucault in their discussions of crime, crime control, risk, or what have you, they tacitly advance the idea that studies of crime are limited to that which can be ob-served because of the acceptance of an empiricist reading of his work. This is to limit enquiry to the realm of the empirical. The category "crime" as Shear-ing (1989) has rightly argued, refers to much more than an outcome. Rather, it indicates the existence of a complex process of social ordering. Such a process consists of the instituting and policing of boundaries by experts within a broader social, political, and economic context consisting of shifting and changing sets of priorities, values, and norms that, in turn, can engender further forms of social action, including those that constitute failed or suc-cessful attempts at producing and applying categories of crime and criminal-ity. One major implication of this empiricism is that, in terms of ontology, depth is lost as the relations between the different orders of the real, actual, and empirical are obfuscated. This means that distinguishing between regu-latory objects and their constitutive relations is made very difficult if not impossible. In other words, the process of emergence and the potential rela-tions that may be actualized or impugned as part of this process cannot be accounted for and thus can never be theorized as themselves objects of crim-inological investigation. Thus, the ability to disentangle and discern the presence and absence of the different sorts of constitutive relations (discursive, material, necessary, contingent) at a level that is deeper than what we can readily see, anterior to the domain of the empirical, is lacking.

## Getting Real

We have argued in this chapter for a critical realist-informed practice for criminology. We believe it to be the most appropriate metatheory for social scientific investigations because of its attention to ontology. We find instructive Pawson's (1989, 139) elaboration of a realist-informed methodology and agree with his assertion that "research cannot simply dwell at the level of events" because if we were "to confine observations solely to the business of monitoring events" we would "end up with endless descriptions of more or less random sequences." The point is to understand the "underlying mechanism[s] which bring about particular sequences of events" (128). The events are not discrete but parts of an object or system. For Pawson, "the causal link between these events is a matter of the 'causal powers' or 'liabilities' or 'ways of acting' or 'tendencies' of the underlying objects or systems" (ibid.). Talk of "causal powers" and "liabilities" or "mechanisms" may not sit well with some readers. However, it is important to accept that there are a wide array of tendencies and potentialities that *will* result in some causal sequence if activated. The properties of gunpowder can be activated under the right conditions (for example, dryness, presence of a spark) to cause an explosion or can be impugned so no explosion is actualized (presence of spark as well as lack of dryness/presence of dampness). It has the potential to explode but will only do so under the right circumstances.

Processes or mechanisms germane to the social sciences that we are all familiar with include racialization, criminalization, gentrification, urbanization, and so on. These can all be viewed as internally or necessarily related to any number of events or outcomes that a criminologist may be immediately concerned to explain. We might also think of opportunities as mechanisms that can activate or impugn social action. In this case, we may want to look at how social programs might work to produce and distribute such opportunities, and how this is necessarily connected to outcomes such as criminal events (see Pawson and Tilley 1997, 157). That "events" such as "crime" are internally or necessarily connected to what is often an unobservable generative process provides the context for Woodiwiss's (1998, 26) astute observation and critique that within governmentality studies "there is a danger that once one has provided a reasonably detailed account of the pertinent 'deliberations, strategies, tactics, and devices' that comprise governmentality ... one might think that one has fully explained the phenomena involved." Viewed as an outcome or regularity, such events cannot be explained by searching for a recurring pattern or attending only to the self-understanding of participants. This would be to produce descriptions, albeit rich and interesting, rather than explanations. Because the phenomenon consists of more than that which is empirically apprehendable, empiricism proves to be inadequate.

The protocols outlined by critical realism and the nuanced model of social reality furnished can allow criminologists to develop post-empiricist- or realist-informed research strategies for the production of criminological knowledge and to work toward building an (ontologically) realistic social justice-oriented political practice. Approaches such as left realism that attempt to be realistic without being realist, or the anti-realist strain of governmentality studies, risk becoming complicit in the reification of abstractions that support existing relations of domination or the very things that such approaches wish to reveal and change.

As Blaikie (1993, 2000), Sayer (1992), and Pawson (1989) have shown, research strategies (methodologies) are different from techniques of data collection (methods) in that they provide us with a mode of reasoning and sets of concepts that can be used to construct substantive theories and to develop and evaluate methods as well as social programs (compare with Pawson and Tilley 1997). They not only offer us a way to understand the relationship between us and the things we seek to describe and explain but also a systematic way of attaining knowledge and promoting social transformation. All research strategies (methodologies) offer a theory of what knowledge is and how it can be attained (epistemology), as well as offering a theory of the nature of social reality/objects of investigation (ontology). A crucial aspect of these strategies is that they are tools that allow us to conceptualize the production of knowledge and our objects of investigation, and they each offer us a different way of doing this in that they offer different analytical tools for the crafting of descriptions and explanations.

Critical realism, as an alternative to both positivism and conventionalism/ interpretivism, offers not only a more rigorous theory of knowledge but also a developed ontology that can be utilized to strengthen and extend criminological enquiry. Positivistic and conventionalist research strategies emphasize *how* knowledge is to be generated, with little regard for *what* the object of investigation must be like in order for it to be known in the way proposed. As critical realism is not a theory but a metatheory, or a philosophy of (social) science, it is also a methodology. As such, it can be used to produce or reformulate a number of substantive theoretical positions and be fruitfully employed for social enquiry (Layder 1990, 19; Sayer 1992, 4-5). What we are suggesting here is that new theories of crime and crime control can be crafted by using the developed sets of concepts and premises furnished by critical realism. This alone means that substantive theories generated would have begun from a different set of questions and thus would make them very different from those produced using either a positivistic or a conventionalist/ interpretivist metatheoretical framework. It then moves to questions of epistemology or how best to go about attaining knowledge of our object. The demarcation of questions of ontology from epistemology in critical realism and the taking of the former as the starting point make it unlike either of its competitors.

## Conclusion

Perhaps some readers will think that we exaggerate what are only minor differences between critically minded scholars. We do not suggest that scholars positioned from within different or conflicting metatheoretical frameworks cannot combine to further critical criminological practice. We do think, however, that theory is *not* a matter of "perspectives" that can be applied or eclectically combined. We stress the issue of whether we are making too much of what may appear to be minor differences between criminologies because, too often, differences are not given enough credence as to their significance to how social science is carried out. How one comes to understand what the real challenges are and what might be done about them, and how to go about this, will be shaped by the sets of concepts available to them through which they can fashion a description and explanation. Accordingly, although there may certainly be minor differences of opinion between scholars who are basically like-minded, there are always more than these small differences between them if they come at things from different theoretical lineages. The differences between positivism, interpretivism, and critical realism, as outlined above, will be reflected in respected positions taken. These differences, of course, might be "worked out" through negotiation and compromise, but they are only held in abeyance. An example of not-so-minor differences is found in comparing Marxist criminology with that indebted to symbolic interactionism (for example, labelling theories). We think it would be easy to find critical scholars on both sides committed to social justice, but each would hold very different positions on, for example, what crime is, how it is produced, reproduced, and transformed, and the implications of this for how and why it is managed in the way that it is. Another example is found in the different ethical commitments within criminology and sociology surrounding the agency-structure debate. Some social scientists study social action only (symbolic interactionists, for instance), others study social structure only (structural Marxists). There are more than simply small differences between these scholars.

Our chapter attempts to highlight the role epistemology plays in orienting social science practice and to challenge the received wisdom and orthodoxy in criminology. Unfortunately, although critical realism offers a powerful analytic that can be combined with social theories such as those proffered by Foucault on governance, Bourdieu on subject formation, Marx on capitalist production, and Durkheim on social integration, many criminologists and sociologists have neglected this analytic because of a category mistake: they hold "realism" to be an outdated theoretical position and believe that there are more fruitful "perspectives" that can be employed in the study of crime and its control. The problem with this position is that critical realism – the "realism" we are concerned with – is not well understood in North American social science and is not the same as the more familiar substantive realisms that criminologists and sociologists are likely familiar with. Moreover, the proliferation of certain readings of Foucault that render him anti-realist is a symptom of inattention to important epistemological issues we have endeavoured to highlight. We believe instead that many critically minded scholars would be predisposed to critical realism if they were made aware of this epistemological alternative. We think this is important for critical inquiry and social science, in general, to move forward.

NOTES

1   The notion that theories are merely perspectives is theoreticist and disregards the fact that theories comprise interconnected sets of concepts that have been produced and can be – and are often in need of being – refined. Rather than holding theories to be perspectives, we agree with Anthony Woodiwiss (2001, vii) that theories furnish us with conceptual lenses that allow us to produce "somewhat artificial representations of social reality" and that these lenses often require refinement.

2   For a useful discussion of the various forms of "science," see Frauley and Pearce (2007). On the broader theoretical and political implications of social science practice, see Datta, Frauley, and Pearce (2010).

3   Although the primary reference point for our text is the work of Roy Bhaskar (1975), we find valuable works by social scientists that have adapted and developed his work for social science (see Layder 1990, 1993; Sayer 1992, 2000). We note

also that our orientation toward scientific realism has been tempered by scientific realists such as Keat and Urry (1975) and Benton (1977). We should also mention that we employ the traditional meaning of "science": systematic and rigorous analysis. We advocate a theoretically sophisticated scientific practice.

4   See Blaikie (2000) and Frauley and Pearce (2007) for a discussion of modes of reasoning.

5   Another example: more men than women participate in white-collar crime. This is so not because of some inherent difference between men and women that makes the former more suitable to white-collar crime; it is because, structurally, women do not have the opportunity to engage in white-collar crime to the same extent as do men. Men have traditionally occupied more positions of power and authority in the public sphere than women, and therefore abuses of power and authority are more likely to be perpetrated by men rather than women. The public face of an organization or corporation is usually the people themselves, but what lies behind this is an organizing structure that positions the people and provides them with roles, expectations, duties, and so on. It is this organizing or structuring element that is not readily visible but which is vitally important. The realm of potential and tendencies in the case of white-collar crime is to be found in organizational structure, including stratification. Action is enabled and constrained through this organizing structure.

6   For Rom Harre (1986, 2001), social structure does not exist in any ontological way. Concepts such as class, race, and gender (and presumably risk) are merely taxonomic categories devised by people to group "powerful particulars" such as "skill acquisition" and other human activities – the latter have causal power, the former categorizations do not. Only humans (like electrons) are causal agents; their discursive productions are not. Even when people talk about some event, they are actually talking about how they talked about what happened. Pearce and Woodiwiss (2001) are sympathetic to Bhaskar's (1975) critical realism but do not see how an intransitive notion of the social helps to enable emancipatory politics.

7   Foucault ranked fifth (see Wright and Friedrichs 1998, Table 1, p. 219).

## REFERENCES

Arac, J. 1980. The Function of Foucault at the Present Time. *Humanities in Society* 3: 73-86.

Archer, M.S. 1995. *Realist Social Theory: The Morphogenetic Approach*. New York: Cambridge University Press.

Benton, T. 1977. *Philosophical Foundations of the Three Sociologies*. London: Routledge and Kegan Paul.

Best, S. 1995. *The Politics of Historical Vision: Marx, Foucault, Habermas*. New York: Guilford.

Bhaskar, R.A. 1975. *A Realist Theory of Science*. London: Verso.

–. 1993. *Dialectic: The Pulse of Freedom*. London: Verso.

Blaikie, N. 1993. *Approaches to Social Enquiry*. Cambridge, UK: Polity Press.

–. 2000. *Designing Social Research*. Cambridge, UK: Polity Press.

Bryman, A. 1988. *Quantity and Quality in Social Research*. New York: Routledge.

Burchell, G., C. Gordon, and P. Miller, eds. 1991. *The Foucault Effect: Studies in Govern-mentality*. Chicago: University of Chicago Press.

Cain, M. 1986. Realism, Feminism, Methodology, and Law. *International Journal of the Sociology of Law* 14(3-4): 255-67.

–. 1990. Realist Philosophy and Standpoint Epistemologies or Feminist Criminology as a Successor Science. In *Feminist Perspectives in Criminology*, ed. L. Gelsthorpe and A. Morris, 124-40. Bristol, PA: Open University Press.

–. 1993. Foucault, Feminism and Feeling: What Foucault Can and Cannot Contribute to Feminist Epistemology. In *Up Against Foucault: Explorations of Some Tensions between Foucault and Feminism*, ed. C. Ramazanoglu, 73-98. New York: Routledge.

Cavallari, H.M. 1980. *Savoir* and *Pouvoir:* Michel Foucault's Theory of Discursive Practice. *Humanities in Society* 3(1): 55-72.

Chan, W., and G.S. Rigakos. 2002. Risk, Crime and Gender. *British Journal of Criminology* 42(4): 743-61.

Collier, A. 1994. *Critical Realism: An Introduction to Roy Bhaskar's Philosophy*. New York: Verso.

Datta, P., J. Frauley, and F. Pearce. 2010. Situation Critical: For a Critical, Reflexive, Real-ist, Emancipatory Social Science. *Journal of Critical Realism* 9(2): 227-47.

Dean, M. 1994. *Critical and Effective Histories: Foucault's Methods and Historical Sociology*. London: Routledge.

Ericson, R., and K. Carriere. 1994. The Fragmentation of Criminology. In *The Futures of Criminology*, ed. D. Nelken, 88-109. Thousand Oaks, CA: Sage.

Fairclough, N. 1992. *Discourse and Social Change*, 37-55. Cambridge, UK: Polity Press.

Fattah, E. 1997. *Criminology: Past, Present and Future – A Critical Overview*. New York: St. Martin's Press.

Foucault, M. 1965. *Madness and Civilization*. Toronto: Random House. (Orig. pub. 1961.)

–. 1971. *The Order of Things: An Archaeology of the Human Sciences*. New York: Vintage Books. (Orig. pub. 1966.)

–. 1972a. *The Archaeology of Knowledge*. New York: Pantheon. (Orig. pub. 1969.)

–. 1972b. The Discourse on Language. In *The Archaeology of Knowledge*, by M. Foucault, 215-37. New York: Pantheon.

–. 1973. *The Birth of the Clinic: An Archaeology of Medical Perception*. New York: Vintage. (Orig. pub. 1963.)

–. 1977. *Discipline and Punish: The Birth of the Prison*. Toronto: Random House. (Orig. pub. 1975.)

–. 1978. *The History of Sexuality*. Vol. 1. New York: Vintage. (Orig. pub. 1976.)

–. 1991. Questions of Method. In *The Foucault Effect: Studies in Governmentality*, ed. G. Burchell, C. Gordon, and P. Miller, 73-86. Chicago: University of Chicago Press.

Frauley, J. 2004. Race, Justice, and the Production of Knowledge: A Critical Realist Consideration. *Canadian Journal of Law and Society* 19(2): 177-97.

–. 2005. Representing Theory and Theorising in Criminal Justice Studies: Practising Theory Considered. *Critical Criminology* 13(3): 245-65.

–. 2007a. The Expulsion of Foucault from Governmentality Studies. In *Critical Realism and the Social Sciences: Heterodox Elaborations,* ed. J. Frauley and F. Pearce, 258-72. Toronto: University of Toronto Press.

–. 2007b. "Toward an Archaeological-Realist Foucauldian Analytics of Government." *British Journal of Criminology* 47: 617-33.

–. 2008. Heterodox Criminology: Rethinking Methodology and Criminological Knowledge Production. In *Criminology: Challenges for the 21st Century,* ed. W. Ventura, 1-25. New York: Nova Science.

–, and F. Pearce. 2007. Critical Realism and the Social Sciences: Methodological and Epistemological Preliminaries. In *Critical Realism and the Social Sciences: Heterodox Elaborations,* ed. J. Frauley and F. Pearce, 3-29. Toronto: University of Toronto Press.

Garland D. 1997. "Governmentality" and the Problem of Crime: Foucault, Criminology, Sociology. *Theoretical Criminology* 1(2): 173-214.

–, and R. Sparks. 2000. Criminology, Social Theory, and the Challenge of Our Times. In *Criminology and Social Theory,* ed. D. Garland and R. Sparks, 1-22. Toronto: Oxford University Press.

Harre, R. 1986. *Varieties of Realism: A Rationale for the Natural Sciences.* Oxford: Blackwell.

–. 2001. How to Change Reality: Story v. Structure – a Debate between Rom Harre and Roy Bhaskar. In *After Postmodernism: An Introduction to Critical Realism,* ed. J. Lopez and G. Potter, 22-28. New York: Athlone Press.

Hunt, A. 1978. *The Sociological Movement in Law.* London: Macmillan.

Jones, T., B.D. MacLean, and J. Young. 1986. *The Islington Crime Survey: Crime Victimization and Policing Inner-City London.* Aldershot: Gower.

Keat, R., and J. Urry. 1975. *Social Theory as Science.* London: Routledge and Kegan Paul.

Kerruish, V. 1991. *Jurisprudence as Ideology.* New York: Routledge.

Kraska, P.B. 2006. Criminal Justice Theory: Toward Legitimacy and an Infrastructure. *Justice Quarterly* 23(2): 167-85.

Lacey, N. 1994. Introduction: Making Sense of Criminal Justice. In *Criminal Justice,* ed. N. Lacey, 1-35. Toronto: Oxford University Press.

–. 1995. Contingency and Criminalisation. In *Frontiers of Criminality,* ed. I. Loveland, 1-27. London: Sweet and Maxwell.

Layder, D. 1990. *The Realist Image in Social Science.* London: Macmillan.

–. 1993. *New Strategies in Social Research.* Cambridge, UK: Polity Press.

Lecourt, D. 1975. *Marxism and Epistemology: Bachelard, Canguilhem and Foucault.* London: New Left Books.

Leiter, B. 1996. Legal Realism. In *A Companion to Philosophy of Law and Legal Theory*, ed. D. Patterson, 261-80. Malden, MA: Blackwell.

López, J., and G. Potter, eds. 2001. *After Postmodernism: An Introduction to Critical Realism*. London: Athlone Press.

Manicas, P.T. 1987. *A History and Philosophy of the Social Sciences*. New York: Blackwell.

–, and P.F. Secord. 1983. Implications for Psychology of the Philosophy of Science. *American Psychologist* 38 (April): 399-413.

Marx, K. 1978. Contribution to the Critique of Hegel's Philosophy of Right. In *The Marx-Engels Reader*, ed. R.C. Tucker, 16-25. New York: W.W. Norton.

McMullan, J., and R.S. Ratner. 1982. Radical versus Technocratic Analyses in the Study of Crime: Critique of *Criminal Justice in Canada*. *Canadian Journal of Criminology* 24(4): 483-94.

Menzies, R. 1992. Beyond Realist Criminology. In *Realist Criminology: Crime Control and Policing in the 1990s*, ed. J. Lowman and B. MacLean, 139-56. Toronto: University of Toronto Press.

–, and D.E. Chunn. 1999. Discipline in Dissent: Canadian Academic Criminology at the Millennium. *Canadian Journal of Criminology* 41(2): 285-97.

Menzies, R., D. Chunn, and S. Boyd. 2001. Introd. to *[Ab]using Power: The Canadian Experience*, ed. R. Menzies, D. Chunn, and S. Boyd, 11-24. Halifax: Fernwood.

Miller, P., and N. Rose. 1995. Political Thought and the Limits of Orthodoxy: A Response to Curtis. *British Journal of Sociology* 46(4): 590-97.

Norrie, A. 1993. *Crime, Reason and History: A Critical Introduction to Criminal Law*. London: Weidenfeld and Nicolson.

Olssen, M. 2003. Structuralism, Post-Structuralism, Neo-Liberalism: Assessing Foucault's Legacy. *Journal of Education Policy* 18(2): 189-202.

O'Malley, P. 2001. Discontinuity, Government and Risk: A Response to Rigakos and Hadden. *Theoretical Criminology* 5(1): 85-92.

–, L. Weir, and C. Shearing. 1997. Governmentality, Criticism, Politics. *Economy and Society* 26(4): 501-17.

Palys, T.S. 1989. Ideology, Epistemology, and Modes of Inquiry: Aboriginal Issues, Trajectories of Truth, and the Criteria of Evaluation Research. Paper presented at the Symposium of the West Coast Law and Society Group, Vancouver (unpublished).

–. 1992. *Research Decisions: Quantitative and Qualitative Perspectives*. Toronto: Harcourt Brace Jovanovich.

Pawson, R. 1989. *A Measure for Measures: A Manifesto for Empirical Sociology*. New York: Routledge.

–, and N. Tilley. 1997. *Realistic Evaluation*. Thousand Oaks, CA: Sage.

Pearce, F., and L. Snider. 1995. Regulating Capitalism. In *Corporate Crime: Contemporary Debates*, ed. F. Pearce and L. Snider, 19-48. Toronto: University of Toronto Press.

Pearce, F., and S. Tombs. 1996. Hegemony, Risk and Governance: "Social Regulation" and the American Chemical Industry. *Economy and Society* 25(3): 428-54.

–. 1998. Foucault, Governmentality, Marxism. *Social and Legal Studies* 7(4): 567-75.

–. 1999. *Toxic Capitalism: Corporate Crime and the Chemical Industry*. Toronto: Canadian Scholars' Press.

Pearce, F., and A. Woodiwiss. 2001. Reading Foucault as a Realist. In *Realism after Postmodernism: An Introduction to Critical Realism*, ed. J. Lopez and G. Potter, 51-62. New York: Athlone Press.

Purvis, T., and A. Hunt. 1993. Discourse, Ideology, Discourse, Ideology. *British Journal of Sociology* 44(3): 473-99.

Quinney, R. 1974. *A Critical Philosophy of Legal Order*. Boston: Little Brown.

Ratner, R.S. 1985. Inside the Liberal Boot: The Criminological Enterprise in Canada. In *The New Criminologies in Canada: Crime, State, and Control*, ed. T. Fleming, 13-26. Toronto: Oxford University Press.

–. 1987. Rethinking the Sociology of Crime and Justice. In *State Control: Criminal Justice Politics in Canada*, ed. R.S. Ratner and J. McMullan, 3-20. Vancouver: UBC Press.

Rigakos, G.S. 1999. Risk Society and Actuarial Criminology: Prospects for a Critical Discourse. *Canadian Journal of Criminology* 41(2): 137-50.

–. 2001. On Continuity, Risk and Political Economy: A Response to O'Malley. *Theoretical Criminology* 5(1): 93-100.

–. 2002. *The New Parapolice: Risk Markets and Commodified Social Control*. Toronto: University of Toronto Press.

–. 2009. Risk, Realism, and the Politics of Resistance. *Critical Sociology* 35(1): 79-103.

–, and R.W. Hadden. 2001. Crime, Capitalism and the Risk Society: Towards the Same Olde Modernity? *Theoretical Criminology* 5(1): 61-84.

Rose, N. 1999. *Powers of Freedom: Reframing Political Thought*. Cambridge: Cambridge University Press.

–, and P. Miller. 1992. Political Power beyond the State: Problematics of Government. *British Journal of Sociology* 43(2): 173-205.

Sayer, A. 1992. *Method in Social Science: A Realist Approach*. New York: Routledge.

–. 2000. *Realism and Social Science*. Thousand Oaks, CA: Sage.

Shearing, C. 1989. Decriminalizing Criminology: Reflections on the Literal and Tropological Meaning of the Term. *Canadian Journal of Criminology* 31(2): 169-78.

Spitzer, S. 1975. Toward a Marxian Theory of Deviance. *Social Problems* 22(5): 638-51.

Sprinker, M. 1980. The Use and Abuse of Foucault. *Humanities in Society* 3(1): 1-22.

Stenning, P. 1999. Implications of Public Service Reform for Criminal Justice Research and Policy in Canada. *Canadian Journal of Criminology* 41(2): 179-90.

Taylor, I., P. Walton, and J. Young. 1973. *The New Criminology: For a Social Theory of Deviance*. London: Routledge.

Veyne, P. 1997. Foucault Revolutionizes History. In *Foucault and His Interlocutors*, ed. A. Davidson, 146-82. Chicago: University of Chicago Press.

Woodiwiss, A. 1990. *Social Theory after Postmodernism: Rethinking Production, Law, and Class*. London: Pluto Press.

–. 1998. *Globalisation, Human Rights and Labour Law in Pacific Asia*. Cambridge: Cambridge University Press.

–. 2001. *The Visual in Social Theory*. New York: Athlone Press/Continuum.

Wright, R.A., and D.O. Freidrichs. 1998. The Most-Cited Scholars and Works in Critical Criminology. *Journal of Criminal Justice Education* 9: 211-31.

Young, J. 1997. Left Realism: The Basics. In *Thinking Critically about Crime*, ed. B. MacLean and D. Milovanovic, 28-36. Vancouver: Collective Press.

# 10
# The Right to the City on Trial

*Lisa Freeman*

> Despite more defeats than victories, there is no sign that squatters and
> homeless people will suddenly give up the struggle for housing.
>
> – Neil Smith, *The New Urban Frontier:*
> *Gentrification and the Revanchist City*

Participating in a criminal trial hardly reflects radical politics. Grassroots
activists have long used the criminal courts as a venue to push for political
change, challenge injustices, and vocalize dissent. Activist legal advocacy
takes many forms. Some activists have been known to transgress the hierarchy
of the courts, resembling Abbie Hoffman and the Chicago Seven's famous
theatrical mockery trial, through performances negating and "spoofing"
law's power. Others have worked with the courts to advance public policies
(Marshall and Barclay 2003).

Canadian grassroots activists have consistently taken their political
struggles into the criminal courts. When the trial of Ottawa's Seven Year
Squatters *(R. v. Ackerley et al.)* began in September 2004 – although not surprising – it did seem odd for five anarchist squatters to fully comply with
legal rules and procedures.[1] Defending their actions in court was not a choice;
deciding to work *within* the court was. The assumption that anarchists would
work against rather than with a system may seem a logical one. Yet, in this
case, the non-hierarchical grassroots political tactics used during the occupation and eviction of the squat were effectively brought into the courtroom.
The social interactions that ensued substantially altered the organization,
procedures, and interpersonal relations of the trial.

It is precisely this *system*, that *process*, and the *social relations* produced
within the physical space of the court itself that are the focus of this chapter.

What happens when activists, who previously attempted to carve out an autonomous space in the city, defend themselves in a criminal trial? Does the process of self-representation and non-hierarchical organizing neatly transfer from the city streets to the criminal courts? An acquittal is not always the sole purpose for defending oneself in court. Pushing boundaries, challenging hierarchies, and asserting politically motivated arguments are sometimes equally as important. The space of the courtroom itself becomes a differently defined political terrain.

When struggles over urban space are brought into the criminal courts, I argue that *the right to the city* itself goes on trial. In such a trial, the criminal charges of break and enter and mischief are intertwined with arguments against private property and for political claims to the city. The Gilmour Street squatters resisted dominant understandings of urban space by occupying a previously abandoned building. They asserted their *right to the city*. When they entered the courtroom, this claim and struggle for urban space did not disappear.

Urban and legal geography literature effectively explores the nexus of law and space (Brigham and Gordon 1991; Blomley 1994; Mitchell 1997; Blomley, Delaney, and Ford 2001; Holder and Harrison 2003). Past studies have predominantly examined the intersection between law and space in the city. In this chapter, I explore the nexus of law and space in formally established legal spaces. Instead of placing the legal in geography, I place the geography in the spaces of the legal. What happens in the spaces of the criminal courts when the *right to the city* is challenged? David Harvey (1973) has noted that the interpretation of law in the city becomes a significant form of governance that shapes the social spaces of control in our cities. When the interpretation of law becomes a form of governance that controls our cities, how does an interpretation of social and procedural relations in court, when confronted with urban resistance, shape the spaces of legal control in our courtrooms and cities? Would such an analysis align the criminal courts with a form of urban governance?

In this chapter, not only do I re-emphasize how legal geography provides useful tools for studying power relations in urban space, but I hope to reveal how urban geography is equally important for re-examining the social relations of the criminal courts. The research for this chapter stems from my participant observation of the trial of Ottawa's Gilmour Street squatters in a previous research project. My initial analysis attempted to prove that the squatters created a new space for resistance within the criminal courts, which may still be the case. Here, I attempt to show how Henri Lefebvre's (1991, 1996) notion of "the right to the city" and the "production of space" can provide useful tools for further analyzing the social relations that affect the space of the courts and potentially reveal an additional (indirect) role the criminal courts play in urban space. I then discuss the connections between the Gilmour Street squat and the rights to the city discourse, how legal and urban geographic tools are useful for studying legal spaces, and how putting "the right the city" on trial can alter the divisions between resistance, compliance, and governance in the courts.

## Squatting your "Right to the City"

The Gilmour Street squatters exercised their right to the city by occupying an abandoned house and attempting to convert it into social housing. They were not alone in this attempt (Corr 1999). For at least thirty years, urban geographers and community activists alike have been documenting and analyzing such claims to the "right to the city." Inspired by Lefebvre's (1991, 1996) writings on the social, political, and economic structuring of urban space, a substantial amount of literature has focused on how urban forms of resistance do not simply act upon space but occur through using, challenging, and focusing on the political implications of the organization of social space itself (Davis 1990; Blomley 1994; Cresswell 1996; Merrifield and Swyngedouw 1997; Purcell 2002; Mitchell 2003).

By opposing the gentrification of working-class neighbourhoods, occupying parks, and reusing already established spaces, people are asserting their right to the city by revealing the radical potential of everyday life and exposing the displacement of power in urban space (Harvey 1973; Castells 1983; Brigham and Gordon 1991; Smith 1996; Mitchell 2003; Slater 2008). In his piece *The Right to the City*, Henri Lefebvre (1996, 158) critiqued scientific approaches to urban studies that viewed the city as object and instead claimed that this right to the city was not a simple return to traditional cities but could "only be formulated as a transformed and renewed right to urban life." For Lefebvre, this right to the city cumulated in a "cry and demand" growing from the class relations and conflict generated from social inequality within capitalism (ibid.). As noted by Don Mitchell (2003, 5), the right to the city is usually contested, has never been guaranteed, and "has only been won through concerted struggle, and then, after the fact, guaranteed (to some extent) in law." Fighting for the right to the city involves claiming space, remaking it, and defending it.

On June 28, 2002, a group of Ottawa anti-poverty activists, homeless youth, and anti-G8 protesters occupied an abandoned house, effectively igniting a debate around affordable housing, disrupting moral claims to private property ownership, and asserting their right to the city. The house at 246 Gilmour Street had been left unused for seven years, and squatting the building – consciously occupying an owned property without the explicit permission of the owner – was a confrontational response to the ongoing housing crisis then underway in Ottawa. In a pattern similar to other Canadian urban squats, the Gilmour Street squatters held the house for a short time, built substantial community support, raised legitimate concerns about the lack of affordable housing in the city, and were subsequently arrested by the police (Freeman and Lamble 2004).[2]

The Gilmour Street squat came to an end on July 3, 2002. During a police operation that took place between approximately 2 a.m. and 9 a.m., several police sections, "including the Tactical Unit, Public Order Unit, Forensic Evidence Unit, and a Command Station" evicted the squatters (*R. v. Ackerley et al.* 2004, 388). In addition to a police force armed with the "regular weapon, a MP-5 machine gun, a rubber bullet, less than lethal type of weapon and ... a gas gun," fire engines, a battering ram (used to breach window frames from the outside), and the deployment of "a number of different gas substances" were used in the removal and arrest of the twenty-two remaining Gilmour Street squatters (ibid., 669, 560). According to Mandy Hiscocks (2004), a squat defendant, the arrests initially resembled those of other squats in Montreal, Toronto, and Vancouver, but the police force used was at a different level. According to Hiscocks, "it was really brutal ... A guy with a machine gun, I don't think that is very common in a political operation to evict people from an empty building." Twenty-two of the Gilmour Street squatters were detained, charged under multiple sections of the Criminal Code, and given restrictive conditions. This arguably excessive use of force and indictable criminal charges represented an ongoing accelerated militant police response to urban squats in Canada.

The Gilmour Street squatters were held in police custody for thirty-six hours following the initial arrests and then released, despite their refusal to sign the original bail conditions, which included a curfew, a clause forbidding the defendants from associating with each other, a ban on all participation in political activity, and a restriction from being within five hundred metres of 246 Gilmour Street (*Official Disclosure of Evidence* 2002).[3] Each of the twenty-two squatters was initially charged with break and enter with intention to commit mischief, three counts of mischief over $5,000, and obstruction of a peace officer (ibid.).

Over the two years of administrative court proceedings, fifteen of the squatters opted to make a deal with the Crown prosecutor and obtained court diversions instructing them each to complete forty hours of community service in lieu of standing trial. The criminal trial of the five remaining squat defendants ensued from September 27 to October 22, 2004.[4] *R. v. Ackerley et al.* marked the first major case against squatters in recent years. After spending nearly four days in deliberations, the members of the jury were unable to unanimously agree on a verdict. The jurors remained deadlocked on all but two charges for two of the accused.[5]

A couple of months later, the Crown prosecutor declared a mistrial. The charges were dropped, and the squatters declared victory. A victory did not guarantee a direct right to the city claim. It did, however, signify that a jury could not wholeheartedly convict people for claiming this right to urban space. The political saliency of taking the right to the city to court results in more than an acquittal or tangible political gain.

The methodological approach to this research was cumulative of my affiliation with the squat defendants, Ottawa-based community activism, and ongoing passion for activism in the courts.[6] My primary research methods included participant observation, semi-structured interviews, and analysis of court documents (including but not limited to the official transcripts). I observed and documented the trial of *R. v. Ackerley et al.* at the provincial courthouse in Ottawa from September 27 to October 22, 2004. My interviews with the squat defendants and several defence lawyers informally affiliated with the case took place from September 2004 to February 2005. The Crown prosecutor, judge, and other court officials declined my invitation to be interviewed. My research was strongly informed by my previous involvement with the squat and accompanying administrative hearings. The grassroots strategies of the squatters were not only documented for this research but also personally experienced.

When the house at 246 Gilmour Street was occupied, people throughout the city of Ottawa, ranging from the landlord, city officials, and police to neighbours, voiced concern or support over how this particular piece of urban space was being used. Space mattered. More importantly, how space was being used mattered. Similarly, when the five squat defendants sat behind the lawyers' bench, represented themselves in court, and submitted legal arguments, once again it became apparent that space mattered. The experiences of the Gilmour Street squatters, in the streets and in the courts, highlights how one political action can broadly influence (and alter) social understandings of grassroots activist engagement with, and the governing power of, the criminal courts.

## From Law and Geography to Geography in Law

Legal geography is useful not only for understanding how law works in the city but also for understanding how geography works in law. Shifting this analysis from the streets to the courtroom provides an opportunity to reinterpret social relations and legal spaces in the courtroom. Previous literature on the spatiality of the courtroom has focused on how particular uses of defined spaces in the courtroom affect judicial processes and power dynamics by emphasizing how social relations are moulded by the physical architecture of the courtroom (Murdoch 1998; Moore 2007; Mulcahy 2007). Building from this literature, I take initial and careful steps in unveiling the usefulness of legal and urban geography for the study of social relations in the courtroom. I argue that the theoretical tools used to examine the interactions between law and space, as well as Lefebvre's notion of the production of space in the capitalist city, open the horizons for understanding subtle yet powerful forms of resistance and governance in the criminal courts.

A law and geography approach identifies and critiques the political production of space by emphasizing how legal meanings and social relations are interpreted through particular spaces. Legal geography challenges the manner in which certain laws and spaces "are frequently presented in life as objective, asocial, and 'innocent'" (Blomley 1994, xii-xiii). It explores how laws, regulations, and legal meanings attached to particular spaces are represented and perceived in society, rather than unquestioningly accepting written legislation as the norm. Challenging how legal spaces are represented is central for making social change, whether in the city streets or in the courtroom.

In critiquing the dominant relationship between law, space, and power, legal geography explores how the subtle yet overt influences of law are not simply a mechanism of state power that outwardly controls behaviour within a defined territory (Johnston 1990; Pue 1990). Legal meanings are created through a specific locality, social interpretations of legal boundaries define particular spaces, and material space itself helps produce legal meanings. This critical approach to socio-legal studies is invaluable for studying the socio-spatial relationships in the courtroom because it shifts our focus from normative understandings of law and order.

The space of the courtroom has rarely been viewed as innocent, and its objectivity has been frequently questioned. Well-defined hierarchies and designated roles are historically established. The political power and legal meanings espoused from the physical space of the courtroom are palpable. Still, courtrooms are represented as *the* home of law. Despite the perceived rigidity of the courts, room exists to explore the subtle and social influences of law through social relations in this specific locality. Moving beyond a critique of the perceived objectivity of the court or of the established power differentiations requires a theoretical tool that can expose the political importance of seemingly mundane orderings of space and social relations. A critical examination of space and law sheds light on how critical examinations of power in the city, when moved into the space of the court, can provide a new light on (urban) resistance.

The theoretical understandings of space developed by Lefebvre are helpful for exploring how certain spaces, particularly in the city and potentially in the courtroom, are perceived and conceived. Lefebvre's theoretical understandings of absolute and abstract space reveal how the hierarchical spatial organization of social life is produced and reproduced while simultaneously opening up a discussion centred on how these spaces can be challenged and contested. His notions of absolute and abstract space are important in regard to this discussion of the space for resistance within the criminal courts because they identify the composition of this dominant space and carve out a space for political resistance.

Absolute space is a lived space that includes symbolic dimensions and an assumed strict form. Based on a Marxist interpretation of primitive accumulation and societal changes from agro-pastoral lands to urban settings, absolute space evolved throughout history and adopted social meanings attached to different spaces represented by technological, religious, and political symbols. It continues to exhibit a material form in the ordering of objects and people and is immersed in "assumed meanings addressed not to the intellect but to the body, meanings conveyed by threats, by sanctions, by a continual putting-to-type test of the emotions" (Lefebvre 1991, 52). According to Lefebvre, absolute space imposes meanings on particular spaces yet is not confined to one location. It is both abstract and concrete.

The difference between absolute space and abstract space is not always easily distinguishable. Even though Lefebvre differentiates absolute space as "conceived space" and abstract space as "perceived space," both notions of space are similarly political, powerful, and institutional (ibid., 51). As a product of capitalism and neo-capitalism, abstract space – the space of power, of the bourgeoisie, and of capitalism – resembles a lens, a specific orientation from which to view the world (57).[7] Although it is political and instituted by a state, it is not a lived space comprising real threats and sanctions. Instead, abstract space consists of "an ensemble of images, signs and symbols" that is "at once lived and represented, at once the expression and the foundation of practices" (58). According to Lefebvre, abstract space is the perceived space where dominant ideologies can be challenged and states that are alternatives to abstract space must stem from social movements focused on dismantling abstract space while simultaneously reconstructing new spaces for resistance. These new spaces of resistance are not uniform and may disrupt abstract space at varied scales. It could be argued that *right to the city* claims, such as urban squatting, disrupt abstract space but are not necessarily a social movement. However, when such claims are brought before a judge, the grassroots tactics and organizational strategies do become more visible and effective.

The concepts of abstract and absolute space fit quite comfortably within the historical context of Lefebvre's critical view of the capitalist organization of urban space. In the context of the courtroom, however, these two concepts are more pronounced and potentially seem out of place. After all, the space of the courtroom is markedly different from a city, is it not? Can resistance and social movements in the city be viewed in the same manner when transferred into the criminal courts? It is the framework for analysis provided by the classification of abstract and absolute space that is useful here. The theories developed by Lefebvre provide an illustration of space as a politically charged and socially influenced medium. The dominant abstract and absolute spaces in society are not viewed as impermeable and resistant to change, and neither are the spaces of the court. Lefebvre's theoretical approach does not merely describe "space"; it gives social and political agency to the production of space.

In the circumstances of *R. v. Ackerley et al.*, and potentially other cases of the *right to the city* on trial, the categorization of absolute and abstract space can reorient everyday occurrences in court. For example, sanctions, orders, the physical placement of actors (for example, the judge's bench, the witness box, and the public gallery) and formalized procedures can be viewed as embodiments of absolute space. Together, they represent a "total space," an "absolute political space," and a "strategic space which seeks to impose itself as a reality despite the fact that it is an abstraction, albeit one endowed with enormous powers because it is the locus and medium of power" (Lefebvre

1991, 52). Sanctions and other judicial rulings are not necessarily confined to one space; they assume a strict form; impose themselves as a reality, as they impose a particular set of ideas; and are endowed with enormous powers. Abstract space, then, may be best illustrated through actions, words, and social interactions, often but not limited to the perspectives of the presiding judge.

Abstract space in the courtroom cannot be uncritically equated with abstract space in the city. The history and locality is different. However, that lens, that specific orientation from which to view the world, including relevant signs and symbols, is prevalent. Justice McKinnon asserted his view that grassroots politics, especially in the procedural conduct of the court, did not have a place in the courtroom[8] – clearly asserting a real yet symbolic abstract space in the courtroom.

The presiding judge Justice McKinnon's reaction to the squat defendants' closing arguments and his final address to the jury is one example of abstract space in the courtroom. After hearing their closing arguments, Justice McKinnon reprimanded one of the accused for making a political speech and "stepping outside of the boundaries of proper closing arguments," demanding that "all you can do is comment on the evidence" (*R. v. Ackerley et al.* 2004, 1258-60). He clearly defined the boundaries of abstract space within the courtroom by re-enforcing the apolitical nature of law and by bluntly asking the accused if they were "going to make a political speech or ... [were] going to talk about the evidence" (1259). By asserting his ideological perspectives of proper court procedures, Justice McKinnon attempted to confine many of the political arguments and claims made by the accused within a purely legally structured abstract space (1216, 1249, 1234).

Justice McKinnon's final charge to the jury outlined his strict legal perspective, clearly representing the role of abstract space in the courtroom. He directed the jury to decide solely on the facts of the case and to make all decisions within the boundaries of the charges (ibid., 1323-24). In addition, he asserted his authority by addressing the jury to

> accept all the rules of law that I tell you apply [to the case] ... even if you disagree with or do not understand the reasons for the law, you are required to follow what I say about it. You are not allowed to pick and choose among my instructions or the law ... it is manifestly important that you accept the law from me and follow it without question. (1324)

By telling the jury to "accept all the rules of law," Justice McKinnon was simply following court procedures, but he was also asserting the "abstract" space of the court. His directives represented how abstract space influences and restricts the space for social agency or resistance in the courtroom.

Social relations, particularly those between the judge and the jury, highlight the abstract space of the court. The categorization of abstract and absolute space, when read through the lens of legal geography, can lead us to examine how such meanings were produced through the locality of the court and guide us to explore other spatial relationships in the court. Lefebvre claims that abstract and absolute space are disrupted only through resistance brought on by social movements. In the courts, this binary between resistance and dominant power, while at times obvious, is not always so simple. Reading between the lines of Justice McKinnon's charge to the jury (or assertion of abstract space), glimmers of spaces of resistance emerge. Why was he so insistent on outlining these procedures? It is possible that he was aware of a disruption going on his court – a disruption possibly instigated by urban strategies of resistance being transferred into the court.

## Self-Representation: Resistance or Complicated Compliance?

Political resistance in the court looks different from other criminal court cases. The Gilmour Street squat defendants represented themselves in court. Acting in accordance with court procedures and decorum was part of their political resistance. It was nuanced and subtle. Working with the courts provided room for the squatters to challenge the dominant abstract and absolute space of the courtroom. They did not simply dismiss the legal procedures of court, nor did they comply with every rule. By politicizing the act of self-representation, they created a space for resistance within the criminal court. The squatters established a space for activist-led legal advocacy, a thirdspace – as Edward Soja (1996) calls such counter-space, discussed in more detail below – by strategically working with the court, representing themselves, and utilizing consensus-based decision making in their trial.

The squatters' approach to self-defence was neither sensationalized nor theatrical but was most certainly intentional and arguably very effective. Self-representation enabled the squatters to frame their own arguments, question witnesses, actively participate in the trial process, and retain their autonomy. They approached the task of self-representation as part of a broader political perspective, thus their choice was not openly discouraged and did not seem to adversely affect the outcome of the case. In fact, the actions of the squat defendants were consistently viewed in a positive light, even by skeptics. Defence Counsel James Ford (2005) commented that "they were good, articulate, intelligent and better than some lawyers," while Duty Counsel Susan Morris (2005) noted that they were "very well prepared. [They] knew how to prepare law [and] knew case law." Defending themselves in court enabled the squatters to consistently insert their grassroots political arguments within the confinement of legal procedure.

The squat defendants used consensus-based non-hierarchical decision making. Important decisions were made collectively, and the squatters embodied one voice before the court. Each of the five squat defendants contributed to the formulation of their defence strategy and presented their case to the judge and jury. According to squat defendant Mandy Hiscocks (2004),

> We brought politics into the courtroom in how we were organized
> ... The court had to adjust their own process to accommodate us.
> The judges didn't really mind [it was] an effective way for a lot
> of people to represent themselves ... stop, huddle, take discussion
> outside. Then one person would speak for everyone. Highly ab-
> normal for the courts[, but it] ran smoothly. Judges were really
> tolerant of that, all the way through to the end. A big shift they
> had to make, [it] worked really well. An extension of how things
> happened in the squat.

Each of the defendants questioned and re-examined witnesses and presented different sections of the opening and closing statements. The self-represented accused submitted factums and charter motions, wrote opening and closing arguments, participated in jury selection, and used the traditional defences of necessity and colour of right (Freeman and Lamble 2004).[9] They clarified questions about court procedures, sections of the Criminal Code, rules for evidence, and legalities with the duty counsel and judge. During the six weeks of trial, interactions between the squatters, the judge, and the Crown appeared to be professional, cordial, and mutually respectful.

As worthwhile as self-representation may have been for the Gilmour Street squatters as self-represented accused and as activists, the squatters occupied a marginalized position in the courtroom. They were not familiar with the detailed procedural aspects of a trial, did not have any formal legal training, and were conducting their defence in a manner unfamiliar to the court. However, they used the strategic space of the courtroom to defend the political action of squatting, to reinforce attributes of non-hierarchical decision making, and to continue the fight for the rights of homeless people by bringing it into the courts. In doing so, they created a new political *thirdspace* within the criminal courts.

The squatters continued to redefine forms of resistance (and transferred knowledge from right-to-the-city tactics) and to challenge abstract and absolute space by generating new uses and interpretations for an already defined material space. Initially, in their attempts to create permanent shelter in privately owned but neglected property, the squatters exercised their grassroots politics to establish a space resembling Edward Soja's (1996, 69) *Thirdspace*, a counter-space "of resistance to the dominant order arising precisely from [its] subordinate, peripheral or marginalized positioning" developed from political choice and/or social (class-based) marginalization. *Thirdspace* is an important concept in analyzing both squatting and activist legal advocacy because it embodies "a politics of space but at the same time goes beyond politics inasmuch as it presupposes a critical analysis of all spatial politics as of all politics in general" (ibid.). It challenges dominant spaces by creating a politically charged space.

*Thirdspace* has the potential to become a place of social struggle because it starts from a marginalized space and uses "lived space as a strategic location from which to encompass, understand and potentially transform all spaces simultaneously" (ibid., 68). In representing the radical potential within a given space, the concept of *thirdspace* reveals how squatting and activist legal advocacy (in the form of self-represented accused) challenges the dominant ordering of space by simply interpreting meaning through taking over a material space. The squatters took over space. However, in the courtroom, the visible reclamation of space is not as obvious. The political motivations behind self-representation were evident in the content of their arguments. Still, in the courtroom, resistance may appear to be more veiled than initially intended.

## Is This What Resistance Looks Like?

When the Gilmour Street squatters occupied the abandoned house, they resisted prevailing norms of private property in urban space. They exercised their right to the city. When they represented themselves in court, they resisted the procedural rules of court space. They exercised urban grassroots organizing tactics in the courtroom.[10] But what tactics and strategies were used as a result of their resistance? Was there any direct reaction on behalf of the judge? The jury? The public?

Looking at how the crime is defined, understood, and punished, as noted by Michel Foucault (1995), may tell as much about the person committing the crime as it does about the society defining the crime. In this case, the crime has been defined as (urban) resistance. What, then, does this form of resistance tell us about the society in the court? If the good governor does not have a sting, as Foucault indicates in his writings on governmentality (1991), could the acquittal of the Gilmour Street squatters be viewed less as a form of resistance and more as a form of governance?

Social gains, although not legal precedents, were made in the trial of *R. v. Ackerley*. Most gains were thought of as a direct result of the organizing strategy of the squat defendants. The inability for the jury to make a unanimous decision and the subsequent lack of a conviction indicates a level of public awareness about the criminality of squatting during a housing crisis. Mark Ertel (2005), an Ottawa-based defence counsel, surmised that the twelve jurors may have adjusted their political opinions and even possibly incited a "long-term ripple effect" on the public at large. Similarly, Yavar Hahmeed (2005), an Ottawa-based civil liberties lawyer who provided support and advice for the squat defendants, noted that going to trial, self-representing, and not being convicted under criminal law is a tremendous victory for the squatters because it extends beyond the immediate needs of the accused and provides an opportunity for "constituents and publics" to observe how it is possible for activists to fight their charges in court and win.

In addition, the trial of *R. v. Ackerley* contributed to the development of new legal resources for disadvantaged groups. During pretrial motions, the squatters presented an argument outlining the reasons why they (as self-represented accused) deserved financial support from Legal Aid Ontario. Even though the Legal Aid documentation and testimony clearly indicated a lack of jurisdiction for the squatters' request, the presiding judge suggested that the Crown appeal to the attorney general for a set sum of money in order to ensure a fair trial for the accused. In the end, the Office of the Attorney General provided financial support for the basic costs of trial, including paying for daily court transcripts, photocopies, and other court-related costs, amounting to over $1,000 (*R. v. Ackerley et al.* 2004, 57). It should be clear, however, that although the allocation of this money was a "victory" for the squat defendants, it did not establish any legal precedent. The Crown plainly indicated that the circumstances of *R. v. Ackerley* were exceptional and that future self-represented accused may not receive the same funding.

Despite the lack of a substantive legal precedent, this "victory" established two social precedents. First, it contributed to Justice McKinnon's awareness of the inadequacies of Ontario Legal Aid's ability to financially support self-represented accused. Second, the case law that the squatters used in asking for financial support may have provided an unofficial guideline as well as motivation for other defendants in similar situations. Even if strict legal gains were not made, the social precedents cultivated by *R. v. Ackerley et al.* definitely broadened the scope and acceptability for such arguments in the future.

There is no doubt that the space of the courtroom was substantially altered and room for alternative forms of court representation fostered by the actions of the Gilmour Street squatters. During my six weeks of court observation, I witnessed a palatable change in the space of the court. Even though the squatters respected the basic hierarchy of the courtroom, referred to the judge as "Your Honour," and were cordial to the Crown prosecutor, this trial had a different feel from most trials. A space for resistance was most definitely created. The squatters maintained their political perspective, organized themselves in a manner not usually accepted by the courts, and stood by their decision-making process. However, were these actions forms of resistance or a new form of urban governance?

To govern, from a governmentality perspective, does not imply to rule. Power is not centralized in one state apparatus. People are governed through policies, regulations, and devices granted by those in authority (Rose 1996). Forms of governance and the criminal court converge when we carefully examine how social relations create legal meanings in a specific space. The social relations exhibited in *R. v. Ackerley et al.* did not represent the law-and-order model of court structure. The altercation of proper court order was initiated by the squat defendants. In addition to creating a space for political resistance, this altercation created a space for governance within the criminal courts. "Governance directs attention to the nature, problems, means, actions, manners, techniques and objects by which actors place themselves under the control, guidance, sway and mastery of others, or seek to place other actors, organizations, entities or events under their own sway," and those actors in control must be subject to change (Rose 1999, 16). And, indeed, the court – the actor in control – was subject to change. It allowed a form of resistance (or could we call it "community governance"?) in the space of the court. The criminal aspects of the charges appeared second to the political and social context of the trial. The gains the squatters made potentially reflect liberal aspirations of the judge and/or the "true" nature of the criminal justice system. However, in the context of right-to-the-city claims and political resistance in the courts, choosing resistance over governance or governance over resistance will lead only to a muddled decision over dispersed versus structured forms of power.

In the case of R. v. Ackerley et al., perhaps both governance and resistance played a role in challenging the space of the criminal courts. The right-to-the-city claims and the grassroots tactics brought into court potentially created a space for alternative forms of urban governance. Another squat did not happen as a result of the trial. The squatters felt satisfied and supported in their claims to urban space. Still, the power differentiations in the spaces of the courtroom exist: the judge governed through the abstract space of the court; the squatters resisted prescribed roles for the accused.

As Valverde (2005) noted, it is important to document and analyze the *how* of governance, which is overlooked in Marxist analysis of the *why*. I contend that when exploring the *how* of governance, we must first ask the *if* question. If taking the right to the city to trial shifts punitive characteristics of criminal courts into the realm of governmentality, then how are these forms of governance resisted? If power is dispersed and implicated through regulatory mechanisms of governmentality, then how do forms and techniques of governmentality, when confronted with specific cases, constitute the spaces beyond the courtroom?

Exploring the *how* of governance is indeed important. Our society is governed by and through complex mechanisms of power. Studies of governmentality enable us to understand how power is formed, administered, and dispersed. However, such studies do not directly help us understand how this power is to be resisted. Identifying power is an essential part of resistance, and resistance is "a purposeful action directed against some disliked entity with the intention of changing it or lessening its effect" (Cresswell 1996, 22).

## Conclusion

Urban and legal geography do have a place in the courtroom. Derived from a critique of the capitalist structures and governance in the city, urban and legal geographies further complicate the power implicit in the social relations in the courtroom. Documenting the production of space by legal procedures and analyzing how space is reproduced by grassroots strategies reveal alternative geographies in the courtroom. The production and reproduction of social/

power relations in the courtroom is not natural. Exploring how spaces of resistance are fostered through activist trials can provide another framework for understanding and exploring the architecture of the courtroom.

Victories in the courts do not need to be defined within an explicitly legal framework. In establishing a nuanced space of resistance in the courtroom, the Gilmour Street squat defendants were helping to redefine the space for activist achievements in the criminal courts. Shortly after the trial, the house at 246 Gilmour Street was demolished. The lot lay vacant, filled with weeds, debris, and dirt, for a couple of years afterward. This empty and abandoned lot to some may signify a failure of direct action and political struggles in the court. Yet, it clearly reflects the uncompromising capitalist context in which these legal struggles are fought. Unlike the house at 246 Gilmour Street, the anarchist politics of the squatters did not vanish. They were not abandoned. Their organizing tactics, critique of private property, and example of alternative approaches to criminal trials was quite visible. Their victories do not need to be defined (or constituted) within the parameters of legal language.

Activist resistance in the courtroom, resulting from large sensational and confrontational political actions, need not reproduce the action that landed activists in court. Sometimes, as in the case of the Gilmour Street squat, defendants with a nuanced, knowledgeable, strong, and determined grassroots political approach will inch by inch carve out the spaces for resistance in the courtroom. The squatters worked with the criminal courts to establish a place of, and for, resistance without overtly compromising their politics and created a space for political resistance in the court by challenging predominant legal spaces. The organizing tactics, critique of private property, and alternative forms of resistance worked in court. In this example, and there are not many in Canada, squatters were not convicted of a crime. Squatting is illegal, yet the squatters walked free.

NOTES

1   In the official court transcripts, the court refers to the matter as *R. v. Ackerley et al.* The complete name at the time of the trial was *R. v. Ackerley, Hiscocks, Miller, Sauvé and Sawyer.*

2   Many cities have recently experienced a proliferation of public squats. From Montreal's Overdale squat (2001) to the Woodward's squat in Vancouver (2002), the Infirmary squat in Halifax (2002), the Pope squat in Toronto (2002), and the Water Street squat in Peterborough, Ontario (2003), many anti-poverty activists

have become more confrontational and direct in their political organizing and strategizing.

3    The arrests at 246 Gilmour Street occurred at two separate times. Six squatters were arrested on the front porch at approximately 3:00 a.m. on July 4, 2002. The majority of the squatters remained in the house and were arrested closer to 7:30 a.m. (participant observation, July 4, 2002).

4    After obtaining a diversion, many squatters returned to their lives, whether in housed or under-housed circumstances. Many of the squatters continued to support the defendants by regular attendance in the court gallery during the trial, and shared meals before, after, and during a long court date and at the subsequent and preceding fundraising events.

5    Mandy Hiscocks and Dan Sawyer were the only two accused acquitted on the break-and-enter charges (Lisa Freeman, author observation, October 22, 2004).

6    I was a supporter of, and organizer with, the Seven Year Squat during its occupation, was arrested during the eviction, represented myself and others during administrative proceedings, obtained a court diversion for my criminal charges, and continued legal and media support during and after the trial.

7    I interpret Lefebvre's categorization of neo-capitalism as similar to neo-liberalism in a capitalist state.

8    It is important to clarify that Justice McKinnon was openly dedicated to ensuring a fair trial for the self-represented accused. On several occasions, one could even claim that his actions were in the realm of progressive.

9    The main charter motion was 11B – unreasonable delay. It took two years for the squat defendants to stand before the judge at trial.

10   It is important not to sensationalize this squat. The squatters did not contest their privileged position. They were able to take off work for nearly three weeks, could make regular meetings and court dates for nearly two years, and had access to court materials and knowledge that many other self-represented accused do not. Still, the privileged nature of the squatters does not dismiss or diminish the significance of this trial. They occupied an abandoned but privately owned house and were not convicted. This set a social precedence in Canada.

## REFERENCES

Blomley, N. 1994. *Law, Space and the Geographies of Power*. New York: Guilford Press.

Blomley, N., D. Delaney, and R.T. Ford, eds. 2001. *The Legal Geographies Reader*. Oxford: Blackwell.

Brigham, J., and D.R. Gordon. 1991. Law in Politics: Struggles over Property and Public Space on New York City's Lower East Side. *Law and Social Inquiry* 21(2): 265-83.

Castells, Manuel. 1983. *The City and the Grassroots: A Cross-Cultural Theory of Urban Social Movements*. Berkeley: University of California Press.

Corr, A. 1999. *No Trespassing: Squatting, Rent Strikes and Land Struggles Worldwide.* Cambridge, MA: South End Press.

Cresswell, T. 1996. *In Place/Out of Place: Geography, Ideology, and Transgression.* Minneapolis: University of Minnesota Press.

Davis, M. 1990. *City of Quartz: Excavating the Future in Los Angeles.* New York: Verso.

Ertel, Mark. 2005. Personal interview. January 6. Ottawa.

Ford, James. 2005. Personal interview. January 13. Ottawa.

Foucault, M. 1991. Governmentality. In *The Foucault Effect: Studies in Governmentality,* ed. G. Burchell, C. Gordon, and P. Miller, 87-104. Chicago: University of Chicago Press.

–. 1995. *Discipline and Punish: The Birth of the Prison.* New York: Random House.

Freeman, L., and S. Lamble. 2004. Squatting and the City. *Canadian Dimension* 38(6): 44-46.

Hahmeed, Yavar. 2005. Personal interview. January 7. Ottawa.

Harvey, D. 1973. *Social Justice and the City.* Baltimore: John Hopkins University Press.

Hiscocks, Mandy. 2004. Personal interview. December 2. Ottawa.

Holder, J., and C. Harrison, eds. 2003. *Law and Geography: Current Legal Issues.* Vol. 5. Oxford: Oxford University Press.

Johnston, R.J. 1990. Territoriality of Law: An Exploration. *Urban Geography* 12(6): 548-65.

Lefebvre, H. 1991. *The Production of Space.* Trans. D. Nicholson-Smith. Oxford: Blackwell.

–. 1996. The Right to the City. In *Writings on Cities: Henri Lefebvre,* ed. E. Kofman and E. Lebas, 147-59. Oxford: Blackwell.

Marshall, A., and S. Barclay. 2003. In Their Own Words: How Ordinary People Construct the Legal World. *Law and Social Inquiry* 28(3): 617-29.

Merrifield A., and E. Swyngedouw, eds. 1997. *The Urbanization of Injustice.* Washington Square: New York University Press.

Mitchell, D. 1997. The Annihilation of Space by Law: The Roots and Implications of Anti-Homeless Laws in the US. *Antipode* 29(3): 303-5.

– 2003. *The Right to the City: Social Justice and the Fight for Public Space.* New York: Guilford Press.

Moore, Dawn. 2007. *Criminal Artefacts: Governing Drugs and Users.* Vancouver: UBC Press.

Morris, Susan. 2004. Personal interview. December 16. Ottawa.

Mulcahy, L. 2007. Architects of Justice: The Politics of Courtroom Design. *Social and Legal Studies* 16(3): 383-403.

Murdoch, J. 1998. The Spaces of Actor Network Theory. *Geoforum* 29(4): 357-74.

*Official Disclosure of Evidence.* 2002. Ministry of Attorney General, Province of Ontario. Submitted to L. Freeman. August 21.

Pue, W. 1990. Wrestling with Law: (Geographical) Specificity vs. (Legal) Abstraction. *Urban Geography* 11(6): 566-85.

Purcell, M. 2002. Excavating Lefebvre: The Right to the City and its Urban Politics of the Inhabitant. *Geojournal* 58: 99-108.

*R. v. Ackerley et al.* Official court transcripts, September 30-October 30, 2004. Ontario Provincial Criminal Superior Court. Transcribed by L. Carriere.

Rose, N. 1996. Governing "Advanced" Liberal Democracies. In *Foucault and Political Reason*, ed. A. Barry, T. Osborne, and N. Rose, 37-64. London: UCL Press.

–. 1999. *Powers of Freedom: Reframing Political Thought*. Cambridge: Cambridge University Press.

Slater, T. 2008. "A Literal Necessity to Be Re-Placed": A Rejoinder to the Gentrification Debate. *International Journal of Urban and Regional Research* 32(1): 212-23.

Smith, N. 1996. *The New Urban Frontier: Gentrification and the Revanchist City.* New York: Routlege.

Soja, E. 1996. *Thirdspace: Journey to Los Angeles and Other Real and Imagined Places.* Cambridge, MA: Blackwell.

Valverde, Marianna. 2005. Taking "Land Use" Seriously: Toward an Ontology of Municipal Law. *Law Text Culture* 9: 34-59.

# 11
# Anarcho-Abolition: A Challenge to Conservative and Liberal Criminology

*Kevin Walby*

Many criminologists, penologists, and socio-legal scholars self-identify as critical. The American Society of Criminology and the Academy of Criminal Justice Sciences even have special sections for critical criminology. Yet, it is not always apparent with who or with what critical criminologists are self-identifying. There are many theoretical and practical distinctions between the various projects laying claim to the "critical criminology" label. There are profound cleavages between socialist, feminist, abolitionist, and other critical criminologies when it comes to perspectives on policing, punishment, law, and sentencing, as well as on overarching issues such as capitalism and governance in contemporary societies.

Numerous scholars (for example, Gamberg and Thomson 1984; Tifft and Sullivan 1980; Braswell and Whitehead 1999; Melossi 2000) argue that contemporary criminology has cleaved in two directions: critical criminology on the one hand, conservative and liberal criminology on the other. Provocative about this argument is the suggestion that conservative and liberal criminology share much in common. Both conservative and liberal criminology reify "crime" and "criminals," it is claimed. Both also naturalize the sovereign nation-state as the legitimate unit of politics. There are differences, of course. Conservative criminology expresses a "tough on crime" approach. Liberals express a far less punitive discourse. Yet, liberals do not find criminal justice institutions problematic per se. What is called "left realism" is one example of liberal criminology. Few criminologists in Canada self-identify as left realist, but there is a larger set of criminologists who can be defined as liberal realists since they share similar visions of justice and the political, only wishing to reform the existing system.

In this chapter, I discuss the challenge that anarcho-abolition offers to conservative and liberal criminology. Penal abolition promotes the dismantling of the prison-industrial complex. Surprising, however, is the reluctance of some penal abolitionists to borrow from anarchism's rich history of insurrection, as well as its anti-statist and anti-capitalist politics. Consolidating some complementary tendencies in anarchist activism and abolitionist criminology, anarcho-abolition contributes an anti-authoritarian commitment to dealing with conflict based on voluntary, non-hierarchical sociations and collective decision making. Thinking of justice beyond the criminal justice industry, and thinking of the political beyond sovereignty, provides a significant challenge to the theoretical and practical problems associated with conservative and liberal criminology. It is this challenge provided by anarcho-abolition that I focus on below.

This chapter is organized in four parts. First, I assess the conservative and liberal branches of criminology. Second, drawing from anarchist and abolitionist thought, I describe what I mean by anarcho-abolition. I argue penal abolition needs an explicitly anarchist posture, since many abolitionists have never been clear about their broader political aims. Yet, anarchism needs abolition to continually provide concrete sites for rebelliousness. In the third section, I position anarcho-abolition in relation to developments in peace-making criminology. Fourth, I point to already existing anarchist and abolitionist critiques of, and struggles against, imprisonment, punishment, criminalization, and the criminal justice industry.

## Conservative and Liberal Criminology

Braswell and Whitehead (1999) argue that even though conservative and liberal criminology take divergent approaches to policing, sentencing, and imprisonment, they are two sides of the same coin. Liberal criminology can be characterized as involving state-supported community policing as a balance to conventional policing, opposing mandatory minimums for sentencing, and supporting health and counselling services inside prisons as well as jails.[1] Conservative criminology, being more retributive, calls for greater policing powers, more arrests, mandatory minimum sentences for many offences, "no frills," and privatization or private/public "partnership" approaches to imprisonment. Despite these differences, both conservative and liberal criminology sponsor policing, sentencing, and imprisonment as the way to deal with conflict, which makes the two positions more similar than different. Braswell and Whitehead argue that conservative and liberal criminology both pursue arguments about cost-effectiveness, excluding questions about the categories "crime" and "criminals" as well as what social justice might entail (ibid., 54). Questions of economic and political self-determination are not on the map for conservative and liberal criminologists.

This conservative/liberal dualism is oversimplified. Yet, Braswell and Whitehead are not the only authors who demonstrate how conservative and liberal criminology give precedence to the already existing criminal justice industry. For instance, Gamberg and Thomson (1984) argue that although conservative criminology is retributive and stresses the ostensive deterrence effect of suffering, and although liberal criminology pokes holes in some conservative arguments, both accept the basic institutional features of our existing social and political order. Melossi (2000) demonstrates how conservative and liberal tendencies emerge in response to socio-economic conditions. He argues that the conservative tendency, marked by a punitive mentality, a hankering for "crime" solving, as well as an antipathy toward those marked as "criminals," emerges in times of economic and political crisis. Melossi situates his claims with reference to criminology after the 1973 oil crisis, which he argues "took it upon itself not so much the task of criticizing and innovating ... but the opposite task of restoring and shoring up," trying to reinforce criminology as a distinct discipline based on the "science of crime" (ibid., 309). The conservative criminology characteristic of the Thatcher, Reagan, and Bush years provided a new criminological consensus, which naturalized ideas about "crime" and "criminals" even within liberal criminology.

Pavlich (1999) has also been critical of conservative and liberal veins of criminology. Pavlich argues that Taylor, Walton, and Young's *The New Criminology* (1973), as well as the left realism offshoot pursued by Young and colleagues, mirrored many problematic tendencies of liberal criminology. I discuss Taylor, Walton, and Young below, but let me briefly discuss left realism here since it is a manifestation of liberal realist criminology.

Left realism emerged during and after Thatcherite conservativism in the United Kingdom. It is a form of liberal criminology that entails a plea for socialist-oriented scholars to be "relevant" and "take crime seriously" (Lea 1992) in response to calls from conservative criminologists for more intensive policing (see Wilson 1975). Concerned with violence in socio-economically deprived neighbourhoods, left realism's focus is on how economic shifts relate to changes in "crime" rates and the ghettoization of racialized urban areas. Left realism offers the "square of crime" (Young 1997) as a conceptual device for understanding responses to undesirable events, which draws multiple policing agencies, offenders and their acts, victims, and the public into mechanistic flow chart relationships. The relationship between the police and the public determines policing efficacy, the relationship between the victim and the offender determines the impact of the "crime," and so on. Left realists advocate short-term policy initiatives to increase social integration. They are also interested in conducting surveys to help police manage deviant populations efficiently (Pease 1992). The left realist perspective argues that intra-class "crime" is frequent and often goes unreported (Matthews and Young 1986). But left realism demands strong interventionist state agencies to engineer reform and rehabilitation projects. Left realists can be faulted for operating with a commonsense knowledge of what constitutes "the crime problem."

Although only a few Canadian criminologists have self-identified as left realists (for example, Lowman and Maclean 1992), liberal criminologists continue to operate with the same positivist premises and reformist goals. Pavlich (1999) argues that liberal realists end up defining "crime" in individual terms instead of as some acts conducted by an institution. The pragmatism of liberal left realism has led it to reify "crime" and also be overly concerned with increased managerial efficiency. For instance, Matthews (1992) engages in conservative cost-effectiveness discourses as it regards the penal system. This technocratic and reformist attitude has "rendered left realism's precepts commensurate with those of administrative criminology, diluting the new criminology's quest for radical criticism" (Pavlich 1999, 34; see also de Haan 1987).

I do not want to be accused, as Garland (1992) accuses Foucault (1977), of painting criminology as a monolithic discourse affiliated with the disciplinary practices of criminal justice institutions. I am arguing, however, that most criminologists fail to challenge the ontological reality of "crime" (see also Hulsman 1986). Naturalizing "crime" and "criminals" as dangerous to the social body is even more glaring with conservatives. A criminology that incorporates in its own position the dominant approach of criminal justice can never be transgressive and is unable to challenge authority, hierarchy, and violence.

Pavlich (2001) argues that the distinguishing feature of critical criminology – critique – has been conspicuously purged in liberal criminology. He argues that we need to nurture subjugated knowledges, otherwise conservative and liberal criminology will continue to be the only positions accepted. Likewise, Tifft and Sullivan (1980) argue that liberal criminology is a grand mystifier. Both conservative criminology and liberal criminology naively suppose that only state sovereignty can provide economic and political organization, yet liberal criminologists stand alone in their rhetoric of state benevolence.

Anarcho-abolition posits the primacy of critique and struggle as the basis of radical criminology. The danger of critique is that it risks the indignation of speaking for others. However, as I explain below, critique is simply a form of analysis, and the main thrust of anarcho-abolition is to reduce the gap between critique and struggle.

## Anarcho-Abolition

Abolitionism is often critiqued as idealist. Turning such criticism around, Piché (2009) points out how many abolitionists have personal experience with the unjust and costly failures of the criminal justice industry. Driven by the failures of prison reform, prison abolitionists have long sought to abolish coercive institutions or drastically reduce their size and number. A broad focus on penal abolition emerged in the 1980s with a critique of the prison industrial complex. But there are divisions here: some abolitionists call for prisons to be torn down, whereas others focus on numerous criminal justice institutions in addition to prisons and jails. For instance, many contemporary abolitionists argue that state-planned alternatives to prisons should be resisted, since these only widen the net of control, creating new coercive institutions that extend out into the public (see Gaucher 1988). The abolition of trans-carceration – abolition of all carceral and coercive institutions – is the aim of many contemporary abolitionists. Anarchists have always been highly critical of carceral and coercive institutions (see Kropotkin 1970, for example), hence my impetus to integrate anarchist and abolitionist thought and practice.

The most cited statements regarding abolitionism are found in Mathiesen's *The Politics of Abolition* (1974). Mathiesen argues that a radical social justice platform should be built around the idea of "the unfinished." The unfinished articulates its premises and goals in its own terms, not in the terms of the existing power structure. A radical social justice strategy will have a foreign message and a message that is not fully formed. "Foreign" means the message does not belong to what it critiques but is a new discourse. "Not fully formed" means the consequences of carrying out the message are only approximately clarified, making them less susceptible to co-option. As Mathiesen (1986, 82) puts it, "the abolition of prisons is not exactly imminent"; it is to be worked for. Abolitionism is not limited to Mathiesen's contributions, however. Many scholar-activists have forwarded an abolitionist position (see Knopp et al. 1976; Culhane 1985; Bianchi and van Swaaningen 1986; Morris 1989; de Haan 1990; Davis 2003; Ryan and Sim 2007; Larsen 2008; Piché 2009). There is a biannual International Conference on Penal Abolitionism (ICOPA) that keeps the idea of abolition alive in the academic world. Countless activists take on social justice projects from an abolitionist perspective.

Let me briefly position abolition in relation to critical criminology. Much of critical criminology emerged out of labelling theory or responses to it. The ultimate goal of labelling theory in the 1960s and 1970s was to debase the way criminal justice industry practices produce deviancy. In his book *Against Criminology*, Stanley Cohen (1988) chronicles the rise and fall of labelling theory and critical criminology. Labelling theory's undermining of mainstream criminology lost its effect when "the emperor underneath tacky clothes of positivism, was revealed not in his full moral nakedness but in his new underwear of naturalism and appreciation" (118). Mainstream criminology remained standing as an industry with ties to state agencies and capitalism, recuperating in status what it had lost to those who were with all their hearts against criminology. Critical criminologists were criticized for romanticizing undesirable acts.

Socialist-oriented thinkers such as Taylor, Walton, and Young in their 1973 book *The New Criminology* challenged the idea that crime is politically inconsequential. The book asserted that, since "crime" is a name for acts prohibited and punished by the state, state power is a central theoretical question for criminologists. Questioning the importance of the state was new terrain for Marxist-socialist criminologists because most socialists previously were concerned with leadership coordinating state takeover to use the state as a vehicle to abolish class. Marxist-socialist criminologists were not (and are not) concerned with dismantling statism itself. Marxist-socialists and liberals believe state authority is necessary. The point is that socialist criminology is ambiguous as it concerns the state in relation to criminal justice policy because of an underlying ambiguity concerning the state in Marxist-socialist thought. *The New Criminology* was not a new radicalism. Pavlich (2000, 48) argues that Taylor, Walton, and Young's notion of change was still ensconced within a Marxist tendency to judge theory and practice by how well it met socialist expectations. The positing of state power as a theoretical question for criminologists does not go as far as anarcho-abolition, because the Marxist tradition and the anarchist critique of state authority are at odds.

Anarchism emerged in the nineteenth century alongside and in a bitter feud with Marxism. There are many varieties of anarchism, and I draw more from the collectivist approach than the individualist or primitivist veins. Anarchists conceptualize state agencies as arbitrary authorities. Anarchists differ from Marxists because they believe political sociation should be based on voluntary and non-hierarchical relations instead of representation and that decisions should be made collectively. Sociations are the voluntary bonds that allow for the possibility of mutual aid: networks of self-organizing affinity groups providing solidarity (see also Day 2005).

Plamenatz (1954, 119) argues that a "bourgeois morality" on the part of Marx's followers signals the greatest differentiation between Marxists and anarchists. Socialists and anarchists oppose private property and the capitalist division of labour, whereas anarchists further oppose state-organized production and state-based forms of administration. The institutionalization of government in the state is an undesirable act. For Stirner ([1845] 1982, 227), "the State seeks to hinder every free activity by its censorship, its supervision, its police, and holds this hindering to be its duty, because it is in truth a duty of self-preservation." This is a very old characterization of state function, but it still holds up. Just as egalitarians oppose inequalities in economic power, anarchists oppose inequalities in political power. Political inequalities are linked to the appropriation and institutionalization of the human capacity for political sociation under bourgeois liberal democracy.

It is been put by Barclay (1990) that anarchists are a people without government, but I think a Foucauldian understanding of government is a helpful corrective.[2] Anarchists are people who want to enact sociations that are not subject to the rule of representative political institutions, since state politics for anarchists are alienating. For Foucault (1982, 221), government refers not simply to the management of states but "designates the way in which the conduct of individuals or states might be directed." Anarchists are interested in modes of self-organizing that are quite different from the conduct of subjection that characterizes life under technocratic liberalism. To enact such sociations based on self-organization would put the governmentalization of the state out of business, on a scale of participation that would exit the rule of representative political institutions from the grid of intelligibility. Anarchism is based on direct decision making, which does not necessitate collapse into individual hedonism. There is still an order to anarchism. Social coordination is organized directly by those who are voluntarily subject to it. The pamphlet "management without managers" offers an anarchist theory of organizations.

The question of what an anarchist society would look like, as put by critics of anarchism, is badly posed. Foucault (2004) takes apart the metaphor of "society" and argues that the impulse to defend "society" is at the heart of a war by other means between the powerless and the powerful. The question of politics cannot be concerned with "what are the troubles with society" or "what to do with society." This way of posing the problem assumes that a societal or national scale of politics is the best or the only possible scale. Questions of scope and scale are key when discussing direct political participation (see Magnusson 1986).

I now hope to explicitly join anarchist analysis with abolitionism. The promise of anarcho-abolition is to identify perversions of power and subvert them through self-governing, anti-authoritarian, non-hierarchical relations. First, anarcho-abolition is both a practice and a theoretical approach. As a practice, anarcho-abolitionists are concerned with decentralization, decriminalization, demedicalization, and decarceration. These practices entail community-based strategies for social change. Abolitionists have argued that the ideas of rehabilitation, individual, and general deterrence have little merit and that incapacitation creates only more violence (see Knopp et al. 1976). Abolitionists are not averse to improving conditions and facilitating harm reduction services inside prisons and jails – Mathiesen (1980) argues that a viable abolitionist project needs both short-term and long-term goals – but reforms do not displace the focus on abolition of coercive institutions. As a position in social and political theory, anarcho-abolition is important because it conceptualizes state agencies as intimately linked with reproducing conditions of political and economic inequality.

Second, anarcho-abolition views the left idealist argument that dissolving capitalism will dissolve "crime" as misguided. Beyond capitalism and state sovereignty, conflict would still exist. Forms of local, self-governing sociality would be needed. Related, and third, many Marxist-socialists believe fully in state revolution. They view the possibility of life beyond capitalism as more or less cinched because, in their heads, such relations are the logical outcome of historical processes. Anarchists have always been critical of movements depending on the notion of a revolutionary dictatorship:

> The only difference between revolutionary dictatorship and the
> state is in external appearances. Essentially, they both represent the
> same government of the majority by a minority in the name of the

presumed stupidity of the one and the presumed intelligence of the other. Therefore they are equally reactionary, both having the direct and inevitable result of consolidating the political and economic privileges of the governing minority and the political and economic slavery of the masses. (Bakunin 1990, 137)

Because of such criticism, Bakunin and the anarchists were excluded by the Marxists from the First International at The Hague Congress in 1872. For anarcho-abolitionists, such a focus on state revolution and historical evolution focuses politics on a singularity (that is, the state or history). This all-or-nothing conceptualization of revolution is linked to a Marxist authoritarian and centralizing urge, a desire for authority (C. Ward 1973). Focus on revolution displaces the active organizing that can be done as it concerns imprisonment, policing, victimization, and punishment. The fundamental aim of collective autonomy can be achieved only by formation of workers councils, networks of affinity, and so on, not by taking state authority. The point is to reject the problematic conflation of justice with the criminal justice industry. Anarcho-abolitionists propose community transformative justice projects organized non-hierarchically. The symbolically violent language and physically violent practices of the criminal justice industry must be rejected. Hil and Robertson (2003) even chastise critical criminologists for focusing narrowly on "crime."

Fourth, traditional anarchists such as Proudhon and Bakunin share with liberals a kindness toward reason, thinking that humans could realize their "true" human natures through science. Anarchism must do away with its presuppositions about the true nature of human beings. Anarcho-abolition must be "anarchism without essences and the guarantees of moral and rational authority" (Newman 2001, 161). Finally, anarcho-abolition exists as both a practice and a theoretical knowledge contra conservative and liberal criminology to the extent that it concerns state interventionism as a purported guarantor of protection from victimization and contra conservative and liberal criminology to the extent that it challenges the conventional scale of politics.

Scull (1984) believes that the community forms of dealing with conflict that anarcho-abolition entails are impossible. He argues that previous alternatives to incarceration failed because they diverted people into a subsidiary correctional system governed not by prison wardens and "crime" policy bureaucrats but by halfway house operators. This defeatist standpoint assumes authority will always colonize the self-organizing capacities of people.

It assumes that alternatives to incarceration will always emulate the logic of state-organized prison administration. It also assumes that the sheer number of people in the world, and the complex division of labour, necessitates governmentalization of the state or a world government. Organizing toward voluntary, non-hierarchical relations and a rotational delegation of power too often appears as delusional to conservative and liberal criminologists.

Anarcho-abolition is what Pavlich (1999) calls a paralogical genre of criminology: a modality of conduct concerned to disrupt what is concealed by conservatism and liberalism, yet open to its own contradictions. Young (2002, 262) misunderstands Pavlich's approach when writing that Pavlich advises scholars "to dig a deep and insurmountable moat around the ivory tower of the academy." Pavlich invites scholars to learn from existing struggles, to break down links between insurrectionary knowledges and one's own analysis. As Pavlich (2000, 128) argues, anarchists do not view justice as being guaranteed through formal institutions. Likewise, for Tifft and Sullivan (1980, 74), "direct justice means no institutionalization of the resolving of conflict ... there is no base on which institutions such as civil law, involving restitution, can be distinguished from punitive, penal or retributive law."

There are a couple of troubles with anarcho-abolition. The first would be that anarcho-abolition analytically sets up the state as mutually exclusive from the social, instead of the social being coextensive with the state. In fact, anarchists have long thought of the state as an assemblage of relations that appears in concrete state-like manifestations. But retaining a level of exclusivity between the state and the social can also remind us that the governmentalization of the state is predicated on the expropriation of individuals' means of political sociation. Liberal forms of political representation are self-justifying regimes that maintain myths about the purported infeasibility of alterative political organizing (see Vahabzadeh 2001).[3] Counter-discourse and counter-conduct are important by virtue of attempting to disrupt alienating political systems.

The second issue has to do with victimization. It is argued that abolitionists do not care about victims. Because of restorative justice's focus on community and management of undesirable behaviours at the local level, it would appear there is a link between anarcho-abolition and restorative justice to be explored. One conundrum with restorative justice is that sometimes sentencing circles and victim-offender mediation will not work because the offender has committed a heinous and undesirable act yet feels no remorse. Nils Christie (2004) suggests that abolition cannot work for this remorse reason. He offers minimalism as an alternative, where punishment in small levels is unavoidable. The decarceration movement in Canada and elsewhere follows this minimalist line (McMahon 1992). But prisons and jails do not allow for reconciliation or restoration. Comack (2008) reiterates that prisons are places that foster and practice violence. For Ferrell (1998, 13), "anarchist criminology serves if only by standing outside the law, by stopping short of the seductive ideologies of obedience and conformity."

Sometimes sentencing circles and victim-offender mediation starts in the community but becomes institutionalized or taken over by some state agency. Pavlich (2005) has levied a devastating critique against institutional varieties of restorative justice, arguing that victims, offenders, and communities are all defined by state law, so that restorative justice is parasitic on the state-based retributive justice system. Restorative justice cannot be an alternative to re-tributive justice if restorative justice borrows from the symbolic capital and the discourse of retributive justice. Pavlich's work is therefore a critique of sovereignty. Restorative justice fails through its inability to escape the limita-tions of sovereignty. Criminal justice industry apparatuses still technocratic-ally define "crime" in the restorative paradigm, leading to paradox. The paradoxes of restorative justice demonstrate that an "attempt to open up to justice anew" (ibid., 120) is intimately linked to the possibilities of a politics beyond state sovereignty.

## ANARCHO-ABOLITION AND PEACEMAKING CRIMINOLOGY

The most obvious proponent of anarcho-abolition is peacemaking criminol-ogy (see Pepinsky 1988, 1991). Peacemaking criminology argues that polit-ical and economic relations must be reorganized before justice can be realized. There are similarities between anarcho-abolition and peacemaking criminol-ogy. First, both problematize the capitalist system of wants/needs instead of targeting individual behaviour. Second, non-violence and praxis are common to both. State agencies and capitalism are to blame for so much already existing violence. A focus on the symbolic and physical violence of state apparatuses and how these accumulate in the bodies of those shuffled through the crim-inal justice industry is a tactic for critiquing arbitrary authority. In terms of physical violence, state-led genocides are an example and so are the terrorist attacks of the US government in Central and South America and elsewhere since the early twentieth century, which has led to numerous blowbacks and more violence. Dahl (1967, 958) writes that "the fatal flaw of the nation-state is its inability to eliminate interstate [and intrastate] violence." Fatal, because the state is implicated in violence as much as it aids in thwarting it: "It is not the social harms punishable by law which cause the greatest misery in the world. It is the unlawful harms, those unpunishable crimes justified and protected by law, the state, the ruling elites that fill the earth with misery" (Tifft and Sullivan 1980, 9). In terms of symbolic violence, the legal system enforces warlike separation of people into criminal and citizen subjects. The state calls its own valorization of violence "law and order" and calls any individual deviance "crime" or "terror." Third, peacemaking criminology and anarcho-abolition both emphasize activism.

Despite these similarities, anarcho-abolition differs from peacemaking criminology. First, the religious overtones of tolerance and spirit in peacemaking criminology are supplanted in anarcho-abolition by the sober inquiry of atheism. Quinney (2000, 25) naively argues that "love makes a different world, a world without crime." This is absurd. Self-organizing is not simply a matter of feeling the spiritual energy. Confrontation still needs to be reconciled in anarchist networks. I agree with Barak (2005) that peacemaking criminology does not take adversarialism seriously. Anarcho-abolition with its forms of reconciliation and direct decision making also needs to account for adversarialism. Second, anarcho-abolition inherits more direct action and permaculture tactics with its collectivist anarchist orientation. Peacemaking criminology translates from theory into practice through restorative justice, but as Pavlich (2005) has shown, restorative justice works to reinforce the primacy of the state.

## Examples of Anarcho-Abolition

Nothing I have written about anarcho-abolition is pulled out of thin air. I am referring to an active field of anti-prison, anti-police, anti-statist, and prisoner-support activism.

Anarcho-abolitionists have identified, critiqued, and struggled against the prison-industrial complex (PIC), in which prisoners are treated as raw materials benefiting corrections businesses. The PIC is based on more austere prison and jail conditions, mandatory minimums for many offences, and cutbacks on in-prison health services. Prisons and jails are provided funding for each prisoner, and then some other corporation makes money off prison labour. Key US participants in this include Corrections Corporation of America, Correctional Services Corporation, Wackenhut Corrections (rebranded as GEO Group Inc.), and government agencies (for example, the Bureau of Justice Assistance), as well as professional institutions, including the American

Bar Association and the American Correctional Association. CORCAN as operated by the Correctional Service of Canada is another example. There is also a giant corporate scheme of food supply, transportation, construction, interstices with public service administration, and outsourcing of correctional services. Facilities housing thousands of prisoners, known as superjails, are now common in the United States and increasingly elsewhere. Superjail architecture indicates a particular approach to punishment (Sudbury 2004) based on the three principles underpinning PIC expansion: incapacitation, deterrence, and fiscal efficiency. There is a cementing of the prison into local economies (see G. Ward 2004). For rural areas devastated by economic restructuring and free trade, prisons have become sought after to stave off economic stagnation and population loss. Prisons and jails cost money, but they have also moved front and centre in the circulation and self-valorization of capital and thus attract investors, creditors, and speculators of all kinds eager to turn a profit off prison labour.

It has been documented how black communities in America and Aboriginal peoples in Canada are subject to disproportionate sentencing and higher levels of incarceration, as well as racialized violence and marginalization (see Royal Commission on Aboriginal Peoples 1996; Davis 2003). Mass imprisonment going on in North America has been discussed by abolitionists in terms of classism and racism (Davis and Rodriguez 2000). Pointing out that penal abolitionists often ignore the racialized character of state violence, Davis (2003) associates the rise of the penal system with the abolition of slavery. Voting rights were truncated by the tailoring of felony disenfranchisement laws to include "crimes" supposedly committed more often by blacks. Slavery still happened as a punishment for "crime," so the South continued to economically benefit from the unpaid labour of blacks. As Davis notes, convict lease system expansion and the county chain gang made the emerging criminal justice industry a chief means for controlling black labour. The PIC exists now not so much as a form of slavery but, rather, as a form of warehousing racialized populations categorized and treated as useless, itinerant, or dangerous. Groups such as Critical Resistance and INCITE! in the United States challenge the racialized violence of the criminal justice industry and actively seek alternatives to incarceration.

Anarcho-abolitionists have been vocal on issues pertaining to racial profiling and criminalization of immigrants and refugees, as well as detention and deportation policies concerning migrants and non-status people post-9/11. In the last several years, the division between national security practices and criminal law enforcement in North America and Europe has almost completely dissolved (Welch and Schuster 2005a, 2005b). Related to racialized state violence, Immigration and Naturalization Services (INS) and later Immigration and Customs Enforcement (ICE) in the United States have responded to the market imperatives of the prison-industrial complex, creating a situation where undocumented immigrants are commodified as raw materials for private profit. INS detainees were known as a "cash crop," since the INS payed institutions $45 per detainee daily (see Welch 2000; Pratt 2005). More covert than the INS, ICE now sets up its own detention centres in warehouses, underground parking garages, and other makeshift locations. The exceptionalism of policy changes post-9/11 (regarding freedom of movement, immigration, and border security) remains to be more fully challenged. We do not need detention centres or a special cadre of police and spy agents. Groups such as No One Is Illegal, anti-poverty coalitions, and the many campaigns against secret trials and renditions to torture and detentions all across North America are examples of those engaged in active struggles against the so-called war on terror.

We also need to learn from those who have first-hand experience with criminal justice industry violence (Hulsman 1986). Alternatives to coercive institutions must involve the direct participation of people who have been brutalized by them (Gaucher 1988). Part of this involves privileging the voices of prisoners. There are many examples of publications that privilege the analysis of prisoners, including *4strugglemag* and *Prison Legal News*. Since 1988, the *Journal of Prisoners on Prisons* has been a forum where prisoners can contribute peer-reviewed articles that document their lived experiences of incarceration.

Groups involved with the Anarchist Black Cross Network, Books to Prisoners, Books Through Bars, as well as prisoner writing publications, are all involved in prisoner support, outreach, and advocacy. Many of these groups work together in coalitions. Coalition building can be difficult (Lee 2008) but is necessary. Alternatives to incarceration and coercion are possible and only a question of organizing. People are already trying to introduce decentralized decision making in large, urban, technologized, and globalized contexts; in this sense, ideas for more concrete strategy best emerge from activists themselves (Gilbert 2008; Graeber 2009). One could list a thousand more groups involved in the struggle against the prison-industrial complex and related state agencies. The point is not to list but to get involved, to stray, as far as possible, from the label "criminologist" and what that has customarily meant. Yet this new life must intersect with the domain traditionally belonging to criminology, since conflict will not dissipate no matter how well anarchist ideals are achieved.

## Conclusion

Issues such as imprisonment and policing intersect with the political and political theory more than we often pretend in criminology departments. I have argued that conservative and liberal criminology begin with questions of control and order, remaining ensconced within a correctional discourse. Anarcho-abolition is the opposite of shoring up the discipline. Anarcho-abolition is not about building a moat around the university. Instead, it points to active and ongoing struggles engaged in by abolitionists and anarchists, calls for them to work together on alternatives to imprisonment and policing, and calls for academics to support and engage in these struggles.

Many people in prisons and jails today are prisoners of class war, recriminalized because of parole breaches and the inability to pay bail. Taylor (1999) argues that these trends in imprisonment and capitalist production evince the need for old orthodoxies to be reinvigorated. As I have argued, the Marxist-socialist paradigm of criminology is limited by a reliance on state sovereignty as a necessity, which only vouchsafes state-centric forms of political thinking and acting (see also Magnusson 1992). There is a danger of criminology being too closely linked with the symbolically violent language and physically violent practices of the criminal justice industry if alternatives to conservative and liberal criminology are shunned. Abolitionist criminology is important to counter the tendency among conservatives and liberals to accept prisons, jails, police, criminal law, and courts as "realistic" responses to conflict. The sense of immediacy characterizing liberal realism is also found in anarcho-abolition: we desire a drastic shrinking of the criminal justice industry and a moratorium on the creation of new coercive institutions.

Lastly, if one advocates abolition of prisons but not abolition of state agencies and capitalism, if abolitionists do not critique broader forms of authority and hierarchy, then they have a lesson to take from anarchism. Prisons are only the most outward expression of hierarchy and authority. The abolition of prisons will be for naught if the spy agencies, the sweatshops, the animal torture labs, and the slaughterhouses are not also put out of business. The persistence of imprisonment, representative politics, and capitalist production corroborates the need for decentralization and post-sovereignist sociations. Anarchism transforms through the practising of it, fostering voluntary and egalitarian relations while abolishing authority and hierarchy.

ACKNOWLEDGMENTS
Thanks to Aaron Doyle, Kevin Haggerty, Bob Gaucher, Michael Welch, Jeff Monaghan, Justin Piché, and the anonymous UBC Press reviewers for comments.

NOTES
1 Rather than use "prison" as an all-encompassing term, I distinguish between prisons and jails as distinct sets of institutions with different sources of funding, goals, and organizational protocol. There are major dissimilarities between prisons and jails in North America, having to do with service provision, overcrowding, sentence length, and so on.
2 De Lint (2006) argues that Foucault has been poorly appropriated by criminology. Yet there is much useful in Foucault for informing an anarcho-abolitionist perspective. Foucault's approach to power as productive and ubiquitous is similar to the ways anarchists describe power as "overflowing" (Antliff 2007; May 2009). Foucault's critique of domination is important for anarchists to consider, since it facilitates consideration of how power operates even in anarchist networks. There are no discourses of non-power, not even anarchist discourses.
3 For Stirner ([1845] 1982), liberalism is a kind of humanism that frees people from religious control while making them more amenable to rule that operates through aligning their desires with the state. Liberalism appropriates people into the universal discourse of rights, but liberal universalism is revoked in the way rights are always already distributed unequally. The language of rights and state-based citizenship is not sufficient for those interested in politics beyond the liberal democratic state. In Emma Goldman's (1969) pamphlet "The Tragedy of Women's Emancipation," we find an anarchist critique of the liberal version of justice. Goldman argues that the primary modality of action under representative democracy – the vote – failed to liberate men and so neither votes nor rights could secure the emancipation of women. The emancipation of women must come from women themselves, Goldman argued, through the refusal of subordination to man, to family, to state, or to God.

REFERENCES
Antliff, A. 2007. Anarchy, Power, and Poststructuralism. *SubStance* 36(2): 56-66.
Bakunin, M. 1990. *Statism and Anarchy*. Cambridge: Cambridge University Press.
Barak, G. 2005. A Reciprocal Approach to Peacemaking Criminology: Between Adversarialism and Mutualism. *Theoretical Criminology* 9(2): 131-52.

Barclay, H. 1990. *People without Government: An Anthropology of Anarchy*. London: Kahn and Averill.

Bianchi, H., and R. van Swaaningen, eds. 1986. *Abolitionism: Towards a Non-Repressive Approach to Crime*. Amsterdam: Free University Press.

Braswell, M., and J. Whitehead. 1999. Seeking the Truth: An Alternative to Conservative and Liberal Thinking in Criminology. *Criminal Justice Review* 24(1): 50-63.

Christie, N. 2004. *A Suitable Amount of Crime*. London: Routledge.

Cohen, S. 1988. *Against Criminology*. New Brunswick, NJ: Transaction.

Comack, E. 2008. *Out There/In Here: Masculinity, Violence and Prisoning*. Halifax: Fernwood.

Culhane, C. 1985. *Still Barred from Prison: Social Injustice in Canada*. Montreal: Black Rose Books.

Dahl, R. 1967. The City in the Future of Democracy. *American Political Science Review* 61(4): 953-70.

Davis, A. 2003. *Are Prisons Obsolete?* New York: Seven Stories Press.

Davis, A., and D. Rodriguez. 2000. The Challenge of Prison Abolition: A Conversation. *Social Justice* 27(3): 202-23.

Day, R. 2005. *Gramsci Is Dead: Anarchist Currents in the Newest Social Movements*. Toronto: Between the Lines.

De Haan, W. 1987. Abolitionism and the Politics of "Bad Conscience." *Howard Journal* 26(1): 15-33.

–. 1990. *The Politics of Redress: Crime, Punishment and Penal Abolition*. Boston: Unwin Hyman.

De Lint, W. 2006. Governmentality, Critical Criminology and the Absent Norm. *Canadian Journal of Criminology and Criminal Justice* 48(5): 721-34.

Ferrell, J. 1998. Against the Law: Anarchist Criminology. *Social Anarchism* 25: 5-15.

Foucault, M. 1977. *Discipline and Punish: The Birth of the Prison*. New York: Vintage.

–. 1982. The Subject and Power. In *Michel Foucault: Beyond Structuralism and Hermeneutics*, ed. H. Dreyfus and P. Rabinow, 208-26. Chicago: University of Chicago Press.

–. 2004. *"Society Must Be Defended": Lectures at the College de France, 1975-1976*. Trans. D. Macey. London: Penguin.

Gamberg, H., and A. Thomson. 1984. *The Illusion of Prison Reform: Corrections in Canada*. New York: Peter Lang.

Garland, D. 1992. Criminological Knowledge and Its Relation to Power: Foucault's Genealogy and Criminology Today. *British Journal of Criminology* 32(4): 403-22.

Gaucher, B. 1988. The Prisoner as Ethnographer. *Journal of Prisoners on Prisons* 1(1): 1-6.

Gilbert, D. 2008. A System within the System: The Prison Industrial Complex and Imperialism. In *Abolition Now! Ten Years of Strategy and Struggle against the Prison Industrial Complex*, ed. CR10 Publications Collective, 31-40. Oakland, CA: AK Press.

Goldman, E. 1969. The Tragedy of Women's Emancipation. In *Anarchism and Other Essays*, 89-93. New York: Dover.

Graeber, D. 2009. Anarchism, Academia and the Avant-garde. In *Contemporary Anarchist Studies: An Introductory Anthology of Anarchy in the Academy*, ed. R. Amster, A. DeLeon, L. Fernandez, A. Nocella II, and D. Shannon, 103-12. New York: Routledge.

Hil, R., and R. Robertson. 2003. What Sort of Future for Critical Criminology? *Crime, Law and Social Change* 39(2): 91-115.

Hulsman, L. 1986. Critical Criminology and the Concept of Crime. *Contemporary Crises* 10(1): 63-80.

Knopp, F., M. Morris, B. Boward, M. Brach, S. Christianson, M. Largen, J. Lewin, J. Lugo, and W. Newton. 1976. *Instead of Prison: A Handbook for Prison Abolitionists*. Syracuse, NY: Prison Research Education Action Project.

Kropotkin, P. 1970. Prisons and Their Moral Influence on Prisoners. In *Kropotkin's Revolutionary Pamphlets*, ed. R. Baldwin, 219-35. New York: Dover.

Larsen, M. 2008. Abolition and the Universal Carceral. *Journal of Prisoners on Prisons* 17(2): 1-5.

Lea, J. 1992. The Analysis of Crime. In *Rethinking Criminology: The Realist Debate*, ed. J. Young and R. Matthews, 69-94. London: Sage.

Lee, A. 2008. Prickly Coalitions: Moving Prison Abolition Forward. In *Abolition Now! Teen Years of Strategy and Struggle against the Prison Industrial Complex*, ed. CR10 Publications Collective, 109-12. Oakland, CA: AK Press.

Lowman, J., and B. Maclean, eds. 1992. *Realist Criminology: Crime Control and Policing in the 1990s*. Toronto: University of Toronto Press.

Magnusson, W. 1986. Bourgeois Theories of Local Government. *Political Studies* 34(1): 1-18.

–. 1992. Decentering the State, or Looking for Politics. In *Organizing Dissent: Contemporary Social Movements in Theory and Practice*, ed. W. Carroll, 69-80. Toronto: Garamond Press.

Mathiesen, T. 1974. *The Politics of Abolition: Essays in Political Action Theory*. Oslo: Universitetsforlaget.

–. 1980. *Law, Society and Political Action: Towards a Strategy under Late Capitalism*. London: Academic Press.

–. 1986. The Politics of Abolition. *Contemporary Crisis* 10(1): 81-94.

Matthews, R. 1992. Developing a Realist Approach to Penal Reform. In *Realist Criminology: Crime Control and Policing in the 1990s*, ed. J. Lowman and B. Maclean, 73-87. Toronto: University of Toronto Press.

–, and J. Young. 1986. *Confronting Crime*. London: Sage.

May, T. 2009. Anarchism from Foucault to Rancière. In *Contemporary Anarchist Studies: An Introductory Anthology of Anarchy in the Academy*, ed. R. Amster, A. DeLeon, L. Fernandez, A. Nocella II, and D. Shannon, 11-17. New York: Routledge.

McMahon, M. 1992. *The Persistent Prison? Rethinking Decarceration and Penal Reform*. Toronto: University of Toronto Press.

Melossi, D. 2000. Changing Representations of the Criminal. *British Journal of Criminology* 49(2): 296-320.

Morris, R. 1989. *Crumbling Walls: Why Prisons Fail.* Oakville, ON: Mosaic Press.

Newman, S. 2001. War on the State: Stirner's and Deleuze's Anarchism. *Anarchist Studies* 9(2): 147-63.

Pavlich, G. 1999. Criticism and Criminology: In Search of Legitimacy. *Theoretical Criminology* 3(1): 29-51.

–. 2000. *Critique and Radical Discourses on Crime.* Aldershot: Ashgate.

–. 2001. Critical Genres and Radical Criminology in Britain. *British Journal of Criminology* 41(2): 150-67.

–. 2005. *Governing Paradoxes of Restorative Justice.* London: Glasshouse.

Pease, K. 1992. The Local Crime Survey: Pitfalls and Possibilities. In *Realist Criminology: Crime Control and Policing in the 1990s,* ed. J. Lowman and B. Maclean, 303-12. Toronto: University of Toronto Press.

Pepinsky, H. 1988. Violence as Unresponsiveness: Towards a New Conception of Crime. *Justice Quarterly* 5(4): 539-63.

–. 1991. Peacemaking in Criminology. In *New Directions in Critical Criminology,* ed. B. Maclean and D. Milovanovic, 107-10. Vancouver: Collective Press.

Piché, J. 2009. Penal Abolitionism: A Different Kind of Reform. *Criminal Justice Matters* 77(1): 30-31.

Plamenatz, J. 1954. *German Marxism and Russian Communism.* London: Longmans, Green.

Pratt, A. 2005. *Securing Borders: Detention and Deportation in Canada.* Vancouver: UBC Press.

Quinney, R. 2000. Socialist Humanism and the Problem of Crime: Thinking about Erich Fromm in the Development of Critical/Peacemaking Criminology. In *Erich Fromm and Critical Criminology: Beyond the Punitive Society,* ed. K. Anderson and R. Quinney, 21-30. Chicago: University of Illinois.

Royal Commission on Aboriginal Peoples. 1996. Ottawa: Indian and Northern Affairs Canada.

Ryan, M., and Sim, J. 2007. Campaigning for and Campaigning against Prisons: Excavating and Reaffirming the Case for Prison Abolition. In *Handbook on Prisons,* ed. Y. Jewkes, 696-718. Portland: Willan.

Scull, A. 1984. *Decarceration: Community Treatment and the Deviant – A Radical View.* 2nd ed. New Brunswick, NJ: Rutgers University Press.

Stirner, M. (1845) 1982. *The Ego and Its Own: The Case of the Individual against Authority.* Repr. London: Rebel Press.

Sudbury, J. 2004. A World without Prisons: Resisting Militarism, Globalized Punishment, and Empire. *Social Justice* 31(1-2): 9-30.

Taylor, I. 1999. Crime and Social Criticism. *European Journal of Crime, Criminal Law and Criminal Justice* 7(2): 180-96.

Taylor, I., P. Walton, and J. Young. 1973. *The New Criminology: For a Social Theory of Deviance.* London: Routledge.

Tifft, L., and D. Sullivan. 1980. *The Struggle to Be Human: Crime, Criminology and Anarchism.* Orkney, UK: Cienfuegos Press.

Vahabzadeh, P. 2001. Technological Liberalism and the Anarchic Actor. In *Anarcho-Modernism: Toward a New Critical Theory in Honour of Jerry Zaslove,* ed. I. Angus, 341-50. Vancouver: Talonbooks.

Ward, C. 1973. *Anarchy in Action.* London: George Allen and Unwin.

Ward, G. 2004. Punishing for a Living: More on the Cementing of Prisons. *Social Justice* 31(1-2): 35-38.

Welch, M. 2000. The Role of the Immigration and Naturalization Service in the Prison-Industrial Complex. *Social Justice* 27(3): 73-88.

–, and L. Schuster. 2005a. Detention of Asylum Seekers in the UK and US: Deciphering Noisy and Quiet Constructions. *Punishment and Society* 7(4): 397-417.

–. 2005b. Detention of Asylum Seekers in the US, UK, France, Germany, and Italy: A Critical View of the Globalizing Culture of Control. *Criminal Justice* 5(4): 331-55.

Wilson, J. 1975. *Thinking about Crime.* New York: Basic Books.

Young, J. 1997. Left Realism: The Basics. In *Thinking Critically about Crime,* ed. B. Maclean and D. Milovanovic, 28-36. Vancouver: Collective Press.

–. 2002. Critical Criminology in the Twenty-First Century: Critique, Irony and the Always Unfinished. In *Critical Criminology: Issues, Debates, Challenges,* ed. R. Hogg and K. Carrington, 251-75. Cullompton, UK: Willan.

# Contributors

**GILLIAN BALFOUR** is Associate Professor in Sociology at Trent University, where she specializes in critical criminology and feminist socio-legal scholarship. Her research interests include the impacts of sentencing law reform on Aboriginal women, imprisonment as state violence against women, and the role of sexual assault nurse examiners as expert witnesses at trial.

**AARON DOYLE** is Associate Professor in the Department of Sociology and Anthropology at Carleton University. His research interests include risk, insurance and security, crime and media, visual surveillance, and risk at work. Other book projects currently underway include *Breaking Criminological Convention: Selected Essays of Richard Ericson* (co-edited with Janet Chan and Kevin Haggerty) and *Eyes Everywhere: The Global Growth of Camera Surveillance* (co-edited with Randy Lippert and David Lyon).

**BENOÎT DUPONT** is Associate Professor of Criminology at the Université de Montréal, where he holds the Canada Research Chair in security, identity, and technology. He is also the Deputy Director of the International Centre for Comparative Criminology. His research interests include the governance of security and the co-evolution of technology and crime.

**JON FRAULEY** is Assistant Professor of Criminology at the University of Ottawa. He is primarily interested in social theory, epistemology, theoretical and policy issues pertaining to governance and regulation, and cultural criminology. He is co-editor of *Critical Realism and the Social Sciences: Heterodox Elaborations* (2007) and has published in a number of anthologies and journals, including the *British Journal of Criminology, Critical Criminology*, the *Canadian Journal of Law and Society*, and *Current Issues in Criminal Justice*.

Lisa Freeman is a researcher, writer, community activist, and PhD candidate in the Department of Geography and Planning at the University of Toronto. Her research interests span anti-poverty campaigns, municipal government and planning initiatives, affordable housing in the suburbs, and legal geography. She is currently a Junior Fellow at the Centre of Criminology at the University of Toronto and a Trudeau Scholar.

Stacey Hannem is Assistant Professor in the Department of Criminology at Wilfrid Laurier University (Brantford campus). She serves as chair of the policy review committee of the Canadian Criminal Justice Association and researches in the areas of stigma, criminal justice policy, and sex offending.

Bryan Hogeveen is Associate Professor of Sociology at the University of Alberta. He is author of *Youth, Crime and Society: Issues of Power and Justice* (2009). His SSHRC-funded research examines neo-liberalism's impact on marginalized inner city populations and neighbourhoods.

Laura Huey is Assistant Professor of Sociology at the University of Western Ontario. Her research interests include policing, surveillance, and victimization. Her work has appeared in both national and international journals and her book *Negotiating Demands: The Politics of Skid Row Policing in Edinburgh, San Francisco and Vancouver* was published in 2007.

Dawn Moore is Associate Professor in the Department of Law at Carleton University. Her first book, *Criminal Artefacts: Governing Drugs and Users*, is available through UBC Press. She is currently working on a book that explores the experiences of people participating in drug treatment courts.

George Rigakos is Associate Professor of Law, Criminology, and Political Economy at Carleton University. He has published widely on public and private policing, risk, security, and critical theory. His most recent books include *Nightclub: Bouncers, Risk and the Spectacle of Consumption* (2008) and *A General Police System* (2009, co-edited with John McMullan and Joshua Johnson).

Kevin Walby completed his PhD in Sociology at Carleton University in 2010 and is currently SSHRC Postdoctoral Fellow at the Centre of Criminology at the University of Toronto. He is the Prisoners' Struggles Editor for the *Journal of Prisoners on Prisons*. He has published in numerous journals and edited volumes, recently including the *British Journal of Criminology* (2010, with Justin Piché) and *Qualitative Research* (2010). Areas of interest include surveillance, policing, and law as governance.

JAMES WILLIAMS is Associate Professor in the Department of Social Science at York University. He has published extensively in the areas of white-collar crime and financial governance, including work on the contributions of private-sector firms to the investigation of financial crime. He recently completed a multi-year study of the policing of financial markets in Canada.

ANDREW WOOLFORD is Associate Professor of Sociology at the University of Manitoba. He is author of *The Politics of Restorative Justice: A Critical Introduction* (2009), *Between Justice and Certainty: Treaty Making in British Columbia* (2005), and co-author, with R.S. Ratner, of *Informal Reckonings: Conflict Resolution in Mediation, Restorative Justice, and Reparations* (2008). His current research is focused on post-genocide reparations, genocide, the Indian Residential School Truth and Reconciliation Commission in Canada, and neo-liberal social regulation in Winnipeg.

DIANA YOUNG is Assistant Professor in Carleton University's Department of Law, where she teaches courses in criminal law and law and film. Her research interests include discretion in the criminal justice system, feminist theory, and the relationship between social and legal theory.

# Index

Andrew S. Thompson
*In Defence of Principles: NGOs and Human Rights in Canada* (2010)

Joanna R. Quinn
*The Politics of Acknowledgement: Truth Commissions in Uganda and Haiti* (2010)

Patrick James
*Constitutional Politics in Canada after the Charter: Liberalism, Communitarianism, and Systemism* (2010)

Louis A. Knafla and Haijo Westra (eds.)
*Aboriginal Title and Indigenous Peoples: Canada, Australia, and New Zealand* (2010)

Janet Mosher and Joan Brockman (eds.)
*Constructing Crime: Contemporary Processes of Criminalization* (2010)

Stephen Clarkson and Stepan Wood
*A Perilous Imbalance: The Globalization of Canadian Law and Governance* (2009)

Amanda Glasbeek
*Feminized Justice: The Toronto Women's Court, 1913-34* (2009)

Kimberley Brooks (ed.)
*Justice Bertha Wilson: One Woman's Difference* (2009)

Wayne V. McIntosh and Cynthia L. Cates
*Multi-Party Litigation: The Strategic Context* (2009)

Renisa Mawani
*Colonial Proximities: Crossracial Encounters and Juridical Truths in British Columbia, 1871-1921* (2009)

James B. Kelly and Christopher P. Manfredi (eds.)
*Contested Constitutionalism: Reflections on the Canadian Charter of Rights and Freedoms* (2009)

Catherine E. Bell and Robert K. Paterson (eds.)
*Protection of First Nations Cultural Heritage: Laws, Policy, and Reform* (2008)

Hamar Foster, Benjamin L. Berger, and A.R. Buck (eds.)
*The Grand Experiment: Law and Legal Culture in British Settler Societies* (2008)

Richard J. Moon (ed.)
*Law and Religious Pluralism in Canada* (2008)

Catherine E. Bell and Val Napoleon (eds.)
*First Nations Cultural Heritage and Law: Case Studies, Voices, and Perspectives* (2008)

Douglas C. Harris
*Landing Native Fisheries: Indian Reserves and Fishing Rights in British Columbia, 1849-1925* (2008)

Peggy J. Blair
*Lament for a First Nation: The Williams Treaties in Southern Ontario* (2008)

Lori G. Beaman
*Defining Harm: Religious Freedom and the Limits of the Law* (2007)

Stephen Tierney (ed.)
*Multiculturalism and the Canadian Constitution* (2007)

Julie Macfarlane
*The New Lawyer: How Settlement Is Transforming the Practice of Law* (2007)

Kimberley White
*Negotiating Responsibility: Law, Murder, and States of Mind* (2007)

Dawn Moore
*Criminal Artefacts: Governing Drugs and Users* (2007)

Hamar Foster, Heather Raven, and Jeremy Webber (eds.)
*Let Right Be Done: Aboriginal Title, the Calder Case, and the Future of Indigenous Rights* (2007)

Dorothy E. Chunn, Susan B. Boyd, and Hester Lessard (eds.)
*Reaction and Resistance: Feminism, Law, and Social Change* (2007)

Margot Young, Susan B. Boyd, Gwen Brodsky, and Shelagh Day (eds.)
*Poverty: Rights, Social Citizenship, and Legal Activism* (2007)

Rosanna L. Langer
*Defining Rights and Wrongs: Bureaucracy, Human Rights, and Public Accountability* (2007)

C.L. Ostberg and Matthew E. Wetstein
*Attitudinal Decision Making in the Supreme Court of Canada* (2007)

Chris Clarkson
*Domestic Reforms: Political Visions and Family Regulation in British Columbia, 1862-1940* (2007)

Jean McKenzie Leiper
*Bar Codes: Women in the Legal Profession* (2006)

Gerald Baier
*Courts and Federalism: Judicial Doctrine in the United States, Australia, and Canada* (2006)

Avigail Eisenberg (ed.)
*Diversity and Equality: The Changing Framework of Freedom in Canada* (2006)

Randy K. Lippert
*Sanctuary, Sovereignty, Sacrifice: Canadian Sanctuary Incidents, Power, and Law* (2005)

James B. Kelly
*Governing with the Charter: Legislative and Judicial Activism and Framers' Intent* (2005)

Dianne Pothier and Richard Devlin (eds.)
*Critical Disability Theory: Essays in Philosophy, Politics, Policy, and Law* (2005)

Susan G. Drummond
*Mapping Marriage Law in Spanish Gitano Communities* (2005)

Louis A. Knafla and Jonathan Swainger (eds.)
*Laws and Societies in the Canadian Prairie West, 1670-1940* (2005)

Ikechi Mgbeoji
*Global Biopiracy: Patents, Plants, and Indigenous Knowledge* (2005)

Florian Sauvageau, David Schneiderman, and David Taras,
with Ruth Klinkhammer and Pierre Trudel
*The Last Word: Media Coverage of the Supreme Court of Canada* (2005)

Gerald Kernerman
*Multicultural Nationalism: Civilizing Difference, Constituting Community* (2005)

Pamela A. Jordan
*Defending Rights in Russia: Lawyers, the State, and Legal Reform in the Post-Soviet Era* (2005)

Anna Pratt
*Securing Borders: Detention and Deportation in Canada* (2005)

Kirsten Johnson Kramar
*Unwilling Mothers, Unwanted Babies: Infanticide in Canada* (2005)

W.A. Bogart
*Good Government? Good Citizens? Courts, Politics, and Markets in a Changing Canada* (2005)

Catherine Dauvergne
*Humanitarianism, Identity, and Nation: Migration Laws in Canada and Australia* (2005)

Michael Lee Ross
*First Nations Sacred Sites in Canada's Courts* (2005)

Andrew Woolford
*Between Justice and Certainty: Treaty Making in British Columbia* (2005)

John McLaren, Andrew Buck, and Nancy Wright (eds.)
*Despotic Dominion: Property Rights in British Settler Societies* (2004)

Georges Campeau
*From UI to EI: Waging War on the Welfare State* (2004)

Alvin J. Esau
*The Courts and the Colonies: The Litigation of Hutterite Church Disputes* (2004)

Christopher N. Kendall
*Gay Male Pornography: An Issue of Sex Discrimination* (2004)

Roy B. Flemming
*Tournament of Appeals: Granting Judicial Review in Canada* (2004)

Constance Backhouse and Nancy L. Backhouse
*The Heiress vs the Establishment: Mrs. Campbell's Campaign for Legal Justice* (2004)

Christopher P. Manfredi
*Feminist Activism in the Supreme Court: Legal Mobilization and the Women's Legal Education and Action Fund* (2004)

Annalise Acorn
*Compulsory Compassion: A Critique of Restorative Justice* (2004)

Jonathan Swainger and Constance Backhouse (eds.)
*People and Place: Historical Influences on Legal Culture* (2003)

Jim Phillips and Rosemary Gartner
*Murdering Holiness: The Trials of Franz Creffield and George Mitchell* (2003)

David R. Boyd
*Unnatural Law: Rethinking Canadian Environmental Law and Policy* (2003)

Ikechi Mgbeoji
*Collective Insecurity: The Liberian Crisis, Unilateralism, and Global Order* (2003)

Rebecca Johnson
*Taxing Choices: The Intersection of Class, Gender, Parenthood, and the Law* (2002)

John McLaren, Robert Menzies, and Dorothy E. Chunn (eds.)
*Regulating Lives: Historical Essays on the State, Society, the Individual, and the Law* (2002)

Joan Brockman
*Gender in the Legal Profession: Fitting or Breaking the Mould* (2001)

Printed and bound in Canada by Friesens

Set in Scala Sans and Giovanni by Artegraphica Design Co. Ltd.

Copy editor: Judy Phillips

Proofreader: Stacy Belden

Indexer: Christine Jacobs